GENDER
COMMUNICATION

GENDER COMMUNICATION

LAURIE P. ARLISS
Ithaca College

PRENTICE HALL
Englewood Cliffs, New Jersey 07632

P96.S48A47 1991

Library of Congress Cataloging-in-Publication Data

Arliss, Laurie, (date)
   Gender communication / Laurie Arliss.
      p. cm.
   ISBN 0-13-351610-5
   1. Communication—Sex differences. 2. Sexism in communication.
3. Interpersonal relations. I. Title.
P96.S48A7 1991   90-6725
306.4'4—dc20   CIP

Editorial/production supervision and
   interior design: KERRY REARDON
Cover design: 20/20 SERVICES, INC.
Manufacturing buyer: ED O'DOUGHERTY

©1991 by Prentice-Hall, Inc.
A Division of Simon & Schuster
Englewood Cliffs, New Jersey 07632

Printed in the United States of America

10 9 8 7 6 5 4 3 2 1

ISBN   0-13-351610-5

PRENTICE-HALL INTERNATIONAL, INC., *London*
PRENTICE-HALL OF AUSTRALIA PTY. LIMITED, *Sydney*
PRENTICE-HALL HISPANOAMERICANA, S.A., *Mexico*
EDITORA PRENTICE-HALL DO BRASIL, LTDA., *Rio de Janeiro*
PRENTICE-HALL CANADA INC., *Toronto*
PRENTICE-HALL OF INDIA PRIVATE LIMITED, *New Delhi*
PRENTICE-HALL OF JAPAN, INC., *Tokyo*
SIMON & SCHUSTER ASIA PTE. LTD., *Singapore*

For Meghan, Amanda, and Bethany—
Watch out world!

CONTENTS

PREFACE

Ironically, it is often the aspects of life that are most meaningful, most central to our understanding of self and other, that are the most difficult to isolate and discuss. Gender is no exception. Our world is a gender-specific world. A child's first memories of life, of language, of self, and of others are gender specific. Indeed, by the time he or she is old enough to develop a social conscience, which prompts him or her to examine gender categories as cultural, not biological, divisions, he or she is undoubtedly well prepared to "act out" the appropriate category with remarkable precision.

For many readers, this will not be the first time that gender issues have been of concern. The daily comings and goings of the socially aware adult often prompt the discussion of gender issues. Perhaps the reader has already developed, or inherited, some very strong notions about gender appropriateness. I hope, though, that this book provides a comprehensive examination of gender as communication. More specifically, it is argued here that gender is an influence on communication, not only as a key perceptual category, but as a variable affecting human interaction. At the same time, though, it is argued that gender is the product of communication, that individuals both learn and teach lessons about gender-specific expectations in their daily interaction with others.

Obviously, the proposed connections between communication and gender cannot stand without support, particularly among readers who fancy themselves to be already quite liberated from gender- specific politics. Many young people are resistant to any suggestion of sex differences in behavior and are particularly resistant to the suggestion that their own behaviors and perceptions may be sex typed. (Please note: no effort has been made in the preface to differentiate between the terms *sex* and *gender*; this issue will be discussed in detail in the first chapter.) Still, communication researchers have provided evidence that indicates clear sex differences in behavior, in evaluations of behavior, and in expectations of behavior. A substantial body of that evidence is presented here, but not without the understanding that it is charged with implications for each reader, a gendered reader, living in a gendered world as well as in a socially aware world that demands gender distinctions be reasonable.

The task of segmenting the world for discussion is always difficult, but particularly difficult in this case because of the mutual influence of communication and gender. The approach taken here, stated simply, is to address the *what* questions first, then the *why* questions, and then finally the *so what* questions. In other words, it seems worthwhile to begin by discussing the specifics of sex differences in communication that have been proposed in the communication literature, providing answers to the "what" questions. These questions are addressed in Parts I and II of the book. The primary distinction between the two is that Part I focuses on communication influences that are portrayed as societal, not personal—namely, sex stereotypes and sex-specific language practices. Presumably, it is easier for readers to acknowledge that they have inherited sex-specific standards if they conceive of the originators as faceless and nameless.

Part II discusses empirical evidence that men and women continue to communicate somewhat distinctly. Proposed sex differences are examined, answering "what" questions about verbal behavior (communication with words), nonverbal behavior (communication without words), and interactional behavior (communication that is meaningful based on how it is interstructured). Students invariably want to explain *why* differences were found, *why* times have changed, *why* people should or should not behave in certain ways. Despite their willingness to do so, readers are discouraged from offering explanations until after thoroughly examining the literature depicting sex differences. As a result, it becomes increasingly apparent that observed sex differences in behavior (at least some of which students may notice themselves exhibiting or expecting from others) are not unrelated to the prevailing gender stereotypes and the inherited biases of language usage. Indeed, it can be argued that we inadvertently perpetuate overly rigid visions of gender appropriateness in our daily communication with others.

Given such a discovery, explanations for sex differences in behavior may take on additional significance for readers. Part III provides a detailed discussion of scholarly efforts to explain gender-specific behavior, efforts that compete on many points. Early on in the discussion of sex differences, students often want to debate the nature–nurture distinction and/or argue vocally for or against political positions. In the midst of examining innate factors, sociological factors, and cognitive developmental factors that have been proposed to affect gender communication, students are often forced to acknowledge that simple yes-no, either-or answers are seldom appropriate. I only hope that they develop a sensitivity for the intricate network that weaves gender conceptualizations into our day-to-day experiences with others.

Part IV attempts to address a number of "so what" questions, assuming that readers are at least partially convinced that gender is, at once, firmly established in the present and open to chance in the future. Implications for male–female communication in various relationships are discussed, including professional relationships, friendships, and family relationships.

The approach taken in this book admittedly does not do justice to the nonsegmentable world of gender communication. Readers are asked to respect the author's best judgment, not only about which questions to address, but about the order in which to address them. Despite concerted efforts to the contrary, it is entirely possible that the process of gender communication may appear simple, linear, and static. Happily, the reader need only put the book down and venture back into the interpersonal world to be reminded that gender communication is complex, circular, and in a constant state of change—but worth considering after all.

ACKNOWLEDGMENTS

The author and publisher would like to thank the following professionals whose efforts and consideration are greatly appreciated in reviewing *Gender Communication:* Cynthia Berryman-Fink, *University of Cincinnati*; Judi Brownell, *Cornell University*; Karen A. Foss, *Humboldt State University*; David Lau, *Oakland University*; Marcia C. Moore, *State University of New York/Oswego*; and Julia T. Wood, *University of North Carolina*.

Thanks, too, to the many students who inspired me to pursue this work. Student voices can be heard throughout this work in all their optimism and enthusiasm. I continue to enjoy discussing gender issues with them and learn immeasurably from the wisdom only they can bring. I wish them all success and happiness in the gender-neutral world they claim is just ahead. Special thanks to my family, my colleagues at Ithaca College, and my many supportive friends. I am particularly indebted to the individuals who have helped me, largely by example, to have the courage and confidence to pursue my own career in my own way, among them Judi Brownell, Arthur Jensen, Constantine Perialas, Charles Petrie, Stuart Sigman, and Sarah Trenholm.

GENDER
COMMUNICATION

CHAPTER 1

THE IMPORTANCE OF STUDYING SEX DIFFERENCES IN COMMUNICATION

Imagine the embarrassment that is suffered each day by countless numbers of innocent friends, acquaintances, and strangers who unknowingly commit the unspeakable error of referring to a newborn girl as "he" or, worse yet, a newborn boy as "she." The insulted parent in this situation cannot understand how anyone could make such a silly mistake—the baby has all the qualities of one sex and none of the other. The unfortunate admirer, of course, blames the parent for dressing a girl in blue or for putting a lace bonnet on a boy.

It seems a stranger must rely on *gender displays,* or deliberate efforts by the parent, in this case, to identify the baby as one sex and not the other. Such displays typically consist of gender–specific styles and colors for clothing and accessories. Recently a team of researchers, wondering about the prevalence and effectiveness of such infant labeling, observed babies and their caregivers at shopping malls. They report that no less than 90% of the youngsters (ages one month to thirteen months) were dressed in sex–typed clothes. Color was the most obvious method of labeling: pink and other pastel colors for girls; blue and red for boys. In terms of style, little girls were adorned with ruffles and puffed sleeves, but boys were dressed in more tailored attire. Babies' toys and accessories were similarly sex specific.[1]

The efforts of the adults were rewarded, according to the researchers: strangers were successful in identifying the sex of all but the 10% of the infants who were dressed generically. Curiously, given the obvious efforts of adults to provide ample information about their child's sex, it is worth noting that, when questioned, most of them said they assigned little importance to sex typing when selecting clothing and toys for their dependents.[2] It may well be that external labeling is so prevalent and so effective that it is done unconsciously. Judging the child's sex based on these displays is preferable, of course, to "checking" the otherwise unidentifiable infant. Except for the very first moment, when the onlookers in the delivery room anxiously look for anatomical information about what sex the baby is, admirers' behavior toward the baby will be sex-typed based on gender displays.

Even some adult strangers would be difficult to place with total certainty as male or female without sex-typed clothing and shoes, hair styles, jewelry, etc. Our ability to quickly cast strangers as male or female based on merely superficial clues—and not biological evidence—is taken for granted until that rare and disturbing instance when the stranger's outward appearance is ambiguous and we are just not able to tell.

It seems fair to say that we are largely preoccupied with dividing the human race into males and females, regardless of age and regardless of our vested interest in knowing. We feel unbelievably anxious if we do not know this particular information about another person. Certainly, there are instances when it is quite important to be absolutely sure about the sex of an individual. But the preoccupation with sex differences extends far beyond the very pragmatic concerns of sexual activity. Otherwise, why do we become so concerned about not knowing the sex of a stranger, even when that stranger is just a baby?

Perhaps we want to know because we understand and evaluate behavior, even that of strangers, as more or less sex appropriate. That is, once we classify another individual as male or female, usually based on available visual information, we begin to draw inferences about "invisible" emotional and psychological attributes. This is even true of babies. Research indicates that "adults are likely to perceive children's behavior in terms of gender stereotypes."[3] Until we become aware of the standards by which we differentiate appropriate male from appropriate female behavior, it seems unlikely that we will become fully aware of the boundaries of sex discrimination in our day-to-day interactions with others. Ironically, however, few of those standards exist in any sort of permanent form, so that we can examine, accept, or challenge them. Rather, many of the judgments we make about sex-appropriate behavior are based on implicit standards. We learn and teach these standards, sometimes unknowingly, through communication.

YOUR PERSONAL STAKE IN UNDERSTANDING SEX DIFFERENCES IN COMMUNICATION

Prior to presenting a single study or a single theory, however, it seems worthwhile to mention that the discussion of sex differences in human behavior is not without implications for each reader. We live in a world in which harmony and understanding between men and women affects nearly every important aspect of our lives—marriage, family, career, politics, religion, and friendship, to name just a few. Yet, what little predictability may have surrounded male–female relationships in the past may well have been (rightfully) shaken by the feminist movement.

Among other things, the feminist movement of the late 1960s brought attention to patterns of daily interaction that had gone largely unnoticed by the participants—and almost completely unstudied by researchers. Although studies of sex differences in communication could be found prior to the establishment of the National Organization for Women (an historical event largely taken to signify the inception of the feminist movement), such studies were few. Of the 147 studies listed in a recent summary entitled "The Status of Research on Women and Communication," only eight were published prior to 1960 and only nineteen more were published during the 1960s. The authors of the summary report stated that the "rebirth of feminism was accompanied by a surge of research....Communication scholars began to explore the relationship between sex, gender and virtually every aspect of communication behavior."[4]

The 1970s was a decade in which attention to gender issues flourished. The discussion of women's and men's lives became so commonplace, according to Pearce and Rossi, that *feminism* is today no longer treated as a proper name, identifying a particular social reform movement. Rather, it has become "a construct, a state of mind or a cultural resource which persons use to interpret various practices...ranging from matters of traditional courtesy (a gentleman opens doors for a lady and allows her to precede him into a room) to employment (over 98% of the highest positions in American business are held by men) to gender-based stereotypes...."[5]

The confusion about the exact status of feminism in our lives seems particularly significant for those who set out to examine studies that have implications for male–female interaction. It seems clear that we do not treat the label as a neutral term identifying participation in an active political group. It seems equally apparent that we do not treat the label as a philosophical stand on social equality. After all, it is quite different to say "I endorse the civil rights movement" and "I endorse the feminist movement." In truth, most people attach an attitude to the label *feminism* (either positive or negative), which Pearce and Rossi assume is related to the fact that "feminism has succeeded better in identifying practices which are offensive than in guiding the performance of appropriate practices." Thus, "it is fairly obvious why feminism has been a source of great disruption of interpersonal relationships: obstinate males and unliberated women do not satisfactorily coordinate their behavior with that of a 'liberated' woman with whom they might live or work, and both offend and are offended by her."[6]

Radical feminists undoubtedly take pleasure in the notion of having ruptured discourse between men and women; they believe that discourse has served for decades to keep women oppressed.[7] Indeed, women and men alike must acknowledge the various social reforms concerning occupational and educational opportunities for which the feminist movement takes credit. However, it is equally clear that a backlash movement against feminism has formed, with both male and female supporters. I cannot help but notice the pride with which men (some of them very young men) are now declaring, "I admit it; I'm a male chauvinist." Try to imagine the same prideful voices uttering, "I admit it; I'm a racist." Young female voices can also be heard advocating traditional patriarchal values on issues ranging from the division of labor in the home to the perpetuation of chivalry to the wisdom of electing a woman president.

It seems fair to conclude that we are still struggling with the concept of feminism, both on a political level and on an interpersonal level. For many individuals, incorporating sexual equality into their daily lives has not proven especially easy or desirable. Others still question the idea of sex-appropriate behavior, but, in some cases, pay the price of alienating others. The difficulties inherent in sustaining relationships with people of divergent political viewpoints is not unique to the discussion of gender differences. But these difficulties may be particularly poignant in the lives of young people about to embark on adult life in a society dominated by the practice of heterosexuality and anchored by the tradition of the nuclear family. Add to the importance of family and romantic relationships the desire to find a comfortable place in a competitive, work-oriented society, struggling with the relatively new issues of affirmative action and reverse discrimination, and it becomes clear that today's young adults will face difficult choices in both the public and private spheres.

The importance of communication practices in all relationships, whether family, friendship, or professional, cannot be discounted. Communication is both a tool that we can use and a system of power that can "use" us. As individuals, our participation in communication practices that perpetuate sex differences may be more or less active and deliberate and need not be based on a strong conviction concerning feminism. Certainly, we all have a sense of ourselves as male or female and a sense of how others treat us based on gender. Many of my students, both male and female, have told me that they feel completely unrestricted by gender. Others have expressed a philosophy akin to *Vive la différence*. But some have voiced dissatisfaction with the way members of the "opposite sex" behave toward them and with the limits that are sometimes placed on their behavior.

Regardless of the attitude they express about their own experiences as a male or female, many young people become most thoughtful when asked hypothetical questions about how they might approach the issue of gender restrictions with their own children. After all, hypothetically, would you let your three-year-old son wear a barrette in preschool? Take ballet lessons? Even if you offer a resounding "yes" to these questions, wouldn't they require no second consideration in the case of a three-year-old daughter? Would you punish physical aggression exhibited by a girl? Perhaps not, but wouldn't it concern you more (or perhaps amuse you more) coming from a daughter than a son? Of course, you cannot foresee yourself saying, "Little girls don't do that!" or "Act like a lady!" Still, many young parents are utterly amazed to hear the very phrases they resented so as children, and especially as adolescents, coming from their own lips, despite their liberal attitudes.

Each reader is asked to consider, then, not only his or her participation in communication from the standpoint of a male or female student, but also his or her possible role as teacher of maleness and/or femaleness. In particular, the reader is encouraged to evaluate his or her personal stake in the existence of sex differences in communicative behavior. These differences, delineated in Part II, seem to contribute to the perpetuation of cultural norms for behavior that differ for males and females. In essence, they underscore the lines that distinguish "us" from "them"—and, as a result, limit the behavioral choices for all of us.

YOUR REACTION TO THE PROPOSED SEX DIFFERENCES IN COMMUNICATION

The notion that we may not have complete freedom of choice is particularly disturbing to a generation of young men and women who think they have been raised on sexual equality. Many students are troubled by research studies suggesting that individuals must communicate gender appropriately or suffer the consequences. In advance, four possible reactions to the proposed differences delineated in the communication literature are predicted. These are borrowed from my students, and reflect some of the various attitudes readers may adopt as a result of being asked to examine studies proposing sex differences in communication:

1. The studies that report sex differences in communication are ill conceived and misreported with an unnatural emphasis on a single variable: gender. Actually, the differences are small or nonexistent, but the reports exaggerate them. More than anything else, these studies have taught me to distrust such research.
2. The studies are outdated. Things have changed since these studies were conducted. Sex discrimination no longer exists. Studying sex differences can provide an interesting lesson in history but has no relation to current events.
3. The studies represent the way people who cling to stereotypes think and act—not the way I and those who are important to me think and act. However, knowledge of these stereotypic standards allows me to be more sensitive to them when I perceive them in others.
4. The studies help me to see how I have perpetuated sex differences in communication by the way I behave. I may (or may not) choose to change my own behavior based on my improved understanding of sex differences in communication.

It might be argued that these attitudes range from the impersonal to the very personal. I hope that each reader will at least consider the possibility that there are differences, even if ill conceived, misreported, and exaggerated in the literature, and that we often participate unknowingly in perpetuating those differences.

The process by which we learn about being male or female within a given society is thought to be very complex and largely invisible. In the next section, some of the constituent elements of the process are isolated for discussion.

KEY TERMS

Sex and Gender. The terms *sex* and *gender* are often used interchangeably, in everyday speech and in scholarly writing. Unless speakers and authors consciously monitor the use of these terms (as I am doing now), it seems that we invariably cross the line that we claim distinguishes the two. In other words, we may define the distinction between sex and gender carefully, noting the important difference between biological characteristics, which are similar across time and place in the human experience, and cultural characteristics, which vary greatly from generation to generation and around the globe. Yet, when we reference the categorical distinction between "us" and "them," we generally take little care to honor that difference.

For example, a researcher may say that he or she observed *sex* differences in a given study, but surely he or she did not verify anatomically the sex of each subject. Rather, the researcher probably assumed that each individual was male or female based on observable gender displays. Yet the fascinating stories about individuals who pass for the opposite sex suggest that gender displays are not necessarily conclusive evidence of sex, although they may effectively clarify questions about *gender*. The fact that we treat *sex* and *gender* as synonymous in our daily interactions might become especially obvious if we were to adopt the unlikely habit of verifying our assumptions about sexual assignment by asking others "Are you a male or a female?"

The practice of equating sex and gender, both in everyday conversation and formal research, continues, despite the efforts of many feminist scholars from a variety of academic disciplines to stress the distinction and advocate the accurate use of these and related terms.[8] Having examined a number of proposed systems for identifying divisions of people and their behaviors (a number roughly equal to one per author), I have opted to treat the terms *sex* and *gender* virtually synonymously throughout the text, but implore the reader to bear with the obligatory discussion of the actual distinction, primarily because it serves the purpose of focusing attention on the interface between the individual and his or her culture—an interface made possible by communication.

Sex refers to a biological category. Each of us can be labeled either male or female at birth based on observable physical evidence, i.e., the nature of the genitalia. We assume that, except in very extreme cases, most individuals are clearly one sex or the other and will grow and develop accordingly. The standard assumptions about the physical distinctions between adult men and women may be categorized in three groups, which Birdwhistell labels *primary, secondary,* and *tertiary.* Primary sexual characteristics relate to "the physiology of the production of fertile ova and spermatozoa." Secondary sexual characteristics are also "anatomical in nature," although not directly involved in reproduction. However, tertiary sexual characteristics are "patterned social-behavioral in form...are learned and are situationally produced."[9] The following list summarizes some of the proposed sex differences in each category:

1. primary sexual characteristics:
   (a) maturation of the genitalia in both sexes to allow for participation in reproduction
   (b) development of mammary glands in the female to allow for nurturance of offspring
   (c) hormonal differences
2. secondary sexual characteristics:
   (a) variant body size (usually, but not always, adult males are larger than adult females)
   (b) slight differences in skeletal structure (specifically, women have a different pelvic structure, undoubtedly to aid in bearing children)
   (c) contrasting distribution of body hair (usually, but not always, adult males have more body hair)
   (d) an unequal proportion of muscle to fat tissue (specifically, women have an extra layer of fat tissue, also apparently related to child bearing, while men have an extra layer of muscle tissue and longer, thicker muscles)
3. tertiary sexual characteristics:
   (a) sex-typed body movements (walking, sitting, etc.)
   (b) sex-typed vocabularies
   (c) sex-typed displays of humor
   (d) sex-typed facial reactions to stress
   (e) other sex-typed behaviors (to be discussed in later chapters)

Obviously, it is the tertiary sexual characteristics that are the most controversial and that vary the most from culture to culture. Some scholars stress that it is the composite of the tertiary characteristics that constitute *gender*, as opposed to *sex*, the composite of the primary and secondary characteristics.[10] Thus, the labels *masculine* and *feminine* may be understood as gender terms that cannot be assigned at birth, but must be inferred based on an individual's behavior. Usually a child assigned *male* at birth behaves *masculinely,* according to cultural standards, and a child assigned *female* behaves *femininely*. Happily, most observers allow for a certain amount of overlap between masculine and feminine behavior. For instance, some may consider it all right for a boy or man to cry in certain circumstances, even though crying is considered a feminine behavior; and some may deem it all right for a girl or woman to become part of a fistfight—given provocation, of course—even though fighting is considered masculine behavior.

Gender must be enacted, then, while *sex* is assigned. Numerous comedies, both classical and contemporary, have amused audiences with plots in which a character, identified to the audience as male, dresses and behaves as a female, or vice versa. On a more serious note, we sometimes use the derogatory label *effeminate* to refer to a male who behaves "too" femininely. A female who behaves "too" masculinely may be referred to as *emasculating,* although, notably, this adjective seems to focus more on the effect of her behavior on the men in her life than on the behavior itself.

In any case, it appears that *sex* is a biologically determined category, while *gender* is a behaviorally determined category. As noted, however, the distinction is largely ignored in everyday discussion of male and female behavior. We seem to interchange the terms at will. Granted, this may be simply another instance of careless language use. But, it could equally well be indicative of the rather restrictive view that biology somehow determines behavior, such that males just naturally behave masculinely, and females cannot avoid behaving femininely. It's only natural!

Sex-Typed Behaviors.   As cited, the terms *sex* and *gender* are used synonymously in this text to refer to the division of human beings into two mutually exclusive categories. It is assumed that most of us learn very early in life into which category "nature" has placed us—and that we feel some motivation to behave "appropriately," although we may be unsure about what that entails. Most cultures provide newcomers with arbitrary lessons about sex-specific behavior, which are passed from generation to generation. These patterns are herein labeled *sex-typed* behaviors.

In many cases, behaviors may be selected consciously and deliberately in an effort to be seen as sex appropriate in a given society. For example, in our culture, carrying a purse is usually regarded as a feminine behavior, and only the most fashion-conscious male will assent to this even if Gucci or Lauren claims it is "in." Similarly, smoking cigars is generally seen as a masculine behavior that most women would forgo in public even if they found it pleasurable. In essence, many sex-typed behaviors are adult versions of the same effort a new parent makes to plainly identify an infant as male or female.

It is important to stress that conscious behavioral displays of gender are very common and often taken for granted. But they can be isolated, described, and challenged. Many of the gender-based behavioral contrasts discussed in this book, however, are not deliberately chosen and are not readily identifiable for discussion and challenge. In fact, some of the sex-typed behaviors proposed in Part II of this book may be met with disbelief and even resentment by many readers. It seems that, although studies indicate that certain communicative behaviors appear to be quite clearly sex specific, the existence of identifiable differences is acknowledged with surprise and regret. Most students of sex differences in communication discover that they do not consciously choose to enact certain supposedly sex-typed behaviors, and do not consciously expect them from others.

In a very real sense, then, a number of sex-typed communicative behaviors are involuntary by the time we reach adulthood. They are culturally taught and learned, to be sure, but seem to elude the "would you allow" questions mentioned earlier in the discussion of parenting practices. How silly to ask "Would you allow a girl to interrupt as much as a boy?" or "Would you allow a boy to ask as many questions as a girl?" or "Would you allow a boy to smile as much as a girl, or say 'Mmm-hmm' as often?" Yet these and many other verbal and nonverbal contrasts have been reported to distinguish male from female communication. Such behaviors, whether or not they are consciously chosen, may serve to display gender and to perpetuate standards of gender appropriateness.

To reiterate, the terms *sex* and *gender* are used interchangeably in this text to identify the categories—the "opposites" as they are fondly referred to more often than not. But the specific, learned behaviors that constitute maleness and femaleness in our culture will be referred to as *sex-typed behaviors* or *gender-specific behaviors*. So we may speak of an individual as behaving sex appropriately to the extent that he or she enacts the communicative behaviors typical of the category to which he or she belongs.

Sex Stereotypes.   It seems important to define *sex* stereotypes at this point, even though they will be discussed in detail in the next chapter. The term is adopted herein to refer to society's standards for determining maleness and femaleness. These standards are proposed to be largely mythological. In other words, society—that invisible entity to which we refer so freely—seems to communicate to its members myths about "pure" masculinity and femininity. In a sense, the stereotypes represent the ends of a continuum. Very few individuals adopt these extremes as standards for their own behavior, nor for judging the behavior of others. But part of the myth is that most people endorse the standards, at least as broadly interpreted, and that some people, seldom anyone we know personally, believe in the stereotypes and actively perpetuate them.

So we may refer to behavior as *sex stereotyped,* which provides a convenient vehicle for contrasting male and female behavior in a general or hypothetical sense. The discussion of stereotypes, of course, has little to do with the discussion of real life—or at least not our lives, we assume. Most of us are outspoken about not wanting to be stereotyped by sex, just as we are about not wanting to be stereotyped by race or ethnicity or age. Conversely, most of us report that we do not use stereotypes to judge others, although we can identify the stereotypes of various racial, ethnic, and age groups with remarkable consistency. The fact of the matter is that stereotyping is a very common and somewhat useful activity in a highly complex and mobile world. We all make assumptions about individuals we do not know based on information we believe about a category of individuals. The danger rests in being overly restrictive— ruling out the possibility of being wrong and learning something new. Thus the line between reacting systematically to a complex world and discriminating against others is a fine one.

The process by which stereotypes are conceived and communicated within a given society is a fascinating subject, but one that will not be addressed here. Still it seems important to acknowledge, at the very least, that sex stereotypes are communicated, with amazing consistency, to the members of our society—and at a very young age. In Chapter Two, researchers' attempts to investigate and describe the prevailing sex stereotypes are examined.

Communication.   One final term, *communication,* seems to warrant attention at this early stage in the discussion of sex differences in human behavior. Admittedly, it seems that every text in our discipline takes as its preliminary task choosing (or, more frequently, creating) a definition for the term. The abundance of definitions is at once frustrating and understandable, but, apologetically, it will not be resolved here. Rather, the broadest possible notion of communication is adopted, such that (1) humans are thought to be social creatures constantly in search of meaning in a social world, and (2) all human behavior is thought to be communicative in the sense that it may be interpreted as meaningful by others.

Communicative behavior, then, is simply human behavior that is perceivable, interpretable, and, above all else, meaningful in a social world. So, while physiological states—such as illness or fatigue or nervousness—are usually not directly perceivable to others, they are communicated, sometimes intentionally and sometimes unintentionally, in behaviors that others may notice and believe they understand. Similarly, while we cannot see or touch the emotions of others, we have great faith in our ability to share them via communication and we constantly seek perceivable information about "what's going on" inside of others. So communication is, in a sense, the thread that binds us as we seek to create and maintain a meaningful existence in the midst of others. It is by no means a perfect process, because varying perceptions and multiple interpretations are always available.

The meaning of *maleness* and *femaleness* appears to be particularly important to us, even as prepubescent children. We actively seek to understand the social meaning of being a man and of being a woman long before we understand the primary sex differences necessary for procreation. The communication of gender is the focus of this book. The process by which we learn and teach sex-appropriate behavior is assumed to be part of the larger process—communication—by which we come to understand our world and our place within it. At the same time, what we have already learned about the nature of being male and being female is assumed to influence our interaction with others. So, communication is thought to be, at once, the process by which we learn to be male or female, and the product of our attempts to behave sex appropriately.

Certainly, the communication of gender is a complex process. As individuals we receive countless messages about the meaning of maleness and femaleness even before we are old enough to realize that these are, for the most part, arbitrarily chosen messages. We come to believe that traditional values concerning male–female interaction are somehow "natural." So, at this point in the process, each of us must attempt to deconstruct the various messages we have already learned so well and question, at every juncture, the logic that connects them. Understanding the process by which we communicate gender can only improve our ability to understand those around us and increase the likelihood of effective male–female communication.

CONDUCT YOUR OWN RESEARCH

1. Visit the nursery at a local hospital and note markers that distinguish newborns according to sex (e.g., color-coded labels to mark bassinets, sex-specific toys placed near babies,

information about the baby's name, etc.). Listen for messages from other visitors that reference the sex of the babies.

2. Survey catalogs and/or retail outlets that sell consumer products designed for children (clothing, toys, furniture, gifts, etc.). Pay special attention to emphasis on gender in describing the content, arrangement, and methods of promotion.

3. Ask two of your friends, one male and one female, to assist you in an experiment. Tell them you want to observe reactions to "inappropriate" gender displays, so you need them to carry or wear items usually carried or worn by the other. Then have them venture out into the world for a brief encounter with the public. Of course, you will record others' reactions, according to plan, but also notice how your friends choose items to swap and how they behave when adorned "inappropriately."

DISCUSS THE ISSUES

1. Can equality between the sexes be legislated? Should it be? In what areas?

2. Why are the sexes characterized as opposites despite biological evidence that men and women are more alike than different? What are the possible consequences of this polarization? Discuss other variables that might be used in place of sex to conceive of humans as opposite.

3. What is your reaction to a woman who refers to herself as a feminist? A man who refers to himself as a feminist? Also, how do you react to men and women who describe themselves as chauvinists or sexists? If your reactions are gender specific, why?

CHAPTER 2

RESEARCH ON SEX STEREOTYPES

The term *stereotype* was first used in the 1920s by a journalist attempting to describe how members of a given society create shared "mental pictures." These pictures were believed to serve those who shared them in two ways: (1) by providing a shortcut for dissecting the continuous world into identifiable categories and (2) by providing a comfortable sense that the status quo was intact. As originally conceived, stereotypes were useful, though by no means neutral. They involved a decided edge for the dominant groups in a society and indirectly served to guarantee their superior position. On the optimistic side, it was thought that individuals were open to new information, even if contradictory, and were constantly recreating the stereotypes in line with new experiences.[1]

Although the connotation of the term has changed considerably over the years, it is helpful to consider the original meaning. We treat stereotypes as narrow, usually negative images that individuals impose on others who they believe belong to a category based on race, age, occupation, place of origin, and, of course, gender. Despite the generally negative view of the practice, it is easy to see the practicality of inferring information about an unknown individual based on previous interaction with similar individuals. For example, this assumption helps you to identify the employees in a restaurant, based on the similarity of their appearance and demeanor to other restaurant employees you have encountered. But stereotyping, as we now know and hate it, extends beyond the original definition, which stressed matching new instances to established "mental pictures." It involves making hasty assumptions about invisible and often irrelevant personal characteristics of the pictured individuals.

Indeed, we are now so preoccupied with stereotypes that we not only assume characteristics of identifiable groups, but we actually create and name new groups based on outward appearance. We refer to someone as a "jap" or a "jock" or a "redneck," often on the basis of the slightest information, and draw assumptions about his or her family background, intellectual capacity, political opinions, etc. Of course, some of us are more open than others to being proven wrong, but the prevailing stereotypes tend to operate on a guilty-until-proven-innocent basis.

There is a certain equity in the current practice of stereotyping, however, which the coiner of the term apparently did not anticipate. It is not only the members of dominant groups who generate stereotypes: anyone, it seems, can play the game—provided they have teammates. So, regardless of membership to the majority or minority group, individuals construct oversimplified descriptions of other people. In fact, the construction process is so well developed that most of us can state, quite fully, the prevailing stereotypes of groups to which we belong or that we encounter often—and even groups about which we have no firsthand knowledge.

Notably, most of us are familiar with multiple derogatory names for various groups and are aware that speakers create new ones all the time. These terms allow for the generation of new jokes and, unfortunately, often spark violence. Regardless of the outcome, there is a clear connection between the perceptual practice of stereotyping and the linguistic practice of labeling: both demonstrate the user's narrow thinking and make it less likely that the user will perceive others without bias in the future. In the case of sex stereotypes, this unhappy situation is especially puzzling. How is it that narrow visions of the sexes can endure when we come into contact with so many different individuals of each sex—individuals of all sizes, shapes, ages, and "personalities"? It simply seems impossible to generalize about the two unbelievably large and varied groups. It seems equally unlikely that the prevailing labels alone can account for stereotypes, given the sheer amount of contact each individual has with members of each group. Perhaps most curious is our willingness to perpetuate stereotypes that logically limit our ability to know ourselves and the individuals who matter most to us—our parents, children, siblings, friends, etc.

The puzzle that surrounds the prevailing system of perceptual and linguistic distinctions based on sex is not likely to be explained by logic, although scholars have attempted to support the "kernel of truth" theory and the "inversion of cause and effect" theory as they pertain to sex stereotypes.[2] Rather, it seems that the communication of sex stereotypes across generations is decidedly illogical—a process that proceeds based on fantasies referred to here as *myths*.

SEX STEREOTYPES AS MYTHS

All societies hold certain myths, or stories about the human experience that are passed from generation to generation. For certain individuals, these myths direct their behavioral choices; for others, the myths serve as conventions of the past to be criticized and challenged. Regardless of the perceived validity and generalizability of the dominant myths, most members of a given society can articulate them with remarkable accuracy. Yet, myths are not recorded stories, learned in public school classrooms. They are communicated, both implicitly and explicitly, in daily face-to-face interaction between members of a given society.

The precise process by which societies create, maintain, and modify various myths through communication remains a mystery. Many analysts have attempted to link conceptions of maleness and femaleness to specific aspects of the human experience, such as the division of labor, the distribution of resources, the allocation of decision-making power, etc. Still, it is difficult to examine the process by which visible differences in the structure of everyday life are translated into perceptions of behavior as characteristically male or female.

Smith and Midlarsky hypothesize that the communication of society's myths about masculinity and femininity first began in folklore. In other words, people learned that men and women were inevitably and irreversibly different (if not opposite), and this lesson was learned through intergenerational storytelling. Smith and Midlarsky go on to speculate about the content of these stories: "From folklore and legend come descriptions of women as gentle, beautiful, calm and faithful; men have been described as brave, aggressive, forceful and able."[3] As most children know, today's adults still repeat legendary tales about able male heroes and their gentle ladies.

However, psychologists could hardly accept fairy tale images, so they set out early in the 1900s to empirically derive the prevailing conceptions of maleness and femaleness in American society. Now joined by scientists from several disciplines, they continue to search for those conceptions and for indications that the conceptions are subject to change. Perhaps the most striking aspects of the resultant body of research are the precision with which sex stereotypes are communicated and the resistance of the stereotypes to change. In the next section, empirical studies of sex stereotypes are discussed.

STUDYING SEX STEREOTYPES

Prior to examining the studies that attempt to delineate the content of male–female stereotypes, it is important to acknowledge the methodological difficulties involved in this endeavor. Although numerous investigators have done extensive research on gender myths, the fact is that most of us are unwilling to declare our faith that gender myths are a valid indication of actual male–female behavior, and almost no one is ready to state that his or her behavior is stereotypic. In fact, a recent study concluded that the greatest change concerning traditional male–female stereotypes may well be that "the social desirability of expressing" knowledge of stereotypes has diminished.[4] In other words, we probably all know and may even accept the stereotypes to some degree, but most of us are reluctant to express them for fear of being labeled *sexist*.

(However, the new term *traditionalist* may make it easier to endorse sex stereotypes; this term is being used more and more, both in everyday speech and in scholarly writing).[5]

Based on the assumed social stigma attached to expressing stereotypes, most researchers have opted to avoid the term entirely as they attempt to extract the information they need from their subjects. Typically, researchers construct scales that they reproduce in written form and distribute to anonymous respondents, who fill them out. Usually, the questionnaires list personality traits judged by the researcher(s), or by a sample pilot group, to be masculine, feminine, or neutral. Of course, the items included on the list limit the range of responses, but using a standardized questionnaire eliminates the need to directly address the issue of stereotyping. Another methodological barrier is encountered in phrasing the instructions to the respondent. As critics have debated (at length), the instructions may influence the outcome of such a study.

These two methodological issues require careful attention whenever survey research of gender stereotypes is examined, along with obvious concerns about the makeup of the group of respondents. My students are usually most concerned about age, educational status, and, of course, gender. They are variously disgusted and reassured to learn that, due to the pragmatic nature of scholarly research, the respondents are usually quite predictable on all counts—a mix of age-homogeneous male and female college students.

In the early 1970s, empirical investigations of gender stereotypes flourished.[6] Although their published titles often included phrases like "a current appraisal" or "a new approach," the reports demonstrated that traditional images of masculinity and femininity were alive and well across age groups, across educational levels, and among both men and women. As Broverman et al. stated the situation in a 1972 summary, "despite the apparent fluidity of sex-role definition in contemporary society as contrasted with the previous decades, our own findings to date confirm the existence of pervasive and persistent sex-role stereotypes."[7]

Notably, the same images of men and women seemed to emerge regardless of the researcher's approach to extracting the information from the respondents. Some researchers asked individuals to rate items as "typical" masculine or feminine behavior.[8] Others asked them to identify "ideal" masculine or feminine traits.[9] Still others asked them to indicate "traditional characteristics" of masculinity and femininity.[10] Perhaps the most renowned and widely used scale, the Bem Sex Role Inventory (BSRI), was constructed by asking people to mark items as "socially desirable" for a man or for a woman, thereafter listing only items that appeared to be "significantly more desirable" for one sex or the other in American society, at least according to the judgment of the respondents.[11]

Apparently, the prevailing gender stereotypes, at least in the early 1970s, continued to influence generalized perceptions of masculinity and femininity. Research reports varied only in terminology and degree, summarizing conceptions of maleness and femaleness along the same lines as the legendary images. The following list of opposites highlights the typical findings:

Feminine:	*Masculine:*
Submissive	Aggressive
Emotional	Rational
Dependent	Independent
Fragile	Strong
Gentle	Rough
Quiet	Loud
Tactful	Blunt
Sensitive	Insensitive
Yielding	Competitive
Verbal/language oriented	Physical/activity oriented

Obviously, this list has personal implications that most readers will find offensive regardless of their gender. Adult feminine behavior seems to be roughly equivalent to that adopted by a beauty contestant, while adult masculine behavior seems to qualify an individual for the marine corps! (Please excuse the seemingly negative insinuation about these two thriving cultural institutions.) However, according to certain critiques, the stereotypic image of femininity is considerably less desirable than the stereotypic image of masculinity, particularly in a capitalistic society that covets strength, rationality, and competitiveness—and distributes power accordingly.

As one team of analysts concluded after comparing depictions of masculinity and femininity with depictions of "healthy" adult behavior, "women are clearly put in a double bind by the fact that different standards exist for women and for adults. If women adopt the behaviors specified as desirable for adults, they risk censure for their failure to be appropriately feminine; but, if they adopt the behaviors that are designated as feminine, they are necessarily deficient with respect to the general standards for adult behavior."[12] Admittedly, a comparison between stereotypically masculine behavior and the qualities valued in a good friend or effective parent may present a similar double-bind for men. If they behave like men, they are necessarily deficient friends and limited parents; if they adopt behaviors deemed appropriately nurturing and gentle, they may appear unmanly.

In any case, the offensiveness of the proposed list of opposite traits is reduced somewhat in view of what the list attempts to report—after all, these are "just" stereotypes. As stereotypes, the two contrasting depictions may even be valuable to those who are personally offended, as they provide detailed information about the nature of the misconceptions of maleness and femaleness. Still, it is important to keep in mind that, although we may react to these extremely limited characterizations of masculinity and femininity with anger and resentment, they delineate the ends of a continuum of expressed perceptions of sex-specific behavior (i.e., the stereotypes or the myths). In fact, when presented with noncategorized adjectives from the Bem list and asked how they believed a "narrow-minded individual" might react to them, most of my students were able to predict the correct label (masculine, feminine, or neutral) for nearly all the items. Most errors involved sex typing a neutral trait.

Perhaps their ability to sort the items into stereotypically masculine and feminine traits is evidence of the precision with which they have learned the societal myths, while their anger and regret are evidence of the growing dissatisfaction with sexist evaluations of personal behavior. Students often echo Bem's pronouncement that many adults would be better characterized as *androgynous* or possessing traits from both lists.[13] Still, the available generalizations about maleness and femaleness in our society, generated anonymously across ages by both men and women, provide a fascinating and undeniable, albeit restrictive, image of the what Bem labels the "culture's definitions of gender-appropriateness."[14]

It would be remiss, at this point, not to address the possibility that the aforementioned narrow, stereotypic images of American masculinity and femininity may be explained by the fact that the studies reported thus far were all conducted in the 1970s. Students assure me that things have changed, that, whereas their grandparents may have communicated these stereotypic notions, and possibly a trace of indirect communication was passed along through their parents, children of the future will have little or no knowledge of sex stereotypes. However, there are at least two convincing counter arguments for this position: (1) recent research conducted with college students suggests that traditional attitudes concerning masculinity and femininity are far from extinct, and (2) research conducted with children and adolescents suggests that they tend to be even more traditional than their older brothers and sisters.

Sex Stereotypes among College Students.   As mentioned, the academic community has not been able to gather empirical evidence that counters the proposed existence of rigid sex stereotypes, although the number of convincing theoretical and methodological critiques continues to grow.[15] Several analysts have questioned the validity of masculinity–femininity inventories, most commonly the BSRI, for reflecting contemporary attitudes. Surprisingly, though, the original scale devised by Bem in the early 1970s and first administered to undergraduate students at Stanford University in 1974[16] has survived multiple examinations concerning validity. Critics have suggested only minor changes, such as the deletion of redundant items like "masculine" and "feminine."[17] Notably, most of the follow-up investigations have also been conducted among college populations, which have been identified as among the most liberal concerning sex stereotypes[18]—particularly when asked directly whether or not they endorse the traditional images that they communicate so accurately and consistently.

In the meantime, scales like the BSRI were widely accepted and utilized during the 1980s to measure differences in behaviors and self-concepts of men and women, substituting "psychological gender" for "biological sex."[19] Scholars apparently recognized the BSRI as a viable description of extremely sex-typed behavior in American society, although they allowed for individual freedom in emphasizing that any adult, male or female, could possess traits associated with masculinity, femininity, or both.

Hence the label *androgyny:* a hybrid combining the root *andro,* derived from the Greek word for *male,* with the root *gyny* derived from the Greek word for *female.* Many of the studies reporting sex differences in communication behavior are presented in line with these conceptualizations. That is, while they allow for overlap, they accept the inventories as indicative of sex-typed behavior. In truth, a careful reading of Chapters Four through Seven of this volume suggest that empirical evidence concerning gender-specific communication is not at all inconsistent with the stereotypes.

Of course, it could be argued that none of this research is valid for today's college students, despite the various statistical analyses conducted by professors housed in ivory towers. If the professors want to know whether or not the stereotypes still exist, why not just ask the "new generation" of Americans (presumably tomorrow's parents and the agents of change)? Those researchers who have done just this have discovered that many traditional attitudes concerning men and women have survived the feminist revolution. Serbin and Unger report, having reviewed the content of the journal *Sex Roles* during its first decade (1976–1986), "we were struck by the relatively small number of either empirical or theoretical articles dealing with change. Those that did often documented or discussed lack of change rather than sweeping success in modifying gender roles or gender-related behaviors."[20]

Among the articles alluded to above are several that directly addressed the extent of change concerning sex stereotypes. Typically, researchers predicted change. As Werner and LaRussa wrote in 1985, "given the large amount of debate, discussion, activism and legislation relating to sex-role change in the last decade, it is relevant to assess the extent to which stereotypic conceptions of the two sexes have changed in recent years."[21] However, the expected change was usually limited. According to the self-report data collected by Werner and LaRussa, which replicated a study done twenty years before, "in many particulars sex-role stereotypes have changed little over the intervening two decades."[22] Specifically, they observed that 65% of the adjectives rated as "in general true of men" twenty years before were rated identically by their respondents. Men were still perceived as more independent, more aggressive, and more forceful than women; but also as more stubborn, reckless, and hard-headed. A slightly higher percentage (68%) of the female-stereotypic adjectives survived the twenty-year period. Among other things, women were stereotyped as more sociable, more tactful, and more affectionate than men. These were listed as favorable traits; some of the unfavorable traits were submissive, moody, and emotional.[23]

Despite the persistence of these stereotypic images, only about two-thirds of the traits were reidentified in the replicated study. One might conclude that it is becoming increasing difficult to label adjectives *male* and *female.* Thus, given time, the stereotypes will gradually disappear. However, it must be noted that adjectives that had previously been labeled *nondifferentiating* were added to the stereotypes! Fifteen new stereotyped adjectives appeared for men, of which just one, resourceful, was listed as favorable. The remaining fourteen were judged unfavorable adjectives, including bossy, demanding, and self-centered. Similarly, new stereotypes of women emerged, mostly favorable, including friendly, sincere, cooperative, enthusiastic, and optimistic.[24] Whether or not these images aid women in achieving political, social, and economic power remains to be seen. It may be that the negative male traits are of more value in competitive situations.

Still, the identification of favorable descriptors for women seems worth noting, since the tendency reported in the 1970s literature was clearly to stereotype women in unfavorable terms and men in favorable terms. The reversal of this tendency is also reported by Smith and Midlarsky, who obtained self-reports from respondents in 1985. These researchers used an open-ended questionnaire allowing each participant to generate an original list of "traits and behaviors of females and males." However, based on these lists, Smith and Midlarsky concluded that it was primarily "female conceptions of femaleness" that had improved, "in marked contrast to the relatively negative portrait of women provided by men."[25]

In another replication study, McKinney specifically attempted to gauge the change in male and female college students' attitudes toward women. Using the same design as a 1972 study, she published self-report data from college students in 1987. McKinney asked subjects to respond to a list of statements designed to identify their attitudes as "conservative vs. liberal." For example, "A woman should be as free as a man to propose marriage," or "The modern girl is entitled to the same freedom from regulation and control that is given to the modern boy." The statements were intended to span political, social, and occupational issues. McKinney concluded that there had been an "increase in liberalism on the part of both men and women," but that women continued to report "more liberal or nontraditional attitudes" than men—at least when it came to political and occupational issues. However, it seems worth noting that the college women in this study joined their male counterparts in reporting traditional attitudes on personal issues, including "proposing marriage, paying for date expenses, sexual intimacy before marriage," etc.[26] This trend suggests that contemporary women may be favoring gender-neutral standards in the public sphere, but preserving gender-specific standards in the private sphere—a theme that recurs in this book.

Since McKinney also paid attention to the age of her respondents, she was able to note another trend that may be rather telling in the future. Research conducted in the 1970s revealed that age was negatively correlated with liberalism (e.g., college students held less traditional attitudes than their parents). However, in 1982—after several years of such comparisons—Helmreich, Spence, and Gibson reported a "leveling off trend" in this correlation.[27] Presumably, liberal attitudes had successfully permeated the ranks of young parents. Remarkably, McKinney's 1987 data suggested that age was positively correlated with liberal-thinking. This means that today's college students may be more conservative than their predecessors.[28] This trend is very meaningful in light of what Renzetti has called "the new conservatism of American college students."[29]

Keep in mind that the post-suffragette period in our history was more oppressive to women, in many respects, than the period during which they were denied the vote. Women were overworked, underpaid, and generally excluded from positions of any real significance. Many analysts believe that women became complacent after gaining the vote. Others argue that economic influences prompted a return to conservatism.[30] Both conditions seem to hold implications for the 1990s. Perhaps the reported backlash

against feminism will successfully effect a return to conservatism in personal relationships and/or will foster complacency in the realms of business and education. Some
of these issues are discussed again in Part IV. Here, it is important to note that a second
era of post-reform conservatism seems to be sweeping the United States, enabling the
perpetuation of traditional stereotypes of men and women.

Sex Stereotypes among Children and Adolescents.   Perhaps the failure to find
significant changes in sex stereotypes among college students is due to some sort of
time lag. That is, although today's college students were conceived well after the first
meeting of the National Organization for Women (the proposed rebirth of feminism),
it is unreasonable to expect an instant effect on their attitudes. After all, change takes
time. Therefore, the decline of traditional myths about males and females ought to be
more visible in the voices of even younger Americans—children and adolescents.
However, the contention that children are currently being raised free from sex
stereotypes is debatable.

Even in dual-career homes, where the most immediate models are logically
androgynous, it seems that young children learn and articulate the dominant traditional
myths about sex-typed behaviors. Of course, the difficulty of communicating with
preschoolers has complicated the determination of the exact age at which children can
articulate a knowledge of sex stereotypes, but studies have shown that children seem
to be aware of gender-specific standards at a remarkably young age.[31]

Even brief interactions with preschoolers will demonstrate their knowledge of
arbitrary symbols for masculinity and femininity. I recently queried a group of
youngsters at my daughter's nursery school as to the correct sex of each of the Care
Bears. Those who have seen the likable little characters may have noticed how clearly
neutral they are with regard to sex. Still, both the boys and the girls agreed that the
pink bears were girls and the blue and brown bears were boys. They cited the names
of these bears as evidence—e.g., Lots of Love, a pink bear, was a girl; and Champ
Bear, a brown bear, was a boy. The yellow and green bears, however, were more
controversial. Several of the children imagined the ambiguously colored bears to be
whichever sex they were—i.e., the boys said they were boys, and the girls said they
were girls. One little boy commented, "I saw the movie, and Birthday Bear had a boy
voice." Some of the children became quite excited when I suggested that one of their
favorite toys may not be the same sex as they were! Finally, my daughter prompted
me to stop asking when she announced, "Oh Mom, they're not anything! Just bears!"

This informal study, and more formal studies mentioned in this section, suggest
that children are very conscious of the categorization of characters as male or
female—with little room for overlap. According to Bem's gender schema theory, this
is not surprising, since "our culture communicates both explicitly and implicitly that
sex is one of the most important categories in human social life." Therefore, even very
young children "see reality as carved naturally into gender categories."[32]

The development of a young child's cognitive conceptions of gender are
discussed in Chapter Ten. However, it must be emphasized here that children learn
language at approximately the same time they begin to demonstrate knowledge of sex

stereotypes. Obviously, it may be that they hold this knowledge at a much younger age, but simply cannot express it. Nevertheless, the cultural emphasis on gender as a two-category system, coupled with the polar nature of our language (discussed in the next chapter), seem to facilitate the development of rigid stereotypes among young children.

Thus, it is not shocking that children have also been found to categorize abstract symbols, such as adjectival traits, according to gender. As early as age two-and-one-half, children reportedly respond that someone who is "strong or big" is a male, and someone who is "pretty or small" is a female.[33] It also appears that children are willing to predict behavior based on their knowledge of stereotypes. In another recent study, preschool children ages three to five were presented with a hypothetical scenario and asked which of two pictured figures, one male and one female, would be more likely to behave in a particular way. For example, "Which person cries a lot when things go wrong?" or "Which person gets into a fight when there's a problem?" According to the authors, the children demonstrated "significant stereotypic knowledge" as they aligned behavioral descriptions with the dominant adult stereotypes.[34]

A number of studies have attempted to measure the extent to which children combine information to form gender stereotypes of occupational roles. Conceivably, young children are exposed to multiple images of what adult men and women "do," whether the adults in question are parents, strangers, or television characters. Children reportedly categorize photographs, uniformed dolls, and even occupational labels as male or female in line with tradition.[35] In a study where children were shown a film depicting a female doctor and a male nurse, the children reversed the images in line with traditional stereotypes, identifying the man as the doctor and the woman as the nurse. Of course, this seems like an excusable mistake for preschoolers, but the same reversal was also cited by fourth-graders.[36]

Zuckerman and Sayre adopted a somewhat more complex approach in their interviews with preschoolers. They compared "generalized impressions" of sex stereotypes with responses to "personalized" questions. This approach allowed for a fascinating comparison between the knowledge of sex stereotypes at an impersonal level and the restrictions children imagine for their behavioral choices. First, the investigators asked the youngsters open-ended questions about their own aspirations and attitudes. For example, children were asked what they would like to be when they grew up—and what they would like to be if they were the opposite sex. They were also asked if they liked being a boy or girl and why. Then the children were asked if a predetermined list of sex-specific occupations and activities were all right for a man or a woman.[37]

The results indicated that the children seemed to be fairly liberal in approving what the authors labeled *nontraditional* activities and occupations for males and females. Of the fourteen traditionally sex-typed items, the most restricted, according to the children, were "being a soldier" and "being a nurse." Still, even on these items, almost half of the boys and girls said it was all right for a woman to be a soldier and a man to be a nurse. The percentages were significantly higher for other occupations— e.g., 60% thought it was all right for a woman to fix a car, and 94% thought it was all right for a man to take care of young children. However, the personal aspirations expressed by the children were rather traditional: 83% of the boys and 68% of the girls chose careers in traditionally sex-typed fields. The most popular occupations chosen by girls were nurse, teacher, and dancer. Boys' favorites were athlete, fireman, police officer, and truck driver.[38]

Thus, while children in this study expressed acceptance of nontraditional career choices on a generalized level, they also made clear a preference for traditional choices on a personal level. Notably, many children chose different careers when they were asked to imagine themselves as the opposite sex. Fifty-four percent of the girls thought they would like to be doctors if they were boys; 46% of the boys imagined themselves becoming nurses if they were girls. In addition, 18% of the children refused to answer the question, which the authors believe indicated discomfort with the idea of changing sex.[39]

There is little formal research that focuses on the ability of young children to identify subtle sex differences in communication behavior. Researchers have discovered that children differentiate male from female figures on the basis of hair length and dress, but as yet we have no evidence that they distinguish men from women based on verbal and nonverbal communication. Recently, however, I conducted some informal research on this subject with a group of three-year-olds that belong to a local play group. Several mothers had arranged for their children to play together once a week, with the location rotating among each of the children's homes. When I hosted the gathering, I seized the opportunity to talk individually with several of the children. I asked them to identify figures in a book as male or female. These figures were very simplistically drawn and largely neutral in body shape, size, and hairstyle. The absence of these contrasts was apparently a deliberate effort by the illustrator to bring attention to subtle differences, such as facial expressions or posture. To my utter amazement, each of the children I spoke with was very adept not only at correctly categorizing the figures but also at pointing to the details that influenced his or her decisions: "the eyebrows...the mouth...the shoes...the way she's sitting." Certainly, systematic research in this area is limited, but there is reason to believe that even young children are most willing (and not altogether unable) to categorize individual behaviors as male or female.

In sum, it seems that today's children are fairly knowledgeable about sex stereotypes. Most of the studies indicate that young children are generally narrow-minded when it comes to sex-specific behavior. According to one source, there is reason to believe that children seem to become increasingly knowledgeable and concerned about sex appropriateness until they "mature and become exposed to the public debate regarding the issues."[40] Therefore, it may be unreasonable to expect very young children to articulate nontraditional attitudes toward sex stereotypes.

Investigations of adolescent perceptions of sex stereotypes, then, may hold more information about social change. In fact, even studies conducted in the 1970s indicated that middle school children (grades five through eight) were far more tolerant than preschool children on the issue of nontraditional occupational roles.[41] Notably, though, adolescent girls seem to be more willing than adolescent boys to endorse a break from tradition, particularly in career choice.[42] It seems that young girls in America assert that they are suited for traditionally male careers, and see males as suited for traditionally female careers. However, the boys appear to be far less willing to cross the traditional lines. This contrast may be explained by a perceived status distinction (i.e., that being male is somehow better than being female in terms of occupational status and power). According to Lewin and Tragos, "the higher status person will emphasize distinctions that are to his social advantage and increase his power, while the lower status person has an interest in minimizing that which lowers her social status or power."[43]

The image of today's teenage girls asserting their interest in improved status for women seems noteworthy, akin to the liberal attitudes expressed by college women concerning occupational and educational freedom. However, an article published in 1987 casts doubt on the breadth of change in adolescent stereotypes—among girls as well as boys—when it comes to general images. According to the authors, "young people apparently engage in as much, or more, sex role stereotyping as they did a quarter century ago." The authors did not speculate as to the reasons for this failure of progress, but went on to specify that "these students do not hold a 'unisex' social role model with respect to the desirable interests and personality traits of girls and boys." Many of these sex-stereotyped traits relate to male dominance and female subordination.[44] It seems adolescent girls, like their older counterparts, tend to assert their freedom to make nontraditional choices in public matters, but decline to do so in matters of personal interests.

Ultimately, today's children, like those of decades past, learn about the importance of sex as a category that influences their self-knowledge as well as their knowledge of others. Some of the restrictions imposed by youngsters are gradually "undone" with age, particularly if the youngsters in question are female. However, a healthy knowledge of sex stereotypes and, to some extent, a positive endorsement of tradition survives into adulthood—even in a society governed by laws that mandated the end of sex discrimination over twenty years ago.

SEX STEREOTYPES AND COMMUNICATION

Although there may still be lingering doubt that the "list of opposites" presented earlier in this chapter appropriately reflects the prevailing sex stereotypes in contemporary society, it seems worthwhile to discuss the implications of the stereotypes for communication. Perhaps the doubting reader can withhold judgment about the exact content of the list, at this point, and think abstractly about the relationship between stereotypes-in-flux and communication.

The list consists of proposed traits that people associate, in the form of stereotypes, with males and females. Certainly, we come to know many men and women on a personal level, i.e., through communicating with them, and need not rely on stereotypes to characterize their behavior. In other words, we come to expect our family members, friends, colleagues, etc., to behave in certain ways—for instance, aggressively or nurturantly—based on our past interaction with them; we have witnessed these behaviors firsthand. Therefore, we do not need stereotypes to understand people we know well—although it is interesting to notice our own reactions when someone close to us behaves in a surprising way or merely asserts his or her freedom to do so.

Still, stereotypes operate as a powerful and ever-present influence on communication. We live in a highly mobile, complex society that requires us to interact with strangers on a daily basis. In addition, there are times when a relative stranger's impression of us matters to us deeply—e.g., when interviewing for a job, meeting your date's parents, or approaching a professor. Certainly, we would prefer that sex stereotypes did not contribute to our expectations of others' behavior, much less to others' expectations of our behavior. But it seems safe to say that we are far more concerned with sex-appropriate behavior in initial interactions and formal situations than in ongoing relationships.

Sex stereotypes are perhaps most apparent, though, when we communicate with an individual who clearly crosses the lines. Many individuals are extremely uncomfortable in the company of men who are *emotional, fragile,* or *quiet* and women who are *aggressive, rough,* or *loud.* The fact remains that most of us are so well versed in the traditional stereotypes that we at least notice, if not criticize or laugh at, behavioral displays that cross the lines. Our sensitivity to such "atypical" displays is evidence of our knowledge of stereotypes and the effect they have on our expectations.

In sum, sex stereotypes may be assumed to influence communication with strangers, particularly in situations in which one or the other individual is attempting to make a certain impression, and in situations that challenge traditional expectations. But stereotypes may be more influential than we would like to imagine. At this point, it is tentatively proposed that sex stereotypes provide a template against which all male and female behavior is initially judged.

In other words, while we may be very accepting of others' freedom to behave in any way they like, we may find we take special notice of a particularly nurturant male. Why is it that we comment on a father who spends time with his children, but expect it of a mother? We may hear remarks like, "He even changes the diapers!" How silly to offer the same remark about a woman. My sister is especially sensitive when people state that a given father is "babysitting." Yet, the notion of referring to a mother as "baby-sitter" seems ludicrous. On the other hand, why do we notice an unusually strong or athletic female, and even comment how well she plays "for a girl." Why do we notice and admire, over and above the males in her world, an aggressive, capable young business woman?

Perhaps the reason that certain behaviors are more noticeable in a male or female stems from our unwilling adherence to the stereotypes we often speak against. In fact, it will become more and more apparent that the investigation of sex differences in communication suggests that there are two styles, quite opposite in nature, of communicating. These styles are not unrelated to the traits listed earlier, and, although we may be unaware of the fact, it is hypothesized that each of us adheres, more or less, to the appropriate communication style, thereby perpetuating the stereotypes.

It is certainly premature to describe with certainty, male and female communication styles, previous to reviewing the empirical literature on sex differences in aspects of communicative behavior. But, to logically infer the styles, based on the prevailing stereotypes, it seems that we might expect men to be *direct, forceful, rational,* and somewhat *self-centered,* in their communication with others. We would, in turn, expect women to be more *indirect, emotive, yielding,* and *other-centered* in their communication. I hope that hypothesizing male and female communication styles based on proposed sex stereotypes will provide a framework for understanding (and perhaps criticizing) the various studies of specific communication behavior presented in the next five chapters.

CONDUCT YOUR OWN RESEARCH

1. Ask a number of friends, classmates, and/or acquaintances to respond anonymously to a questionnaire you design intended to provide information about gender stereotypes. Think carefully about the format of your questionnaire. (Should the questions be open-ended? close-ended? checklist? true–false?) Consider the approach you use to define stereotypes: are they physical traits? social behaviors? psychological tendencies? activities and occupations? life goals? Also consider the way you want respondents to conceive of a stereotype: as typical behavior? desirable behavior? socially acceptable behavior? Compare your results to the studies conducted during the 1970s.

2. Conduct a content analysis of three of the top ten television shows using the information available in any television section of a magazine or newspaper. Write down each character as he or she appears and look for evidence that the character acts stereotypically and/or is treated stereotypically.

3. Ask your friends to retell favorite fairy tales they were told as children. Tape record their stories and look for evidence supporting or countering the argument that sex stereotypes are mythological.

DISCUSS THE ISSUES

1. What are the differences and similarities between sex stereotypes and other common stereotypes (e.g., racial, religious, ethnic)? Are sex stereotypes more widely known? more comprehensive in content? more resistant to change? less offensive? If so, why?

2. Certain stereotypic "truths" appear to be contradicted by statistical evidence. For example, women are stereotyped as poor drivers, but are better insurance risks. Also, marriage is stereotypically "good" for women and "bad" for men, although statistical evidence reveals that married women and single men are among the poorest health risks, both mentally and physically. Which are correct, the myths or the statistics?

3. Even though we may find them distasteful and dangerous, stereotypes can effectively reflect and/or reinforce certain political and economic realities. If so, what are the implications of being stereotypically male and female in our culture? Are males and females stereotypically right for some jobs, positions, pastimes and wrong for others? What is the price to be paid for being cross-qualified? Is it possible to be right for all of life's positions? What are the consequences of this condition?

CHAPTER 3

DEBATES ABOUT LANGUAGE AND SEXISM

The use of language is so integral to the human experience that most of us seldom stop to think about the fact that we are symbol-using creatures in a world inhabited predominantly by non-symbol-users. Children around the globe develop the ability to communicate with amazing ease. In fact, it is surprising that most children learn to communicate competently at roughly the same age, regardless of the language they speak, and regardless of the attention paid to this project by the adults around them. Still, good parents everywhere are careful to teach youngsters the right names for things, correct the inevitable grammatical errors, and blame one another if a child should utter a profane phrase.

The attention we pay to the rules of language use, however, may serve to cloud our awareness of the tremendous impact that language use in general has on the human experience. We may be overly conscious of language as a tool that we may or may not use to express our thoughts and feelings but be unconscious of the role that language plays in determining which thoughts and even which feelings we experience. To borrow an overused metaphor, we tend to see the ability to use language as opening doors and are generally uncomfortable with the notion that language may simultaneously close doors.

Those who have recognized the narrowing effect of language in the human experience have variously referred to it as linguistic relativity, determinism, the world view problem, and the Sapir-Whorf hypothesis (after its authors). Essentially, they have argued that the particular language we speak serves to segment a continuous world—to divide it into parts that we can identify and talk about—and to put it back together according to a given set of "rules." In this way, each language system embodies a particular "world view" and probably influences not only what its speakers can say but also what they can think.[1] For instance, our language has words that serve as symbols for a variety of human emotions: sorrow, pride, greed, etc. Perhaps we would be less likely to feel a particular emotion in a particular situation if we had no word to name it. Certainly, we would have difficulty describing the emotion, and the feeling might fade or even disappear having gone unshared.

In this chapter, aspects of language use with regard to the sexes are examined in light of the possibility that our language system, despite our good intentions to the contrary, may serve to limit what we can say and possibly what we can think about men and women. Examples are provided suggesting that there are identifiable trends in our language that subtly distinguish the sexes along the very same lines to which most readers probably took offense in the "list of opposites" presented in the previous chapter. Each reader, whether male or female, will undoubtedly respond to the forthcoming examples individually: "I don't say that!" or "I say that and there's nothing wrong with it!" or perhaps "I guess I do say that once in a while, but I don't mean anything by it." But, regardless of the individual reader's habits, it is suggested that the examples delineate trends in our language system that, at a collective level, define *maleness* and *femaleness* in our experience and, in the process, close certain doors to a segment of the population.

THE GENERIC HE

Our language is noticeably laden with nouns. Much to the surprise of elementary school students who struggle with verb tenses, adverbs, participles, etc., the majority of the words in the dictionary are plain old nouns or words that modify nouns. Most of us use a very small range of verbs in our speech. We say we *love* ice cream, Mom, and a comfortable article of clothing, although the emotions we feel in each case are clearly distinct. We *are* tired and poor, but talented, although the present tense does not relate any distinctions about the permanency of each condition. We also use an extremely small number of adverbs: mostly *really, very,* and, oh yes, *mostly.*

Since we use so many nouns in our communication, both written and spoken, we also tend to rely heavily on pronouns (short words that take the place of nouns). Americans appear to be conscious of efficiency and accuracy in communication, as evidenced by the popular phrase "short and sweet." Therefore, pronouns are used often, and those same elementary school students who must learn participles, must encounter the generic *he.* The rule for the generic *he,* roughly stated, is: When the referent of a pronoun is not specifically male or female, the correct pronoun is *he* and the correct possessive pronoun is *his.* As a result, it is correct to say "Each citizen is entitled to his day in court," although we know that women have to stand trial too, and "He who hesitates is lost," even though females are often thought to be less adventurous than males.

The use of the generic *he* has been called into question since the feminist movement. Alternative forms such as *s/he, he/she, he or she,* and *they* are becoming more common and some form of nonsexist treatment is mandated in most public, legal, and educational writing. Still, the generic *he* rule is worth our attention for several reasons. This grammatical form continues to characterize a good deal of literature, some of which was written before authors were asked to consider its implications and some of which continues to be published despite objections. Newspaper editors, for example, continue to resist the adoption of a nonsexist form, due to their emphasis on brevity and clarity.[2]

Also, this form continues to be a characteristic of spoken English. Sources as recent as 1988 report that "overall, the masculine generic remains an integral part of [the] English language usage of most Americans, particularly in the case of oral language."[3] Because speech is a more spontaneous form of communication than writing, the masculine generic's appearance there indicates just how firmly embedded it is in our way of thinking. However, regardless of the prevalence of the generic *he*, it is worthwhile for students to examine the debate over the adoption of a nonsexist alternative because it brings into focus some of the prevailing attitudes in our culture, not only about men and women but also about language and experience.

At the onset, it should be stressed that the linguistic problem we encounter when we attempt to use a pronoun to refer to a person, unidentified as male or female, is evidence that our language emphasizes the division of the species into two biological groups. In fact, we can refer to a mixed group of men and women neutrally by simply saying "The citizens are entitled to their rights." Our language easily allows for such an uncontroversial statement. But there is no sex-neutral, uncontroversial form providing for a reference to one person. Our neuter singular pronoun is *it* and we are taught not to refer to a person as an it. As a result, we can opt to use the masculine singular *he* or the feminine singular *she*. Another feasible solution is, of course, to adopt a less efficient but more accurate alternative, such as *he or she*.

The generic *he* solution to this problem is consistent with other linguistic habits. We refer to the entire species as *mankind* and refer to ourselves collectively as *man*. We talk about the "*man* in the street," a "*man* for all seasons," and the "common *man*." The language used in our dominant religions references the supreme being as masculine: "Our Father," "The Lord." Even some of our seemingly gender-neutral terms are derived from the emphasis on the male (e.g., hu*man* and per*son*).

The tendency to use male forms of language to refer to both men and women has been summarized as the *he/man approach* by Wendy Martyna. She contends that, although it is not the only issue in the debate about sexism in language use, the he/man issue has received the most attention due to the fact that the practices in question occur so frequently in our interaction and that the treatment of women is so obviously discriminatory.[4]

The he/man approach has been said to discriminate against women through two categories of practice: exclusion and exception. The former has already been demonstrated by terms such as *mankind,* and statements such as "Every citizen deserves his day in court." Women are apparently excluded, at least in literal translation. The latter is exemplified by pairs of terms like man/woman and male/female, which call attention to one sex as a "special form" of the other by adding a prefix to a root word. So, just as cranberries, raspberries, and strawberries are specified types of berries, so is a woman a particular type of man. This makes sense, given the generic label *man,* except that there is no term for the other particular type of man—*man!* If this discussion begins to seem circular and confusing, the reader may be indirectly arriving at one of the arguments against the generic *he,* i.e., it causes confusion. The reader or listener has no way to be sure whether the term *man* is used as a specific biological category or as a generic label. The term *woman,* though, always denotes a biological class.

Studies have consistently demonstrated that the generic *he* is often confused with the specific *he.* It appears that the pronoun is used far more often as a specific reference to males, so that when it is used as a generic reference, the reader or listener is likely to perceive it as male-specific.[5] Perhaps the greatest evidence of this lies in our sense that something is wrong with the sentence, "Each nurse will wash and iron *his* uniform daily." My students have told me that this construction is ridiculous because, like it or not, most nurses are still women, so the pronoun should be *her.* The fact that the exceptional male nurse is excluded by this construction demonstrates the point (in the inverse) that our language system suffers from both confusion and exclusion when we try to use generic pronouns.

It is worthwhile to consider the way children tend to use pronouns when confronted with the problem of speaking or writing about an unspecified other. According to several studies, a young child will simply use the gender-specific pronoun appropriate to himself or herself. (How egocentric!) Of course, these children can hardly be blamed, due to their tender years, and studies confirm that children cease this practice as they learn the "rules of language."[6] But, those who subscribe to the theory of linguistic relativity have argued that this particular grammar lesson may have serious consequences for female children, as they suddenly find themselves "excluded," even in their own utterances.[7] Conversely, learning to use the masculine generic provides a seemingly effortless extension of the egocentric practice already adopted by young male children.

Indeed, a 1988 survey of children in grades three to twelve revealed that the vast majority of young boys are most likely to refer to a nongendered other as *he.* Among high school males, presumably aware of the social implications of the masculine generic and/or required to follow nonsexist requirements, some boys opt for a neutral referent (e.g., he/she or s/he) (but a larger percentage simply continue to use the masculine referent. Virtually none of the boys in the study, regardless of age, used a female referent, evidence either of their egocentricism or the widespread dislike of the proposed generic *she*—or both).[8]

Girls are more likely to use the female referent, particularly girls in grades three to six, but not as many as one might expect (only 12%). The number steadily declines as the age of the subjects increases; only 3% of the girls in grades ten to twelve reportedly supported the use of a female referent. Perhaps the most provocative information in this recent survey concerns the pronoun-usage habits of today's young women, whom may be assumed to be aware of the debate surrounding nonsexist language. As might be expected, more girls than boys adopt a gender-neutral style. Still, 43% of the high school girls surveyed used the generic *he*![9]

Thus, many of us born "XX" (to use chromosome talk for lack of a nonsexist term) find ourselves to be linguistic exceptions and exclusions even in our own communication. Clearly, we have all inherited this language system together, so the male reader who becomes defensive and shouts at his book, "Well, feminists say *women* and that's a form of *men!*" need not take the blame for this situation. The language practices in question predate us all and will undoubtedly survive us all. In fact, efforts to legislate nonsexist forms have only called attention to the intricate network of sexism that is woven into the very fabric of our thinking. The sheer difficulty of locating, much less agreeing to use, terms for women that do not involve the exception rule or the exclusion rule is demonstrated at the beginning of this paragraph. The thought of referring to women as *XX*s and men as *XY*s seems inconsistent with our way of thinking and living.

In addition to pointing out the drastic change a truly neutral language system would involve, those who oppose legislating neutrality have argued that linguistic discrimination need not be equated with other, more serious, forms of discrimination. They suggest that the energy being directed toward changing the language is futile and misguided and only detracts from more important issues, such as equal employment and educational opportunities. The term *trivial* is often used by those who oppose paying attention to linguistic practices. The trivialization argument may tell us more about an attitude toward language than an attitude toward women. This claim voices the assumption that language is not of consequence—in this case that how we refer to groups of people need not influence how we treat them.

To be sure, the discussion of language peculiarities like the generic *he* is generally lighthearted, in sharp contrast to discussions of inequality in the public sphere. In my classes, discussions of household responsibilities and chivalrous manners become more heated than the debate over the generic *he*. Most of us tend to treat language as a system somehow separate from our lives; as long as we are aware of inconsistencies in the system, they need not cause serious problems. We ought to consider, though, the effects of the exclusion and exception rules on early language users. After all, young children are unlikely to be aware of the subtle difference between the sex-specific *he* and the generic *he*. How might they be affected by the famous utterance "One small step for man; one giant leap for mankind"?

Perhaps the possibility that young girls may feel excluded from space exploration is too farfetched to be convincing. Another analogy may demonstrate the power of linguistic exclusion more vividly. Imagine that we agreed, in symbolic form only, to refer to a population of many colors according to just one of the colors (albeit the most commonly seen one). The term *white* could be used in some utterances to refer to all Americans, and in other utterances to refer to just white-skinned Americans, right? Need our many people of other colors feel excluded, as long as we used the label *generically*? Such a practice is sadly not without historical example, but would be labeled discriminatory in no uncertain terms, and would probably not be taken nearly as lightly as the continued use of the generic masculine.

OCCUPATIONAL LABELS

Traditionally, the male form has also been used to identify occupational categories. Usually the practice involves adding the suffix -*man* or one of the suffixes -*er* or -*or* to a root word which denotes a skill or product someone controls or delivers for pay. Thus, we learn as children about the "people in our neighborhood": the mail*man*, the police*man*, the fire*man*. Later we learn about the people in our government: the congress*man*, the senat*or*, and the legislat*or*. Again these labels are exlusionary since they seem to deny the possibility of a woman occupying these roles.

But youngsters soon learn that there are, in truth, "*lady* mailmen," "police-*women*," and even "fire*ladies*"! It might be argued, though, that these forms all suffer from the exception principle, since a special form must be chosen in order to label a female of this general category. In any case, it is less unusual, both linguistically and perceptually, for a man to occupy these positions. Certainly, it is redundant (as well as difficult) to say "male mailman." Linguistic relativists would argue that the use of the male label for the general category and the specific case in which a male belongs to the category, coupled with the tendency to adopt a special language form for a female who belongs to the category, is evidence and also possibly the cause of our understanding that these are not "women's jobs." In essence, the symbol system we use to describe occupational categories often suffers from both the exclusion and the exception rules in dealing with females.

Those who respond that noting biological detail is simply identifying specific information about a particular instance of a given group (i.e., giving a "fuller description") and does not involve noting it as exceptional might ponder his or her reaction to the label "short mailmen," or "fat firemen." We seldom include such specific biological details in occupational labels. So the fact that we attend to gender in this regard probably demonstrates our expectations about employment based on our learned gender prejudices.

Other occupational labels reveal the assumption that women will be the rule, not the exception. Traditionally, nurses, secretaries and strippers have been females. Admittedly, these labels do not include a specific female reference, and, appear to be gender-neutral. But the common practice of adding the word *male* when a man occupies one of these positions demonstrates that these are female labels. For instance, if certain dance ensembles did not advertise themselves as consisting of "*male* strippers," they would surely fail to attract the intended audience.

In some cases, we adopt the practice of learning pairs of gender-specific complements to describe occupations, which is further evidence that we pay close attention to gender even when we have no particular expectations about who is more qualified to perform a given task. We accept service from wait*ers* or wait*resses*; we enjoy performances by act*ors* and act*resses*; we attend parties given by hosts and host*esses*; we listen to bands led by drum maj*ors* and drum major*ettes*. In each case, although the female form is easy to say and commonly used and therefore females need not suffer from exceptional linguistic treatment, the male form is generally adopted for the plural in the category or in cases where gender is unknown. Therefore, while you can get away with calling a female an *actor*, you probably ought not call a male an *actress*.

Admittedly, we do employ many sex-neutral occupational labels with success. We speak of teachers, technically a male form, but most people identify the term as gender-neutral (although when asked to identify which of two pictures was probably a teacher, the clear majority of children studied chose the female).[10] We use terms like *principal, judge*, and even *president* as gender neutral. In these examples we need not be bound by any linguistic inference, although we cannot help but be influenced by the expectations of tradition. So it is not unusual to hear about a female judge debating the merits of a woman president.

Efforts to impose the usage of sex-neutral occupational labels have been undertaken since the onset of the feminist movement. For instance, mailmen and their female counterparts are now asked to identify themselves collectively as *letter carriers*, and policemen and policewomen refer to themselves officially as *law officers*. In these cases, the uniform adoption of the male suffix -*er* seems preferrable to the continued use of the more overt suffix, -*men*. In identifying a single case, though, a very interesting trend has revealed our resistance to sex-neutrality. It has become common practice to use the neutral term for a woman, but the sex-specific term for a man. Thus, we have either a chair*person* or a chair*man*, a congress*person* or a congress*man*, a sales *representative* or a sales*man*. Apparently, our language habits are beginning to reflect the impropriety of referring to a female as a type of -*man*, but they have not yet succeeded in withholding the gender of the occupant in naming the person by position.

The tremendous strides that we have taken in recent decades toward equal opportunity for employment have apparently not resulted in an abrupt change in the forms we use to identify our work. Without question, the words we use are less important than the actions we take, but they may serve to gently close doors that have been slammed shut in the past.

FORMAL TERMS OF ADDRESS

Perhaps the most well-publicized request of the feminist movement was that females no longer be identified as married or unmarried when formally addressed. The popular magazine *Ms.* appears to have gained its title, if not its readership, as a side effect of the campaign for equality with men in this regard. In reality, the use of the nonspecific form *Ms.* is very helpful in highly impersonal communication in which the marital status of a female is unknown. But this linguistic change, which might have been seen simply as pragmatic, has become a symbol of the struggle for equal treatment of women.

Traditionally, it has been easy to signify formality, thereby maintaining distance and respect, when addressing a man. The speaker or writer need only attach the formal term *Mr.* to the other's surname regardless of the age or marital status of the addressee. In contrast, linguistic tradition has called for dual labels of respect when addressing a female: *Miss* or *Mrs.* Each term, coupled with a surname, not only denotes respect and distance, but indicates marital status as well. The term *Miss* has also come to connote youth, since it is assumed that only young women are "maidens." Therefore, a woman who retains the title *Miss* into adulthood is often labeled an "old maid."

It has been argued that marital status is more important for women than for men regardless of the formal term by which they are addressed. After all, we are all familiar with the myths about women "chasing" husbands and men maneuvering to avoid being "trapped" into marriage. In fact, at least one study shows that married men are happier than single men, while single women are happier than married women.[11] In any case, the suggested change to *Ms.* for all women might be taken as another trivial issue that detracts from more important problems caused by false stereotypes. This argument demonstrates once again the position that "words cannot hurt us." Those who have little faith in the power of language simply have not seen the need for changing the traditional practices.

The universal convention of addressing women with a single formal term would certainly uncomplicate matters for the addresser and probably help to alleviate some common prejudgments about the addressee. Following this logic, some critics have agreed to this practice in theory but have been critical of the specific label *Ms.* After all, is it a word or an abbreviation? Strict grammarians need to know whether or not to follow it with a period! It cannot be a word because it has no vowel, but what is the longer form of this abbreviation? Certainly, it is not consistent with *Mr.,* which, as an abbreviation for *Mister,* clearly necessitates a period at the end.

Both *Mr.* and *Ms.* are listed in the most recent edition of *The American Heritage Dictionary* and are followed by periods. However, a second form of the latter term also appears as capitalized, but without a period. According to definitions which follow the listings, *Mr.* is "an abbreviated form," while *Ms.* or *Ms* is "a title of courtesy." Thus, the inconsistencies between the traditional male form and the invented female form are obvious. Yet, wedged firmly between the two listings in the dictionary is a listing for *Mrs.,* which reads a "title of courtesy," even though it appears as an abbreviation according the inclusion of the period![12] In searching for the longer version of this title, I discovered that it is an "archaic" form of "Mistress."[13] (Imagine the surprise of the woman who thinks she is the "Mrs." and finds out, technically, she is the "Mistress.") Add to these complications the use of *Miss,* a full word with no standard abbreviation, to refer to an unmarried woman. Apparently, grammatical consistency does not even characterize the traditional forms.

Other critics have argued that *Ms.* is harder to pronounce than the traditional titles. Apparently, forming the voiced sound "z" is more difficult for these speakers than forming the unvoiced "s" in *Miss,* although the spoken title *Mrs.* contains both sounds. More likely, because it is a new form, it calls attention to itself, making the transition to *Ms.* difficult for speakers.[14]

While the status of the new term has not been of great interest to researchers, my mail suggests that the title currently serves the pragmatic purpose of simplifying matters for those sending mail to a recipient whose gender is assumed, but whose marital status is not. I have received a good deal of *Ms.* mail, both as a single and a married woman. On the other hand, I am formally addressed by hundreds of students (and a handful of others wishing to show respect) but cannot recall the last time I was addressed as *Ms.* in person. Granted, tradition dictates other formal terms for professional educators, such as *Professor* and *Doctor,* but I am referred to as *Mrs.* far more often than by any other title. I understand from my single teacher friends, however, that they are currently called *Ms.* both in speech and in writing. So it may well be that we are in the process of replacing the title *Miss* with the title *Ms.* If so, we may have succeeded in simplifying mailing lists, but probably have not made progress toward eliminating attention from the female's marital status.

A related area of this issue surrounds the proper way to formally address a married couple. Although the IRS may want a woman to sign her "given" name, and she is even asked to call herself by her "maiden" name when filling out an offspring's birth certificate application, formal etiquette calls for a woman to be treated essentially as Mrs. Somebody Else. That is, the woman takes not only the last name of her husband, but the first. Thus an invitation sent to a married couple should read *Mr. and Mrs. John Doe.* Moreover, an invitation sent to only Mary Doe should read *Mrs. John Doe.* The dictionary suggests the alternate form *Ms. Mary Doe,* but *Mrs. Mary* Doe is clearly as improper as *Ms. John Doe.*

There are other formal titles, though, and a woman can earn the title *Dr.* even in a "man's world." By rights, she should then be called *Dr. Mary Doe.* If she is unmarried, the title is proper; if she is married, addressing her in this way calls for only a slight breach of etiquette. But, when addressed in tandem with her husband, a married woman may not be properly titled *Dr.* The proper formal address remains *Mr. and Mrs. John Doe,* which ignores her earned title.[15] Alas, she remains Mrs. Somebody Else despite her accomplishment.

The reality is that the current system of formal address does not accommodate the strides that our "governing fathers" claim we have made toward equal rights for women. Those married women who have chosen to retain their maiden names (which, by the way, were probably inherited from their fathers) and those married couples who have chosen to hyphenate their names are breaking tradition, but not without having to declare their politics with every self-introduction. Those of us who have not wanted to be stereotyped as "feminist so-and-so's" or unwed mothers have taken the coward's way and adopted our husband's name. But, again, this linguistic option opens certain doors and closes others. Women who formally take their husbands' names, first and last, may lose more than a little of themselves in the process.

The language of courtesy titles provides a fascinating commentary on the differential treatment men and women receive concerning marital status. My young students assure me that times are changing such that my three daughters will not feel pressured to land a husband and will feel free to aggressively pursue their own identity. Despite their confidence, I wonder about a society that has not been amenable to language change in the face of these attitudinal changes. Clearly, at least on a linguistic level, we seem to be unwilling to abandon practices that mandate recognition of marriage for women (but not men) and make problematic the recognition of earned titles for women (but not men).

FAMILIAL TERMS

There are also noticeable distinctions in the terms by which we describe men and women in relation to their families. This is just one of several areas in which we see an absence of "gender complements." As with some of the occupational labels described in the previous section, and with some of the metaphorical terms described in the next section, there are noticeable gaps in our linguistic tendency to have a male form and a female form for most of our family labels. Admittedly, we can always invent gender complements by adding a word or perhaps a suffix. Thus a "male nurse" is the gender compliment of a nurse, while a "lady cab driver" is the female version of a cab driver. But, as these examples demonstrate, the special forms are longer and more difficult to say. It seems they draw attention, via their irregularity, to the minority status of the person they describe. One might argue that special linguistic forms can do little to draw added attention to a phenonmenon already noticeable in itself. We comment on hearing a male telephone operator and notice a female construction worker because they are still in the minority in these positions. We are just not used to affirmative action yet.

But family positions are occupied by both sexes and always have been, so the absence of gender complements in familial labels is particularly revealing. For instance, it was mentioned earlier that we have a term that describes the sad case of a woman who grows old without ever landing a husband—*old* maid. We even named a card game after her, in which everyone avoids getting stuck with the poor, singular, and usually very ugly *old maid*. In real life, we have euphemistic names for her, such as *spinster*. This term is widely understood to denote an elderly never-married woman and to connote an undesirable woman who failed to find someone to marry her. Although logic might tell us that there are also men of this general type, we have no special term to denote an elderly never-married man. We use the same term used to refer to any never-married man—*bachelor*. This term connotes a more favorable image of an individual who chooses to remain single and could be married in the future if he wishes. There is no card game named after this man, and we have seen no need to adopt euphemistic expressions to refer to him. It appears that the term *bachelor* is neither a denotative nor a connotative gender complement for the term *old maid*.

In fact, there is simply no male version of the label *old maid*, presumably because remaining unmarried beyond the conventional age does not appear to be as salient for men as for women. Predictably, there is also no female version of the label *bachelor*. A popular television game show invented the term *bachelorette*, but it is not listed in any dictionary I consulted. Dictionaries are commonly believed to reflect usage, so the absence of the term probably means that it is not widely used to refer to an unmarried woman. Certainly, we do not refer to "confirmed bachelorettes" or "eligible bachelorettes." This is consistent with the myth that women actively pursue marriage, and men actively avoid the institution. Another noun for which there is no gender complement according to *The American Heritage Dictionary*, is *divorcée*. This term refers to a woman whose marriage has been legally dissolved.[16] But there is no single word form to refer to her husband—he is referred to as a *divorced man* or even as a *bachelor* again. Following the logic of linguistic relativity, the absence of a workable noun form for a man who has "failed to make his marriage work" may reinforce the myth that it is the woman's responsibility to succeed at the goal she actively pursued. Admittedly, all of these marital conditions can be attached to our standard gender labels using adjectives. That is, we can refer with equal ease to a single man and a single woman, to an unmarried guy and an unmarried gal, to an ex-husband and an ex-wife. In fact, since the divorce rate continues to rise, and since more people are choosing to remain single, we will be referencing these conditions with increasing frequency. It will be interesting to note, though, whether or not gender complements emerge, or perhaps workable noun forms emerge that are gender-neutral. The feminist movement would have us adopt terms like *singles* and *nevermarrieds,* although it might be argued that even these terms would still be more applicable for women than for men in a society that subscribes to the myth that women chase husbands. This myth, and related myths, are discussed in more detail in Chapter Fourteen.

Other linguistic inequities surround the habits we employ in using possessives to describe family relationships. I find it interesting, for example, that we have workable gender complements for individuals whose spouses are deceased: *widows* and *widowers*. Presumably the latter is an altered version of the former, since it requires a suffix, but it is nonetheless a word we use and a word that is both denotatively and connotatively similar to its complement. Perhaps *widow* is the primary term because, statistically, more women than men outlive their spouses. Whatever the reason, it seems that this is a case of a language change that promotes sexual equality. However, it is unheard of to refer to a man as *Mary's widower,* although we commonly refer to a woman as *John's widow.* Even though my students tell me this is especially trivial, it demonstrates that the language practices for naming and categorizing individuals by family relationships continue to be used more for describing women than men.

Along the same lines, we have invented and adopted a noun which is very useful to describe a female who does not work outside of the home—she is a *housewife.* It is easy to say this; it doesn't sound amusing or silly. Granted, the linguistic construction bears a disturbing resemblance to words such as *houseplant* and *housefly,* but it is useful in identifying a now diminishing number of women who agree to take the role of domestic partner, presumably to complement the men who take the role of "breadwinner." The particulars of the *housewife* occupation are fascinating and controversial. After all, does this woman have to have children to be a true housewife? The dictionary does not specify this, but says she must be "a married woman," and oddly, that she must "run the household."[17] Apparently, the term could be used to refer to a woman who supervises a staff of servants from a nearby tennis court, even though it connotes a woman in an apron.

In fact, even my most doubting students agree that the connotations of this word are more than trivial. They agree that it connotes a woman who is "just" a housewife, important, perhaps, in the privacy of the home, but largely incapable of carrying on an interesting conversation at a cocktail party. When I ask them to tell me what she does all day, given the wonders of modern household appliances, they invariably allude to soap operas and lengthy coffee breaks. Surely, this image is damaging to the number of highly capable women who choose to manage a household—some who may have left important positions in the public sector to do so and some who could occupy such positions in the future if they choose to. The connotative value of the term *housewife* further diminishes the difficulty of maintaining the home and often of raising children, although adding *mother* to the occupational description (*housewife and mother*) has become a convention on game shows.

Recently, some have called for women to declare proudly, "I'm a housewife and mother," when asked what they "do," in order to undo the damage of those who sheepishly responded "Oh, I'm just a housewife." This seems to suggest that connotations are more flexible than dictionary definitions. Yet, it is interesting to note that, once again, there is no gender complement listed in the dictionary for "a married man who manages a household."[18] Perhaps it is grammatically consistent to call him a *househusband*. In truth, the phenomenon has been referenced in human interest magazine stories and has even been the subject of a popular movie, *Mr. Mom*. But the fact remains that we do not use *househusband* as commonly and unproblematically as *housewife*. If a man were to refer to himself as such, we might wonder, "Did he lose his job?" (Mr. Mom did, by the way.) We might wonder "Doesn't he hate staying home? Does he actually sit around and watch soap operas and change dirty diapers? (Mr. Mom did both.) Certainly, the term may gain utility if it continues to be used in reference to real people that we know and, hopefully, respect, but at present it is apparently as odd to hear as *male nurse*. Therefore, choosing to be a married man who takes the role of domestic partner is a decision likely to complicate responses to the question, "What do you do?"

The various linguistic depictions of men and women with regard to marital status may become more significant to each reader as he or she finds himself or herself contemplating the institution that appears to be at the center of our lifestyle. Many perceive remaining single through adulthood as abnormal and undesirable. Perhaps because it is natural, and perhaps because it is made to seem so, most of us at least try marriage and often encounter unexpected threats to our individuality. For a woman, the linguistic conventions may seem particularly threatening and permanent.

SEXUAL METAPHORS AND LABELS

Few speakers ever stop to contemplate the power of metaphorical language, although most readers may occasionally admire the poet's use of metaphor. Yet, the tendency to refer to one entity as though it were another is hopelessly woven into our speech. Some scholars have argued, in fact, that language-speakers inevitably think metaphorically, and may become blind to the practice.[19] For example, we might speak of a sunrise as "a fire in the sky." While most of us realize that it is not, in reality, a *fire,* we lose track of the fact that it is also not a sun*rise.* Similarly, while we might speak of our past as "an open book," realizing that it has not been committed to the printed page, we take for granted that our activities are "behind us," although this is only another metaphor for visualizing our movement forward through time.

The intricacy with which metaphors are woven into our language and thought is worthy of a book in itself, but the reader is asked to open his or her mind (not literally, please) to the possibility that the metaphorical labels by which we refer to men and women may interact with our perceptions of the two classes of individuals. It seems that there are very definite trends that characterize the metaphors we hear and sometimes use to reference the sexes. Perhaps we realize that these metaphors are not to be taken literally and perhaps not.

For example, certain metaphors liken women to food, available (and generally desirable) for consumption. A female may be called a "dish" or a "feast for the eyes," or it might be said that she looks "good enough to eat." Of course, only a male chauvinist would call a woman "cupcake" or "cookie," but don't we appreciate it when our beaus call us "sweetie" or "honey"? Men may consent to be called by these names, but seldom in public. Also, women have "peaches and cream" complexions and "strawberry blonde" hair, but not men—how insulting! When food metaphors are applied to men, they are predictably manly: the "big cheese," or, perhaps, "hunk." On the other hand, what could be worse than being called a "fruit"?

The food metaphors may seem obviously figurative and largely harmless, but animal metaphors are somewhat more descriptive. Ironically, we refer to people as animals often, and may use the generally neutral term *pig* to denigrate another, whether male or female. But, in the absence of other information, the term is usually taken to mean a fat, undesirable female. The statement "he is a *pig*" may also refer to obesity, but more likely references the use of obscene language or bad table manners. The same woman who is referred to as a pig may be labeled a *moose,* but the nickname "Moose" is often given to males of impressive muscular strength (and is far less demeaning). Calling a woman a *dog,* or even a *bow-wow,* is a common way of describing her as ugly, but calling a man a *dog* is entirely different, a short version of "you *lucky dog.*" Certainly, we would be mistaken if we called a man a female dog or a female horse. The metaphors *bitch* and *nag* are reserved for women with irritating behavioral tendencies.

Other animal names are more complimentary to women, it seems. They are *chicks, fillies, kittens, and bunnies.* Notice that all are youthful or diminutive images. Metaphors for men generally conjure up bigger, stronger, and more sexually mature animals. They are *studs* who attend *stag* parties. The names chosen to identify all-male sports teams are typically big, strong animals: *lions, rams, bulls, and bears* (but never *teddy bears*).

Metaphorical expressions come and go in the form of slang names, but the general trend toward describing females as edible objects and soft, cuddly animals remains a sharp contrast to male metaphors. Several notable exceptions seem to have emerged, though, apparently with the trend toward sexual liberation for women. My younger and wiser female friends tell me we can now call both men and women *foxes,* among other things. In addition, we can now reference parts of their body, although the fact that women's bodies are referenced more frequently is demonstrated by the long list of slang terms for breasts, legs, hips, and the incredibly long list of metaphors for the female genitalia. It is both amusing, on an X-rated level, and informative to contrast the metaphors for the sexual apparatus of men and women. Clearly, images of women as mattresses and playthings of various sorts, along with images of men as weapons and manipulators, are not accidental in our society, even though women now claim to be outspoken about their sexuality.

LANGUAGE AND COMMUNICATION

The various linguistic habits discussed in this chapter may constitute just that—habits—at least on one level. Those who have little faith in the power of words may be amused by the metaphorical contrasts and label other trends trivial. Certainly, the reader would not be alone if he or she took this stance. Those who pay heed to the power of language, however, can take one of two positions. The reader who believes that it is important to provide predictable, stable lines by which to delineate men and women such that we, as members of a given society, can continue to teach youngsters how to be male and female, can call for the perpetuation of language practices that assist in conceiving of men and women as different. This reader, in my opinion, must respond privately to the implications of the exclusion and exception rules.

Other readers may now be cognizant of common language practices that serve to discriminate against men, or more likely, women, and may begin to wonder about the etymology of these practices and their significance in a society that collectively voices the desire for equal opportunity. I suggest that these readers carefully examine their own speech. The choice to change habitual language behavior is somewhat like the choice to exercise or diet—working to make your speech (or your body) what you decide it should be—and is a very individual decision that cannot be legislated. Those who choose not to undertake a program of self-change or (like me) are not sure of exactly what language practices are feasible or desirable in the midst of a well-developed patriarchal system such as ours, can still develop an ear for practices that are discriminatory and can be especially careful to not be influenced by the exclusion or exception rule.

I hope all readers will realize that language is not a neutral tool that we each manage on an individual basis. To the contrary, language is a collective decision. We cannot decide to use a given word in a particular way without ramifications for our communication in a world that necessitates human interaction and expects stability.

The uniform adoption of language practices must be understood to facilitate communication and also to influence communication, i.e., to open some doors and close others. On the other hand, language can change, although it is understandably slow to change in a world where people rely on its stability as a system. We must be patient with the sluggish nature of language change, but constantly alert to the implications of the habits we have inherited.

CONDUCT YOUR OWN RESEARCH

1. Ask respondents to write a story, providing them with only the first sentence. Be sure the introductory sentence mentions an individual, but does not identify him or her as either male or female. (samples: "A student goes to the bookstore for the very first time"; "An accused criminal faces the truth about the future"; "Every citizen has certain rights.") After gathering several versions of the story, describe the pronoun-usage. Does the story continue to reference a single individual or adopt the plural form? If singular, does the writer adopt a gender-neutral format (he/she, he or she, s/he) or a gender-specific format? If specific, is it "egocentric" (male writer uses he; female uses she)?

2. Check dictionaries across several decades for evidence of language change. Look up words that describe women and men (family labels, terms of address, etc.). Also look up words that are not denotatively gender-specific, but may be connotatively restrictive (e.g., housekeeper, nurse, soldier, astronaut).

3. Visit a store that sells toiletries and/or personal hygiene products. Note the kinds of products designed for men and those designed for women. Are the differences all related to anatomical differences? Notice trends in the naming, packaging, and marketing of sex-specific articles.

DISCUSS THE ISSUES

1. Share with your classmates the specific nicknames you have been called from childhood through the present. Provide background about each—who coined the name; what it meant; how you reacted. Discuss apparent sex differences in the way nicknames portray boys and girls, men and women.

2. Brainstorm about the names you use to refer to strangers who anger you (such as a driver who cuts in front of you) and strangers upon whom you want to make a good impression (a clerk who can waive a requirement or extend a deadline). Are these names gender specific? Does it matter if the communication is "with" the individual or "about" the individual?

3. Make of list of gender complements and decide which are denotatively but not connotatively equivalent. Notice how the male form and female form differ. Look for evidence of the exclusion rule and the exception rule. Then, brainstorm about words that have no gender complements and discuss what these words reveal about our cultural images of men and women.

SUMMARY OF PART I

The discussions of sex stereotypes and sex specific language habits can provide a useful framework for viewing, or perhaps reviewing, how that invisible force "society" influences our understanding of what constitutes being male or female. Undoubtedly, each individual has unique experiences that also influence his or her understanding of maleness and femaleness, but it would be very naive to believe that each of us gets to create these categories based on our own experience. We are, at least to a certain extent, at the mercy of the invisible force that teaches us how to be sex appropriate.

It is argued here that the perpetuation of sex stereotypes is essential to the process by which youngsters are taught to conceptualize behavior as sex appropriate. Even though they may infuriate us, myths about masculinity and femininity are widespread and surprisingly uniform. They may serve only to provide a grounds for arguing about change and inequity but it is important to realize that our willingness to dispute a given stereotype is evidence that we pay attention to behavior as being sex specific. If we notice and evaluate behavior as inappropriate for a man or a woman, society has effectively taught us its myths. Most likely, every reader pays more attention to sex as a variable in his or her communication than any other variable. Admittedly, we also have learned stereotypes of age, race, occupation, etc., but few are as widely known or as universally employed as sex stereotypes. Realizing their importance is crucial to understanding the communication of gender.

Just as we inherit a well-established mythology about gender in the form of stereotypes, we also inherit a well-established language system that encourages us to acknowledge that men and women are different, or at least must be treated differently in language practice. We have sex-specific nouns and pronouns and use grammatical constructions such as the generic *he* that influence our perception of men and women. It is undeniably difficult to speak of a person without acknowledging, in some way, the sex of the person. The fact that our language systematically differentiates many of its constructions according to two categories influences us to perceive ourselves as essentially unlike the sex we refer to as opposite.

Developing an awareness of language, specifically of the manner in which linguistic practices treat men and women, has been proposed as integral to the communication of gender. Both male and female readers have inherited essentially the same language practices. Like sex stereotypes, language practices precede and usually outlive each individual. We have faith in our power to change the world into which we are born, but ought not be overly optimistic about the speed or the ease of implementing such change. The belief that we can collectively legislate equal treatment for men and women is integrally tied to our faith in democracy. But even a cursory review of American history must alert us to our resistance to change, even for the "right." Each reader is encouraged to consider our society's traditional beliefs about males and females, communicated in the form of stereotypes and language, and to develop a sensitivity to his or her own expectations about sex-appropriate behavior in light of these influences.

Part II examines some of the communication behaviors that have been proposed to differ predictably according to gender. It appears that we have developed styles of communicating in line with our perceptions of ourselves and others as male or female. The behaviors that have been found to differentiate male and female communication are proposed to be logically aligned with expectations that have been demonstrated in Part I to be embodied in our society's stereotypes and linguistic system. Thus, understanding the empirically grounded descriptions of sex differences in communication in light of inherited conceptualizations of the sexes can facilitate the reader's understanding of his or her own interaction with others.

CHAPTER 4

VERBAL ASPECTS OF COMMUNICATION

Cheris Kramarae has provided a valuable term for referring to the specific aspects of communication that are inherent in the culture's stereotypes and widely held to be true; she calls them *folklinguistics*.[1] It appears that there are well-circulated "tales" about how men and women communicate. Knowledge of these tales is invariably demonstrated in my classes when I ask male students to role play females in particular situations and female students to role play males. The same students who deny belief in or even knowledge of folklinguistics enact the mythological behaviors with remarkable accuracy. The relationship between the folktales about male and female communication behaviors and the actual behaviors we encounter in our daily interaction with others is a topic that recurs throughout this text. Each reader is encouraged to conduct informal research by observing his or her own behavior and the behavior of others. The results of individual observations, coupled with the results of the studies discussed in this text, may help the reader to develop a sense of the impact of folklinguistics in his or her life.

QUANTITY OF TALK

One of the widely held myths pertains to sex differences in quantity of talk. Put plainly, most people believe that women talk more than men. We have a number of expressions which verify this myth. We say that women spend their time "gabbing," "chatting," or "visiting" (particularly on the telephone), but we seldom use these verbs to describe male–male interaction. Men simply "talk," or perhaps "shoot the bull," which is an amended profanity related to the verb "to bullshit," apparently derived from the noun form of the same word and indicative of the quality of the information shared. Women have been referred to metaphorically as "cackling hens" and elderly women referred to as "old biddies," both terms that liken women's speech to the sounds chickens make when laying eggs. The gender complement of the "cackling hen" is the "man of few words" or the "strong, silent type." The myth about men is that they keep their interactions brief, saying all that need be said in a few words. Apparently, we see men as doers, not talkers.

In fact, it appears that the mythology about females enjoying talk as an activity is related to well-documented sex differences in early childhood activities. Play has been observed to be remarkably sex segregated during the time when children are achieving *gender identity*—a sense that being male or female is permanent and important in their lives.[2] Opportunities to play in mixed groups are rare until children begin school. Even when parents attempt to force integration, mixed groups of two- and three-year-olds invariably divide into male and female subgroups, not entirely unlike their adult counterparts. Therefore, contrasting playtime activities for boys and girls, paying particular attention to the importance of talk, may help to clarify the influence of the mythology on sex-specific behavior or vice versa.

Boys' activities tend to be active and organized. They tend to play war games at a young age, for example, that necessitate a good deal of action and at least a crude understanding of "us" and "them."[3] Even in the midst of recent objections to toy guns, the popularity of fighting games has not waned. Many mothers tell me that their young sons substitute sticks for guns when toy guns are not available. These simple feuds eventually develop into more civilized wars in the form of organized sports. Even very young males are encouraged to develop basic skills used in popular sports like baseball, football, and hockey. While the rules may be too complicated to be fully comprehended by three-year-olds, the development of an interest in these structured games seems to entail an emphasis on activity, on rule-governed behavior, and on the accomplishment of some goal.[4] Notably, highly structured activity does not rely on talk to proceed, as long as all the participants know the rules and the goal. You are either safe or out; you either win or lose. There is no need to decide on a new set of procedures each time you play.

Girls' play, in contrast, is typically unstructured. They often play games like house or school, which are essentially verbal activities.[5] The participants must identify themselves and behave according to the assigned roles. There are clearly "right" and "wrong" behaviors, but the range of choice in each category is considerably larger than in baseball. Therefore, girls playing house are likely to be observed talking about how the game should proceed, while boys playing baseball talk only as needed to clarify and enforce the rules.

It is not surprising that, as they grow older, boys tend to associate in age-heterogeneous groups and girls in age-homogeneous dyads or triads.[6] After all, a number of players are needed to stage boys' games, and games requiring a large group can hardly afford to exclude players based on age. For girls' games a smaller number of players, similar in age, facilitates the negotiation of roles and standards for behavior.

The continued movement toward talk as an activity for women is apparent in common adolescent experiences—pajama parties for girls, which feature talk about clothing, grooming, and boys, as opposed to Little League practice for boys, which involves little talk except about the game. Following practice, the boys are likely to talk only about the game. Even while attending college, an experience which is probably less sex segregated than any other, men's and women's activities have been found to differ along the same lines. Caldwell and Peplau report that, even though both women and men reported valuing friendship in their lives, "compared to men, women showed a greater preference for 'just talking' with friends [and indicated] that talking was an important thing to do with a friend...In contrast, men were more likely to prefer doing some activity...and were more likely to talk to their friends about activities."[7] Wheeler and Nezlek also conclude that college women are more likely to spend their time talking, while college men more frequently share a sport or hobby.[8] In a recent study of conversation among same-sex adults, the authors reported: "The overall impression is that women are likely to talk about more subjects more often with different people of their own sex compared to the male pattern."[9]

In sum, the empirical evidence seems to be largely consistent with the myth that women enjoy talking for its own sake, at least in sex-segregated situations, while men prefer engaging in sports or other activities that essentially discourage lengthy verbal interactions. The implications of these sex differences in preference for talk as an activity are discussed later in this chapter in relation to topics of conversation, in Chapter Nine as they relate to social learning explanations of sex differences, and in Chapter Thirteen in relation to sex differences in friendship. But, at this point, the research findings are presented to demonstrate one of two well-supported portrayals of sex differences in quantity of verbal interaction, i.e., women do more of it, just like the folk wisdom says.

Other research efforts have presented portrayals of sex differences in quantity of speech that directly counter the myth that women talk more than men. These studies are not necessarily inconsistent with those just presented, since they are generally concerned with which sex talks more in mixed groups, not same-sex groups. This claim has implications for the ongoing discussion of how power and status relate to gender. In order to fully comprehend the political significance of this and other reported sex differences in communication, it is necessary to conceive of gender as a variable that can generate status in and of itself.

I encourage my students to suspend their objections to this contention at least long enough to liken a hypothetical male–female interaction to a high status–low status interaction with which they are familiar. For instance, we know all too well that in a parent–child interaction, certain behaviors are appropriate for the parent that are not tolerated from the child. Recently, I found myself offering consolation to my six-year-old by forecasting, "When you're the Mommy, you can tell your children what to do, too!" In any case, most of us are familiar with the unequal status of a parent–child relationship, at least from the subordinate position.

Other superior–subordinate positions may be less universally experienced: professor–student, employer–employee, law enforcement officer–speeding driver, etc. But if the reader can imagine the nature of an interaction in which the participants are clearly not equal, he or she can compare these cases to some of the empirical research about communication between men and women in such a way as to better understand those who argue that specific communication behaviors serve to make and keep women subordinate to men.

In the case of quantity of talk, it seems that women talk less than men, just as subordinates talk less than superiors. Granted, other forms of status may intervene, but all other things being equal, women have been found in several studies to talk less often than their male counterparts and for shorter periods of time. Eakins and Eakins recorded and transcribed faculty meetings with the knowledge of the participants and discovered that the women spoke far less than the men. In fact, the man with the fewest utterances spoke twice as often as the woman with the fewest, and exceeded all the other women except one in terms of the number of utterances he offered over a seven-meeting schedule. In addition, the male speakers held the floor longer than the female speakers. The shortest average speaking time for a male participant was 10.66 seconds, which was longer than the longest average speaking time for a female participant, 10.00 seconds. As mentioned, several other factors may affect status, and thus can also influence who will talk most. In faculty meetings, rank and length of experience may also affect length and number of turns taken. Eakins and Eakins report that these factors were influential within the same-sex rankings, but no factor was as telling as gender in predicting the amount of participation.[10] As one female member of the governing faculty body at a small private college, I have had the opportunity to witness firsthand both the growing number of women serving on the council and the relative reticence of the women compared to the men. The sex difference in quantity of participation is striking, across age, rank, and experience. Even women who hold elected positions typically serve by listening and taking notes, but do not seize the floor to speak.

Sex differences in quantity of participation have also been reported in educational settings. Student status, of course, may also be influenced by other factors, but all other factors being equal, male students have been reported to speak more often and for longer periods of time than female students in elementary school classrooms,[11] secondary school classrooms,[12] and college classrooms.[13] Other studies indicate that male students initiate communication with teachers more than female students,[14] and receive more feedback on their performance, both positive and negative.[15]

The influence of the teacher's sex on these findings is also well researched, but results are somewhat confusing. In one study, it was discovered that female instructors were involved in more interactions with male students than with female students.[16] Thus, it may seem that female-instructed classrooms increase the likelihood of male student participation and simultaneously decrease the likelihood of female student participation. However, in another study of college classrooms it was discovered that male students talked more than female students regardless of the sex of the person teaching the course, but female participation increased in classes taught by women.[17]

At first these appear to be contradictory findings, but both studies point to a common possibility: women may allow others to talk more, even from a position of higher status.

Many studies have reported similar sex differences in quantity of talk across a wide range of mixed groups. Women have been reported to talk less often and/or for shorter periods of time in laboratory groups,[18] in jury deliberations,[19] and in professional meetings.[20] In each case, researchers concluded that gender did indeed influence who was willing and able to speak in mixed-sex groups.

Other studies have focused on the distribution of talk in male–female dyads. Perhaps the most unique study of this type, at least in terms of its methodology, was conducted by Soskin and John, who used radio transmitters to monitor the talk of a husband and wife during a sixteen-hour period at a summer resort. They calculated that, during one episode of interaction with his wife, the husband spoke about 79% of the time. This provides a sharp contrast to another situation, in which he spoke only 29% of the time, but to another man. Soskin and John point out that, in the male–male conversation, the husband was clearly less expert on the topic than the other man.[21] Perhaps he was clearly "more expert" than his wife in their conversations. In a study which specifically examined the association between expertise and quantity of talk, Leeft-Pellegrini discovered that neither expertise nor gender alone could predict which of two partners would talk most. However, males identified as "experts" talked more than females identified as "experts." Again, with other factors equal, sex may function as a predictor of conversational dominance.[22]

The association between dominance in terms of quantity of talk and status of the participants in mixed-sex groups and dyads is well researched, but the findings are by no means conclusive. After reviewing the literature in this area, Berger, Rosenholtz, and Zelditch hypothesized that sex does function as a status characteristic, since men seem to have more opportunities to "perform" and since they provide more "performance output."[23] Other studies report inconclusive findings as to which sex talks most in mixed groups.[24] Still, there remains a paucity of findings that women talk more often than men or for longer periods of time, all other things being equal. As women gain assigned status, the examination of their interaction with male peers and subordinates during group and dyadic interaction may be very telling.

At present, it appears that the folktale that women "gab" refers primarily to the probability that same-sex female dyads spend more time just talking than same-sex male dyads, who are likely to engage in some sort of activity that hinders conversation. However, there is a good deal of research suggesting that women do not "gab" in the presence of male peers. Rather, women appear to be less willing and/or less able to seize and hold the floor than their male counterparts.

Admittedly, sheer quantity of talk is not necessarily indicative of status. Therapeutic interactions, for instance, are usually dominated by patient talk, even though the doctor may be assumed to be the higher-status participant. But our participation in superior–subordinate relationships of all types provides evidence that the higher-status individual has more freedom, or privilege, in this regard than the lower-status individual. The common adage "children should be seen and not heard" is evidence that they occupy a subordinate position to adults. Instructions like "just answer 'yes' or 'no' " remind a courtroom witness that he or she occupies a nonpowerful position in that setting.

Male–female interactions, of course, vary as to the status relationship of the participants. But it seems that, all else being equal, gender in and of itself may be a determinant of status. In Chapter Five, certain sex differences in interaction are examined that, taken together with differences in sheer quantity of talk, suggest that men and women often collude in maintaining a relationship that is, at least interactionally, unequal.

TOPICS OF TALK

Since there seems to be some empirical support for the folk myth that female–female interaction tends to feature talk as an activity more than male–male interaction, it may be worthwhile to examine just what it is that women discuss. The linguistic mythology portrays women at a dinner party (probably in the kitchen prior to and after the meal) talking about recipes, fashion, and children. The complementary mythology portrays their men (probably in a more comfortable setting) discussing sports, money, and politics.

Researchers have been interested in sex differences in topics of conversation for quite some time. It is not surprising that out-of-date research is consistent with the myths. In 1922, a study concerned with sex differences in topics of conversation in public places reported that women walking down Broadway were overheard to be talking mostly about men, clothing, and other women, while men talked mostly about business, sports, and other men.[25] A similar study conducted just two years later in Ohio yielded remarkably similar stereotypic results.[26] It appears that women of the 1920s could be overheard talking mostly about people (men and women) and about clothing; men of the 1920s could also be overheard talking about people, but most likely those people would be other men, and were usually being discussed in relation to their professional and athletic endeavors.

It might be assumed that participation in business and athletics increases the likelihood of discussing these activities. Thus, if we can safely assume that these arenas are more open to women now than they were in the 1920s, we might expect to find significant changes in the topics of female–female conversations. Conversely, male–male conversations might be expected to involve topics like fashion and family.

But Haas and Sherman recently tabulated the most common conversational topics of 110 adult men and 166 adult women of various ages, occupations, and socioeconomic backgrounds and reported findings remarkably similar to those reported sixty years prior. According to their 1982 summary, women reported a higher frequency of talk on many topics, such as family, relationship problems, other women, men, and clothing. The authors concluded that women's topics are most concerned with "personal matters and things dealing with daily life.…This is in keeping with expectations, since even when both adult members of the household are employed, women typically assume primary responsibility for family matters."[27]

The men reported a higher frequency of talk about money, news, spectator sports, and participation in sports. In fact, the Haas and Sherman study, like nearly every study of conversation topics conducted in the last six decades,[28] concluded that "most clear-cut is the sex difference in talk about sports."[29] Developing a proficient knowledge of sports and a working vocabulary of sports terms seems to be a traditional male activity that transcends time and social class.[30] Although women's sports are becoming more popular, both as spectator and participant activities, most women still do not seem to be as proficient as men, nor as interested as men, in discussing sports. Women (like the author) who do enjoy playing and talking about sports are typically greeted with remarks like, "You know a lot about sports *for a woman*," but are usually not taken seriously in discussion of the greatest moments in sport.

Other common male topics also surround public, as opposed to personal, business. Men report talking with other men about news and money—presumably topics that can be discussed on a less personal basis than popular female topics. In a sense, the women of today seem to be demonstrating their interest and expertise in private matters: people (both males and females), relationships, and clothing. Like the women of yesteryear, they do not report talking often about news, sports, or money. Moreover, the men of today are following tradition by discussing less personal matters. Specifically, men are still not talking a great deal about their relationships with others.[31]

The Haas and Sherman survey indicates indirect support for the commonly held belief that women "gossip." However, one team of researchers set out to examine sex differences in gossiping. Levin and Arluke reported that, in a sample of nearly two hundred college students, women were only slightly more likely than men to participate in "conversations about third persons," i.e., gossip (71% vs. 64%). However, the third parties talked about by men were more likely to be distant from their lives—acquaintances, attractive women they had seen, or even celebrities. The third parties of interest to the women tended to be friends and family members.[32] So, it does seem that women continue to spend time talking about personal relationships—whether their own or those of persons close to them.

Overall, the investigation of conversational topics in same-sex talk has not provided clear evidence of the gradual merging of male and female perspectives on the world. However, several findings pointing to such a trend have been revealed: (1) today's men report "women" as a frequently discussed topic, while yesterday's men reported "other men"; (2) today's men and women both report talking about work; and (3) today's men and women both report talking about sexual partners. The first finding points to a rather comfortable complementary situation, in which both men and women talk a good deal about members of the opposite sex. Of course, this talk could cover a wide range of subtopics. When I mentioned this new trend to a group of my husband's male friends, they "joked" that I ought to note that the women that men talk about are usually not their wives and daughters. Still, this trend indicates a narrowing sex difference in conversational content.

Similarly, Haas and Sherman believe that the second finding is evidence of "changing patterns in employment in society." However, I have noticed in my conversations with female friends who also work outside the home that we inevitably discuss work and family in the same conversation. Granted, work emerges often as a conversation topic, but typically leads to a discussion of the tension between work and home. This tension in women's lives is discussed further in Chapters Ten and Twelve, but here it is important to note that the topic "work" may be different for men and women. The third finding is undoubtedly empirical verification of increasing freedom for women to acknowledge their sexuality in conversation—a freedom that men have enjoyed for decades. In fact, it is interesting to note that, when the respondents listed suggestions for improving same-sex conversation, 11% of the men cited "less sex talk" as a potential improvement! Men also cited "less bragging" as a potential improvement.[33] (Perhaps these concerns are related in male conversation!)

The survey-type investigation of same-sex topics, of course, is only as reliable and honest as the respondents, so the trends discussed here and the interpretations offered must be considered speculative. Also, Haas and Sherman discovered that topics vary according to the relationship between the same-sex participants. Hence, female coworkers are more likely to talk about work than female friends and male family members are more likely to talk about family matters than male coworkers, etc.[34] Despite the predictable variance among relationship types, however, sex differences emerged that seem to both support traditional trends and indicate new freedoms.

It is also important to note that clear sex differences persist with regard to the perceived importance of same-sex conversation. In reported evaluations of same-sex talk, also obtained by Haas and Sherman, three times as many men as women thought these conversations were "not important." The implication of this finding is that men still devalue talking together. However, women do value same-sex talk: twice as many females in this study responded that such talk is "necessary," and three times as many reported receiving "empathy" in conversations with others of the same sex.[35]

VOCABULARY

At first, it may seem difficult to imagine that men and women use different vocabularies, even though they supposedly "speak the same language." But can you imagine a man calling a new shirt "divine," or referring to a baby as "precious"? Would you think twice if a man described his new car as "persimmon"? The problem lies not in the color of the car he purchased, but in the word he used to describe that color. Shouldn't he just say "red" like a man?

Robin Lakoff was one of the first scholars to attempt to delineate sex differences in language use. In 1973, Lakoff pointed out that, although most of the debate about gender and language at that time focused on how women were referred to (a topic discussed in Chapter Three), a second area of difference also contributed to the relative powerlessness of women. She contended that women were expected to speak in ways that communicated uncertainty and demonstrated detailed knowledge of topics considered trivial in the "real world."[36]

While these claims may seem antiquated and/or outdated, Lakoff succeeded in focusing researchers' attention on the specific traits of female speech. Based on her study of female communication—both her own and that of women she encountered in person and through the media—she reported distinct female linguistic patterns. Her observations provide a useful framework for examining sex differences in language use. Many of the differences she proposed have since been examined in scholarly research and debate.

Color Words. Lakoff proposed that women have a larger color vocabulary than men.[37] Your reaction to the hypothetical use of the word *persimmon* in the earlier example may be evidence of your perception that men do not use detailed color descriptors. Women, however, can be heard comfortably referencing such colors as mauve, peach, and aquamarine. Seldom do students in my classes argue that a sex difference exists with regard to color language, but, very commonly, they deem the difference unimportant. However, they seem to enjoy debating the possible explanations for this trend. Indeed, this debate helps to illuminate the lives of men and women in our society.

Linguistic anthropologists report a tendency for a group to develop a large vocabulary to describe environmental phenomena that they value.[38] Thus, while Eskimos may use any of twenty-five (or more) terms when referring to snow, we generally call any form of the dreaded white precipitation by a single name. Conversely, we can hardly enumerate the many labels we use to describe automobiles: brand names, such as *Ford* and *Chevy;* body names, such as *station wagon* and *convertible;* category names, such as *sports car* and *economy car;* etc., etc. But most Eskimos would refer to all the cars in the average parking lot with but one word, roughly translatable as *automobile.*

Following the same logic, women probably have larger color vocabularies because color is important in women's lives. Women are, at least stereotypically, more concerned with fashion and home decoration. In addition, our culture encourages the use of makeup to "color" a woman's appearance, but discourages this practice by men, except in special contexts such as the theater. If, indeed, women are occupied with making the world beautiful, an extensive color vocabulary is a logical outcome. But consider the implications of this conclusion, according to Lakoff's argument. She proposed that women could be heard elaborating on "subject-matter deemed *trivial* to the *real* world" (italics in original) and cited the ability to discriminate among colors as evidence of this condition.[39] After all, matters of corporate, political, or social significance seldom hinge on whether a blouse is lavender, mauve, or lilac.

In a rush of eager honesty, one male student in my class offered another explanation for the proposed sex difference in color vocabulary. He admitted that he possessed a large color vocabulary, related to years of part-time employment in a paint store, but explained that he did not use most of the terms for fear of sounding "femmy." His rationale for possessing a large vocabulary is clearly consistent with the theory of linguistic relativity, but his rationale for not using it demonstrates that word usage can serve as a type of gender display. In this case, men may not be inferior linguistically, but may want to appear so to demonstrate their association with the correct gender.

Expletives. Lakoff delineated other categories of words that appear to connote femininity. She argued that women use weaker expletives than men.[40] An expletive is technically an exclamation, a remark followed by an exclamation point in writing. In speech, any utterance can be an expletive with the appropriate vocal character. But Lakoff noticed a sex difference in terms of verbal expletives that communicate the strength of expression of a speaker's utterance. For example, a woman might phrase an observation, "Oh dear, I left my umbrella home and it looks like rain." Similarly, a woman might introduce a remark with "Oh my," "Oh my goodness," or even "Good gracious." But imagine your reaction to a man's use of these expletives!

The expletives traditionally used by men are stronger sounding, and often involve profanity. "Oh shit" comes to mind immediately, but other expressions, such as "Jesus Christ," "God damn it," and the "F-word" seem more credible for a male speaker who forgot his umbrella. Of course, the young women in my classes usually claim that it is all right for women to swear, and most of them report having used all the expressions in this paragraph at some time. But recent evidence suggests that profane expletives continue to be (1) used more often by male speakers, (2) evaluated more favorably by male listeners, and (3) even explained by males as a demonstration of social power.[41] Even if this evidence is incorrect, if women are swearing more than they used to, it is worrisome that their greatest achievement may be the privilege of using profanity in public.

Less obvious is the continued restriction of weak expletives to female usage. Beyond the obvious restrictions surrounding expressions like "oh dear," there is other evidence that weak expletives are used exclusively by women. For instance, there is a widely used female practice of substituting weak words for profane words based on their phonetic similarity. In the midst of a heated tennis match, I have often heard female partners and opponents utter "Oh, sugar!" after hitting a bad shot. "Sugar" has little denotative value in this context, but it begins with the same initial sound as "shit." Similarly diluted expletives include: "shoot," "Gosh darn," and "Oh fudge." While both sexes are familiar with the verbal practice of substitution, it appears that women use it far more often than men. In fact, male students asked to role play females invariably utter expletives of this type.

In the case of expletives, then, change may be occurring in terms of condoning the use of traditionally male-appropriate language by females, but not in terms of condoning the use of traditionally female-appropriate language by males. This pattern was also cited in Chapter Two with reference to adolescent endorsement of females in traditionally male careers, but not vice versa. It is a pattern that will be cited again, and one that may be related to the broad contention that male behavior is perceived as standard, while female behavior is perceived as exceptional.

Evaluative Adjectives.   Lakoff also pointed out that there are several adjectives that women use freely, but men generally do not use without cost. These adjectives usually express "approbation," or approval.[42] During a dinner party, for instance, women may describe the surroundings as "charming," but men would probably just call them "nice." Women can call the main dish "divine," but men might say it is "really good," or maybe "delicious." When complimenting the baby pictures displayed on the mantel, the female guests can call them "adorable" or "sweet," but the males usually go no farther than a simple "cute." If, on the way home, a woman wants to express disapproval, she can call the dessert "dreadful" or "ghastly," but the man would seem overexpressive if he used these adjectives. He might call the dessert "bad" or even "awful," but never "ghastly." Again, all of the linguistic options open to the man are also open to the woman, but an additional set of evaluative adjectives appears to be reserved for female use.

Generally, women seem to employ an extended vocabulary in referencing color, in expressing their emotions verbally, and in evaluating the world. Females can use what Lakoff labeled "neutral" language, also used by men, or they can express themselves with words traditionally restricted by gender. Except for profane words, which may be becoming more available to women, very few adjectives are restricted to male usage. At first evaluation, then, it may seem that the sheer size and latitude of women's vocabulary should elevate the status of women with regard to communication. But remember the student who deliberately avoided being accurate in referencing color discriminations for fear of sounding effeminate. It appears that women's language may be more precise in certain areas than men's language, but that the attention to detail, in this case, is evidence of attention to the trivial. It will be argued later that women also pay more attention to propriety in other linguistic concerns and in their nonverbal demeanor as well.

GRAMMATICAL CONSTRUCTIONS

Other sex differences in language use can be found in grammatical constructions, or the way speakers put words together. Lakoff suggested that women seem to be unwilling to use grammatical constructions expressing certainty, while men are typically more straightforward.[43] The term *female register* has been used to identify a distinct set of grammatical forms that Lakoff claimed are used predominantly by women.[44] The register has been portrayed as containing the following linguistic devices: (1) qualifiers, (2) disclaimers, (3) tag questions, (4) polite forms, and (5) intensifiers.

Qualifiers.   One common claim is that women use more qualifiers than men use in constructing statements. Qualifiers, or "hedges," are words that soften the strength of statements. For instance, if a speaker describes a friend as "somewhat slender," or "kind of chubby," the phrasing seems to soften the evaluation of the friend's build. Similarly, if the speaker clearly describes the friend as "chubby," but adds "I guess," the evaluation is weakened by the expression of uncertainty. In both constructions, the speaker has included a qualifier, which may be indicative of subordinate status in communication.

Crosby and Nyquist examined the use of qualifiers (among other things) in interaction between college students, between information givers and seekers at a public information booth, and between police personnel and their clients. Obviously, these dyads vary as to their developmental stages and the relative status of the participants. Therefore, the authors were able to examine the influence of a variety of factors on the use of qualifiers in dyadic interaction. They concluded that, while other factors, particularly role relationships, influenced the use of qualifiers, such grammatical constructions appeared to be used more by women than by men.[45]

Another study found that both men and women used qualifiers, but that the effect of the grammatical construction on credibility varied with gender. As you might guess, qualifiers were not as damaging to male credibility as to female credibility.[46] Perhaps, then, the practice of qualifying statements does not cause powerlessness in conversation, but reinforces expectations of power based on gender. Or, it may be that nonverbal information counters the verbal expression of uncertainty by men and reinforces the same sort of verbal construction by women.

Disclaimers.   Another grammatical formulation that has been associated with expressed uncertainty is the disclaimer. Put simply, a disclaimer is a grammatical construction in which the speaker begins with an excuse for some aspect of the communication to follow. This can be accomplished through admitting to some personal weakness that might be used to disqualify the remark: "I know I'm not an expert in this area, but...." Another sort of disclaimer can be used to point out that the communication that follows is atypical of the speaker: "I usually don't gossip, but...." Still other disclaimers predict a possible negative reaction from the listener: "You'll probably think I'm crazy, but..." or "Don't get mad at me, but...."

The precise wording may vary, but all disclaimers express some sort of defense, in advance, against criticism by the listener. The speaker seems to anticipate a negative reaction and begins his or her defense or apology even before an objection is voiced by the listener. Like qualifiers, disclaimers seem to soften critical or controversial remarks. Therefore, it is not surprising that they have been proposed as part of the female register. One study concluded that disclaimers appear to be used less often by all speakers than qualifiers. Nevertheless, the women in this study used disclaimers more often than the men.[47]

Taken together, qualifiers and disclaimers seem to cause a definite weakening of the speaker's position. This function may be useful in situations where a speaker wishes to voice a tentative position. After all, there are situations in which a speaker is not absolutely certain and linguistic formulations communicating this condition are useful. The issue is not whether qualifiers and disclaimers constitute inferior communication, but whether these linguistic habits are used more by women than by men across situations. If they are part of a female register, a second issue arises: do these linguistic habits diminish a woman's power in communication?

Tag Questions. Lakoff contended that incorporating expressions of uncertainty with declarative statements is a female tendency and that this tendency does indeed render women less powerful than their male counterparts. Besides qualifiers and disclaimers, Lakoff identified a linguistic construction, the "tag question formulation," which she claimed was used predominantly by women.[48] The tag question formulation proved to be somewhat controversial in subsequent studies. Understanding the nature of this formulation and its association with the speaker's status may be especially enlightening.

The tag question is a grammatical construction in which a brief question is added to a statement. For instance, an assertion such as "The play begins at eight-thirty" becomes a quasi-question when a tag is added: "doesn't it?" Lakoff noted that adding the tag usually involves transforming the statement into a yes–no question, a practice that seems particularly illogical. If the speaker is unsure of what time the play begins, why not just ask "What time does the play begin?" If, on the other hand, the speaker knows the time, why add the tag? Several interesting explanations are possible. Lakoff, predictably, associated the use of the tag question with the speaker's unwillingness to express certainty and risk confrontation. By adding the tag, the speaker invites verification, but also legitimates negation, of his or her assertion. Lakoff said that women use this construction more than men and that it signifies subordination. She admitted, nevertheless, that the tag question is a useful and logical linguistic construction in circumstances calling for an indication of an opinion about which the speaker is unsure.[49] "You have an eight o'clock class on Friday, don't you?" or "You don't eat meat, do you?" In each case, the speaker demonstrates his or her tentative knowledge of the listener's circumstance, but seeks verification from a more informed source. The tag question communicates this condition accurately and succinctly.

The tag question also serves as a device for opening conversation. "Small talk" often begins with a tag question, such as "Nice day, isn't it?" The blended assertion-question seems preferable in its indirectness to either alternative: "I think it's a nice day" or "What is your opinion of the weather?" The isolated assertion seems to be too final and self-centered for an opening remark, while the isolated question seems to be too demanding for an initial encounter. Thus, the tag question may be used deliberately to create small talk in uncomfortable initial interactions.

In sharp contrast, I find myself using the tag question construction when disciplining my children: "You have been told not to do that over and over, haven't you?" In this example, the tag demands that the child verify the parent's hard work in carefully communicating the rules. Similar instances can be imagined in police interrogations: "You thought you could get away with this, didn't you?" In courtrooms, individuals with superior status often use the tag to demand verification: "You were present at the scene, were you not?" In each of these examples, the use of the tag signifies superior, not subordinate, status. When coupled with the appropriate nonverbal behavior, such tag questions can effectively render the addressee powerless.

It may well be that there are various types of tag questions, and that they serve different purposes, just like other grammatical constructions. Questions, for example, can be used to seek information, provide information, make accusations, make counter accusations, and so on. The multiple meanings that participants can attribute to tag questions must be considered in judging whether or not they signify (or contribute to) subordinate status.

Several studies have, in fact, verified Lakoff's suspicion that women use this construction more often than men, particularly when addressing men. Women have been observed to use tag questions twice as often as men in small groups with same-sex participants, and three times as often as men in small groups with mixed male and female participants.[50] But at least one study found contradictory results. After listening to taped group discussions in which both men and women participated, Dubois and Crouch reported that men uttered thirty-three tag questions, while women uttered none.[51]

The apparent contradiction among studies focusing on the use of the tag question construction may be evidence that there are no sex differences in the use of this device, or that its usage is multifunctional in relation to the status of the participants. Perhaps the most accurate statement that can be made about the tag question construction is that, while several researchers have been able to isolate the form described by Lakoff and delineate its use according to gender, no one has been able to verify, nor counter, her contention about its effect on status.

Polite Forms.   Whether the tag question is associated with expressed uncertainty remains in doubt, but other linguistic habits associated with female behavior seem to clearly endorse Lakoff's proposition that women are less straightforward than men. Perhaps the strongest evidence of this distinction lies in the documented female tendency to use polite forms. Lakoff suggested that female speech is, by prescription, more polite than male speech. "Little girls are indeed taught to talk like little ladies...in many ways [to be] more polite than boys or men, and...politeness involves an absence of strong statements...."[52] Thus, a female, even in a position of superiority, would be likely to use polite speech to achieve the same end as her less polite male counterpart.

Following this logic, an overt order may be perceived as less polite than a request, although either may serve the function of communicating the speaker's wish. Arguably, giving an order draws attention to the superior status of the speaker. In effect, an order such as "Meet me at my office," does not call for a verbal response (although in many superior–subordinate communications a required ritual response like "Yes, sir" reinforces the subordinate status of the respondent). Phrasing an order as a question, in contrast, seems to inflate the status of the listener, at least on the surface, by suggesting that he or she can decide how to respond. Take, for example, the question "Can you meet me at my office?" It may be understood, based on the status of the participants, that the listener cannot refuse, but the question seems undeniably more polite than a command.

Subsequent research has endorsed the assertion that women are more likely than men to phrase imperatives as questions. In one investigation, females used this type of construction three times as often as males in peer group interaction.[53] In addition, women have been observed to add obligatory polite forms, such as "please" and "thank you." One study, which examined communication behavior across status relationships, concluded that both gender and status proved useful in predicting the use of polite speech. As might be expected, being female and being subordinate were conditions that statistically increased the likelihood of being polite.[54]

Intensifiers.   There is one linguistic behavior that has been associated with the female register, but seems contrary to the general claim that females are tentative and uncertain in speaking. Intensifiers are adverbs that exaggerate the strength of an expression. For example, by adding the word *so,* the speaker seemingly intensifies whatever word follows: "I am so hungry." Thus, it might seem that including an intensifier would add to the perceived strength of an expression. But linguists have suggested that, due to overuse and hyperbole, intensifiers tend to focus attention toward the emotional message and away from the cognitive meaning of the statement.[55]

In one study, it was reported that women used six times as many intensifiers as men during group discussions. The authors were careful to note that intensifiers were defined as "syntactic constructions rather than particular words...[in which] heavily emphasized adverbs were included."[56] Thus, the singular occurrence of an adverb such as *so* or *just* does not constitute the use of an intensifier. But imagine hearing a speaker complain, "I am so-o-o-o hungry." The elongation of the adverb and its placement in this construction verify that the word *so* is used as an intensifier to stress the misery of the condition. It seems that the speaker wants to emphasize the extent of his or her emotional message, as opposed to accurately phrasing a cognitive statement.

Of course, people are emotion-feeling creatures, as well as language-using creatures, so it seems logical that we have developed linguistic habits to facilitate the expression of emotions. But it has been argued that female speech, which seems to be characterized by an abundance of intensifiers, is often perceived as overemotional and imprecise. Certainly, the indiscriminate use of intensifiers may be damaging to a speaker's credibility.

Many linguists have argued that our society prescribes linguistic habits for women that contribute to their powerlessness. These habits may be roughly summarized as communicating intellectual uncertainty and excessive attention to emotions and other concerns considered trivial by the rest of the world. Robin Lakoff, who was in large part responsible for drawing attention to these concerns, acknowledged the limits of her own research and stated her hope that she might "goad" subsequent research into male–female speech habits.[57] Right or wrong, she played an instrumental role in inspiring scholars to pay attention to gender differences in communication and to the possibility that certain differences may contribute to discrimination.

The resultant research has gathered a good deal of information about male and female communication styles, but has also provided few conclusive answers. Questions remain about the extent to which women's speech is truly distinctive and, if it is, the effect of the differences on the status of female speakers. Some scholars have concluded that the female style of communication does indeed exist, but that it need not be viewed as inferior.[58] Rather, it may be that females are more other-centered in their communication, which necessitates expressions of tentative judgment and emotionality.

CONDUCT YOUR OWN RESEARCH

1. Observe conversations in a public place where you are not likely to be conspicuous (e.g., in a shopping mall, library, fast food restaurant). Record and compare the conversational topics you overhear in male–male, female–female and male–female dyads.

2. Ask for permission to observe a group that allows visitors to its meetings. Record and compare the number of turns and length of turns taken by the men and women in the group discussion. If appropriate, make notes about formal status (elected offices, seniority, power to make decisions, etc.). Rank the order of the participants in terms of power as "achieved" through quantity of talk and as "assigned" through formal channels.

3. Conduct a survey in which you ask respondents to describe as fully as possible what they see in photographs clipped from magazines. Record their responses and look for sex differences in vocabulary, length of description, and grammatical constructions.

DISCUSS THE ISSUES

1. Do you agree with Lakoff's contention that women's speech reflects and perpetuates subordinate status in our culture? Is your agreement or disagreement based in specific claims about the truth or falsehood of language habits or about the relationship between these habits and status? As you debate the issues, try to imagine the speech habits of individuals who have been assigned subordinate positions and compare them to women's speech habits.

2. Share some of the lessons in politeness that you learned as you were growing up. Be specific about the words you remember hearing, the voices and situations that surrounded the lessons, and the way you reacted. As adults, what purpose(s) do you think polite forms serve in human interaction? What lessons *should* parents pass along to children?

3. What evidence in support of linguistic relativity can be found in the discussion of sex differences in vocabulary? Is it possible that our perception of the world is shaped, to some degree, by the words we use to think about and talk about sensory information? Or, conversely, is it more likely that we develop a working vocabulary that serves the end of discussing, in detail, aspects of our world that matter to us? In defending your position, try to think of sex differences in vocabulary not mentioned in the reading.

CHAPTER 5

INTERACTIONAL ASPECTS OF COMMUNICATION

For the most part, the proposed language habits discussed in the previous chapter serve as an index of how men and women have been observed to express themselves without regard to a particular other. In fact, with only a few exceptions, studies of verbal behavior have categorized and counted some aspect of a speaker's message with little regard for the influence of the dyadic context. Yet, in most situations we are keenly aware of that other as we speak and listen—activities that are far less discrete than content analysts would have us believe.

Interaction is seldom neatly divisible into logical verbal units that differentiate speaker from listener. In fact, automated situations attempting to simulate an action–reaction model of communication are typically either frustrating or laughable, depending on the circumstance. Struggling to communicate with mechanical voices, no matter how pleasant or life-like they may be, only serves to make us aware of the futility of the action–reaction model of communication.

Many research scholars have argued that the organization and management of talk is a complex human capacity. Therefore, regardless of content, the structure of conversation is worthy of investigation. Attempting to study the structure of talk creates the somewhat unlikely task of "undoing" what we do so naturally. Even though we usually do not pay attention to how we talk and may not be able to express the rules by which our participation is governed, the fact is that most of us are proficient at interaction even before we know the meaning of the word *conversation*. But decades of investigation into the structure of *ordinary interaction* has resulted in a working vocabulary that can be used to discuss the rules by which conversation is informally governed.

TURN-TAKING

Conversation analysts have adopted the practice of referring to talk as organized by *turns*.[1] This is consistent with some of the formal rules we were taught as children: "Wait your turn," "Don't speak out of turn," and (most important) "It's my turn!" Of course, the turn-taking metaphor is not to be taken literally. Communication does not proceed as a "fair" game, in neatly structured, equally distributed message units. Turns may overlap or be interrupted, and some verbal messages are uttered precisely to indicate that the utterer does not have, nor want, the turn. In addition, most of us are aware that not all players have the same privileges. Turns are often distributed asymmetrically, and certain participants will be penalized for certain moves, while others will be rewarded for the same moves.

Still, it is useful to oversimplify the case by referring to dyadic interaction as organized into turns, and identify overlaps, interruptions, assertions, responses, etc., in an effort to characterize how people manage talk. To the extent that males and females participate differently in the turn-taking system, discernable sex differences may contribute to the understanding of male and female communication styles.

Interruptions.   As mentioned, although early childhood messages may lead us to believe that talk is neatly and politely organized according to turns, the system is seldom perfect in practice. It is fraught with imperfections—the most noticeable of which may be the interruption. In many situations, usually when we feel comfortable with one another and with the discussion, we are untroubled by, and even unconscious of, interruptions. But in other situations, such as employment interviews, decisions about when to speak are as troublesome as decisions about what to say. We are keenly aware of all sorts of imperfections in our own behavior: long silences, false starts, abrupt endings, and, most of all, interruptions. We become so cognizant of the other's turn that we invite the other to speak, to continue, to respond, and we promptly apologize for interrupting. In still other situations, we protect our turn and attack the other's turn, as though at war. Being the speaker, not the listener, becomes so primary that we seemingly abandon the prohibition against interrupting. Sometimes the interruptions are so numerous that we lose track of the content of the conversation. Eventually, the content may disintegrate into mutually uttered profanities or even violent nonverbals.

Thus, it seems fair to conclude that the presence or absence of interruptions, as well as the distribution of interruptions in the talk, may somehow illuminate the relationship between the participants. The interruption, perhaps more than any other conversational move, has been associated with dominance. In sharp contrast to the overlap, which is most often a miscue because it occurs near the apparent end of a speaker's turn (akin to a poor exchange in a relay race), the interruption clearly preempts a turn-in-progress.[2] An interruption signifies a lack of concern for the other's turn, or at least the judgment that the interrupter's utterance takes precedence.

Interruptions vary, of course, as to the apparent intent of the interrupter: to endorse, contradict, ask for clarification, etc. Interruptions also vary as to the extent to which they redirect the conversation. Still, most adult communicators have had the unpleasant experience of interacting with a chronic interruptor and can attest to the frustration of never being able to complete an utterance. In situations where the interrupted party feels particularly unwilling to voice his or her frustration, and the interrupting party feels particularly willing to continue seizing the turn, unequal status can become apparent.

Foundational research into the effect of gender on interruptions produced two primary findings: (1) more interruptions occur in cross-sex conversations than in same-sex conversations; and (2) the interruptions that do occur are likely to be equally distributed between the participants in same-sex conversations, but unequally distributed in cross-sex conversations such that the men interrupt more than the women. In other words, in male–male or female–female dyads, interruptions are relatively rare and both partners interrupt about an equal amount. But in male–female dyads the rate of interruption increases, and men do most of the interrupting. Each of these conclusions has been investigated across relationship types and across research situations, and, predictably, some studies have reported contradictory findings.

The claim that interruptions are more numerous in cross-sex interactions than in same-sex interactions has been well supported by researchers. Zimmerman and West reported a surprising contrast in this regard, when they observed dyadic interaction through naturalistic observation in public settings and listened to audiotapes recorded in private dwellings. Across situations and relationship types, male–male dyads and female–female dyads were markedly less plagued by interruptions than male–female dyads.[3] Even in laboratory-situated discussions between newly acquainted college students (where status is presumably equal), studies have demonstrated that cross-sex dyads display the most interruptions.[4]

Before speculating on the reason why same-sex partners seem to interrupt less, it is necessary to examine the research on cross-sex interruption more specifically. A number of studies have clearly indicated that men initiate most of the interruptions recorded in male–female dyads. Zimmerman and West reported that males initiated anywhere from 75% to 96% of all the interruptions that occurred in the cross-sex conversations they studied.[5] Natale, Entin, and Jaffe also concluded that males interrupted females more often than females interrupted males in their study of dyadic interaction.[6] Similarly, in group situations, males have been reported to be guilty of the majority of cross-sex interruptions.[7] Even in groups composed of three- and four-year-olds, this trend has been supported.[8]

Put simply, the interruption of a female speaker by a male speaker seems to be the most common type of interruption in both dyadic and small group interaction. The prevalence of interruptions in cross-sex conversations, combined with the unequal distribution of interruptor–interrupted roles, serves as evidence of unequal status between men and women according to many communication scholars.[9] After comparing male–female interactions with parent–child interactions, Zimmerman and West concluded "females and young children apparently receive similar treatment in conversations with males and with adults."[10] It is difficult to deny that there is a very obvious status differential in conversations between parents and small children. Just imagine a five-year-old telling a parent, "I'm not finished. Wait your turn!" Similarly, if interruptions are asymmetrically distributed in cross-sex interactions, they may be evidence of unequal status. Indeed, unequal distribution of interruptions in male–female interaction may be the result of a cooperative effort to create or maintain the status differential.

However, as mentioned, some studies have resulted in opposing conclusions. Even though most scholars agree that cross-sex conversations appear to be more plagued by interruptions than same-sex conversations, several researchers have reported that the interruptions are symmetrically distributed. In other words, in some studies, women have interrupted their male partners as often as the men have interrupted them![11] Such findings seem to contradict the proposition that men occupy a superior status position in dyadic interactions with women. Given the rejection of the status-based explanation, Dindia hypothesized that "opposite-sex conversations [may be] more awkward than same-sex conversations thus resulting in more conversational errors [e.g., interruptions]."[12] She apparently likens interruptions, then, to overlaps, as evidence of imperfection in exchanging the turn, rather than as disregard for the other's input.

Still other authors have attempted to study the quality of male and female interruptions, as well as the quantity. LaFrance proposed a difference between interruptive statements and interruptive questions. She observed that males tended to interrupt females to offer statements, while females tended to interrupt males to ask questions. Therefore, she concluded, the female interruptions were less assertive than the male interruptions.[13] Sex differences in offering statements and asking questions are discussed in more detail in the next section. Here it is important to stress that both constructions, as interruptions, can demonstrate interest or disinterest, depending on their content. But the proposed female tendency to interrupt with a question may support the contention that women are less straightforward, or perhaps just more cautious, in managing the interruption of their partner's turn.

Unfortunately, there has been a paucity of research characterizing the nature of interrupting behavior in same-sex dyads. This may be due to the relative absence of interruptions in same-sex interaction, to the proposed symmetry in distribution between the partners, or to the lack of research interest in same-sex conversation. Same-sex interruptions just have not proven to be especially controversial. Still, it seems important to be able to contrast qualitative findings on cross-sex interruption with qualitative findings on same-sex interruption. Perhaps women interrupt in question form regardless of the sex of the partner, or perhaps they question male partners but challenge female partners. Knowledge of distinctive patterns according to the sex composition of the dyad is necessary in order to draw valid conclusions about the effect of interruptions on status and vice versa.

Ideally, studies should combine the investigation of assigned status and sex, since many dyadic relationships, regardless of sexual composition, are superior–subordinate in nature. In one such study, conducted by Greif, sex and status position both proved to be valuable predictors of interrupting behavior. In parent–child interactions, both same sex and cross sex, Greif reported that fathers were more likely than mothers to interrupt children, although both parents interrupted far more than their children. This seems to suggest that parental status legitimates interrupting, and further suggests that males take greater advantage of superiority than females in this regard. In the same vein, daughters were interrupted by parents more than sons, indicating that male children's status may not be quite as subordinate as that of their female counterparts.[14]

The sensitivity that most speakers share toward being interrupted warrants that researchers pay careful attention to this particular imperfection in the turn-taking system. It seems overly idealistic to assume that interrupting behaviors are randomly or evenly distributed in most dyadic relationships. Even in those relationships we label *peer,* status can be achieved conversationally, and being the interrupter (not the interrupted) may be a contributing factor to rising above the other. While the research is not conclusive, the claim that women are interrupted more than men has been made often and interpreted as evidence that females may have more difficulty creating and maintaining status in conversation. Those studies that challenge this claim generally counter that men and women both interrupt other speakers, not that women interrupt men more than vice versa. Of course, any study is limited to a given set of participants and research procedures, but the absence of a single study in which women emerge as doing the majority of interrupting in conversations with men supports the contention that a sex difference characterizes this aspect of conversational dominance.

Questions and Statements.   Conversation analysts have proposed that certain types of turns usually occur in pairs. Some pairs are symmetrical, involving the exchange of similar types of turns. For instance, a greeting is usually followed by a greeting. If another fails to return a greeting with a greeting, the failure needs to be explained: "He's mad at me" or "She didn't hear me." Other turn pairs are complementary. A question, for example, should be answered with a statement, not another question. If someone breaks this convention, we could legitimately scold "Don't answer a question with a question!" We generally operate according to a rule that requires that one question be answered before another is asked, even if it is the same question, as evidenced by the expression "I asked you first." Each of these rules, of course, assumes that a question is a request for information, although as proficient speakers we know that questions can be used for a multitude of other purposes.

Nevertheless, a question usually serves as the first part of a two-part conversational event and therefore may be understood as an attempt to initiate interaction. A statement, in contrast, may or may not be answered. Unlike a question, it can stand alone. A statement does not necessitate, nor even invite, interaction. Granted, statements are as diverse in form and purpose as questions. But given the "rule" demanding that a question be answered, and the option not to respond to a statement, it stands to reason that, if you want to invite another to speak, you ought to ask a question.

In light of the diverse quality of questions and statements as conversational turns, any claim about sex differences in their usage must be offered tentatively and explained carefully. Still, an examination of the empirical data available concerning questions and statements helps to delineate what some scholars have identified as distinctive male and female styles of interaction. Fishman reports, based on conversational data she obtained from over fifty hours of audiotaped interaction between couples, "there is an overwhelming difference between female and male use of questions as a resource in interaction." The wives in her study asked two-and-one-half times as many questions as the husbands during conversations recorded in the privacy of the couples' homes. In contrast, the men offered twice as many statements as the women.[15]

Lakoff also proposes that women tend to ask more questions than men and suggested that this sex difference is another sign of powerlessness.[16] Unlike Lakoff, Fishman argues that the sex difference in question asking serves as evidence that women perform "work" that is essential to successful conversation. She credits women with using strategies that "insure a minimal interaction—at least one utterance by each of the two participants."[17] Obviously, questions can be used to this end.

The women in Fishman's study often used questions to initiate topics of conversation. They used a particular type of question, apparently designed to introduce a topic of talk, twice as often as their husbands. It is a form used commonly by children when they want to insure that they have adult attention: "D'ya know what?" This particular question, of course, calls for a question in response. Hopefully the listener will ask, "What?" At that point, having been invited to speak, the child (or wife, in this case) can offer a statement, comfortable that the listener approves. The use of this question/question/statement sequence, therefore, seems to constitute an indirect route to making a statement. In effect, the speaker asks a question not to seek information but to secure attention.[18]

Taken together, the evidence gathered by Lakoff and Fishman about sex differences in the use of question asking seems to support the contention that women are more other-centered than men, at least in conversation. Women ask others to make statements and ask for an invitation from others when they want to make statements. Fishman refers to these and other practices as the interactional "work that women do."[19] Women's work is examined further in the next section.

Minimal Responses.   A minimal response is a conversational turn that is just that—the bare minimum. Usually, the minimal response may be taken to mean something akin to "message received," but provides very little information about the listener's interest in or evaluation of the speaker's remark. Typical forms of this response in our language are "yeah," "oh," and "mmm-hmm," but certain lengthier responses may communicate a similar reaction: "I see," "right," or "no kidding." Imagine the impact of telling a long, involved story and receiving any one of these responses.

In fact, a familiar comedic scene features a husband hidden behind a newspaper, offering a series of minimal responses to information offered by his wife. After several such responses, she reports, "Also the house is on fire, and I'm having an affair with the milkman." He responds, "That's nice dear." Imagine another comedy routine that uses the same minimal responses, but offered periodically during the speaker's lengthy turn. Typically, this scene features a gabbing or nagging voice on the unseen end of a telephone conversation and a visible listener who merely utters an occasional "mmm-hmm" and sometimes goes so far as to put down the receiver! The effect is, of course, that the speaker continues to talk on and on, ignorant of the listener's fake attentiveness.

These two humorous episodes serve to display two very different effects of using the minimal response. In the first, the listener's disinterest is clear to the speaker based on the brevity of the response, but in the second, the minimal responses apparently encourage a willing speaker to continue. Certainly, faking interest in face-to-face conversation is more involved, since nonverbal information is required, but most of us are surprisingly adept at pretending to listen. Try to recall an incident in which you realized that someone had just finished speaking to you and you had no idea what he or she had said. In some cases, if you pretend well, the speaker may not realize your inattentiveness. But when you respond with an abrupt, meaningless response like "right," the speaker will probably get the message.

Fishman's study suggests a fascinating distinction in the way men and women use the minimal response in their daily conversations. While both sexes used the minimal response about equally in terms of numbers, they differed sharply in terms of the timing and apparent purpose of its usage. The men tended to offer minimal responses at the end of their partners' turns, often after a brief pause.[20] This practice, often called the *delayed minimal* response, was also observed by Zimmerman and West as a characteristic male reaction to a female utterance. They observed that, following a delayed minimal response, the female speaker often "fell silent."[21] Fishman concludes that "such minimal responses operate to discourage interaction."[22]

Zimmerman and West argue that women, in contrast, seldom display the delayed minimal response.[23] The women in Fishman's study did offer minimal responses, but they did so intermittently during their partners' turns. Fishman also noted the skill of the females in placing the responses appropriately: "seldom [did] they mistime their insertions and cause even slight overlaps. These minimal responses [occurred] between the breaths of a speaker...." She concluded that the skillful insertion of the minimal response signified "interest in the interaction and the speaker."[24]

Apparently, the minimal response is fairly powerful in promoting or discouraging a speaker's turn. Fishman and others have concluded that part of the work women do in conversation involves participating in the other's turn, and the minimal response facilitates that work, if carefully timed and uttered. On the other hand, the work men do in conversation may sometimes involve exerting power over the other's turn, and they appear to use the delayed minimal response effectively to that end.

Presumably, the subtle difference in placing the minimal response is learned by children along with other conversational maneuvers. But according to Esposito, sex differences in this behavior do not emerge as early as more obvious power-related behaviors. She reported that children (3.5 to 4.8 years) clearly showed sex differences in interrupting behavior and topic-controlling moves, but did not demonstrate contrasting uses of the minimal response.[25] So it may well be that certain conversational regularities are subtle, perhaps unconscious moves that an adult uses to improve or damage another's participation in talk. Undoubtedly, every reader has experienced a situation in which he or she intentionally offered a sarcastic "no kidding!" as well as a situation in which he or she enthusiastically encouraged another to keep the floor by offering plenty of "really's" and "mmm-hmm's." But given the possible unintentional use of the minimal response and its potential power, each reader is encouraged to attend carefully to his or her own interaction for evidence of sex differences in this aspect of turn-taking management.

TOPIC INITIATION AND SELECTION

While observations about the turn-taking system can be offered without reference to the content of the talk, it is also valuable to attend to the content in order to examine sex differences in the initiation and selection of topics. Conceivably, the power to control the topic of discussion is another indicator of the relative status of the participants. In classrooms, for example, the highest status member (i.e., the professor) usually determines when to move on to a new topic. Similarly, in dyadic situations in which the hierarchy of the individuals' positions is clear (e.g., employment interviews), the higher status individual generally initiates topic changes.

Therefore, topic control appears to be indicative of conversational power. Predictably, the same studies that report male dominance in terms of interruptions report that males control the topics in male–female interactions.[26] It stands to reason that interruptions sometimes function as topic changes in and of themselves. Kennedy and Camden contend that nearly one-quarter of all the interruptions they coded could be categorized as "subject changes."[27]

Fishman's discussion of topic control is especially interesting, since she not only recorded attempts to initiate topics, but noted whether or not attempts succeeded. She defines success as the "mutual orientation" of the two participants to a topic. This requires that both individuals contribute to the elaboration of the topic. Therefore, if one partner offered only a minimal response, Fishman did not consider the topic-initiation attempt successful. The men in her study were consistently successful in initiating topics; twenty-eight of twenty-nine attempts resulted in mutual elaboration by the couple. The female-initiated topics succeeded only seventeen times in forty-seven attempts. In essence, the females attempted nearly twice as many topic initiations as the males, but succeeded only about half as often.[28]

To be sure, the definition of *topic* in Fishman's data is specific to her belief that "it takes two" to make a conversation succeed. So, the men's success in initiating topics may tell more about the "work women do" to maintain conversation than about the fascinating nature of male-introduced topics. In fact, she noticed that the topics raised by men and women were largely similar: public events, the day's activities, friends, food, and work. She concluded that "topics introduced by the women failed because the men did not respond with the attention necessary to keep the conversation going."[29]

HUMOR

Humor is another interactional event that might be attempted by an individual, but cannot be considered successful unless it is appropriately received. A smile, laugh, or verbal remark like "That's funny," typically signals at least minimal success. The ability to make others laugh is sometimes regarded as a talent—like the ability to draw or sing well. Certainly, the world's great comedians are talented performers, but, in daily interaction, the freedom to offer witticisms and the tendency for others to express appreciation may very well be tied to status. After all, there is a risk in offering a remark for the entertainment of others. How many times have you spared someone the truth about a joke that was not funny by faking a hearty laugh? The logic follows that we are more concerned about not offending superiors, so they have less to risk by attempting humor.

Several years ago, Coser studied attempts at humor during hospital staff meetings. She noticed a clear hierarchy: the higher-status individuals predictably offered more jokes than their subordinates. As might be expected, men occupied the highest positions and attempted humor most often. But the sex differences in this regard were even more significant than might be anticipated: nearly 95% of all witticisms offered were spoken by males. Sex, not status, emerged as the most accurate predictor of which members offered jokes. As for the response, nearly every witticism offered was successful, with the females present tending to laugh longer and harder at most of the jokes.[30] In a more recent study of committee meetings among peers, Edelsky found substantiation for the proposition that males offer more witticisms.[31] Another study by Duncan and Fiske provides evidence that women laugh more often and longer than men in dyadic situations.[32]

The tendency for males to entertain others with humor has even been revealed in groups of children. McGhee studied children ranging in age from three to eleven for evidence concerning the frequency and nature of attempts at humor. He reports that "at the Nursery School level, no sex differences were apparent...[but] by the middle childhood years (6–11) boys were rated higher on all aspects of humor." Specifically, their "behavioral attempts to initiate humor included silly or clowning behavior, arranging objects in incongruous positions, teasing through gestures, etc...." Certainly, such behaviors bring back fond memories of schooldays, as do the boys' verbal attempts at humor: "distortion of familiar word sounds, puns, riddles, 'bathroom' words, etc." McGhee contends that the change in behavior from preschool children to elementary school children is evidence of differential treatment of "clowning around" by boys and girls.[33]

Put simply, boys are more likely than girls to get positive attention for this behavior, particularly from those all-important peers. When it came to responsiveness to humor, McGhee reports a similar trend in laughter, i.e., preschool girls responded with laughter as often as preschool boys, but elementary school boys laughed significantly more often than their female peers.[34] Other investigations of sex differences in children's responses to humor have shown that elementary school girls tended to respond to others with smiling, rather than laughing.[35] Thus, it may be that boys learn to participate more overtly in the achievement of shared laughter, but girls tend to assume the more passive role of recipient when it comes to humor. The reason for this is debatable, although there are obvious implications in terms of the active–passive continuum that some scholars have suggested distinguishes male from female communication.

In any case, the development of sex differences in offering and responding to humor during early childhood is fairly well supported by the research and appears to be logically related to research suggesting that adult humor tends to be male-dominated. As mentioned, men have been observed to offer more jokes in mixed-sex groups. In addition, Hassett and Houlihan report that the majority of men and women surveyed as to the sex of the "wittiest person" they knew chose a man.[36] Indeed, this trend has made it very difficult for females to achieve success as professional comedians (sometimes, they are referred to by a special female form—*comediennes*). For his 1968 book *The Great Comedians Talk About Comedy*, Larry Wilde interviewed Phyllis Diller, one of only a handful of women to have broken into the field at that time. Diller remarked, "Almost nobody wants you to be a female comic and they give you a lot of static just because of your sex."[37]

For many female comics, including Diller, the solution to the anti-female bias took the form of self-deprecatory humor, or humor that hinges on self-criticism. Levine compared monologues by Diller and several other females (Totie Fields, Moms Mabley, and Lily Tomlin) to monologues by male comics (George Carlin, Robert Klein, Bill Cosby, and David Steinberg) and reported an overwhelming trend toward female self-derision: 64% of the jokes in monologues by females were self-deprecatory, compared to 11% of the jokes in monologues by males. In addition, Levine points out that men criticized women in their stories twice as often as women criticized men.[38] Cantor comments that jokes targeting female "victims" are perceived as funnier than jokes targeting males, regardless of the sex of the teller.[39]

In another study of comedy, raters were asked to rank comedy routines by men (George Carlin, Don Rickles, David Steinberg, Bill Cosby, and Herman Schnitzel) and women (Lily Tomlin, Fanny Flagg, Joan Rivers, Phyllis Diller, and Rusty Warren). Only one woman was rated to be in the top five—Lily Tomlin. It appears that Tomlin is one of very few women who has been able to break into the male-dominated area of comedy.[40] She is recognized as a talented impressionist and a creative wit who seldom bases her humor in self-criticism. But she is the exception. For the majority of female comics, the same dynamic that makes it difficult for them to be perceived as funny may encourage them to adopt a style of self-deprecation in their routines.

In fact, theorists have long concurred that much of what is funny involves ridicule. *Putdown humor,* as it is often called, typically targets the behavior of groups or individuals believed to be nonthreatening to the listener. Self-disparagement, then, is somewhat unique in that the comic offers himself or herself for the amusement of the audience. This practice seems far less offensive than ridiculing the listener, or some group to whom the listener is sympathetic. Several researchers have attempted to compare the effects of self-disparagement and other-disparagement on the listener. The results are pertinent here based not only on the tendency of female comedians to ground their humor in self-criticism, but because there are some fascinating sex differences in the responses to putdown humor. Zillman and Stocking asked listeners to respond to stories in which the speaker poked fun at his own inadequacies and to stories that ridiculed the same behaviors in a friend and an enemy. Male raters found the disparagement of the enemy most amusing, while females found the self-disparaging version funniest. So the same trend that characterizes professional female comedy seems to be present in female raters' evaluations of what is funny. But, notably, there may be special costs to the self-disparaging humorist. Zillman and Stocking also found that the self-ridiculing speaker was judged less intelligent, less witty, and less confident than the other-ridiculing speaker.[41]

Based on another study, one that tested the effect of self-disparaging humor in speeches made by college professors, Chang and Gruner concluded that "speakers with relatively high status and ethos can disparage [themselves] and thereby raise their ratings on wittiness, funniness and sense of humor without damaging other factors of credibility."[42] The obvious conclusion, then, is that those who have already established themselves as high-status individuals can risk putting themselves down and probably enjoy an increase in status by demonstrating their wit and generosity. But, without preestablished high status, the self-disparager risks being perceived as less capable. In relation to sex differences, the fact that women often rely on self-disparagement for laughs suggests that they may inadvertently reinforce their low status.

The successful use of humor in interaction seems to be a privilege that only a small segment of the population enjoys, much less gets paid for. Humor succeeds for many reasons, to be sure, but much of the literature indicates that it is harder for women to succeed in this interactional endeavor than men and that they may have to sacrifice themselves to some extent in order to do so.

SELF-DISCLOSURE

Many popular and scholarly communication articles have dealt with the effect of individuals "opening up" to one another. In fact, groups intended to provide arenas for sharing deep emotions are currently flourishing. You can join a group to talk about almost any personal problem and you can listen to strangers open up to faceless listeners on a number of popular talk shows. While the appropriateness of sharing deeply personal information with large groups and mass audiences is questionable, the physical and psychological dangers of keeping such information inside are well documented.

Self-disclosure is a term communication scholars use to refer to the face-to-face communication of personal information—information that is true and that the other is presumed not to know.[43] In this text, self-disclosing is termed an *interactional* event because it is assumed that sharing such information, in a dyadic situation, requires the participation of two willing partners and is likely to affect both of them and the relationship between them. Thus, the present discussion is not concerned with the all-too-familiar situations in which a stranger tells fantastic personal stories during a two-hour bus ride or a psychiatrist listens and nods (for pay) while a client voices his or her innermost secrets. The conceptualization of self-disclosure here is far more narrow, in order to examine the reported sex differences in the tendency to share personal information in various relationships. Self-disclosure of this type calls for cooperative interaction and is often reciprocal in nature. Therefore, it is logically related to the development of close personal ties.

The folklinguistic myths about sex differences in self-disclosure are consistent with the conceptualization that women like to talk more than men, especially about people and relationships. Besides gossiping about others, therefore, women are thought to confide information about themselves. The complementary myth, of course, portrays men as "strong and silent," or, as some communication scholars report, "emotionally inexpressive."[44] The operative distinction may rest in the expression of emotions, which women are generally thought to share openly and men are generally thought to hide. Thus, a good deal of self-disclosure research has focused on sex differences in expressing emotions and personal weaknesses, not biographical data or stories of the day's events.[45]

Like stereotypic information, empirical evidence about self-disclosure abounds. Since the early 1970s, many studies have attempted to delineate sex differences in the willingness to self-disclose, the nature of the information disclosed, the sex composition of self-disclosing dyads, and the effect of the disclosure. However, an obvious problem exists in attempting to violate the rules governing self-disclosure in order to examine these factors. Indeed, when a researcher is privy to the information, it cannot be considered real self-disclosure between two relationship members. So most researchers have opted to study either self-reports (i.e., what people say has been shared) or recorded laboratory conversations designed to promote self-disclosure. Understandably, neither of these methods is likely to permit the analysis of genuine self-disclosing behavior. Although the futility of trying to observe self-disclosure is acknowledged, it is still worthwhile to study the results in order to compare them with our own behavior and the behavior we observe around us.

Generally, the literature reports that women disclose more than men, and that they receive more disclosure from others.[46] Using the Jourard Inventory, designed to categorize the subject and depth of disclosed information, as well the person to whom it is disclosed, several studies have reported that women disclose more personal information, across subjects, to more others.[47] Naturally, other studies also exist that report no apparent sex differences in self-disclosure.[48] But it may be most telling that no study has ever reported that males disclose more than women.[49] Overall, therefore, the research can be summarized as substantiating the myth that females participate in self-disclosure, at least according to their self-reported behavior and their behavior in laboratory settings; males may or may not participate as frequently or as openly in self-disclosure, depending on the conclusions of the particular study.

A more fascinating contradiction has emerged, however, regarding the same-sex effect on self-disclosure. Researchers have hypothesized that, in general, people tend to disclose more freely to others they perceive as similar to themselves, thereby reducing the risk of disapproval.[50] This seems logical, since we can assume that someone who shares our experiences probably understands our perspective best. It follows that a drug user might self-disclose about drug-related experiences to another he or she perceives to be a drug user and avoid disclosing this information to a perceived nonuser. Similarly, a disgruntled employee would probably seek out a disgruntled peer to whom he or she might disclose attitudes about work. The same logic indicates the likelihood that a woman would disclose to another woman and a man would disclose to another man. A body of empirical evidence does indeed support this logic.[51]

But some studies suggest that, while females disclose most often and most openly to other females, males disclose more often and more fully to females than to fellow males. Specifically, in terms of the depth and breadth of information the participants share about one another, female–female relationships have been ranked first in many studies, followed by male–female relationships, with male–male relationships rated lowest on degree of intimacy.[52]

This ordering seems to contradict the effect of perceived similarity on the tendency to self-disclose. Instead, it seems that both men and women prefer to self-disclose to women, which is consistent with the findings that women are other-centered in their communication. It seems that a major benefit of self-disclosing in close relationships (one that I hope every reader has experienced) is the securing of support and understanding from the other person. Put simply, it may be that women are perceived as more supportive and understanding, and therefore as better targets for self-disclosure.

But Hacker explains that self-disclosure must be understood as involving two dimensions: intimacy and power.[53] Considering self-disclosure as potentially empowering adds another angle to the intrigue surrounding cross-sex dyads. Henley explains that status does indeed affect the sharing of information, such that self-disclosure is likely to be somewhat "unidirectional" in nonpeer relationships, with the subordinate revealing more personal information than the superior.[54] Presumably, keeping personal information secret helps distance a superior. On the other hand, a subordinate has more to lose by disclosing too much information to someone with the power to damage or improve his or her position. It seems that, if power does affect self-disclosure, the direction of the effect is debatable.

If sex may be assumed to entail status in and of itself, this dimension should not affect levels of self-disclosure in same-sex dyads, but would be very interesting in cross-sex dyads. In other words, male–male dyads and female–female dyads may be assumed to be equal, so same-sex pairs should not be inhibited by status considerations. Yet, male–male dyads are reported in much of the literature to be the least open, while female–female dyads are reported to be the most open. Therefore, it does not seem that equal status necessarily results in high levels of self-disclosure. Rather, equality seems to result in reciprocity of disclosure levels, whether high or low. It may be that higher-status individuals (in this case males) do not disclose as freely as lower-status individuals. This may be due to perceived competition among higher-status pairs or greater need for support among lower-status pairs.

But remember that some studies found no significant sex differences in same-sex disclosure. If these findings are correct, the cross-sex findings may be more telling in terms of the status dimension. Hacker interviewed over one hundred pairs, obtaining information from both partners about the quality and depth of their self-disclosure. She concludes that women are far less disclosing in cross-sex friendships than in same-sex friendships, while men remain about the same. None of the female–female dyads reported what Hacker terms "low levels of self-disclosure," but 13% of the women reported that, in cross-sex friendships, the level was low. In addition, while 40% of the women reported high disclosure with same-sex friends and 60% reported moderate disclosure, both numbers declined in the cross-sex category. The men tended to report moderate levels in cross-sex friendships and same-sex friendships.[55] These findings support the claim that subordinates (females) may be more reluctant to self-disclose to superiors (males) than to peers (other females).

The influence of status in cross-sex friendships is even more obvious in light of Hacker's findings about what information the men and women kept hidden. She reported that one-third of the men in these relationships admitted concealing weaknesses, not strengths, from their female friends, while a similar portion of the women admitted concealing strengths, but disclosing weaknesses! In essence, Hacker's study suggests that, women, as the lower-status members in cross-sex interactions, may be expected to listen to talk about their partners' strengths and conceal their own. But they are more willing than men to talk about weaknesses, which Hacker suggests may increase their level of subordination.[56] Thus, it may be best to conceive of the disclosure of strengths and weaknesses as both a consequence of status differences and a possible cause of those differences.

Admittedly, the empirical research concerning sex differences in self-disclosure is laden with contradictions and competing explanations. But each of us probably has an intuitive sense of the importance of sharing ourselves with others and of protecting ourselves from "overexposure." Sharing personal information, appropriately and constructively, is not an individual activity. Rather, like dancers, the disclosing partners constantly attend to one another's cues as to which moves are appropriate. It is the tendency to select or fail to select a target person based on gender that is of interest here, and each reader is encouraged to consider carefully the interaction of trust and power as these factors pertain to self-disclosure in relationships.

CONDUCT YOUR OWN RESEARCH

1. Ask two friends, one male and one female, to help you with a class project. Tell them you are studying some political issue that relates specifically to women (e.g., affirmative action, funding for collegiate athletics, a woman in the presidency, pornography). Ask them to choose sides and debate the issue, and tape the debate for analysis. As you listen to the tape, ignore the content; focus, instead, on evidence of conversational dominance (e.g., interruptions, minimal responses, questions, topic initiation, etc.).

2. Examine the use of timing to create humor in situation comedies on television. Notice and record the differences in how male and female actors pause, interrupt, and overlap, and use the minimal response to achieve certain communicative ends, e.g., making fun of someone, getting the last word, revealing that they are not being fooled, etc.

3. Conduct a survey about self-disclosure. Choose some specific aspect to examine, such as the content of disclosure to a same-sex vs. an opposite-sex other, the likelihood of disclosing high-risk information to one or the other, the reciprocity of disclosure in same-sex vs. cross-sex dyads, etc.

DISCUSS THE ISSUES

1. What can the examination of telephone conversations teach us about the turn-taking system? Specifically, how do we compensate for the absence of visual information about the exchange of turns? One of the folklinguistics about women's communication is that women enjoy telephone conversations. Discuss this myth in relation to the specific behaviors you used to contrast telephone turn-taking with face-to-face turn-taking.

2. With a friend or group of friends, compile a list of all the professional comics that you can think of. How many names are male? How many female? Discuss the type of humor characteristic of each. Are there sex differences in the content of their humor? In the success of their humor? If so, what do these differences communicate about cultural images of men and women?

3. Is self-disclosure a healthy activity? Under what conditions might it be unhealthy, unwise, or even unfair to the other? Are these conditions related to the type of relationship in which the disclosure takes place?

CHAPTER 6

KINESIC
AND PARALINGUISTIC
ASPECTS
OF COMMUNICATION

Although most of us conceptualize communication as a verbal activity (I talk, you listen, etc.), analysts agree that, when two or more individuals are in a face-to-face situation, a good portion of the meaning created and exchanged takes the form of nonverbal communication. We watch and listen to one another, regardless of the presence or absence of speech. We have all experienced the subtle yet effective communication contained in a knowing glance, a nervous gesture, and an inviting smile. Nonverbal messages are the first messages we learn to offer and interpret, and they continue to influence our interaction with others long after we acquire language.

Unlike verbal communication, which is arguably discrete, nonverbal communication is clearly continuous. That is, nonverbal communication is not divided into turns; both speaker and listener are communicating nonverbally at every instant. Also, while verbal communication is usually uni-channeled (i.e., we are either speaking *or* listening, writing *or* reading, at any given time), nonverbal communication is multi-channeled. We receive information through several senses at once. Because they are continuous and multi-channeled, nonverbal messages are understandably difficult to isolate.

A good deal of effort, nevertheless, has been expended in trying to isolate nonverbal behaviors, determine their meaning, and predict their impact on interpersonal communication. In order to examine proposed sex differences in nonverbal communication, empirical evidence is divided according to the type of nonverbal behavior studied. This is certainly an imperfect system, but one that dominates the communication literature. In this chapter, kinesics and paralinguistics are examined; in the next chapter the so-called "interactive" nonverbals are discussed—proxemics and haptics. If these terms are unfamiliar, it may be because we tend to take nonverbal messages for granted—to treat them as behavior, not as communication. Keep in mind, though, that any behavior can constitute communication when humans are together. Any movement of the body or sound of the voice can be understood to convey meaning if perceived by another. Similarly, any touch, any movement toward or away from another, constitutes potentially communicative behavior.

KINESICS

The area of nonverbal communication referred to as *kinesics* includes the many muscular and skeletal movements that humans consider meaningful. Birdwhistell first used the term in the 1950s and was instrumental in establishing the study of movement in daily interaction as an important research area.[1] Since then, several subcategories have come to be considered integral to the study of human communication:

Facial Expressions—movements of the facial muscles.

Eye Contact—movements of the eye that result in mutual gaze with another individual.

Gestures—movements of the hands and fingers.

Body Movements—movements of the arms, legs, and torso, excluding those specifically labeled by any other subcategory.

Postures—body positions that can be identified in the absence of body movements.

Obviously, except for eye contact, the kinesic subcategories are individually based in the sense that they do not require that another be present in order to be enacted. Most individuals exhibit kinesic behaviors whether someone is there to observe them or not. Victims on the "Candid Camera" television show often demonstrate a continuous production of kinesic information even though they believe they are alone, much to the amusement of the audience. Apparently, it is part of being human, perhaps part of being alive, to react to the environment, and a good deal of human reaction takes the form of movement. If that movement is perceived by another, it can become meaningful, even though the actor may not have intended to communicate at all.

Of course not all kinesic communication is unintentional. Birdwhistell stresses the notion that humans learn culturally transmitted patterns of "body motion communication."[2] In other words, we learn a particular language of movement (although the popular term *body language* surely oversimplifies and exaggerates the learned aspects of kinesic behavior and simultaneously ignores the spontaneous aspects). Most of us can recall several specific lessons we have been taught by parents or teachers about which gestures and postures are inappropriate when trying to make a good impression. Indeed, gestural communication is often so closely tied to verbal communication that a seemingly nonverbal act—raising the middle finger—communicates the same two words to virtually every adult member of our culture!

Communication through movement is particularly complex and confusing because it may or may not be intentional. Most readers have been on both sides of a discussion in which one individual accuses another of giving a "dirty look," and the other denies any such behavior. The issue in this discussion is seldom the presence or absence of a facial expression. Rather, the discussants typically argue about whether or not the facial expression displayed was deliberate. The fact that we can refer to specific communicative acts, such as gestures and facial expressions, and apply adjectives to them, like *obscene* and *dirty,* is evidence that we attend to movement as communicative. But it is important to remember that each culture prescribes standard interpretations, in some cases even quasi-definitions, for at least a subset of the identifiable movements humans can make.

As mentioned in Chapter One, Birdwhistell is also credited with recognizing that many movements function as "gender displays." According to his analysis, all animals need to identify potential mates, but humans are relatively unimorphic, so it may be difficult to be sure who's who based solely on visual information. It may be disturbing to think of human males and females as looking more alike than different, but consider the obvious contrast between many male and female birds: the males are often brightly colored; the females brown or black. During a recent trip to the zoo, I was struck by the number of parents and teachers proudly instructing their children "that's the female lion," or "that one is the daddy." It was not difficult to tell which animal was which. But imagine the information that would be needed to tell humans apart, especially if we all let our hair grow! Because humans are "civilized" creatures, the situation is confounded by the custom of concealing with clothing the biological information that distinguishes us as female or male. We cannot rely on olfactory information, like dogs for instance, so each society seems to have developed "patterned social-behavioral" gender displays.[3]

As a result, it is important to delineate observable gender differences in movement and to consider which appear to be linked to the conscious effort to display gender. In addition, it is crucial to remember that culturally patterned behavior may be adopted long before its significance can be articulated, so many gender displays are enacted purely because the actor believes they are natural. Each reader is encouraged to carefully observe and evaluate nonverbal behaviors, and to hypothesize which are culturally defined as sex appropriate. For many who have concentrated on such observations, discrete behaviors that distinguish male nonverbal communication from female nonverbal communication begin to form patterns related to the mythology of gender.

Facial Expressions.   Facial expressions are often believed to be visible indicators of inner emotional states. Certainly, children seem to have little control over facial configurations, a characteristic that sometimes delights and sometimes troubles the adults around them. Even though most of us develop a fair amount of control as we grow, nearly everyone can remember a time when he or she could not conceal a smile, a frown, or a nervous look, even in the midst of hearty verbal denials of that emotion. In truth, however, facial behavior appears to be far more patterned and predictable than most of us imagine.

Recently, Leathers and Emigh developed a set of ten photographs of the same person, each intended to communicate a specific emotion: anger, bewilderment, contempt, determination, disgust, fear, happiness, interest, sadness, and surprise. The photos were sorted with overwhelming success; the percentages of the 268 decoders who identified the facial expressions "correctly" ranged from nearly 99% for the emotion happiness to 82% for the emotion bewilderment.[4] Granted, the person in the photographs may have been unusually talented in presenting facial expressions, but the uniformity of the coding still suggests that the subjects (as well as the model) shared a finely tuned system for determining facially appropriate behaviors for given emotional states.

This study casts doubt on the common belief that we react spontaneously to our emotions. It may be that we sometimes react as we believe we are expected to—even facially. Surely, every reader can remember one or two situations in which he or she deliberately selected a facial expression to convey a desired, but not necessarily felt, emotion. LaFrance and Mayo explain that facial expressions of this type are common. They label such expressions *presentational* and contrast them with *representational* facial expressions. The distinction is, roughly, that presentational facial expressions are consciously intended to communicate particular emotions, while representational facial expressions are closely linked to actual emotional states.[5] Of course, sometimes the intention is to hide an actual emotional state facially. Henley goes so far as to suggest that "faces are the means by which we attempt to create an impression."[6] Certainly, we are not always consciously controlling our facial communication, but we must be careful not to assume that facial expressions are as individual and spontaneous as the mythology suggests.

In light of the potential of facial expressions to be representational, certain facial behaviors may serve as gender displays. In our culture, women have been observed to be far more facially expressive than men.[7] Ekman and Friesen explain that the female stereotype allows for a wider range of emotional expressions, including positive expressions like giggling (which is hardly perceived as "manly") and negative expressions like crying (which is still evaluated far more negatively for males than females).[8] The tendency for women to be more facially expressive, then, both supports and perpetuates the stereotypes that females are "emotional" and men are "rational."

The fact that women are more outwardly expressive than men raises an intriguing question, one that researchers have attempted to address: does the sex difference in facial expressiveness signify a difference in presented emotions or a difference in represented emotions? If the latter is the case, could it be that women truly react more emotionally to the world than men? In one study, male and female viewers were shown slides intended to inspire emotional reactions, both positive and negative. The researchers videotaped the subjects' outward responses to the pictures and monitored their physiological responses by recording changes in heart rate and glandular activity.

Comparing the two sources of information provided researchers with information about expressed vs. felt emotions. As predicted, the female viewers expressed their emotions externally more than the male viewers; their facial reactions were far more dramatic. In contrast, the males' internal reactions were more pronounced, although they tended to maintain stoic facial expressions.[9] Buck and his colleagues have also conducted experiments comparing overt emotional expressions to monitored physiological changes. They have concluded, as well, that women appear to be externalizers and men internalizers of emotion.[10]

The possibility that the expression or internalization of emotion could be a learned cultural lesson seems remote. But nearly every culture limits its young people's behavioral displays of emotion in some way. Indeed, socialization necessarily requires the tempering of emotional behavior, or we would be subjected to endless adult tantrums and unbridled violence when things go wrong! The prescriptions regarding how emotion may and may not be expressed seem to be gender-specific in most cultures.

Although the age at which we begin to punish, reward, or otherwise direct male and female behavior differently remains in question, some contend that even infants are handled and responded to differentially.[11] Birdwhistell studied videotapes of children in various settings and concluded that visible behavioral evidence of sex differences emerges in the second year.[12] It is difficult to determine when children begin to receive different messages about acceptable and unacceptable nonverbal behavior for their own sex. Yet, it stands to reason that consistent behavioral displays of gender should follow a period of time in which the child observes, experiments, and eventually categorizes actions as gender-appropriate or gender-inappropriate. (Remember the age patterns observed by Birdwhistell as you read the competing explanations for sex differences presented in Part Three.) Certainly, facial communication is one of the earliest and most abundant types of communication in the child's perceptual world. Children may begin to recognize gender differences in facial behavior far earlier than we suspect.

In any case, facial expressiveness eventually seems to become natural for girls in our culture, while facial restraint seems to prevail among boys. Yet, according to Ekman et al., one emotional expression, anger, tends to be regarded as nonfeminine and is not typical of female American faces. He reports that women either do not show anger or "mask" the display of anger with another emotional display.[13] For instance, in a situation that makes a woman very angry, she might display a facial expression that, based on Leathers and Emigh's inventory, typically represents sadness—perhaps even accompanied by crying. Even women who have competed and succeeded in the professional world report reacting to interpersonal tension with tears.[14] As one who has regrettably cried when she ought to have screamed, I can attest to the helpless feeling that accompanies being overcome with tears. On the other hand, as one who has deliberately presented the emotion sadness as a means to an end, I can also attest to the feeling of power that accompanies the freedom to choose this expression. In addition to each of these situations, there are others in which facial sadness is displayed because it represents the actual emotion sadness. Probably, each female reader has a sense of the communication, intentional and unintentional, that results from the facial display of sadness in intense emotional situations.

But the literature on facial communication suggests that it is not nearly as likely that each male reader can recall a variety of situations in which he displayed sadness (or fear) facially. Several studies report that men tend to "neutralize" or "mask" these emotions,[15] just as women tend to not display anger. As a result, men may use expressions of anger to react to feelings of sadness or fear. In addition, men seem to be better able to feign anger than women. Indeed, men seem to have a well-developed array of "watch out" behaviors, some facial (such as lowering the brow and snarling the lip), some bodily (such as exaggerating the size of the chest and placing the hands on the hips). Women are usually not prone to displays of this sort, and might appear unconvincing (in truth, funny!) in attempting to display their anger through these nonverbals.

Although men can and do display sadness at times, and women can and do display anger at times, the visible expression of these emotions tends to be gender-specific, at least in terms of the range, frequency, and credibility of the facial display. Again, this visible sex difference in adult human behavior tends to both demonstrate and perpetuate the complementary beliefs that women are emotional and vulnerable, while men are strong and stoic.

Just as women seem to be free to display their displeasure and sorrow in tears, there is a clear tendency for women to display an excess of positive emotion via the facial expression commonly referred to as the smile.[16] In fact, women have been observed to smile more than men even when they are alone. But, during interaction with another, the discrepancy increases.[17] Based on this increase, LaFrance and Mayo argue that "a man's smile has meaning in terms of his own private state while a woman's smile is essentially an interactional phenomenon."[18] Put in other words, men smile to represent some pleasant inner state, while women smile to promote pleasantness in their communication with others.

Sometimes, in order to create a pleasant atmosphere for communication, it is necessary to fake a smile. Luckily, the smile is relatively easy to "put on"; it is without a doubt the most abundant and ambiguous facial expression in interactive settings. The fact that we learn to smile is apparent in photographs of children. Before they understand what it means to smile "for the camera," they display the most genuine and attractive facial expressions imaginable. Then, sometime after they acquire language, the crooked, forced, unattractive smiles begin to surface. From that point on, they struggle uncomfortably to smile naturally for the camera. Similarly, many adult communicators tend to "put on a happy face" in interpersonal exchanges, but it seems that women are more likely to force a smile than men.

More specifically, it appears that smiling is especially popular among middle-class American women. Several researchers have observed smiling in parent–child interaction, across class borders and gender compositions. In videotaped experiments, middle-class mothers smiled considerably more than middle-class fathers. Generally, the men in the videotaped segments smiled when they offered positive remarks to the children. The women, however, smiled as they offered both positive remarks and negative remarks during the videotaping. Coincidentally, they smiled less when the camera was turned off. The women described as lower class in these studies did not demonstrate the same tendency to smile indiscriminately. Rather, they smiled, as did the lower-class men, when they offered a positive evaluation of some sort.[19] So, there is reason to doubt that the smiles middle-class women direct toward children always represent positive affect.

Similarly, women have been observed to smile predictably in male–female interactions that seemingly call for promoting a positive atmosphere. According to Silveria, who observed interaction in public settings, women are more likely to smile at men than vice versa when they first exchange greetings and, beyond that, to continue smiling more when they know each other only moderately well. Men, on the other hand, tend to smile most in communication with close acquaintances. Keep in mind that smiles sometimes "present" pleasant feelings, although the smiler may not necessarily feel warmth or friendliness.[20] Therefore, it may be that both men and women fake smiles, but it is curious that women tend to do so in the presence of "moderate" (as opposed to "close") acquaintances.

In sum, the empirical evidence concerning sex differences in smiling behavior provides ample reason to suspect that women offer smiles in order to visually demonstrate positive affect, even when that affect may be contradicted by other factors, such as accompanying verbal remarks and the apparent intimacy of the relationship. Henley argues that females are taught the importance of looking pretty and that looking pretty generally involves smiling. To find support for this argument, just notice the so-called "saccharine" smiles that characterize beauty contests. Few contestants choose a serious countenance during these events, even when they discuss world politics. Yet, according to one study, the women who smiled least were perceived as occupying the highest status and demonstrating the greatest intelligence.[21] So, it may be that incessant smiling improves one's appearance, but simultaneously injures one's credibility.

Naturally, it is difficult to be sure why women have been observed to smile more, cry more, and show less facial anger than men. It may well be that women are more prone to feel emotion and so are more prone to show emotion facially. Yet, these differences seem to become more pronounced in adolescence, to stabilize in adulthood, and to diminish later in life.[22] So, it is difficult to deny the possibility that we learn to manage our facial expressions as we are learning other kinds of gender-appropriate behavior. As a result, although we may consciously reject verbal prohibitions against men crying and women scowling, we may perpetuate learned sex differences by unconsciously demonstrating them.

Eye Contact.   Although movements of the eye area are generally studied as part of facial behavior, the study of eye contact is regarded as separate due to the tremendous effect mutual gaze seems to have on human interaction. It seems that, although it is very obviously necessary to look at others during communication in order to perceive various types of visual information, looking directly into the other's eyes has a rather compelling effect. It results in eye contact, a bond that cannot be easily broken without affecting other aspects of communication.

Many scholars believe that the magnetic effect of eye contact is rooted in some sort of instinct that other animals also share. However, across generations and cultures humans have developed prescribed rules regarding eye contact, which indicate that instinctive behavior can be shaped according to established standards. Intercultural studies demonstrate this, as well as contrasts between adult and child behavior within our own culture. Children have to be told, "Look at me when I talk to you!" and "Don't stare." When my three-year-old wants me to establish eye contact with her, she takes hold of my face with both hands and abruptly turns it toward her, demonstrating her lack of subtlety in establishing eye contact, and at the same time, her sense that I cannot help but listen if our eyes meet.

Even experienced communicators who can articulate the importance of eye contact are usually unaware that eye contact serves several functions in communication. Obviously, we know that mutual gaze can indicate that two individuals share intense emotions, both positive and negative. We are also aware that the aversion of gaze can be seen as a sign of nervousness, guilt, or insincerity. Indeed, both extended and averted eye contact draw attention precisely because they serve as violations of the standard rules for eye behavior. Our cultural standards call for attentive eye behavior, but prohibit staring.

Besides communicating emotional involvement and attentiveness, eye contact sends important messages that influence the turn-taking system. In normal conversation, the listener is responsible for maintaining eye contact, while the speaker glances away periodically to eliminate uncomfortable, prolonged eye contact and simultaneously cut down on the amount of visual feedback he or she receives. Some scholars claim that, if the speaker did not look away periodically, he or she would suffer from "information overload" and be unable to encode a coherent message.[23] The speaker usually indicates that the end of his or her turn is nearing by raising his or her eyes to the listener. As expected, when the listener takes the role of speaker, he or she averts the gaze.[24]

The above description of eye behavior probably seems far too rigid and predictable to be realistic. However, this structure will quickly show itself if the reader will develop a sensitivity to the regulatory function of eye contact. Moreover, in conversations that are uncomfortable, the reader will probably be able to diagnose irregularities in one or the other participant's eye behavior.

Thus, eye contact helps to communicate emotional states and also performs the very practical function of helping to regulate the exchange of speaking and listening turns. Also, eye behavior can function to communicate power in dyadic interaction. Generally, the subordinate individual adopts the role of listener, and thereby maintains steady gaze unless the speaker (superior) directs his or her gaze back at the subordinate. When that occurs, the subordinate individual typically yields by averting his or her gaze. When speaking, subordinates tend to be less direct in establishing eye contact than their superiors. That is, they avert their eyes more often and for longer periods.[25]

Clearly, superior–subordinate exchanges are different than peer exchanges in terms of eye contact. The ratio between the amount of looking while in the role of speaker, *look-speak time,* and the amount of looking while in the role of listener, *look-listen time,* has been labeled *visual dominance behavior.* As mentioned, dyadic communication between peers usually involves an uneven ratio, such that participants look more while listening. But the ratio has been observed in numerous studies to approximate one to one for superiors (i.e., they look about the same amount whether they are speaking or listening) and to exceed the norm for subordinates (i.e., they look considerably more while listening and less while speaking).[26]

In situations involving a struggle for power, eye contact may become a weapon. These exchanges typically involve prolonged, direct gazes by both individuals. The assumption is, of course, that whichever participant averts his or her eyes first is the loser. Courtroom lawyers are often well trained in nonverbal indicators of power and may use direct and averted gaze to influence the jury's impression of the proceedings. But even untrained communicators will find that, during intense debates and arguments, direct eye contact is the rule, and breaking that rule is often interpreted as weakness.

Since eye contact serves numerous functions in communication, it is difficult to draw definite conclusions about sex differences in gazing behavior. Although identifiable sex differences have been observed with fair consistency across a variety of research approaches, the trends reported may seem confusing and contradictory, and the multiple functions of eye behavior must be taken into account in order to understand them. Early research identified a clear tendency for female–female interactants to display more mutual gaze than male–male interactants. In addition, early research showed that females gaze more in the direction of the other during interaction, regardless of whether the gaze is returned or not.[27] Subsequent research tended to support these preliminary claims, although relationship type[28] and topic of talk[29] were also shown to influence gaze.

Most of this early research attempted to delineate sex differences in male–male vs. female–female interactions, but a few studies also estimated the amount of mutual gaze in male–female interactions. Generally, the females in male–female interactions were observed to look more often at their partners, and for longer periods, whether speaking or listening, than did the males.[30]

The notion of *mutual gaze* seems to be violated somewhat in crediting the women in these situations with more looking, since it inarguably takes two to establish eye contact. Due in part to this discrepancy, Hall points out that the research characterizing mutual gaze in cross-sex interactions is confusing.[31] When studies report only on the amount of mutual gazing in dyadic interaction, male–female dyads fall between female–female dyads and male–male dyads. But when researchers specify contrasts in visual dominance behavior, it becomes apparent that females do more looking than males in mixed pairs.

Based solely on these observations, sex differences in eye contact might be summarized quite simply: women look in the direction of their conversational partners more than men and, logically, participate in more mutual gaze during interaction. Mehrabian argues that women are more interested than men in establishing positive interaction with others, i.e., that they are more affiliative. This contention has already been discussed in terms of self-disclosure (see Chapter Five). According to Mehrabian, women score higher than men on self-report tests intended to measure the affiliative tendency and also demonstrate this tendency in their nonverbal communication. Availability for mutual gaze is just one of several affiliative nonverbal behaviors.[32]

Certainly, the affiliation explanation is not without support. In Exline's research, females who scored high on affiliative tendency displayed more eye contact than females who scored low on the same measure.[33] Also, there is reason to believe that pairs who believe they share a positive relationship will display more eye contact, particularly when discussing a positive topic,[34] and pairs who believe they are engaged in negative interaction will display less eye contact.[35] Competition between partners, which logically counters the affiliative tendency, has been proposed to reduce the amount of eye contact in female–female interaction.[36]

But it appears that the affiliative tendency does not explain male behavior as well as it does female behavior. In some studies, males who scored as low affiliatives displayed direct gaze, and men in competitive situations displayed direct gaze.[37] Men also increased eye contact during negative interaction with persons they claimed to intensely dislike.[38] Thus, it is clear that the desire for affiliation does not explain all the reported sex differences in eye contact.

Argyle and Cook have suggested that a variety of factors may motivate eye behavior in communication.[39] Perhaps the most simple and straightforward explanation is that women look more than men because they assume the listener role more often and for longer periods.[40] This theory is supported by the research concerning quantity of talk in cross-sex interactions (see Chapter Four). But if it may be assumed that same-sex pairs spend roughly equal amounts of time speaking and listening, doubt still remains about why women display more mutual gaze than men in same-sex interactions.

Those who usually support power-related explanations for sex differences in communicative behavior encounter an apparent contradiction in the eye contact research. If women occupy subordinate status, it stands to reason that they should demonstrate typical subordinate eye behavior, i.e., direct gaze when listening and averted gaze when speaking. Yet women reportedly look at the other more than men, regardless of their position as speaker or listener. Perhaps, as Rubin reports, women gaze toward others in order to obtain information about their own behavior.[41] The mythology suggests (and some researchers agree) that women are more concerned with other-evaluation than men, so women may be seeking cues about how they are being perceived, both as speaker and listener.

To confuse matters, however, women have been observed to avert their gaze more readily than men in situations where mutual gaze is uncomfortable, such as an inadvertent meeting of the eyes in a public place. Gaze aversion, as mentioned, is a behavior often related to subordinate status, even among animals. Henley argues that women may be taught to "steal glances," but not to stare, so females who are caught staring and do not avert their gaze may become fair game for men, who tend to return the stare.[42]

Of course, theories also abound to explain why men may demonstrate gaze aversion. Webbink suggests that men may avoid eye contact with other men because looking at other males can appear aggressive, or worse yet, seductive.[43] The distinction between aggressive looks and seductive looks may be very important, particularly for men suffering from homophobia, the irrational fear of homosexuality. According to a study conducted by Argyle and Williams, women felt sure that men use gaze to indicate sexual choice. But, consistent with our predominantly heterosexual orientation, men in the same study felt sure that when a man gazes at another man, it indicates threat, not sexual choice.[44] This may be a case when contextual information and other nonverbals are very important. But it is still sadly remarkable that neither men nor women seem to conceive of male gaze as motivated by affiliation.

Thus, it seems that we generally learn to understand sex differences in eye behavior as consistent with the mythology about males and females. However, several recent studies by Ellyson and his colleagues demonstrate that males and females can display similar visual dominance behaviors when put in similar, artificially created positions. Specifically, the researchers manipulated subjects' perceptions of one another's status and observed the behavior of those who believed themselves to be superior and those who believed themselves to be subordinate. Both males and females tended to decrease their look–listen time and increase their look–speak time when they believed they were superior to the other in some way.[45]

But it is important to note that these were all same-sex situations, so that perceived status could be based solely on the information provided by the researchers. That is, if status is related to gender, the effect of gender could not be observed in these studies. One study, conducted by Ellyson et al., attempted to simulate cross-sex interaction by showing subjects silent videotapes of a female engaged in conversation; half were informed that the female was talking to another female, and half were told she was talking with a male. Some of the subjects observed a visually dominant version of the tape, and some observed a visually submissive version. The researchers reported that the viewers made the expected judgments concerning power, influence, and relative status of the actress based solely on her eye behaviors, regardless of whether they thought she was talking to a male or female.[46] So, overt signs of dominance, in this case dominant eye behavior, can apparently override gender in the communication of status.

Recent research clearly lends support to the contention that eye contact is both an indication of and a contributing factor to status. But unanswered questions remain in terms of sex differences. Henley may be correct in asserting that men and women use eye contact for different purposes.[47] But as legal and social reforms open new doors, we will need to understand that both sexes are capable of expressing power and affiliation. Competent communicators will need to be able to offer and accept both messages and distinguish between them.

Gestures, Posture, and Body Movement.   Although gestures, posture, and movement are usually separated definitionally for beginning students in communication, they are combined here for discussion because we tend to form an overall impression based on how the body is held, how the arms and legs are moved, etc. So, although individual kinesic behaviors will be isolated for discussion throughout this section, it is important to remember that we tend to perceive them as blended.

The term *body language* has recently achieved a fair amount of popularity, although it is disturbing to those of us who spend semester after semester encouraging students to distinguish verbal from nonverbal behavior. The term served as the title of a former best-seller by Julius Fast. On the cover, and throughout the book, the communicative parts of the body are segmented and particular movements are defined. For example, Fast explains one picture by writing "Her arms say she's available."[48] Approaching the study of kinesic behavior as a language is at once intriguing and futile, in light of the fact that communicative behaviors, particularly nonverbal behaviors, tend to be multifunctional and therefore difficult to define. Shrugging the shoulders, for example, can communicate ignorance, apathy, surrender, or even amusement, depending on the situation.

Still, the popularity of Fast's idea helps to draw attention to the fact that identifiable movements of the body do tend to be associated with invisible correlates, such as confidence, power, affiliation, excitement, etc. Since *Body Language,* numerous handbooks have emerged that attempt to teach people how to convey desired impressions through manipulating their kinesic behaviors, and it seems the "most easily manipulated are gesture, posture and movement."[49] This may well be because they are gross muscle movements (in this context, *gross* means *large,* not *unsightly*).

While they probably will not solve all your communication problems, manuals for successful communication help provide insight into the prevailing meanings attributed to particular gestures, movements, etc. Leathers concludes that behaviors generally taken as positive indicators of "power, status and dominance" include relaxed posture (with variations) and dynamic, purposeful gestures. Conversely, behaviors taken as indicators of "powerlessness" include tense posture (usually the legs and arms are closed) and nonpurposeful (or nervous) gestures.[50]

Nierenberg and Calero coined the term *relaxed aggressiveness* to describe the behavior of the empowered. They identified specific examples of kinesic expressions of relaxed aggressiveness in videotapes, including leaning back in a chair, resting limbs on furniture, and loosening restrictive clothing.[51] Other studies have examined the relationship between body postures and perceived power in reverse—by showing silhouettes or pictures to subjects and asking them to rate the imaginary people as important or unimportant, superior or subordinate, etc. Again, the communication of power appeared to rest, at least in part, in "relaxed, aggressive" poses.[52]

Less research has been done on the bodily communication of affiliation or liking. However, Mehrabian suggests that the communication of affiliation is characterized by a highly predictable set of nonverbal behaviors.[53] Leathers summarizes that positive indicators of affiliation include forward-leaning posture, affirmative head nods, a moderate number of gestures, and general "mirroring" of postures.[54] It seems that people engaged in positive interactions have been observed to coordinate their movements.[55] Conversely, individuals display negative affect in "incongruent postures," according to Leathers, along with bodily tension and a relative absence of gestures.[56]

Since the kinesic behaviors that communicate power and affiliation are articulated in contemporary literature, it is possible to discuss sex differences in movement in relation to these characteristics. As mentioned, Birdwhistell observed kinesic activity across cultures. In *Kinesics and Context*, he offers a careful, albeit highly technical, description of the gender displays specific to our culture. In his observations, Birdwhistell noticed that American males displayed more freedom and breadth of movement than their female counterparts. Male postures were more open, both at the legs and at the arms. Particularly when sitting, females tended to hold their legs tightly together, sometimes locking the knees, ankles, or both. The women observed by Birdwhistell also held their arms closer to their bodies and displayed a limited range of movement, even when walking. It seems that men swing their arms and, contrary to common belief, even their hips more than women.[57]

Recently, Frances examined videotapes of college students and reported that males displayed a greater range of movement, particularly leg movement. But when asked to participate in a second videotaped conversation, females seemed to expand their movements somewhat, which Frances attributed to increased familiarity and comfort with the situation.[58] This study indicates, therefore, that relaxed aggressiveness may be displayed to some degree by women, but that men seem to adapt this stance more readily. It is especially important to note the age of the participants in this study, since Birdwhistell stressed that gender displays are most apparent among individuals of "mating age." My students are quick to point out that they live in a world relatively free of prescriptions about gender-appropriate movement. Males and females tend to dress more alike than differently, participate in largely similar daily routines and, by their own analysis, display similar communicative behaviors. Yet, by using unobtrusive measures (watching when she could not be detected watching), Frances was able to find examples of the same gender displays proposed by Birdwhistell.

Another study described the kinesic behaviors of adolescents communicating in informal groups. They, too, displayed predictable gender displays. The boys displayed more expansive postures, both in standing and sitting, and showed greater range of movement. In view of their relaxed aggressive nonverbal behavior, it is not surprising that the boys seemed more influential in directing interaction in mixed groups.[59] Again, it is important to note that these young men and women (presumably approaching "mating age") displayed gender in movement, despite the fact that the majority of them were dressed in jeans.[60] Therefore, it seems unlikely that sex differences in fashion were the primary determinant of sex differences in movement.

Regardless of the fashion trends, our culture has prescribed gender-appropriate postures that apparently cross generations. Women hold their legs and arms close together whether they're wearing dresses or jeans. Many male comedians have amused audiences by donning female dress while retaining male movements. Even on Halloween night, most men cannot disguise their masculinity in a dress, largely because they have not learned the "moves." Conversely, as I watch my young daughters grow, I can attest to the fact that clothing does not restrict their movement until they learn appropriate gender displays. Youngsters of both sexes must relearn how to sit, how to gesture, how to walk, etc., as they become concerned about gender appropriateness.

It seems important to state at this point the dominant naive explanation for sex differences in body position, particularly when sitting. Put nicely, the argument explains male leg position as a quest for physical comfort. Advocates of this explanation may be surprised to learn that European men, who, one must assume, pursue the same comfort, cross their legs in a similar position to American females—knee-to-knee. In our culture, this sitting posture by a male is often labeled effeminate, but one should not think that it is impossible for men to sit this way comfortably.[61] Of course, intermittent changes in sitting posture also seem to be associated with comfort (and with relaxed aggressiveness). Consequently, males have developed an array of gender-appropriate ways to cross their legs: ankle-to-knee, knees-apart/ankles-crossed, etc. Thus, men in our culture can display a range of leg positions and still be perceived as masculine. Prescriptions for women, on the other hand, usually involve knees together, whether legs are crossed or not. Indeed, one sitting position women often display includes knee-to-knee and ankle-to-ankle crossing with feet to one side. Of course this posture is only possible for the very limber female.

A thorough discussion of gender differences in movement renders a fully biological explanation unlikely, although genital differences are more directly related to sitting posture than to other kinesic behaviors. The assumption that postures are related to genital comfort is countered, however, by evidence that upper body movements for females also tend to be highly restrictive. One researcher concludes that females tend to protect soft tissue, i.e., breast area and pelvic region, by constricting harder tissue, i.e., legs and arms.[62] This explains upper body positioning (closed for women vs. open for men), but the same argument would have men covering their soft tissue, instead of exposing it in widened leg postures.

In any case, movements of the legs and arms tend to be more obviously related to gender than movements of the head. Yet, gender differences in head movement have been observed too. It seems that a head position commonly called head cocking is displayed far more by women than by men. Women have been observed to tilt their heads slightly to the side and back during interaction. When the same head gesture is displayed by dogs and cats, it seems to communicate curiosity. According to Nierenberg and Calaro, females deliberately use this head gesture, particularly in male–female communication, to display interest.[63] Whatever the motive, women have reportedly displayed this head position across a variety of research situations.[64] In one study, 90% of the observed instances of head cocking involved female heads.[65]

If women cock their heads to the side, you might wonder how men hold their heads during conversation. The answer is consistent with the theory of dominance. Unless they occupy a subordinate status, men hold their heads upright, sometimes tilting them forward, not sideways.[66] Henley points out that sex differences in head positioning during conversation may be related to biological differences in height.

That is, women have to look up to talk to men, and it is more comfortable to hold the head sideways than back.[67] But differences in head positioning are more predictable based on gender than on height, since short men do not tilt their heads to the side as often as short women, and tall women do it more than tall men. So, it is likely that women learn to cock their heads in an effort to be perceived as gender appropriate, just as American men learn not to cross their legs at the knee.

While the biological foundations of female and male gestures, postures, and movements remain in doubt, little controversy has arisen as to which kinesic behaviors display gender appropriateness. The important point is that they are learned behaviors, as Birdwhistell concludes based on cross-cultural observation. So, although they may or may not originate from "opposite" physical characteristics, they invariably function to reinforce and emphasize that men and women are different in our culture. The similarity of male behaviors to those exhibited by superiors and female behaviors to those exhibited by subordinates may reinforce and emphasize status differences as well.

A recent study by Davis and Weitz provided empirical verification for the contention that people usually perceive male kinesic behavior as indicative of dominance and female kinesic behavior as indicative of submissiveness. After viewing male–female conversations without sound, raters judged the females as being more submissive than the males. However, females were also rated as warmer and more "partner-oriented."[68] This study demonstrates that kinesic behaviors—facial expressions, eye contact, gestures, posture, and movement—were seen as support for the prevailing mythology about masculinity and femininity in our culture. But, realizing that these reports may be little more than self-fulfilling prophecies (which is an interesting finding in itself), the researchers coupled the analysis by untrained eyes with the analysis of experts in movement. The experts verified that the conversants' behaviors tended to correspond with cultural standards of masculine and feminine display. The males on the tape sat with widened postures, showed a greater range of movement, and used more gestures than the females. Females used more head movements, however, along with greater amounts of gaze and, of course, more smiling.[69]

The Davis and Weitz study provides support, in nonverbal form, for the contention made by Fishman that women perform a substantial amount of the "work" that makes for successful interaction (see Chapter Five). To begin with, the naive raters reported that females appeared most submissive nonverbally when communicating with dominant males, but tended to display slightly more dominant nonverbal behavior when talking with less dominant males. Of course, it is impossible to say that it is clearly the female partner who is working to achieve complementarity and not the male partner, or perhaps both are working toward this end. More convincing, though, is the observation that both male and female partners were perceived as more comfortable when talking with a female partner. Indeed, the expert analysts also pointed out that, when conversing with a female partner, both males and females tended to display increased mobility and animated movements and gestures. The researchers caution that nonverbal indicators should not be equated with status, yet the experts and nonexperts alike noticed that both males and females tended to display more relaxed aggressiveness when interacting with a female.[70]

The empirical research concerning sex differences in kinesic nonverbals, then, seems to provide support for the possibility that there is a male style and a female style of interaction. Taken together, stereotypically masculine bodily actions tend to communicate dominance and power, while stereotypically feminine bodily actions tend to communicate affiliation and warmth. Certainly, most communicators hope to be skilled at encoding and decoding both types of messages and at controlling their behavior so that appropriate nonverbal behavior can be displayed as desired. To the extent that men are less capable of communicating warmth and women are less capable of communicating power, the inevitable conclusion is that all individuals who behave according to sex-appropriate prescriptions are substantially limited.

PARALINGUISTICS

Most human beings are blessed not only with the gift of language, but with two distinct forms of expressing language: speech and writing. In its spoken form, language consists of sounds produced as air passes through the larynx, which are articulated into meaningful patterns as the air passes through the mouth and nose. Humans produce a variety of sounds instinctively, but must learn to articulate them into identifiable patterns in order to participate fully in spoken interaction. Hence, learning language boils down to learning to combine sounds into meaningful units and link those units together in order to communicate increasingly complex ideas. No easy task, to be sure, yet we all seem to accomplish it at a very early age, with little formal instruction.

Besides generating the power to produce audible words, the vocal mechanism also provides nonverbal communication in several forms. The study of vocal nonverbal communication is referred to as *paralinguistics*. The prefix *para-* is used here to mean *assisting agent,* just as it is in the terms *paramedic* and *paralegal.* Laughter, screams, and sighs, for example, are all produced by the voice and assist in communication, but are not at all verbal. Other vocalizations border on verbal communication, such as minimal responses like *mmm-hmm,* and *uh* (see Chapter Five).

When words are spoken, the voice provides additional nonverbal information based on how they are spoken. Inflectional patterns, rate of speech, pitch, vocal qualities, and characteristic articulations all assist in communication. Thus, the voice must be understood to generate both verbal and nonverbal messages.

Usually, the discussion of paralinguistics involves isolating specific vocal characteristics, although it is understood that they are indivisible and mutually influential. The paralinguistic behaviors discussed in this section are those that have been reported to differ most obviously depending on the sex of the speaker: habitual pitch, vocal variety, inflectional patterns, voice quality, and articulation.

Habitual Pitch.   No honest examination of sex differences in vocal nonverbals could proceed without acknowledging the fact that men and women differ, anatomically, in the size of the vocal apparatus. It seems that male maturation usually includes an expansion of the neck and shoulders. When this occurs, the vocal folds also grow longer and thicker—sometimes so rapidly that we can identify a period of voice change. Female bodies expand too as they mature, but in somewhat different ways. A female's vocal pitch may become lower, but usually this is a gradual change and is unnoticed. At any rate, mature male and female speakers tend to differ in terms of their habitual pitch, or the pitch at which they speak by habit, such that females have higher voices than males.

Several scholars have pointed out, however, that the contrast in male and female voices is markedly larger than the physical difference imposes.[71] It seems that every vocal apparatus allows a range of pitches. Within that range, cultural prescriptions may influence habitual pitch. In our culture, males tend to select a pitch that is comparatively low, according to cross-cultural research.[72] Female voices, therefore, are heard as particularly high pitched in comparison. In fact, the contrast between male and female voices, according to Sachs, could not be due entirely to biology, since boys and girls, even prior to puberty, tend to display the "appropriate" vocal pitches—low for boys and high for girls.[73]

This gender display may be of particular importance for women, since high-pitched voices tend to be perceived negatively in our culture, particularly when they are also loud.[74] It is not surprising, then, that females tend to speak more softly than males.[75] The result, in the extreme, is that female voices may not be heard as readily as male voices, regardless of what they have to say. This possibility can hardly be ignored, in light of the research on quantity of talk and number of successful interruptions displayed in mixed groups (see Chapter Five).

Henley reports that, until recently, female voices were deemed unacceptable for broadcasting because they were judged difficult to listen to and difficult to believe.[76] Even now, the females employed by the major networks tend to have unusually low-pitched voices. It is difficult to be sure whether high-pitched voices are evaluated negatively because they are associated with femininity or vice versa, but it is fairly clear that pitch is influenced by both anatomy and cultural expectations.

At any rate, the assumption that pitch is the primary paralinguistic criteria for distinguishing males and females has been countered by many studies.[77] Rather, it seems that other distinctive paralinguistic information is used to identify speech as female. Male speech, then, is often assumed to be "normal" speech—i.e., the absence of the female indicators.[78] Studies of two such indicators will be reviewed: vocal variety and inflectional patterns.

Vocal Variety.   It was mentioned above that humans are physically capable of vocalizations across a range of pitches. *Vocal variety* is a broad term that refers to variation of many vocal characteristics, including rate and loudness. However, the most thoroughly studied aspect of vocal variety is variation in pitch. *Monotone* speech has become a popular label for speech lacking pitch variety. Few speakers actually speak at only one tone, but the range displayed may be so small as to give that impression. Most readers undoubtedly have personal experience with listening to monotonous speech. In our fast-paced culture, it is one of the most negatively evaluated speaking habits—a kiss of death for anyone wishing to hold a listener's attention. On the other hand, too much variation in pitch can also be detrimental to the speaker's effectiveness. Using a great deal of variety may communicate instability, even panic.

Happily, most speakers, in most situations, exhibit a comfortable amount of vocal variety communicating a condition somewhere between boring and unstable. It is commonly thought that each individual chooses to vary his or her pitch according to personality traits, but studies show that vocal variety, like habitual pitch, may be a personal characteristic that is influenced by cultural standards. Male speakers have been observed to use a fairly limited pitch range compared to female speakers. Females tend to use a greater portion of their range in everyday conversation, particularly at the upper end. Brend estimates that most women use four distinctive intonational levels, while most men display only three. Predictably, men tend to eliminate the highest level of pitch in their range.[79]

The result is that female paralanguage may help to create the perception that women are emotional and excitable, while male paralanguage may help to create the perception that men are stable and invulnerable. However, according to Edelsky, it is more likely that messages attain different values and meanings by virtue of being identified as spoken by a male or spoken by a female.[80] In other words, although Brend may be correct in summarizing that women tend to use an extended pitch range, it may be that they would be perceived in accordance with stereotypes even if they did not. Edelsky argues that the listener's perception of various characteristics of the speaker may be based, foremost, on the initial perception of the voice as male or female. The rest of the process may constitute a self-fulfilling prophecy of sorts.

Along the same lines, Aronovitch used subjects' ratings of recorded voices to determine that the degree of variability tends to be highly salient in judging male speaker characteristics, while the average pitch tends to be highly salient in judging female speaker characteristics. (*Salience* refers to the importance of the variable in affecting the raters' judgment.) Aronovitch concluded that a high degree of pitch variability distinguishes a male as an exception, probably because men are expected to be rational and competent, i.e., unvariable. But women are expected to be emotional and irrational, so variability is expected. For female speakers, the average pitch was taken as a more accurate indicator of her personality.[81]

Most researchers agree that perceived vocal variety is a positive characteristic for both female and male speakers.[82] However, there seems to be a fine line separating variety from hysteria, particularly when the uppermost levels of pitch are used. In view of the prevailing stereotype that women are more emotional than men, the display of high pitch levels by women may serve to reinforce the expected image. Some doubt exists, however, as to whether or not eliminating high-pitched utterances can undo the image that women are highly emotional.

Inflectional Patterns.   Inflectional patterns are vocal "melodies," which function in speech much like punctuation in writing. They tell us how certain words are to be understood. For example, one common inflectional pattern features the dropping of both pitch and volume at the end of an utterance. (Try doing this as you say, "I failed the test.") The voice communicates nonverbally that this is a statement. To change the same words to a question, you need only raise the pitch and volume at the end of the utterance ("I failed the test?"). You can even make it into an exclamation by lowering the pitch but raising the volume ("I failed the test!"). Inflectional patterns of this sort are usually specific to a given culture and are learned along with spoken language.

In our culture, it appears that females use distinctive inflectional patterns, which are presumably prohibited in masculine-sounding speech. Inflection is difficult to identify in writing, but try to imagine a woman, and then a man, uttering a single word with a double pitch change, beginning in an excited high pitch, dropping to a lower pitch, then rising again ("Really"). Another inflectional pattern that has been labeled *female* features a sharp upward glide at the end of a question. You will recall that raising the pitch at the end of a statement will signal that it is meant as a question, but it is not necessary to signal the interrogative form through pitch when the words indicate that you are asking a question ("Did I fail the test?"). The result is usually an extreme expression of nonfinality or disbelief. Women also tend to use the redundant upward glide at the end of questions like "Can I help you?" The effect is usually an extreme expression of politeness.[83]

A common expression among my niece and her friends (age thirteen) is "Oh, that's gross." They usually use three consecutive downward glides: "Oh, that's gross." My nephew (age eleven) tends to be a man of few words; he would probably just say "Gross!" or "Man, that's gross." Neither utterance would be spoken with numerous glides. Granted, my family may be extraordinary, but several studies of adults, as well as adolescents, verify the contention that male speakers seldom use these and other characteristically female inflectional patterns.[84]

In fact, these inflectional patterns are commonly adopted by males asked to abandon their normal speech and "talk like females."[85] In many classes, videotaped role-playing exercises in which students "switch" roles typically feature exaggerated inflectional patterns (accompanied by leg crossing and limp gestures) when males portray females. However, while the kinesic nonverbals tend to have predictable counterparts when the females portray males (leg spreading and closed fists), it is fascinating that male speech tends to be displayed as the absence of certain inflections.

Vocal Quality.   Vocal quality is particularly difficult to isolate for discussion because it refers to the listener's perception of the sound produced by the speaker, separate from the words articulated and from the rate, volume, and other characteristics. In fact, because it is so difficult to define, quality is often discussed in terms of abnormalities in the voice, such as roughness, tenseness, breathiness, nasality, denasality, etc. Of course, these characteristics may be permanent or temporary. So, they can provide information (often unintended) about the emotional state of the speaker or about the "personality" of the speaker. In either case, the assumption is that the sound of the voice is somehow linked to invisible, and otherwise unspoken, characteristics of the individual.

In truth, several studies have demonstrated that the voice tends to be a more reliable indicator of emotion than the face.[86] Individuals who force a smile and utter, "No really, I'm fine," may also communicate vocally that they are only saying that they are fine. Somehow, we seem to be able to recognize, often based on experience, the sound of someone who is not all right. Of course, some individuals appear to be more sensitive to nonverbal information about emotion. Women are particularly good at decoding vocal cues. Studies have consistently shown women to be better than men at drawing appropriate assumptions about emotion based on vocal information.[87]

Naturally, the situation is far more speculative when we make judgments about permanent invisible characteristics, such as "personality," based on the quality of the voice. Yet many studies have demonstrated that listeners tend to share perceptions about what particular "types" of people sound like.[88] Aronovitch explains that these perceptions appear to be culturally derived. He compiled one hundred rating sheets of over fifty different male and female voices, and concluded that, overall, perceptions tended to reflect "the widely held American cultural stereotypes."[89]

Addington, who has conducted extensive research on the voice, attempted to determine precisely how various vocal characteristics influenced the perceptions of male and female voices in our culture. He asked two trained vocalists to read and reread the same monologue adopting various vocal qualities. Then he asked untrained judges to evaluate the speakers. The judges, both male and female, demonstrated remarkable consistency in evaluating the voices. However, they tended to provide a more in-depth evaluation of the female voices, which Addington cited as evidence that voice may be more salient for women than for men in our culture. For example, a breathy male voice was consistently perceived as "younger and more artistic," but a breathy female voice was perceived as "more feminine, prettier, more petite, more effervescent, more high-strung and shallower."[90]

Obviously, the judges were willing to identify the female speaker in more detail than the male speaker, based only on the sound of the voice. In some cases, the same vocal quality was positively evaluated in a male, but negatively evaluated in a female. For example, throatiness made the man sound "older, more realistic, more mature and well adjusted," but it made the woman sound "less intelligent, lazier, more boorish, ugly, careless, uninteresting and more cloddish."[91]

Of all the characteristics of voice, quality is the least controllable and the most individual. The sound that an individual's voice makes is not easily categorized, yet cultural generalizations abound. We often use predetermined categories to draw impressions about an individual's "personality," which is a dangerous habit, to be sure. But it is intriguing that vocal categorization seems to provide more information about women than about men. It seems unlikely that we have more experience in hearing female voices. Perhaps the most reasonable explanation is that the sound of an individual's voice may be conceived of as part of an individual's appearance. Whether we like it or not, cultural standards surrounding appearance continue to be more salient for women than for men. In other words, how a woman looks tends to mean more to the average observer than how a man looks. How a woman sounds also seems to be particularly important in forming an impression of her.

Articulation.   Another form of paralinguistic communication surrounds the precision with which words are articulated. In the extreme, misarticulations result from speech disorders, and, unfortunately, are often laughed at or ridiculed. Stuttering is also very common in our society, but largely misunderstood to indicate mental deficiency of some type. The fact is that most normal speakers suffer from an occasional misarticulation or nonfluency.

More importantly here, many (if not most) American speakers develop habits of articulating substandard forms of words: *gonna* instead of *going to;* sposta instead of *supposed to; cuz* instead of *because.* The list is endless. Americans are often accused of being product-oriented when it comes to articulation. We reason, "Who cares how it sounds, as long as it gets the message across?" Those readers who have traveled to other places where English is spoken, or perhaps talked with exchange students, have probably noticed the precision with which they utter English words. Undoubtedly, these speakers have developed articulation habits in line with different cultural expectations.

The theory that articulation habits are influenced by cultural expectations may be extended to explain observed sex differences in articulation. Specifically, males have been reported, in several studies across ages and geographical locations, to use more nonstandard forms than women.[92] In truth, *substandard* describes these forms more accurately: *-in* for *-ing; yeah* or *yup* for *yes; ain't* for *isn't;* double negatives, etc. The fact that men use these expressions more than women seems somewhat confusing, since they are commonly associated with low status. One researcher suggested that women probably use these "casual" expressions, like they use profanity, in informal settings, but put on their "best behavior" in formal settings.[93] This is consistent with other nonverbal indicators (e.g., posture, eye contact) that subordinates, and women, are hyperconscious of when trying to behave properly. Indeed, it may be that correct speech is thought to contribute to the general impression one makes. Using so-called *prestige forms* may be another aspect of looking good.

It has also been argued that men display masculinity in what I call *cowboy speech* or what others have labeled *blue-collar speech.* Sounding (and sometimes looking) rough may be more acceptable, even desirable, for men than the alternative. Being too proper and articulate may be perceived as effeminate. Thus, there may be pressure for males, regardless of educational or professional status, to achieve what one author labels "covert prestige" by demonstrating a rough-and-tough approach to interaction.[94]

Regardless of whether they are perceived as nonstandard or substandard, the speech forms discussed above are often deliberately selected by those who are quite capable of selecting standard forms. But, as mentioned, some communicators suffer from speech disorders, over which they have little control. It is puzzling, to say the least, that boys have consistently been reported to suffer such disorders (of all types, but particularly stuttering) more often than girls.[95] Some experts continue to search for anatomical explanations, while others are convinced that this trend is related to cultural demands. Specifically, boys may suffer special pressure to succeed in difficult public arenas like sports and business, while girls may be rewarded in the private arena for their attractive and caring self-presentation.[96] If this is the accurate explanation, changes in speech disorder rates should accompany the merging of public and private activity for men and women, which my students assure me is well under way.

CONDUCT YOUR OWN RESEARCH

1. Ask a particularly expressive friend to present emotions for a camera. Prepare a series of pictures, each labeled as the emotion your friend claimed to present. Then ask a number of respondents to guess the emotions and discuss sex differences in decoding ability.

2. Observe sex differences in posture and movement around campus. Look for individuals who are alone and look for sex differences in sitting posture, standing posture, and even sleeping posture. (The library may be a good place for this.) Also, look for individuals engaged in dyadic communication and notice sex differences in nodding and "head cocking."

3. Watch any dramatic program that features intense emotional discussions, such as a movie, soap opera, or police show. Take notes on the emotional situations associated with direct eye contact and with averted eye contact, paying special attention to sex differences.

DISCUSS THE ISSUES

1. Discuss the standards by which you deem gaze appropriate and inappropriate. Be clear about the situational, relational, and emotional factors that influence your judgment of appropriateness. Then discuss the differences, if any, as determined by the sex of the participants.

2. Describe past situations in which you suspected (or knew) that someone was not telling the truth. Be specific about the kind of nonverbal behavior associated with keeping information from someone and with exaggerating or misrepresenting information. Then compare the behavior of someone you doubted with male behavior and female behavior as described in this chapter.

3. Brainstorm about famous women who have gained the respect of the public as intelligent, credible, etc. Describe, to the best of your ability, the vocal characteristics of each woman and discuss the implications of your descriptions for "typical" female speech.

CHAPTER 7

HAPTIC AND PROXEMIC ASPECTS OF COMMUNICATION

The common expression "it takes two" might serve to clarify the distinction between the nonverbal communication discussed in the previous chapter and those types of communication about to be examined. It may seem unlikely, or perhaps silly, to exhibit kinesic or paralinguistic behavior while you are alone, but people do talk to themselves in certain circumstances, and it stands to reason that some of the speech is accompanied by expressive gestures, etc. However, when another human is present, at least two additional communicative tools are seemingly available—touch and space. To put it impersonally, haptic and proxemic behaviors require the presence of an "object."

HAPTICS

The study of communication through touch is often referred to as *haptics*. Interpersonal touching is also referred to as *tactile communication*, since it is assumed that any sensory stimulation through the skin communicates meaning. Of course, the perceived meaning of a given touch is dependent not only on the nature of the touch but also on the situation and the relationship between the individuals. In fact, touching may be the most noticed type of nonverbal communication between adults, but the least studied by researchers. Unlike many kinesic behaviors, which are usually learned without explicit discussion, we are often taught prescribed cultural norms concerning whom we can and cannot touch, along with information about where, when, and how.

Our culture has been labeled a *noncontact* culture, which indicates that we tend to be fairly restrictive about who touches whom.[1] More specifically, it seems that touching in our culture is most often associated with sexual behavior, and many touches are evaluated first and foremost in relation to potential sexual ramifications. The fact that touch can communicate sexual desire is obvious in our predominantly heterosexual culture. It has provided the basis for many romance stories, both fiction and nonfiction. But with increased publicity about child molestation and growing openness about homosexuality, even adult–child touches and touches between adults of the same sex may be regarded as potentially sexual.

Perhaps because touch is so closely linked to sexuality, sex differences in haptic communication abound. But it is important for the reader to be able to suspend his or her learned preconception that all touch is sexual in order to be able to understand the variety of messages that can be communicated through touch. We have all experienced unpleasant touches and (hopefully) warm, reassuring, and pleasurable touches of many kinds. Conversely, most readers can remember offering touches expressly intended to communicate displeasure with various others, touches expressly intended to communicate affection or arousal, touches intended to communicate intermediate emotions, and even inadvertent touches for which immediate apologies were probably offered.

Gibson classifies tactile communication as active or passive, to emphasize the distinction between touching and being touched—a distinction that most of us find quite important.[2] In fact, a good deal of the research concerning sex differences in touching has focused on precisely the issue of which sex demonstrates the most touching—both active and passive—in communication with others. As you might guess, men have been observed to be considerably more active than women in this regard, across a variety of situations. According to Deaux's review, "men are more likely to touch others, and women are more likely to be touched."[3] But this simple statement requires a good deal of clarification.

To begin with, it is crucial to specify the gender composition of the dyad in which touching behavior is reported. The obvious conclusion is that the men who are doing the touching are touching women. This conclusion about male–female dyads accounts for a good deal of the research. According to Leathers, "in both intimate and professional relationships men are expected to touch women much more frequently than they are touched by women, and they do so."[4] Research based on self-reports indicates that, indeed, both sexes tend to think that adult males touch adult females more than vice versa.[5] Observational research supports this expectation. In a study conducted during the 1970s, Henley observed what she classified as *intentional touching* in public settings and reported that male-to-female touches were most common, accounting for 42% of all intentional touches observed. This figure is nearly twice that of the female-to-male touches she observed.[6]

In a 1980 replication of Henley's research, Major and Williams reported that the sex differences proposed by Henley were supported, although the contrast in the touching behavior had decreased somewhat: men touched women in 36% of the observed instances, while women touched men in 27% of the incidents. Major and

Williams were also concerned with the extent to which touches were reciprocated. They found that some were and some were not, but men were more likely to initiate touches that their female counterparts did not return than vice versa.[7]

Thus, in male–female dyads, there is good reason to expect that the male will communicate through active touching, while the female will participate in passive touching communication. This empirical observation is consistent with the self-reports of adult Americans, and, coincidentally, with the stereotypic assumption that males should initiate sexual contact. It may be that in cross-sex adult interactions, even when no sexual intent is involved, the norms governing sexuality are observed. Certainly, we have inherited a system of "manners," based on notions about chivalry, which call for men to touch women as they escort them through unopened doors and into empty chairs. Like children and elderly companions, women generally occupy the role of the cared for, which often involves being the passive recipient of touch.

An alternate explanation for the uneven distribution of intentional touches between the sexes has been well articulated in the work of Nancy Henley. She points out that male–female dyads are "mixed" in the sense that there is an unequal distribution of status and power between men and women in our society. Therefore, just as any superior is freer to touch any subordinate than vice versa, so are men freer to touch women than vice versa. The tendency for men to be the touchers not only demonstrates their superiority over women, according to Henley, but also reinforces it behaviorally.[8]

Research based on male–female pairs clearly contradicts the prevailing cultural mythology that women touch more than men. However, this stereotypic portrayal accurately reflects the research on same-sex touching. Self-report data indicates that both men and women believe women are freer than men to touch members of the same sex, whether friends or relatives. Women are reportedly freer than men to dance together, walk hand-in-hand, and hug one another, to name just a few examples. Observational data supports the self-reported findings that female–female touching is more prevalent than male–male touching, and also that female–female dyads are allowed a wider range of permissible behaviors.[9]

In fact, haptic communication among males seems to be highly restricted to specific kinds of touches and specific situations. This is true even in familial communication. Father–son touches are not as common as mother–daughter touches, or, for that matter, as common as mother–son touches.[10] Young boys are often taught to substitute a handshake for a kiss as part of their socialization. Certainly, restrictions of this sort are culturally and situationally influenced, but the tendency for males to save certain touches for females is apparent nevertheless. The touches that are deemed appropriate for male–male dyads, according to Willis and his colleagues, tend to be "purposeful and directed."[11] So, when men do touch other men, their tactile gestures tend to be like their speech—short and to-the-point: a mild punch in the arm or a firm slap on the back.

In sum, the research concerning active and passive touch clearly supports the mythology that men are the touchers and women are the receivers of touch. As expected, opposite-sex touching is the most prevalent type, largely because men initiate touch with female partners. But same-sex touching, which is not nearly as common in our culture, is female-dominated, since men tend to restrict tactile contact with other men. Because they receive more opposite-sex touching and more same-sex touching, women must be perceived as more approachable in terms of passive touch.

In the next section, several meanings that can be associated with human touches are described and examined for sex differences. Several category systems have been proposed to identify the potential messages that can be communicated through touching.[12] The list that follows admittedly does not cover every function of touch in human communication. But the touching behaviors discussed are those most clearly identified with gender differences.

Ritualized Touching.   Nearly all societies share conventions about ritualized touch. The most obvious example of a ritualized touch in our society is the handshake. This mutual gesture is widely practiced and serves as a substitute for a number of verbal messages: "Hello," "Good-bye," "It's a deal," "Congratulations," etc. Sometimes, a ritualized *pat on the back* is offered in place of the handshake, but this substitution seems to be riskier and seldom occurs between strangers or during initial meetings.

Other ritualized touches are not prevalent in our culture today, but are characteristic of other times and places: *the double kiss on the cheek* or *the kiss on the hand.* Certain situations, like weddings and funerals, invoke patterns of ritualized touching that are otherwise not typical. If you stand on the receiving line of either event, you had better be prepared; weddings are rife with simultaneous *cheek kisses,* while funerals require sharing brief *shoulder hugs.*

As stated, the handshake is the most widely used ritual touch in our daily interaction. In fact, it is impressive to note that the handshake is usually accomplished with a minimum of difficulty between men, which indicates its prevalence and importance in the male arena. But many women still encounter some difficulty in accomplishing the handshake. The norms governing when and how to extend one's hand to a female, how long and how firmly to grasp the other's hand, etc., are still indefinite. As women begin to move in political and professional circles requiring more interaction with relative strangers, the female–female and male–female handshakes will undoubtedly be accomplished with greater ease. Nevertheless, at present, the ritual handshake seems more easily and widely practiced by men.[13]

A more locally situated form of ritual touching that also tends to be male dominated at present is identified by Key as *play,* and "comprises a wide range [of touching] from very informal bantering and exchanges to contact sports."[14] It is fascinating to observe the many types of touches that men exchange in the context of their games. Apparently unconscious of any possible sexual overtones, they grab, wrestle with, and pat one another in otherwise restricted areas, whether on or off the field. In the context of the game, the touches function variously as encouragement, consolation, and congratulations.

Women seldom share a carefully tuned system of ritualized touches. In fact, many observers have commented that, when women engage in sports, they borrow an array of male behaviors, including a number of ritualized pats and embraces. Apparently, participation in group athletics, like participation in public interactions with strangers, has not traditionally been part of the female experience. As women gain access to these arenas, special forms of female ritualized touching may emerge.

Sexual Touching.   It was argued earlier that sexuality appears to be a preoccupation among Americans, which renders most any tactile contact potentially sexual. According to Morris, it may well be the possibility for confusing the two which is responsible for a prohibition against touching in middle-class America.[15] Certainly, sexual pleasure is physically and instinctually tied to various types of touching, but due to culturally determined patterns otherwise-nonerotic touches have also come to be identified as sexual. For example, hand-holding has come to be associated with romance and is often identified as a precursor to intimate tactile interaction. Of course, humans join hands for other reasons: members of groups join hands to pray; patients take their nurse's hand to squeeze during painful procedures; and even a stranger can take a child's hand in order to provide assistance.

Despite the exceptions we all acknowledge, holding hands still remains a predictable event during early stages of adult heterosexuality. It is one of a sequence of touches that Morris suggests is "spontaneously reenacted" with surprising regularity. Imagine a past (or fictional) romance and check the touching sequence against that suggested by Morris: "hand to hand, arm to shoulder, arm to waist, mouth to mouth, hand to head, hand to body, mouth to breast, hand to genitals, genitals and/or mouth to genitals."[16] To be sure, the steps become increasingly tied to physically erotic stimulation, but the fascinating truth is that, in early stages of intimacy, the various touches serve as symbols of sexuality and can be very arousing. We have learned to treat these touches as sexual and to understand their place on a continuum of romantic behavior.

Traditionally, men in our society have been believed to be the sexual aggressors and women the passive receivers of touch. Bernard points out that, in terms of sexual intercourse, this tradition appears to be consistent with the physical reality that men must be aroused in order to participate, while women can participate regardless of arousal, or even consent.[17] But with regard to the "moves" that serve as precursors to sexual interaction, there appears to be no such logic prohibiting a female from taking a male's hand or putting her arm around him. Yet, stereotypically, men have also been expected to initiate these touches, while women have traditionally used more subtle and passive techniques, sometimes known as *flirting.*

Although women are certainly freer than ever to acknowledge and cultivate their own sexuality, it is difficult to assert that cultural prescriptions concerning sexual touching are dead and gone. There is substantial evidence that the active–passive myth is real (see the related discussion of "Romantic Friendships" in Chapter Thirteen).

Further evidence that the myth of male dominance lives on is contained in the contemporary language used to reference sexual involvement (see Chapter Three for a full discussion of language use pertaining to gender). Baker points out that sexual metaphors continue to portray women as passive "receptacles" and men as explosive aggressors, and that this distinction is demeaning and dangerous. While the specific sexual metaphors seemingly come and go, the trend remains unchanged.[18] Indeed, the sheer number of slang words that metaphorize women as sex objects is reportedly ten times the number used to refer to men.[19]

Actual patterns in sexual touching are difficult to study, except through self-reports. According to a well-publicized survey, women are experiencing increased freedom to act on their sexual desires.[20] Certainly, media portrayals of sexually aggressive women are increasingly abundant. But each reader is encouraged to question for himself or herself whether or not sexual touching, from hand-holding to sexual intercourse, is now free from traditional prescriptions concerning male aggression and female passivity. Remember to imagine yourself as the future parent of an adolescent boy and girl!

Affiliative Touching.   Certain touches appear to be offered in order to help create or maintain a sense of affiliation between individuals. Sometimes, affiliative touches represent acknowledgment of the relationship between the individuals and are offered upon meeting or parting. Exchanging hugs or kisses or placing one's hand momentarily on the other's shoulder in such situations often symbolizes a positive connection between the participants. Sadly, these tactile gestures sometimes become so ritualized that it is difficult to discern a sincere touch from a feigned expression of warmth. In much the same way that we call almost anyone "Dear," we may overuse affiliative touches of this sort.

Sometimes, affiliative touching is closely tied to an emotionally charged event. We may hug or hold hands with a friend or relative to console them or share their joy. These touches seem especially meaningful, and I hope that each reader has experienced a moment in which a relationship seemed to spontaneously grow closer during such an event. Henley concurs that the amount of affiliative touching seems to be influenced by the relationship between the actors. Logically, friends engage in more affiliative touching than acquaintances, and acquaintances more than strangers. Also, the situation between the actors is influential, i.e., friends would be more likely to touch one another at a party than at work.[21]

As you might expect, though, women report more affiliative touching than men across relationships and situations, particularly with members of the same sex. In addition, women touch children more than men, according to both self-reports and observations.[22] Similarly, women touch the elderly and disabled more often than men.[23] Coincidentally, women dominate professions that seemingly call for affiliative touching, such as elementary school teaching and nursing. As these occupations become better integrated, it will be interesting to see if men adopt similar patterns of touch to communicate affiliation and support. At present, the tendency for women to use touch in this way probably functions both to create and to reinforce the myth that women are more emotionally expressive.

Aggressive Touching.   Many of the scholars who have studied touch as communication have stressed its positive functions in human interaction. We have all heard stories about skin hunger suffered by neglected children and been warned that we need our daily dose of hugging. While the need for physical contact is well documented, it is important not to overlook the potential negative functions of tactile communication.

Some touches are overtly aggressive and obviously harmful. To put it plainly, they hurt! In addition to inflicting pain, tactile gestures like punching, choking, and kicking communicate information about the relationship between the participants. Yet, violent acts of this type are seldom treated as tactile communication.

Rather, physical aggression has been treated as an individual trait, one that is likely to be more pronounced in a male than in a female. Some scholars have speculated that men are biologically predisposed to aggressive behavior.[24] Others have argued that male aggression is a socially learned and rewarded tendency—one that is neither encouraged nor allowed among females.[25] The competing theories explaining gender differences in aggression are discussed in more detail in Part III. Here it is important to note that, regardless of the explanation, men are clearly more likely than women to be both the inflictors and the victims of aggressive contact.[26] Ultimately, Henley argues, women are culturally excluded from physical interaction to the point where they are often incapable of defending themselves against attack.[27]

But actual physical trauma is only one of the possible negative effects of tactile interaction. Several researchers have concluded that active touch is related to status and power, whether it hurts or not. Support for this contention is embodied, first of all, in the observational studies reporting that higher-status people touch lower-status people more than vice versa, across a wide variety of relationships and situations.[28] In addition, self-reports indicate that people believe that status affects the likelihood of active and passive touching such that people are more likely to touch lower-status people than peers and less likely to touch higher-status people than peers.[29] Finally, research suggests that people perceive active touching to be an indication of status. Several experimental studies in which subjects reacted to various types of photographs that depicted touching provide evidence that, at least between members of the same sex, the toucher was seen as dominant. This trend was accentuated in depictions of same-sex unequals, such as a boss and a subordinate. At least one of the studies, however, reports an apparent contradiction in cross-sex interactions, when a female identified as higher status was shown touching a male of lower status. The touch of a female superior did not increase her perceived dominance over the male subordinate. Despite this telling inconsistency, this research indicates "a striking and consistent finding...that the act of touch overwhelmed the impact of any other power indicators, namely gender, age, and initial status."[30]

So, it appears to be a well-researched conclusion that touching can serve to reinforce the power dynamic of dyadic interaction. In light of the observed tendency for men to touch women more than vice versa, it seems that touching may be one behavior by which male dominance is perpetuated. But the aggression explanation does not account for the reported and observed finding that women touch women more than men touch men. To explain this tendency, it is necessary to call on the affiliation explanation. While it may be confusing to combine explanations in this way, it is apparent that the gender composition of a given dyad appears to influence the meaning of touch and therefore to affect sex differences in tactile communication.

PROXEMICS

Obviously, tactile communication can only occur when people are located fairly close to one another. However, human communication can occur at any distance that allows mutual perception. A number of communication scholars have been interested in determining how humans use space to communicate, not only in terms of how close or far they stand or sit from one another, but in terms of how they react to and control space in the environment. The term *proxemics* was coined by Edward T. Hall to refer to the investigation of how humans structure and use microspace.[31] Hall and others have helped to clarify the habitually practiced, but poorly understood, lessons about space that appear to be highly influential in interpersonal communication.

Although this book is specifically concerned with human behavior, it is fascinating to note that many animals also use space to communicate, especially messages about territory and dominance. Most of us have experienced or heard tales of the violent attacks of domestic dogs who sense that their territory has been violated. Even our spoiled pets take care to mark and protect their domain in the midst of suburbia. Also, you may have seen two dogs or cats engage in battle in order to determine which one is dominant. We have even adapted the phrase *tail-between-its-legs* to describe the loser. Furthermore, animals who establish themselves as dominant command greater individual space and are freer to invade the territory of subordinates. Conversely, animals established as subordinate yield more frequently when approached.[32] Indeed, many animal species establish and maintain their hierarchy in relation to the control of space.

The human use of space appears to be far from instinctual, although we may imagine that the way we react to spatial violations is somehow natural. In order to verify that proxemic communication is a learned behavior, it is useful to compare our behavior as adult members of a given culture to that of children, who have not yet learned all of society's lessons, and to that of adult members of other cultures. Children, of course, care little for proxemic rules. They climb over the backs of booths in restaurants, position their faces nose-to-nose with adults when attention is not forthcoming, and scream messages across a room if they are predisposed not to move to the normal conversing distance. Examining their seeming misuses of space leaves little doubt that proxemic behavior must be learned.

Moreover, intercultural communication can result in the painful lesson that members of other cultures have learned quite different norms. Imagine your reaction to conversing with an Arab, for instance, who assumes a distance comfortable for him or her—just a few inches from your face. This close proximity would make most Americans feel very uncomfortable, prompting them to back up, at least slightly. Yet, when we assume a more comfortable conversational distance, about three feet away from the other speaker, members of cultures who practice even greater conversational spacing might feel ill at ease. An individual unaware of these cultural differences might feel slighted or even insulted. Although the distances vary, it is clear that humans do become accustomed to different amounts of space and different uses for space across situations. Each culture perpetuates norms as to how much personal space an individual ought to command, and how to behave when individuals compete for space.

Interpersonal Distance.   In order to understand reported sex differences in proxemic behavior, it is helpful to describe in writing the spatial norms that we all know so well from experience. Hall developed a taxonomy to describe interpersonal distance that is widely used to discuss this aspect of proxemics. He identified four categories of interpersonal distance and approximated the boundaries of a close and far phase for each:

Intimate Distance
    close phase: 0 to 6 inches
    far phase: 6 to 18 inches
Personal Distance
    close phase: 1 1/2 to 2 1/2 feet
    far phase: 2 1/2 to 4 feet
Social Distance
    close phase: 4 to 7 feet
    far phase: 7 to 12 feet
Public Distance
    close phase: 12 to 25 feet
    far phase: 25 feet or more[33]

Hall obviously selected labels specific to the culture he observed in formulating these categories, but it is important not to equate the name of the distance with any imagined relationship between the communicators. Rather, try to imagine some of the situations in which you might have conversed at each distance.

Most individuals in our culture reserve the close intimate distance for relationships that are likely to involve tactile contact. In fact, while tactile exchange is facilitated by extreme physical proximity, other forms of communication are hindered. Eye contact is very difficult; usually only one eye can be gazed into at a time. Gestures cannot be seen, only felt, and verbalizations may be distorted.

The immediate image is, of course, a romantic interlude, full of touching and whispering, but other loving relationships also involve communication at the close intimate distance. Parent–child interactions often take place at this distance, particularly with very young children. Indeed, a lost child is often approached, even by a stranger, at a very close distance. Just imagine how frightful some adult faces must seem to children in such situations. But it is quite clear that children do not command as much space as adults, and they must suffer the consequences.

Under special circumstances nonintimates may communicate at the close intimate distance. Dentists, eye doctors, and hairdressers may converse with customers at this distance. Many people feel quite uncomfortable standing or sitting, much less talking, with so little space separating them from a nonintimate. Sometimes, individuals assume this proxemic distance precisely because it makes another feel uncomfortable. The image of two boxers before a fight comes immediately to mind. Both the discomfort invoked by deliberate intrusions into one's close intimate space and the excitement invoked by invited intrusions into this area serve to demonstrate that the close intimate distance is highly restricted in our culture's system of communicative norms.

The far intimate phase is similarly restricted, although we seem to be able to talk comfortably with friends at this distance when the environment limits our space. In movie theaters, seating is often "too close for comfort," yet we converse with those in the next seats. Similarly, while dancing, conversation sometimes takes place between the participants. Two individuals may also assume this distance to talk quietly, in a library, for example. Still, most of the situations described and others in which we interact at a distance of six to eighteen inches typically feature some adjustment by the participants. In the theater, both people face forward, or, if they do turn face-to-face, they lean back slightly. While dancing, the remarks are usually brief and the dancers often pull their heads apart somewhat. In most discussions that take place within eighteen inches or so, the eye contact between the conversants is limited. Only in intimate relationships is this distance used for prolonged interaction.

Most of our conversing takes place at a distance approximately in the center of Hall's *personal* category—about three feet. This distance seems most natural to us; we can hear and see the other comfortably and are usually not bothered by unseemly odors or touches. The term *three-foot bubble* has been adopted among communication experts to recognize the fact that most of us believe we carry that much space around with us. Some scholars believe it is actually oblong, since we require three feet in front of us, but allow others to be much closer behind or beside us.

Observational studies abound that attempt to clarify the factors that influence us to abandon the three-foot norm. Burgoon and Jones propose that cultural norms probably interact with "idiosyncratic preferences" in determining how strictly the standard conversational distance is assumed.[34] According to this argument, we each learn and know the culture's spatial norms, but also develop a personalized sense of how close is too close and how far is too far in given situations. But, it is difficult to ignore the regularity with which subjects have reacted by backing up, turning sideways, and putting objects between themselves and trained "violators" in controlled experiments.[35] Moreover, it is difficult to overlook the regularity with which these cultural norms are observed in our daily interaction. In open spaces, we move forward and backward as we speak, seldom venturing closer or farther than three feet. We often adjust or abandon furniture that prevents us from assuming a comfortable speaking distance. The cultural standard concerning the expected conversational distance seems to be very well taught and learned, despite possible personal idiosyncrasies.

The *social* distance is used for formal conversations—for example, business meetings. Often these talks take place over counters or across tables designed to separate the participants. One's ability to judge the relative power of an individual in business by the size of his or her desk is consistent with the norm that interactional distance increases with increased formality. The subordinate typically sits across the desk from the superior, who may even lean back to increase the distance. Indeed, some desks are so large that even a very important individual could hardly hope to use the outer portions for work—but the size communicates status nevertheless.

Certain situational irregularities may necessitate that peers communicate at the social distance. We can talk at a distance of four to seven feet with little difficulty hearing or seeing the other. Sometimes conversations take place across rooms, for instance, or along hallways. In fact, when two individuals approaching one another intend to begin a conversation, this is often the distance at which they first speak. Likewise, they may continue the exchange as they move apart. But, all other conditions equal, most Americans will unconsciously gravitate to the standard distance for the bulk of their conversation.

The public distance is one seldom used for interpersonal exchanges in a culture that imagines itself to be largely classless. Hall suggests that people usually reserve this seemingly tremendous space of twelve feet and beyond for communicating with public figures.[36] But even presidential candidates typically make at least a token move into the crowd to be closer to the people. The public distance, it seems, has come to be appropriately associated with public communication—speechmaking, acting, etc. Even small group situations typically call for little more formality than the social distance affords. As evidence of this standard, when a high-ranking college official recently took a seat all alone at one end of a huge conference table across from a small group of faculty, all of whom elected to sit next to one another, he apparently realized his conspicuousness and explained "I'm sitting down here because I have a terrible cold." Coincidentally, he had also assumed a highly formal communicative stance in relation to the rest of us, and, predictably, he spoke while we listened.

It is impressive to recognize the great range of distance at which humans are capable of communicating. It is also impressive to recognize the limited range in which we actually engage in most interpersonal conversation. But only when we come to understand that other cultures have perpetuated, across generations, obviously different spatial norms can we fully grasp the probability that there is nothing whatsoever natural about our chosen standard.

Within the various cultural standards, certain predictable variations have been observed. As mentioned, higher-status people tend to be awarded more space than their subordinates, and adults tend to be awarded more space than their children. Obviously, there appears to be a correlation between occupying a position of power and commanding extra space. In light of this correlation, it is not totally unexpected that males tend to be awarded more space than females. Willis observed what he called "initial speaking distance" and concluded that, across a variety of situations and nearly eight hundred individuals, women were approached more closely than men.[37] Subsequent studies have supported the sex difference cited by Willis across a number of contexts. In addition, the tendency for women to be approached more closely than men appears to hold regardless of the sex of the approaching individual.[38]

Based solely on the approach conceptualization of space, it might be assumed that female–female dyads and male–female dyads should both assume about the same conversational distance, provided that the approached female remains stationery. A stationery male, then, would be awarded greater space, so an approaching male or female would stop approximately the same distance from him, resulting in, again, equal space for the male–male and male–female dyads. These configurations can become very confusing, to be sure. But, more importantly, they tend to overlook the fact that conversational distance is seldom left only to the approacher. Rather, both members of a dyad can influence the space separating them, so interpersonal distance is best understood as interactional.

Therefore, it is not at all surprising that female–female dyads tend to stand closer than male–female dyads, and male–male dyads tend to maintain the farthest distance. It seems that women both approach others more closely and allow others to approach them more closely than men do. In essence, women do not command as much space as men, and they participate in the negotiation of close distances.[39]

Several alternative explanations are possible for sex differences in interpersonal distance. My students are quick to tell me that women do not need as much space because they are smaller. But this simple explanation leaves several unanswered questions. Since there is little evidence to support the contention that we consider the relative size of the other when negotiating conversational distance, why is this factor important in relation to gender? Also, in reality, women and men are not nearly as separated by size as the myth would have us believe. The range of heights and weights of American women and men tend to overlap considerably and the averages continue to grow closer.[40] Given these facts, it seems unlikely that we unconsciously award less space to women because of their diminutive size.

My students retort, however, that women tend to hold their bodies in such a way that they take up less space and this is certainly correct. It appears likely that kinesic behavior and interpersonal distance are closely associated. Recall, from the previous chapter, the concept of *relaxed aggressiveness*. Men have been observed to assume sitting and standing positions consistent with the contention that they command a larger portion of the surrounding space than their female counterparts, who tend to sit and stand in more restricted positions.[41]

Another popular explanation for the observation that women stand closer together than men surrounds the assumption that women are more approachable in the sense of being more interested in and open to conversation. In essence, this is another application of the affiliation theory already offered to explain sex differences in self-disclosure and touching. The affiliation theory clearly explains the reported tendency for women to be approached more closely and even the reported tendency for women to approach others more closely, given the assumption that they value communication with others more than men do.

In one study, though, it was discovered that women tend to employ a greater variety of conversational distances than men, who tend to speak at approximately the same distance regardless of their relationship to the other. In other words, women choose distances appropriate to the formality of their relationship, such that they stand closer to good friends than mere acquaintances and closer to acquaintances than to complete strangers.[42] So, while affiliation does appear to influence conversational distance, it seems to do so among women more than among men.

Thus, explanations of size, posture, and desire for affiliation may serve to explain some of the observed sex differences in personal space. But it is still difficult to ignore the correlation between status and distance that apparently transcends situational influences in our society. The fact that women are awarded less space than men, across a variety of situations and relationship types, suggests that a woman may be assumed to occupy a position of lesser status. It is difficult to deny that space is a valued privilege in most societies, and interpersonal space is no exception. In the next section, the discomfort that can occur from spatial invasions is discussed and the reactions of men and women to such invasions are contrasted.

Spatial Invasions. Regardless of the precise measurements, each culture's norms regarding personal territory are learned by each succeeding generation. When these norms are violated, individuals feel crowded. *Crowding* is an everyday term we all understand in addition to being a psychological concept that has been applied to a number of research areas. Broadly stated, crowding is experienced when an individual attempts (and fails) to achieve a certain amount of privacy.[43] As each reader undoubtedly knows, we can tolerate a certain amount of crowding for relatively short durations. For example, some college students adjust easily to "dormitory living" (for lack of a better term), but others feel anxious and uncomfortable largely due to the effects, both physical and psychological, of crowding (e.g., limited bathroom facilities, shared televisions and telephones, noise, housekeeping considerations, etc.). It stands to reason that these conditions would be most uncomfortable for people who highly value their privacy or who are most accustomed to greater territory.

The concept of crowding can also be applied to the violation of one's invisible personal space—the distance others are expected to keep. According to Leathers, "the violation of proxemic expectations results in consistently disruptive effects on the communication between two or more people."[44] Again, it seems reasonable that those who place a high value on that distance and are most accustomed to separation would find spatial invasions most disturbing. Therefore, it should come as no surprise that men have consistently been observed to respond more negatively to invasions of their personal space than women.[45]

Conversely, women have been observed to yield more readily than men in situations where walking or standing space is limited. For instance, when two individuals approach one another head-on, if there is limited passing space, one or the other has to stop momentarily. Women have been found to yield to men in these situations with remarkable consistency, according to Silveria. In over 60% of the encounters involving a man and a woman, the woman yielded so that the man could pass. Another 20% of the situations resulted in both the man and the woman altering their courses somewhat and, in the remaining cases, the man yielded to the woman. Yet same-sex encounters of the same type were resolved with mutually cooperative movement about 50% of the time.[46] Other research has suggested that people are less threatened by the approach of a female.[47] This conclusion helps to explain why both men and women yield more often to an approaching male.

Each reader is encouraged to conduct some informal research into the fascinating phenomenon of this type of yielding in public places. The obstacles to ready passage through doorways, crowded hallways, and even supermarket aisles are typically managed with little difficulty, yet they require a rather refined sense of communication with strangers. I know this for a fact because I occasionally let my seven-year-old daughter "drive" in the supermarket, and she demonstrates her naïveté concerning the rules in nearly every aisle. As I give her verbal instructions, practically nonstop, I realize the subtle nonverbal cues by which adults manage to move through crowded places.

One would be tempted to declare that chivalry is dead (except, perhaps, on first dates and initial meetings with prospective in-laws). In supermarkets and, indeed, most of the real world, women appear to be far more accommodating than men. Perhaps this is based on a fear of strangers—a fear that our nation's newspapers verify daily is justified for women in particular. Whatever the cause, it seems that reported sex differences in yielding behavior are aligned with a larger trend in proxemic behavior, i.e., women are awarded less space than men.

C O N D U C T   Y O U R   O W N   R E S E A R C H

1. Select a physical environment that limits people's freedom to use space (e.g., a doorway, a stairway, an elevator, an aisle). Observe yielding behavior, paying special attention to sex differences.

2. Break the rules you observed in the physical environment you chose for #1 above. Observe sex differences in the reactions to your deviance. Also, have a friend of the opposite sex break the same rules and observe the reactions.

3. Locate and clip magazine ads that include photographs of men and women supposedly engaged in communication. Ask respondents to discuss the apparent relationship between the characters and to support their impressions with specific evidence. Note references to the use of space and/or touch in categorizing relationships.

DISCUSS THE ISSUES

1. Which factors are most important in determining your reaction to a given touch? The relationship between you and the toucher? Situational variables (such as time or place)? Dispositional variables (including how you feel toward one another at the moment of the touch or how you are feeling about some recent event)?

2. Describe the various messages associated with touch at family gatherings you have attended or observed (even in the movies or on television). Describe how touching norms differ from culture to culture. Be sure to specify whether or not gender predicts norms within and across the cultures you have witnessed.

3. Consider how proposed gender differences in the use of space may be both caused by and reflected in fashion trends. You may want to begin with sex differences in clothing and then look at differences in furniture design, interior decorating preferences, etc.

SUMMARY OF PART II

The reported sex differences in communication described in Part II help to demonstrate that men and women behave, at least in part, as predicted by the mythological stereotypes. Recall the list of "opposites" presented in Part I:

Feminine:	*Masculine:*
Submissive	Aggressive
Emotional	Rational
Dependent	Independent
Fragile	Strong
Gentle	Rough
Quiet	Loud
Tactful	Blunt
Sensitive	Insensitive
Yielding	Competitive
Verbal/language oriented	Physical/activity oriented

Given this list of contrasts, it is possible to summarize the correlation between reported trends in communicative behavior and the prevailing stereotypes. For example, the myth that men are aggressive and women are submissive seems to be embodied in sex differences in interrupting and touching. Similarly, the myth that women are sensitive seems to be upheld by findings that women tend to be other-centered in communication—asking abundant questions, smiling, and gazing attentively at the other during communication. The mythology that depicts men as more rational seems related directly to evidence about facial expressions and vocal variety and indirectly to data concerning control of topics in mixed-sex conversation.

Numerous other correlations may be drawn between gender-specific communication and the prevailing sex stereotypes, even though we tend to reject the stereotypes as antiquated and discriminatory. If the reader acknowledges the possibility that individuals might unconsciously enact gender displays that tend to perpetuate stereotypes of masculinity and femininity, the inevitable question is "why?" Why do individuals participate in sustaining stereotypes on a behavioral level that they reject on an intellectual level? Why have the myths about being male and female survived despite social and legal reforms that plainly communicate that men and women are equal? It is important for the reader to address such questions in detail, not with easy answers like "Change takes time" or "Well, it's not me!"

Each of the next four chapters characterizes an alternative explanation for the observable differences in male and female behavior among members of our society. Each provides a theory (in some cases, multiple theories) about why gender-specific communication behaviors have proven so resistant to change, based on differences in innate factors (determined at birth), social factors (determined by interaction with others), and cognitive factors (determined by the way the mind processes information about the world).

Notably absent from this list are theories positing that those in power (namely men) deliberately perpetuate gender differences in order to maintain control. To be sure, such theories are well articulated elsewhere and are not without strong logical arguments and factual support. However, in this book I have chosen to not include arguments that accuse certain readers and make others victims, if only by association. Each reader, whether male or female, is urged to read the explanation chapters with as little bias as possible. I urge you to be alert for signs of my biases, which may unintentionally color my discussions of these theories. In any case, you may find a favorite explanation or discover that a combination of factors is the best explanation.

CHAPTER 8

EXPLANATIONS BASED ON INNATE FACTORS

In Part I, the physical differences that separate the sexes were discussed very briefly, in order to clarify that references to the two groups as opposite probably ought not be taken literally, even as they pertain to primary sex differences. In reality, the biological contrasts herein labeled *primary* pale in comparison to the biological similarities. Still, many theorists have suggested that the fundamental physical differences between the sexes have real consequences in terms of predisposing (not to be confused with causing) individuals to behave in predictable ways.

PHYSIOLOGICAL DEVELOPMENT

The mythology that Mother Nature created opposite but neatly compatible creatures in order to perpetuate the human race is well communicated in our culture. Certainly, the basics of human procreation suggest that the necessary parts are compatible. But beyond this fundamental complementarity, questions abound about the extent to which reported sex differences in behavior, which also seem to be largely complementary, are inborn. Many disapproving traditionalists have responded to social reform issues with a single, terrifying question: "If women and men become too much alike, what will become of the human race?" This question indirectly states a theory of innate sex differences. The argument follows that males and females possess not only distinct genitalia but also distinct behavioral tendencies from birth. In other words, male and female behavioral differences are in the genes. Challenging the tradition of labeling behaviors as appropriate for one sex but not the other, then, threatens the genetic foundations of the human experience and cannot succeed.

While many of us turn a deaf ear to this argument on the whole, there may be a few specific male and female traits that we must admit seem to be logically linked to sex differences in physiology. In fact, interest in delineating the innate contrasts between males and females has not waned in the scientific community. New research clarifying these contrasts and relating them to behavioral tendencies abounds.

Chromosomal Sex Differences.   We can hardly help but marvel at the astounding precision with which the scientific community has been able to outline the chromosomal determination of gender. Of the twenty-three chromosome pairs contained in every cell of the normal human body one precious pair indicates sex: an individual having an XX sex chromosome pair is a female, while one with an XY sex chromosome pair is a male. We now know, however, that "every embryo has the beginnings of both male and female ducts" until about the sixth week, when the sex hormones kick in and the fetus begins to develop structures consistent with the sex chromosome pair.[1]

Based on the absence of maleness during this period, some women have taken great pride in arguing that all fetuses begin as females. Others have cited *Turner's Syndrome* as evidence that all embryos are fundamentally female. This condition can be found in a female infant who develops with only one chromosome, an X, in the twenty-third pair. Most likely, the sex chromosome in either the ovum or the sperm was incomplete or damaged, but the fetus developed based on the sole surviving X. These women are usually infertile and may suffer some maladies, but they are clearly female. In contrast, no male with one sex chromosome has ever survived. Hence, it seems that the X can survive without the Y, but not vice versa.[2]

Some genetic researchers have associated the chromosomal composition of males and females with indications of physical strength, a trait stereotypically associated with males. The typical argument states that men are naturally stronger, and therefore more rational, competitive, etc. However, it seems that female fetuses have proven to be statistically stronger in terms of health and survival than their male counterparts, just like their older sisters. Specifically, (1) more male fetuses are spontaneously aborted than female fetuses[3]; (2) the infant mortality rate is higher for males[4]; (3) a number of genetic abnormalities, like hemophilia and color blindness, are far more common in men[5]; and (4) women appear to be more resistant to the effects of malnutrition and other forms of deprivation.[6]

In addition, a male's life expectancy is lower than that of his female peer. Many explanations for this difference cite the effect of role-related behaviors. For example, "More men suffer stress-related death because they are involved in high-pressure jobs"; or "Of course women live longer—they don't have to fight in wars!" Ultimately, we have been warned that, if women's lives begin to merge with men's, so will the life expectancy averages. Perhaps it is too early to gauge the effect of feminists' gains on the life expectancy figures, but it seems the strength of women continues. Recent sources indicate that more males than females still fail to survive every stage of development from infancy through old age. According to the National Center for Health Statistics, in 1980 the average life expectancy for white females in America was 78.1 years—in sharp contrast to the average for white males, 70.7 years. The figures for nonwhite Americans were lower overall (which is troublesome in itself), but the nonwhite females were expected to live an average of 8.6 years longer than the nonwhite males.[7]

Certainly, role-related factors may influence these rates. However, some genetic theorists suspect that the female of the species may be stronger chromosomally than the male. In fact, researchers have concluded that the X chromosome is larger and contains more genetic information than the Y. Also, because females have two X chromosomes, they may be able to cancel out any abnormality in one or the other. But, males, having only one of each, must inherit whatever genetic error is present. Therefore, certain diseases (e.g., hemophilia) are said to be "carried" by females and "given" to male offspring since male offspring actually inherit the malady, while female offspring only pass it along to their own male children.[8]

Based on the chromosomal differences between males and females, then, there is little reason to believe that men are innately stronger and more aggressive, while women are born weaker and more passive. To the contrary, it seems that Montagu was correct, at least genetically, in defending the "natural superiority" of women.[9]

Size and Strength Sex Differences.   Despite genetic information to the contrary, perhaps the most commonly held belief about sex differences is that men are stronger than women, probably because they are larger in stature. The differences are far less obvious than most people believe, but statistics do show that, across cultures and environments, average male heights and weights are higher than average female heights and weights. It is difficult to be sure of the precise figures, but one source estimates that adult men are about 7% taller and 20% heavier than adult women.[10] Even among full-term babies, the male is slightly larger than the female in all dimensions except pelvic width.[11] During the childhood years, boys and girls are fairly similar in size and shape, as most elementary class portraits show. To verify this, I requested that my daughters' pediatrician send me copies of the growth and development charts doctors use to compare their patients' growth to percentiles based on national figures. The doctor sent me two such charts, one for boys and one for girls, which made me wonder about the statistical differences.

According to the graph, the smallest infant girls (fifth percentile line and below) are only about one-half pound smaller at birth than the smallest infant boys. The largest boys (ninety-fifth percentile and above) are less than a pound heavier than the largest girls. The center lines (fiftieth percentile) at birth are 7.5 pounds for boys and 7.0 pounds for girls. By age two the differences increase somewhat, but not nearly as much as most people believe. The average-sized boys and girls at age two are about the same size—separated by only a pound or two in weight and nearly the same size in inches. As children grow older, however, size and weight differentials increase, in somewhat predictable patterns. It seems that girls catch up with boys, at least in terms of weight, at about age nine, when the average weight for both girls and boys is sixty-two pounds.[12]

By age eleven, half the girls are over eighty pounds, with the heaviest girls weighing about 120 pounds. But half the boys at age eleven weigh in at less than seventy-eight pounds and the heaviest boys are only about 114 pounds. Girls seem to increase even more rapidly in inches during what is termed their *growth spurt*—so much so that the average thirteen-year-old girl at her first dance measures about 5'2", and more than half of the available partners are shorter! Boys, however, continue to grow in both height and weight after girls' growth has leveled off. As a result, the tallest young men of eighteen are about five inches taller than the tallest young women—a comfortable margin for dancing. The median height and weight differentials for eighteen year-olds also approximate the international figures for adults: young men are about 8% taller and 15% heavier than young women at this age.[13]

The fact that male sexual maturation terminates in a greater growth spurt than female sexual maturation has been cited as evidence that men are *innately* the dominant sex.[14] Obviously, the larger size of men at age eighteen hardly seems to constitute physical superiority, much less inevitable dominance over women. But, sex differences in strength are also accentuated during puberty. Strength differentials are relatively small during early childhood, although girls have more fat tissue than boys and boys have more muscle tissue than girls from birth. It seems reasonable that this difference might eventually contribute to male superiority in muscular strength, although other physical (and many social) factors may be more responsible.

To begin with, at puberty boys muscles begin to develop at a faster rate and the result is absolutely larger muscles. This means that, even without working at it, males muscles are larger (approximately 15% longer and 30 to 40% thicker).[15] Of course, societal norms that encourage or discourage maximizing the absolute size of one's muscles have been sex specific in the past. Some females have recently challenged these norms, and statistical summaries reveal that female athletes are gaining on their male counterparts.[16] Women runners, for instance, are steadily reducing the difference between male world records and female world records. In 1956, the average difference was 13.98 seconds per meter run, while in 1981 the average difference was 8.94 seconds per meter.[17]

Nevertheless, the debate continues as to whether or not women can ever achieve, through conditioning, the same level of muscular strength as men. Skeptics argue that the body Mother Nature provided the female may be durable, but that it is innately limited in terms of the development of muscular strength.

In fact, some have argued that it is decidedly unnatural for women to challenge their body composition—specifically, to try to eliminate fat. It seems that fat tissue facilitates the production of female hormones (which are discussed in detail in the next section). Therefore, women who reduce their body fat drastically, whether due to eating disorders or athletic conditioning, often cease to menstruate.[18] It appears, then, that innate differences related to the female reproductive role do contribute to the difference between the muscular strength of the average man and the average woman.

Other sex differences in growth and development also facilitate physical strength in men. They have larger hearts and lungs and, as a result, their bodies are better suited for strenuous exercise, since their hearts can beat slower and their blood has a greater capacity to carry oxygen to the muscles. These characteristics, combined with an apparently superior power for "neutralizing the chemical products of muscular exercise," suit the male body for sustained exercise that might be more difficult for a woman to endure.[19]

Certainly, societal norms function to emphasize the importance of muscular strength in males and to de-emphasize, even counter, its attractiveness in females. But the recent fitness craze in America has prompted women to challenge norms perpetuating the notion that they are the weaker sex. In the end, it may be that women are able to achieve levels of fitness commensurate with the levels achieved by men, but it seems unlikely that females will achieve equal muscular strength because certain aspects of their physical makeup seem to oppose it.

The connection between muscular strength and social strength is quite another issue. Stereotypically, men are portrayed as stronger, i.e., more rational, more capable in crises, etc. The perception that females are weak in comparison seems closely related to another stereotypic contrast: that men are independent, and women are dependent. This notion, however, is really just one small part of an entire social–economic–political system in which men traditionally hold power. So, although evidence of female genetic strength abounds, those who favor explaining sex differences as biological in origin simply emphasize, instead, differences in muscular strength in order to legitimate the patriarchal structure of our culture.

Ultimately, such emphasis on muscular strength seems inappropriate in an age of high technology that seemingly eliminates the usefulness of a "survival of the fittest" philosophy. It is important to remember, however, that man (in the generic sense, of course) has evolved over many centuries, and many believe that sex differences in strength may be related to the once-necessary division of communities by sex. The men typically ventured out into the wild to hunt, while the women stayed at home to bear and care for children. As a result, presumably, the strongest men survived the hunt, and the most nurturant and fertile women produced healthy (and numerous) offspring. It follows that, via the process of natural selection, men became stronger and women became more nurturant and more dependent.[20]

Lionel Tiger speculates far beyond the simple evolution of muscular strength to other apparent sex differences in public and private activities. He advanced the well-known theory that men invariably bond in groups because of their past participation in the hunt, which required them to communicate rationally and competently in order to conquer animals otherwise superior in size and strength. Conversely, he argues, women are better suited to bonding in dyads, because of their long-standing participation in the home, which required them to communicate effectively on a one-to-one basis in order to manage and nurture the family. Thus, reasons Tiger, men are innately more capable than women to handle business in the public sphere, while women are innately better suited to handle business in the private sphere (i.e., at home). Tiger claims that, in the hunting and gathering days, "unnaturally" aggressive females who joined the hunt were either killed or failed to reproduce. Following Tiger's reasoning, aggressiveness in women died an untimely genetic death during this period. Hence, he bases arguments for male dominance in modern society on the theory of natural selection.[21]

Certainly, it is difficult to deny that adult male bodies are better suited for strenuous muscular activity. But, as mentioned earlier, female bodies are stronger in other ways—on measures of general health, endurance, and resistance to genetic and environmental maladies. Therefore, the theories that establish male dominance in communication as natural hinge on the acceptance of a direct link between muscular strength and aggressive behavior.

Hormonal Sex Differences.   Hormonal sex differences seem to provide the most widely argued explanation for behavioral sex differences, not only in the scientific community but also, regrettably, at many social gatherings. However, few of those who explain with remarkable certainty the effect of a woman's menstrual cycle on her behavior actually understand the role sex hormones play in the human experience. You may be surprised to learn that scientists themselves are still unsure about the mutual influence of hormonal activity and human behavior.

Although most people believe that men and women are opposites hormonally, human males and females both possess all three groups of sex hormones that have been discovered to date. These are labeled *androgens, estrogens,* and *progestogens.* If the reader can tolerate a brief lesson in etymology, the dictionary can help clarify the distinctions. *Andro* is a root meaning *male; estro* derives from the term *estrus,* which refers to the period of time during which most female mammals ovulate and mate; *progesta* is a compound root roughly divisible into *pro,* which means *in favor of,* and *gesta,* which refers to pregnancy.

Based solely on their etymological origins, it would seem that androgens would be found only in males, and estrogens and progestogens would be found only in females. Yet, as mentioned, most normal individuals possess all three types of sex hormones. Most of the time, males have higher levels of androgens than females do, and females have higher levels of estrogens and progestogens than males do. But in order to understand the effects sex hormones have on humans, both physiologically and behaviorally, it is important to remember that women do possess male hormones and men do possess female hormones.

Scientists have been able to chart, with amazing precision, the hormonal activity that seems to be integral to the development of physical sex differences. It is generally believed that hormone distributions are especially important during certain critical time periods in an individual's life; we know them as *prenatal,* before birth, *neonatal,* just after birth, and *pubescent,* during puberty. During prenatal and neonatal development the function of hormones may be understood as *organizational*—they organize the necessary parts as either male or female. During pubescent development, the function of hormonal activity may be labeled *activational*—they activate the parts, which they had previously organized, so the individual can assume the pre-identified reproductive role (mother or father).[22]

Naturally, we know that sexual maturation is not a purely physical process. It occurs in the midst of complex, and sometimes contradictory, sources of information that influence behavior. So, it is especially difficult to identify the link between hormonal activity and observable sex differences in behavior. It is simply impossible to state with confidence the extent to which hormonal differences in normal males and females cause them to behave differently. Nevertheless, scholars continue to speculate about the degree to which hormonal activity is an influence on sex differences in behavior.

In the main, those who have attempted to clarify the importance of hormonal activity in humans have operated from one of two methodological perspectives: some have experimented with animals; others have studied humans who are identified as possessing abnormal hormone distributions. The first approach usually involves the manipulation of hormone levels in some other species, such as rats, mice, guinea pigs, or nonhuman primates.[23] Experts have verified that females can be *masculinized* through the injection of androgens, such that they display behaviors normally known to develop in males but not in females. Certain of these behaviors are directly related to sexual activity, but others have little to do with reproduction (e.g., aggressive play, greater levels of activity, sensitivity to pain). Males, though, if deprived of androgens through a number of methods too cruel to use on humans, develop as females.

Thus, the animal research has been useful in clarifying the effect of androgen manipulation in both males and females. These hormones seem to be critical in determining physical sex assignment. Without them, male animals seem to turn into females. But while excessive androgens clearly masculinize female behaviors, they do not result in cross-development of the genitals.[24]

These and other significant results of experimentation done on animals, particularly nonhuman primates, provide compelling evidence that hormones are very closely linked to physical and behavioral sex differences. Yet, it seems advisable not to assume that human behavior coincides with animal behavior, especially as it relates to sex differences. We have been accused of intellectualizing our sexuality to the point where we can seemingly convince ourselves of our femininity or masculinity without references to physiology, especially to invisible physical characteristics like hormones. Indeed, we use the term as though we know them intimately, but most of us are fairly uninformed about hormonal activity in our own bodies—much less that of the opposite sex.

Considerable proof for the "mind over matter" approach to hormonal activity can be found in the studies of humans who suffer abnormalities due to the injection of hormones into their pregnant mothers and due to genetic imperfections affecting hormone distribution. As the cases discussed below will demonstrate, surgical artistry and hormonal manipulation can seemingly undo what nature originally intended, but only if coupled with socialization into the gender of choice.

Although scant, human evidence supports the theory that without androgens men will develop along female lines, both physically and behaviorally. In rare cases, men who suffer from a condition known as *androgen insensitivity* may develop external genitalia that are female in appearance, even though the sex chromosome pair is XY. The development of female genitalia, coupled with the continued absence of androgens, seems to yield women with the incorrect chromosomal identity. Obviously, these individuals are reared as females and may never know of the internal contradiction unless they are chromosomally charted for one reason or another, the most likely of which would be apparent infertility. A few females of this type have been identified early in life, and they seem to develop on the normal female schedule, both physically and psychologically.[25] In essence, the body ignores the chromosomal information and allows the hormones to run their course.

Certainly, this is a happy ending considering the contradictory situation, but these cases are relatively uninteresting to researchers who seek to clarify the effect of hormones on human behavior. More fascinating, and much sadder, is the case of a male twin who was accidentally castrated during circumcision. The child was reassigned female, both surgically and hormonally. Money and Ehrhardt traced the development of these unique twins—a boy and a boy-reassigned-as-a-girl, genetically identical, raised in the same environment by the same parents. After six years of longitudinal research, they concluded that neither the boy nor the girl was confused as to gender identity and that their behaviors were distinct and gender appropriate.[26] The logical conclusion, based on this case and the antiandrogen condition cases, is that chromosomal information may predispose sex-specific behaviors, but can be overridden by hormonal irregularities and socialization.

Recently, a genetic defect was discovered among natives of the Dominican Republic that inhibited XY individuals from developing male genitals by the time of birth. Of the thirty-eight cases studied, about half were raised as females due to the appearance of the genitalia. Unlike the twin described above, these individuals were not surgically and hormonally reassigned. So, they provided a research team with the rare opportunity to observe the results of contradictions between biological and social information. Before puberty, the ambiguous genitalia and the latent hormonal state did not interfere with the identification of those treated by their parents as girls. However, when the hormones activated male development, additional biological clues as to masculinity began to appear, and all but one of the "girls" took on a male gender identity. This choice could hardly be questioned, given the mounting physical evidence of masculinity, but it is especially fascinating that nearly all of these adolescents adopted male-appropriate behaviors after they "switched" categories.[27]

As critics have pointed out, this situation is clearly unique, due to the complex of biological and social confusion that probably surrounded these unfortunate individuals. Still, it provides evidence that gender identity can be learned and even relearned in conjunction with hormonal activity. Undoubtedly, the relative success of sexual reassignment depends in large part on the social circumstances of the individual.

More abundant, though less dramatic, is the evidence that hormonally mascu-linized females tend to display behaviors typically associated with males, and tend not to display behaviors typically associated with females. You may be surprised to learn that the effects of abnormally high androgen levels in females have been extensively studied, since, at one time, doctors mistakenly recommended the injection of male hormones into certain pregnant women to prevent miscarriage. If the fetus was genetically female, abnormalities commonly resulted. Other masculinized females have been identified as victims of a genetic defect that prompts female fetuses to incorrectly produce extra androgens.[28]

As scientists continue to identify and observe masculinized females, they obtain valuable information not only about the wisdom of hormone manipulation but also about presumed effects of sex hormones in the human experience. In some cases, masculinized females may be born with ambiguous physical characteristics. The internal ducts are usually female, but the genitalia may be seen as a large clitoris or a small penis, depending on the observer's individual perspective.[29] These cases call for parents to choose how to assign the child, a difficult choice to be sure and one that forces these parents to examine their own definitions of maleness and femaleness.

Fortunately, most parents of females with excessive levels of male hormones need not consider reassignment, since their daughters are clearly daughters. These little girls, though, have been observed to differ from other little girls of roughly the same age, intelligence, and background. (In some studies sisters were compared.) Specifically, it seems that they show a greater preference for *rough-and-tumble play,* the name given to energized, aggressive play usually displayed by boys. Also, they are self-labeled and labeled by parents and teachers as *tomboys* far more often than other females. Thus, both observational studies and interviews suggest that these girls display behavioral traits commonly associated with boys. In addition, both methodol-ogies reveal a less-than-average interest in doll-play, baby care, and role rehearsal for motherhood (roughly translated, "playing house").[30] Overall, girls with extra male hormones are both masculinized and defeminized, a distinction that is quite important. Keep in mind that these females still possess the normal doses of female hormones, even though they have received extra male hormones. The "double" effect of the androgens has been cited as evidence that sex hormones may "antagonize each other." In the case of these masculinized females, the male hormone seems to counter the presumed normal effects of the female hormones. Also, according to Ehrhardt, animal studies suggest that progestogens can act as antiandrogens if injected at critical times in proper dosages.[31]

These studies raise questions, then, about the extent to which hormones them-selves are opposites. Indeed, even though men and women usually possess all three, it is difficult not to acknowledge the complications resulting when the normal balance is disturbed. To summarize, there is reason to believe that:

1. Androgens are absolutely essential to men. They must be present during critical periods in male maturation. Without them, genetic males are at the mercy of the small doses of female hormones which, in the presence of active male hormones, are usually ignored.
2. Androgens are not as important to female maturation. Females develop as females with or without small doses of androgens. However, when androgen levels are abnormally high, females do not "turn into" males. Rather, females display more masculine and less feminine behaviors.

Admittedly, the bulk of this research has focused on the influence of male hormones in the human experience. This fact is largely determined by the available data. Questions remain about the effects of higher-than-normal estrogen and progestogen levels in males. As explained, few such cases exist, since these men probably live their lives as women. Still, animal research should continue to clarify the extent to which hormones affect physical and behavioral sex differences.

Most of the research concerning female hormones has been devoted to determining precise cycles of hormonal activity. Of course, the underlying assumption of this research is that adult female lives are cyclic, while adult male lives are acyclic. This assumption has been used to explain stereotypic sex differences in emotionality and rationality. In order to clarify the implications of accepting or rejecting the cyclic vs. acyclic premise, it is necessary to examine and compare the available research. At the onset, though, it must be stressed that studies focusing on female cycles abound, while very few have focused on male cycles. So the research serves as a sort of self-fulfilling prophecy, in that female cycles are well documented and much written about, because they have traditionally been believed to exist and, therefore, have been studied as though they exist. Indeed, most women who reported or were interviewed in the studies were not ignorant of the assumption of cyclic moods, nor of the proposed connection to hormonal activity.

In case some readers are uninformed about the proposed connection, medical experts began to document what folkmyths had long held about female moods in the 1930s: that "women are at their happiest and most self-confident at mid-cycle, at the time of ovulation, but that they become tense, unstable and depressed in the week before and during menstruation...."[32] Many researchers have attempted to clarify the physiological causes of these mood swings, while others have attempted to depict the behavioral outcomes. After all, if women are likely to be depressed and unstable for several days of each month, they ought not be in positions of national security! In truth, some early studies reported that female performance, both intellectual and physical, was diminished during the "low" period. But more recent studies suggest that, for most women, performance is not diminished during that time.[33]

That is not to say, however, that women are no longer experiencing cyclic mood swings, only that the performance of the women studied was not hindered. Studies show consistently that women report positive moods around ovulation and negative moods just prior to menstruation.[34] The difficulties associated with the latter period of time have recently been specified and the label *PMS* (premenstrual syndrome) has become a familiar term identifying a medical condition women need not be ashamed of and men must not ignore. The identification of PMS as a medical condition involving physiological changes may serve to legitimize female complaints, but may also lend support to arguments that females are unfit to function in positions of responsibility. Some researchers have turned their attention to listing the dangers women may inflict on themselves and others during the week before menstruation. One recent source summarizes that "half of the women who commit crimes, have serious road accidents, commit suicide and are admitted to a hospital for a psychiatric disorder, are in this phase of their cycle."[35] Given that the average female cycle is four weeks, logic suggests that only around 25% of these problems would occur during the premenstrual week. Hence, the reported figure is nearly double the statistical prediction.

It may be important to recognize that, as part of the women's movement, female problems have been given greater attention. This attention certainly validates the female experience, which is long overdue, but it also affects the female experience. So focusing popular attention on PMS may have inadvertently hindered young women from being taken seriously. Also, there is reason to believe that the felt effects of hormonal activity, like the felt effects of any internal condition, can be exaggerated, if not created, by learned expectations. So, it may be that young women who are exposed to detailed depictions of the physical and emotional effects of hormonal changes may exaggerate their impact.

Once again, the precise connection between physiological conditions and overt communication behaviors is vague. Perhaps women are more emotional, innately, due to hormonal irregularities. Perhaps they are less rational, less capable, weaker. At the same time, the sensitivity and flexibility required to cope with constant change may enable women to be more sympathetic and nurturing—more other-centered. But, most likely, a tentative and nonuniversal connection between female hormonal activity and mood changes is exaggerated and overgeneralized in the mythology. The myths, in turn, probably influence our perception of others' behavior and even our interpretation of our own experience. In other words, when all else fails, the myths provide a ready explanation for female emotionality and male rationality.

There is some evidence, however, that rattles these myths at least slightly. As mentioned earlier, few studies have attempted to depict male cycles, despite the fact that the level of male hormone in a given body is not necessarily stable. Based on the assumption that levels of testosterone, an androgen, might fluctuate on a cyclical basis and might correlate with periodic mood swings, a group of researchers collected daily blood samples and diary-type reports from male subjects. They reported that 60% of the subjects had a regular cycle with regard to the level of testosterone. However, the cycles varied in length and in reported effect. Some males reported being depressed when the level was high, others reported being aggressive.[36] The inconsistencies in this study may be taken as evidence that men don't have hormonal cycles; that the regularities were misrepresented. On the other hand, the inconsistencies may be evidence that neither the researchers nor the subjects had preconceived notions about what to report, since so little is known about cycles in the male experience. In that light, consistencies in male reports might be seen as more valid than the consistencies in female reports, at least as they pertain to moods and emotions.

An article by Estelle Ramey, appropriately entitled "Men's Cycles (They Have Them Too You Know)," argues that both sexes experience hormonal variations that seem to influence their moods. Yet, both scientific rigor and popular discussion, she suggests, emphasize the impact of cycles in the female experience and ignore the impact of cycles in the male experience.[37] While this discrepancy is not necessarily a problem in itself, it becomes a problem when women are denied the opportunity to be judged as rational and capable based on individual performance. They may be denied employment and/or perceived as emotional and unstable. Conversely, male stability may be overestimated as a result of the assumption that their lives are acyclic. Individual problems and emotions may be trivialized or, worse yet, seen as unmanly. Men may be perceived as nonnurturing and unsympathetic, regardless of individual behavior.

Thus, the continued discovery of sex similarities, as well as sex differences, in hormonal activity must be carefully considered in relation to traditional myths about masculinity and femininity.

PSYCHOSEXUAL DEVELOPMENT

All of the theories in the previous section are grounded in modern knowledge concerning male and female physiology, regardless of the particular sex difference that is emphasized and regardless of the logic connecting that difference to human behavior. The theory discussed in this section was proposed long before detailed knowledge about physiology was available. It emerged during the early 1900s, which one historian remarks was "a time when both the romantic philosophers and Darwin had great status."[38] Despite the dramatic style of his writing, however, and his failure to conform to modern scientific standards concerning size and random selection of his sample, many believe that Sigmund Freud's theory of psychosexual development has received more attention than any other theory of sex differences.

Freud theorized at length about the relationship between personality and primary sex characteristics—more specifically, the genitalia. He claimed his theory described universal sex differences, ones that are innately male and female, regardless of the specific culture into which a child is born. However, Freud took a very narrow view of culture; he equated culture with family, specifically the Western family. Thus, Freudian theory is discussed in this section because of the claim that sex differences are naturally linked to biological development, but is important to remember the historical and theoretical context from which this body of theory emerged.

The theory of psychosexual development depicts what Freud believed to be the chronological stages through which "normal" humans pass on the way to becoming "healthy" heterosexual adults. He assumed that the development of the mind (*psycho*) could be correlated with the development of the body parts (*sexual*). In his earliest work, Freud presented his stage-by-stage development in terms of the experiences of the male child, but, as you will see, his logic failed to account for the female experience. Later, Freud attempted to delineate the developmental stages through which female children pass, but, when he encountered logical dilemmas in explaining how adult heterosexual women reach "full psychological health," he concluded that women are innately inferior in this regard. Thus, as Gilligan points out, "a problem in theory became cast as a problem in women's development."[39] The theory of psychosexual development, therefore, operates according to two sets of logics: one for males (the standard) and one for females (the exception).

According to Freud's theory, the psychosexual development of girls is identical to that of boys during the first two early childhood stages: the oral and the anal. Regardless of sex, he reasoned that humans possess a psychological energy, labeled *libido*, which is appropriately channeled toward different body parts at predictable stages. In early infancy, gratification is centered on the mouth, so the mother's breast, or a substitute bottle, is the first important object of satisfaction. Freud assumed that the successful channeling of the libido in this stage results in feelings of trust and dependency, since the child must rely on assistance from others, especially his or her mother.[40]

Anyone who has spent even a few moments observing the behavior of a baby can testify to an apparent preoccupation with the mouth; as soon as an infant can manipulate his or her hands, any available object is inserted into the mouth. In fact, there does appear to be a very strong drive on the part of babies to get to and consume visible objects of all types, but few of us assume, as Freud did, that this is evidence of the libido at work.

In any case, Freud proposed that children redirect their attention, around the end of the first year, to the *anal* zone, and their interest "involves the retention and expulsion of feces." Freud theorized that children begin to experience feelings of power during the anal stage, as their action or inaction in this regard seems to draw considerable parental attention. So, according to the theory of psychosexual development, children of both sexes have an equal opportunity to assume an active (or passive) stance in relationship to others during this stage.[41]

Now, it is common knowledge among mothers that little boys toilet train later than little girls (a fact that mothers of little girls tend to drop ever-so-casually in conversations with mothers of little boys). Perhaps Freud would interpret this fact as evidence that male children assume a more active stance with regard to when and where they will dispose of their feces. Again, however, it is difficult for most of us to imagine the sort of psychological connections proposed by Freud, as we observe the toilet-related behaviors of the average toddler, male or female.

The third stage of psychosexual development marks the parting of the ways for males and females. Through the oral and anal stages, the objects of gratification and the outcomes of successful passage are equally available to children of both sexes. But in the *phallic stage*, beginning around age three or four, children develop a keen interest in their genitals, and Freud assumed that this experience is clearly different for boys and girls. As one source summarizes, "psychoanalysts claim that there is a connection between people's genitals and their personality. The fact that the penis is an organ which intrudes into the world is said to lead to men being outgoing, adventurous and aggressive, while the internal reproductive system of a women is alleged to make her passive, receptive and peaceful."[42]

Although this quote probably overstates the case, Freud speculated that women inevitably suffer from *penis envy*. It is difficult to be sure exactly how three-year-old girls regard their anatomy in comparison to their perception of the anatomy of three-year-old boys. Perhaps the "bigger is better" philosophy does invoke a temporary sort of envy. In addition, it has been observed that parents tend to directly and correctly reference the male apparatus for urination, but use euphemisms or fail to name the female apparatus. So little girls may be indirectly led to believe that boys have a penis and they have "nothing."[43]

But Freud theorized that the effects of penis envy are far more complex than a simple interest in the biology of urination. To explain, it is necessary to introduce perhaps the most dramatic and well known of Freud's concepts, the fear of castration. Just as passage through the oral and anal stages are assumed to contribute important characteristics to the adult personality (trust and power, respectively), passage through the phallic stage is assumed to contribute a sense of morality. Successful passage through the phallic stage is very difficult and complex, as portrayed by Freud. He theorized that the child soon tires of autoerotic gratification and turns to another for gratification. Obviously, for a male child the most obvious choice is the same individual who has gratified his needs since the beginning—his mother. As most readers undoubtedly know, Freud termed the son's desire for his mother an *Oedipus complex*, after the mythological character who accidentally married his natural mother.

Naturally, the child's fantasy to "have" the mother is discouraged, by the father as well as the mother, and the child fears that the punishment will be castration. This fear, along with an intense feeling of rivalry toward the father (who possesses the mother), is said to drive the male child to emulate the father as the proper and moral solution to his dilemma. During the next eight to ten years, Freud believed that the male child moves into a period of *latency* in which sexual desires are denied. The child postpones his desires initially because of fear, but, as a result, exercises the rational and moral solution to an impossible situation. When puberty occurs, he successfully transfers his desires from the mother to a more "available" female.[44]

All in all, this results in a happy ending for the male adult, now capable of trust learned during the oral stage, full of feelings of power acquired during the anal stage, and equipped with a strong sense of morality as a result of the difficult resolution of the phallic stage. But what of the development for females? Freud's logic fails to cover their development on several counts. To begin with, his critics argue that, despite attempts, Freud was never able to establish a complementary logic explaining a daughter's assumption that her father would become the object of gratification during the phallic period.[45] She, like her hypothetical brother, receives oral gratification and learns trust from the mother, and, given no knowledge of sexual intercourse, can hardly be assumed to reason the redirection of her desires at age three. Also, since so much of the male's healthy psychological development is assumed to hinge on resolution of the Oedipus complex, driven by the fear of castration, what commensurate fear drives the female child to deny sexual feelings for the father?

Obviously, the fear of castration in boys has no logical correlate for girls. But, Freud theorized about female development based on what he believed to be the dominant emotion during the female experience of the phallic stage—penis envy. He proposed that the female child blames her mother for the supposed loss of her penis and redirects her desires to the most available possessor of the *coveted penis*.[46] Both of these decisions seem to be driven by a logic quite unlike that which attracts the male child to his mother, whom he trusts and loves based on a long history of interaction. Moreover, Freud argued that the male child eventually emulates the father, as a means to an end, and, although many question the "end" he specified, it does seem that imitating the same-sex parent is a habit demonstrated by the average three-year-old. Yet, how can we assume that a female who wishes to have a penis like her father does, and blames her mother for her sad condition, will naturally emulate the villain who shares the dreaded affliction?

Logically, it seems that fear is quite different from blame combined with envy, and critics have argued that the identification of the female child with the mother cannot be explained by the dynamics of penis envy, even if it is experienced by female children. Ultimately, Freud himself recognized the absence of a logical and complete resolution to the female version of the Oedipus story, but he concluded, as mentioned earlier, that this resulted in incomplete moral development in females, which is evidenced in a weakened "sense of justice," a ready submission to "the great exigencies of life" and a tendency to be "influenced in their judgements by feelings of affection or hostility."[47]

In addition to these maladies, Freud also proposed that females may "resent" their sexual assignment, since there is no logical resolution to their dilemma of wanting but not having a penis. He suggested that, normally, females opt for gratification through having a child (preferably a male child) which predicates that the formerly active sexuality they desired during the phallic period be replaced by passive sexual aims associated with the womb.[48] But, once again, it is difficult to reason how the desire for passivity naturally evolves from a strong sense of penis envy.

To sum up an already abbreviated discussion, Freud's theory of psychosexual development offers dual explanations linking the development of sex-specific body parts to the development of sex-specific adult personalities. The theory traces the assumed-to-be standard development of the male child as he learns to resolve issues of trust, power, and morality. It also traces the supposedly nonstandard development of the female child as she learns to trust the one she eventually blames for an "inferior" condition they share, and passively serves the one she envies.

At this point you may or may not be convinced by Freudian logic, which dooms females to passivity, dependency, and emotionality and legitimizes male activity, independence, and rationality. However, it is important to recognize the tremendous impact that Freudian theory has had on Western thought about the connection between biology and behavior. Freud argued, perhaps more convincingly than any other individual, that males and females are innately different, even though he was not privy to biological information about hormonal cycles, tissue compositions, or chromosomal structures. One of his supporters points out that "scientists" who attack Freud fail to grasp his "premises" because they are blinded by attention to empirically observable detail.[49] If nothing else, Freud appears to have initiated a long and worthwhile debate about the extent to which biological differences are linked to sex differences such as susceptibility to emotion, ability to resolve conflict, activity vs. passivity, etc. A good deal of scientific research has been generated as proponents and critics attempt to argue the various tenets of psychosexual theory.

On the other hand, Freudian theory may have proven a detriment by limiting our ability to conceive of human experience as unique, both individually and culturally. Surely, early childhood development hinges on a variety of dynamics, not just sexual conflict. Also, not every child is raised according to the Western model of the conjugal family. Even in our own culture, the family dynamics are changing; blended families and single-parent families are becoming more and more prevalent. So, it is very limiting to label as standard a model for the development of sex appropriateness that can only explain these situations as exceptional and dangerous. Ultimately, Freud has been criticized for the most basic of his assumptions: that behavior must be sex-specific to be healthy. Many have argued that he disallowed the freedom to chose, for both men and women, in his rigid approach to human development.

C O N D U C T   Y O U R   O W N   R E S E A R C H

1. Keep a diary for one month in which you rate your "mood" each day on a scale of one to ten and explain the reason for the rating. At the end of the month, prepare a graph that reflects your monthly moods and a brief paper summarizing the factors that caused your moods? Trade graphs with an unidentified opposite-sex classmate and guess about the causes of his or her mood cycle. How did stereotypes affect your attribution of causes to your own moods and the moods of another?

2. Clip photographs of men and women engaging in exercise activities considered more typical for the other sex, i.e., women lifting weights or men in aerobics classes. Ask respondents to react to the pictures. What stereotypic traits survive the situational switch? Is the man still perceived as strong? the woman as yielding?

3. Prepare a survey in which you ask respondents to list actual physiological differences between males and females. Do they stress primary, secondary, or tertiary traits?

DISCUSS THE ISSUES

1. Can females ever achieve equality with men in terms of muscular strength? Can training allow them to run as fast as men? swim as fast? jump as high? Conversely, could changes in lifestyle result in a more equitable life expectancy for men? Fewer incidents of heart disease and ulcers?

2. Should women have drawn attention to PMS as an unavoidable physical condition? Has this attention helped or hurt the feminist movement?

3. Imagine sex differences in behavior in various historical periods (hunting and gathering societies, frontier societies, etc.) and compare them to contemporary sex differences. What factors seem to predict how labor is divided? How is this division linked to invisible, psychological characteristics?

CHAPTER 9

EXPLANATIONS BASED ON SOCIAL FACTORS: SOCIAL LEARNING THEORY

Although students are often intrigued by theories postulating that sex differences are innate, the overwhelming tendency is to argue that sex differences in behavior result from societal influence. When questioned as to exactly how the invisible culprit, society, performs its magic, students usually respond by identifying its more visible agents: parents, teachers, peers, and the media. In the next two chapters, these agents are discussed, along with theories that attempt to explain how children develop socially mandated, sex-specific behaviors. For the purposes of discussion, two seemingly separate theories that emphasize social factors are presented: social learning theory and modeling theory. However, it is widely believed that the two processes work hand-in-hand as various adult influences socialize children and thereby perpetuate societal standards of sex appropriateness.

Social learning theory may be understood as an adaptation of learning theory. In its capsule form, learning theory is often referenced using the simple stimulus-response (S-R) model. Most students do not escape college without being exposed to Skinner's box, so you may have already watched tiny animals react predictably to positive or negative stimuli. In observing human behavior, we generally adopt a somewhat different vocabulary, and recognize a far more complex set of influences, but the basic premise is the same: "humans tend to repeat those behaviors which have been reinforced...."[1]

Social learning scholars usually refer to sanctions, which social agents use to shape gender-specific behaviors (among other things) as a child is socialized. Sanctions may be positive or negative, tangible or intangible, subtle or violent. In order to explain how sanctions affect gender-related behavior, it is helpful to trace a hypothetical child's life as he or she encounters the various agents of socialization.

PARENTS AS SOCIALIZERS

The first agents of society who enter a child's life are the mother and father, so the parents are generally labeled the *primary socializers*—a label that signifies not only that they are the earliest influence, but also that they are the most powerful influence. Naturally, in the absence of one or both parents, a suitable substitute may assume the same powerful position with relation to the child's socialization. According to perhaps the most widely cited source in the field, *The Psychology of Sex Differences* by Maccoby and Jacklin, the bulk of the research concerning social learning of gender has focused on the early childhood period, i.e., under school age. So, most of the literature concerning sanctions has reviewed parental interaction with children.[2]

In the extreme, people may argue that parents are ultimately responsible for the way their children turn out. We often hear parents take credit for a child's good grades or nice manners. Similarly, we may witness the shame and guilt of parents who must take responsibility for a child's failure. Maccoby and Jacklin speculate that the treatment of parents as the primary agents of socialization is appropriate given the family structure in America, as opposed to other cultures where adults other than the parents are given far more freedom to sanction a child's behavior. In our society, children are largely at the mercy of their parents' judgment during the preschool years. Of course, various agencies try to intervene when children are mistreated, but, short of child abuse, parents are given near total freedom to raise their children in any way they deem fit.

According to social learning theorists, parents generally operate through the systematic rewarding and/or punishing of specific behaviors. It follows that, to the extent that the parents endorse the dominant sex stereotypes, vigorously rewarding masculine behavior in boys and feminine behavior in girls and punishing (perhaps more vigorously) cross-sex behavior, society will have made its gender-specific mark long before a child enters the dangerous and unpredictable public arena.

Of course, there is reason to believe that adults are beginning to experience their own lives as free from restrictions according to gender. We have experienced legal and social reforms, which mandate equal treatment of men and women in the public realms of education, employment, government, etc. So, when they (you) become parents, they (you) will probably not reward and punish behavior in line with traditional views of masculinity and femininity, right? As I discuss this question with students, semester after semester, I am impressed with their declarations of independence from tradition in this regard. But when discussion turns to the nuts and bolts of parenting, many students confront the reality that, as primary socializing agents, they will be expected to "teach" gender to children who will probably not be born into an era of total freedom. In the best interest of those imaginary children, many students admit that, to a certain degree, they will be compelled to nurture gender appropriateness.

For the sake of argument, imagine yourself as a primary socializer, a new parent, and agree or disagree as you will with the following assumptions about teaching gender that have been developed from a social learning perspective:

1. The child exhibits a range of behaviors, some of which parents react to and some of which they ignore.
2. Parents react to the child's behavior in light of their conceptions of what the two sexes are like.
3. In some cases, parents deliberately attempt to prepare the child for the appropriate adult sex role.
4. In other cases, parents react to the child's behavior in terms of immediate concerns, exhibiting differential treatment of boys and girls.
5. Parents tend to offer positive sanctions to behaviors deemed sex-appropriate and negative sanctions to behaviors deemed sex-inappropriate.

As the first claim states, parents tend to react to only a subset of the behaviors exhibited by children. This is not surprising, but it is noteworthy if, indeed, the gender of the child predicts which behaviors will draw attention, as the second claim states. Several studies have revealed that parents react differently to boys and girls, even as infants. For instance, some researchers report that both mothers and fathers handle baby boys more roughly than baby girls and believe that boy babies enjoy aggressive play more than girls. Other research studies reveal that baby girls are talked to more than baby boys, and that parents believe girls are more responsive than boys during infancy.[3] In addition, both male and female observers tend to describe baby boys according to stereotypically male traits such as "strong, solid and independent," and baby girls according to stereotypically female traits such as "loving, cute and sweet."[4] In fact, in one study identical behaviors were described differently when exhibited by babies labeled male and female.[5]

From the very beginning, it seems, parents tend to respond to behavior in conjunction with the perception of the infant as male or female.[6] It is difficult to be sure, based on social learning tenets, precisely why children first exhibit certain behaviors, but most theorists speculate that newborns respond instinctively to the outside world, based on physical sensation. Thus, it is possible that innate factors may result in behavioral displays that truly differ according to sexual assignment. Recent research has demonstrated that sex hormones, which had once been thought to be latent between birth and puberty, are fairly active just after birth.[7]

Newborn boy babies may very well act differently from newborn girl babies because of biological differences. On the other hand, parents may exaggerate, or even imagine, behavioral differences that are aligned with myths about sex differences. The important point is that parents react to certain infant behaviors and ignore others, so the process of selectively sanctioning behaviors is proposed to begin very early in the child's life. Maccoby and Jacklin conclude that, in early infancy, "a circular pattern of interaction becomes established based upon an individual child's [behaviors] and the parent's [behaviors]..."[8] Admittedly, the age-old question, "Which comes first?" remains unanswered.

The third claim essentially acknowledges the same reality that my students sheepishly endorse when they admit that parents must assume some responsibility for teaching their little boys and girls how to behave according to the standards established by society for male and female roles. Even though, as adults, we believe in the freedom to contradict those roles, and may sometimes act in ways inconsistent with them, most parents readily see the necessity for communicating gender-specific assumptions to children. In practice, the positive and negative sanctions that follow a child's behaviors linked to gender appropriateness may range from very subtle facial changes by the approving or disapproving parent to verbal directives like "Little boys don't do that!" or "Act like a lady!" The familiarity of these expressions is verified in my classes with knowing smiles and laughter; we lovingly refer to them as the things you learn to say in "parent school," a school that no one ever remembers attending.

What childhood behaviors, then, might be considered preparatory for adult sex roles? Several experts speculate that gender-specific toys are sanctioned by parents because they are logically related to adult sex roles.[9] For example, boys may be encouraged to play with trucks and sports equipment and girls may be encouraged to play with dolls and miniature kitchens. Obviously, encouragement may be either very blatant or very subtle in this regard. It may involve prohibitions against boys playing with dolls. Incidentally, the majority of the college females in my classes report that they would not impose this prohibition, but the males are divided. Many say they might let their sons play with dolls, but not in public. Others say, unapologetically, "no way." Regardless of your response, this is yet another question that simply requires no asking if your child happens to be born XX.

Parental sanctions may include distracting children from cross-sexed toys or, simply, giving the child the toys he or she requests, which are likely to be in line with societal standards.[10] In reality, few children request toys without a certain degree of prompting from outside sources. Toy stores are usually divided into several sections, and the consideration of gender is obvious. Often, there is a gender-neutral infants' section, which features primary colors and developmental toys. For infants, age and stage of development seem to be of primary importance in marketing. Toys for older children, however, are usually divided into two sections: female and male. The former is typically laden with dolls, doll accessories, costumes and makeup, toy furniture, and miniature kitchen appliances; the latter is bountiful with super-hero characters, war toys, sports equipment, and machinery replicas.

Of course, some toys should be appealing to both sexes. Bicycles, swing sets, wagons, etc., are often manufactured in primary colors and marketed for both boys and girls. When my husband and I made purchases of this sort for our first daughter, we appreciated toys that could be inherited by a possible future brother. However, in examining the advertising for some of the very purchases we made, I detected subtle messages about gender. I would probably have never noticed them had I not suspected the validity of a 1974 study reporting that models for gender-neutral toy lines often portray adult sex role expectations.[11] To my surprise, a brand new catalog for a line of toys I believed to be gender neutral contained many photographs depicting boys actively engaged in play and girls in passive poses.

Aware of the limitations of looking at one isolated example, I turned to scholarly research. To my surprise, I found a recent content analysis of toy catalogs in the journal *Sex Roles*. According to the authors, who looked at 392 photographs in toy catalogs, "when toy advertisers present pictures of children with toys, they generally show toys with a child of the appropriate sex." Even gender-neutral play activities tended to be cast as having male and female versions: "girls were shown with tricycles which were pink and blue, with flowers and cute-sounding names. The boys' versions had heavy-duty tires, were typically dark colors, and had rugged-sounding names."[12] A fuller discussion of the effects of media portrayals of gender is included in the next chapter. Here, it is important to acknowledge that children may request toys according to their own image of gender appropriateness at a very young age. Therefore, it is difficult to tell what comes first—the child's desire to choose gender-appropriate playthings in the midst of American consumerism or the parents' readiness to supply gender-specific toys. But the failure of many parents to challenge lines dividing toys by gender may serve as subtle reinforcement of the child's tendency to choose toys aligned with anticipated adult sex roles.

Similar subtle sanctions may surround other aspects of the preschooler's life, such as recreational activities and even housework. Boys, in particular, seem to be expected to behave according to standards deemed manly. The negative sanctions that commonly confront a male child who displays female behaviors are symbolized by the pejorative label *sissy*. The counterpart for girls, *tomboy,* is not nearly as negative. Indeed, the majority of girls are called tomboys at some point in their development, whereas sissies are comparatively rare. This contrast has been attributed both to the strength of parental sanctions of cross-sex behavior and to the apparent attractiveness of boys' activities to active young girls.[13]

Whether the sanctions are negative or positive, the efforts made by parents (and others) to shape behavior according to gender-specific standards may be called *anticipatory socialization*.[14] Most parents undoubtedly have the best of intentions as they diligently prepare their children to live in a world where distinctions are sure to be drawn between male and female behavior. The author is no stranger to difficult choices in this regard and does not deny that the perpetuation of restrictive stereotypes is closely linked to anticipatory socialization by well-meaning parents.

Naturally, parents also sanction a number of childhood behaviors without regard to the long-range future; this is called *nonanticipatory socialization*. As claim #4 on the list of social learning tenets states, parents often respond in terms of immediate concerns, but may do so differently for boys and girls and thereby inadvertently perpetuate societal standards. Of course, certain behaviors are negatively sanctioned regardless of sex. Destructive actions, uncontrolled temper, and deliberately hurtful behavior are not allowed because they are not in accordance with societal standards. Yet some studies show that boys are not sanctioned as negatively for aggressive behavior and may, in fact, be sanctioned against passivity. Take, for instance, the case of a young boy who is told to stand up to the neighborhood bully on his own, despite the risk of being beaten. It is difficult to imagine that the same advice would be given to his sister. Other studies show that girls are not discouraged from outbursts of tears as strongly as their male counterparts.[15] In each situation, parents undoubtedly attempt to deal with immediate concerns. But if parents impose different sanctions for boys and girls, they may inadvertently perpetuate stereotypes about adult male and female behavior. It is difficult not to notice the correlation between studies of parental treatment in such crises and the observed differences in emotional expression discussed in Chapter Six.

Even in situations where parents offer identical verbal sanctions to boys and girls, they may indirectly emphasize gender, since so many of our standard grammatical constructions facilitate this practice. For instance, a parent might remark, "Good little boys don't color on the walls" or "Nice girls say 'Excuse me' when they leave the table." Of course, the parent intends to emphasize the adjectives ("good" and "nice"), but the child may be influenced by the nouns, which are gender specific, in the language tradition detailed in Chapter Three.

One of my daughter's favorite books used to be *The Good Little Girl and the Bad Little Girl,* which, of course, was about one little girl who was sometimes good and sometimes bad. My little girl chose the book from a rack, on which it was flanked by another book, *The Good Little Boy and the Bad Little Boy.* When I compared them, I found that the content was the same; only the pictoral representations and the gender labels differed. Boys and girls alike were labeled "good" because they washed their hands, said their prayers, and cheerfully obeyed parental commands. "Bad" boys and girls were depicted as complaining and defying rules, not to mention pulling the cat's tail. Still, I could not help but wonder why two versions of the book were necessary, until I realized that my daughter, who selected the book at age three, had already received the message that sanctions about girl behavior applied to her, but sanctions about boy behavior did not.

But it is not through language habits alone that primary socializers communicate societal expectations about gender-specific behavior. A short while ago, during a discussion of sex differences in sitting posture, I surveyed a class of college women and men as to whether or not they recalled hearing the specific directive: "Sit like a lady" or "Sit like a man," respectively. All of the young women recalled hearing the female version of the expression, either from parents or teachers. But the young men only recalled hearing "Sit up" or "Sit straight." We tentatively concluded that sitting posture seems to be sanctioned more vigorously for females, which is clearly in line with the sex difference reported in Chapter Six. As the discussion continued, the male students remembered other sanctions, both positive and negative, associated with "acting like a gentleman." These surrounded not only using good table manners (practices presumably not specified by gender), but also manners derived from the age of chivalry, e.g., opening doors, letting females pass first, etc.

In sum, the primary socializers, in the process of fulfilling their responsibility to teach children acceptable behavior, can be understood as perpetuating their own understanding of gender-specific expectations through both anticipatory and non-anticipatory socialization. In many cases, parents prepare children to "fit" into a world that distinguishes people according to sex. In other situations, parents simply deal with the immediate concerns of the day, but in doing so inadvertently reinforce certain behaviors in boys and other behaviors in girls.

Of course, as even this brief discussion indicates, parental socialization does not operate in a vacuum; it occurs amidst an array of outside influences. Still, in our society, where the nuclear family is an accepted way of life, parents are assumed to take primary responsibility for early childhood sanctioning.

TEACHERS AS SOCIALIZERS

A child's experience in the world outside of the home usually begins upon entering school, which, in our country is required by law at approximately age five. However, many children attend preschool, so they encounter the influence of professional educators as early as age two or three. Interaction with teachers, of course, usually involves overt rewards and punishments. In fact, the expression "en loco parentis" refers to the teacher's responsibility to act as parent while the child is in school.

Obviously, teachers seldom assume the same responsibility as parents for a child's development of gender appropriateness. Rewards and punishments seem to surround the social and academic skills necessary to succeed in the educational system. However, several critics have noted that educators may indirectly sanction gender-appropriate behaviors in several ways. To begin with, there is ample evidence that boys receive more negative sanctions than girls for their behavior in school settings.[16] In one observational study of fifteen preschool classrooms, boys were reprimanded, both physically and verbally, about three times as often as girls.[17]

In addition, the negative sanctions boys receive from teachers are likely to be stronger than those girls receive, a fact that one researcher warns must not be taken out of context, since harsh reprimands often follow "a history of interaction in which weaker forms of intervention were ineffective."[18] Observers point out that boys of this age do, indeed, seem to behave in ways that threaten the orderly classroom. They are more physically aggressive with peers, more destructive of property, less willing to follow directions, etc.[19] However, it may be that teacher attention to such behaviors, even though negative, inadvertently encourages boys to continue behavioral patterns scholars label as "active."

If this reasoning seems contrary to social-learning theory, consider the evidence that boys also receive more positive sanctions for acceptable activity. They are praised more often and more vigorously than girls for good behavior in the classroom.[20] Thus, for boys, activity yields sanctions, some positive and some negative. But girls are simply not as noticeable according to a number of studies of teacher–student interaction. One researcher reported, after observing second grade classrooms, that although "problem boys" received more teacher interaction than "non-problem boys," both groups received more interaction than girls, regardless of the girl's behavior. "Problem girls," in this researcher's estimation were usually "passive and withdrawn," and could more easily be ignored than "problem boys."[21]

It is fascinating to posit whether or not girls who behave quietly in order to avoid negative sanctions inadvertently set standards by which girls need not be praised for observing classroom routines. For instance, during a recent visit to my daughter's kindergarten class I noticed that, when the teacher asked that the children "go to their places on the carpet," several little girls proceeded directly and quietly to their spots. While they waited, one active little boy finally arrived at his spot and sat down. The teacher, understandably, praised his behavior, since it was a rare opportunity to offer a positive sanction. I must admit, I too noticed that he had followed directions! Granted, my visit does not constitute a systematic observation, but it is consistent with research indicating that boys receive both more positive and more negative sanctions from early childhood educators.

Of course, it must be stressed that the ranks of preschool and elementary school teaching continue to be dominated by females. Many critical voices have portrayed elementary school walls as containing one of several "female ghettos," due to the preponderance of women and to the comparatively low salaries. Others explain female dominance in the profession as discrimination against males. Traditionalists argue that "teachering" young children may be seen as a natural extension of "mothering" them. Whatever the case, it is important to note that most dyads involving teacher–student interaction in elementary school will probably be either male–female or female–female, which may impact on the number and nature of sanctions given. To date, little is known about how these sanctions may differ from those imposed in male–male teacher–student dyads.

Similarly, men continue to dominate at the rank of principal, and, according to Paradise and Wall, "the vast majority of children [see] the role of principal as punitive. They [see] the teacher's role as considerably more positive...."[22] Therefore, the "ultimate" negative sanction in the school context, may very well involve different sorts of gender dynamics. Presently, though, little is known about those dynamics. Some might argue that the literature that attempts to distinguish mother-imposed vs. father-imposed sanctions has yielded confusing and contradictory results, so why attempt a similar contrast in another context? But since a number of studies have found fairly consistent sex differences in classroom behavior and academic achievement, it seems crucial that the gender dynamics of the educational system be examined. Otherwise, differences in the children's behavior can only be explained by innate factors or parental influence.

Admittedly, the gender dynamics of the elementary classroom impact more directly on other explanations of sex differences (see the discussion of modeling that follows and the discussion of relationship dynamics in Chapter Eleven). But, it seems possible that educators may reward and punish children in patterns consistent with their own sense of gender appropriateness. If so, this is an area that warrants future attention from those who favor the social learning explanation of gender differences.

PEERS AS SOCIALIZERS

Learning theorists generally assume that the stimulus can be manipulated by some higher authority who controls the distribution of sanctions, so it may seem inappropriate to argue that peers participate in one another's social learning. Yet, children are very sensitive to evaluation by their peers, according to a review of the literature on peer influence conducted by McCandless. He concludes that:

1. The peer group is a powerful agent of socialization, second only to the parents.
2. Peer influence increases gradually until, by adolescence, peers are about as influential as parents.
3. The peer group is especially powerful in sanctioning superficialities of appearance and speech.
4. Prior to adolescence, and sometimes well after that time, peer influence is predominantly same sex.
5. Except in extreme cases, peer acceptance (based on friendship and status dimensions) is the best single indicator of a child's personal-social adjustment.[23]

These claims might tend to unnerve many parents hopeful of shaping acceptable behavior in their offspring, and many teachers hopeful of molding today's youth. The fear of peer influence is widespread among adults, despite claim five, indicating that acceptance from peers is essential to the individual's social well-being. Most adults take consolation in the second claim, that it is seldom until adolescence that peer influence equals parental influence. The argument goes that, provided children have a solid foundation of values by that time, they will survive peer influence. Even then, McCandless speculates that peers "may have more influence on the style of expression," while the parents have more influence on the "content of expression" (italics omitted).[24]

Most scholars agree that the core of gender learning takes place well before adolescence. As discussed in Chapter Two, young children seem quite knowledgeable about the prevailing cultural prescriptions concerning masculinity and femininity. Two- and three-year-olds express gender-specific preferences and restrictions seemingly in the midst of learning to speak. So the content of gender learning is likely to be well established prior to the dreaded introduction of peer pressure. It would be hasty, though, to overlook the importance of "style of expression" and "superficialities of appearance" given that many of the sex differences in communication behavior discussed in this text serve to indirectly perpetuate sex stereotypes.

Observational studies of kinesic and paralinguistic behavior among adolescents were discussed in Chapter Six. To reiterate, there is ample evidence that sex differences in posture, movement, vocal variety, etc., are clearly discernable, even exaggerated, in adolescent groups.[25] These exaggerations are especially fascinating since, as McClelland points out, social learning theorists believe the peer group to be "indispensable in role rehearsal" of adult courtship and sex-role behaviors.[26] Apparently, adolescents deliberately experiment with various overt expressions of masculinity and femininity and receive immediate positive and negative sanctions from their peers. As might be expected, their moves are often exaggerated and clumsy, but it stands to reason that the peer group provides the only viable learning atmosphere.

Imagine groups of same-sex adolescents venturing into and out of interactions with the opposite sex and discussing their successes and failures with their cohorts. Most likely, every reader can recall such ventures in his or her own adolescence. As parents, you may hope to guide your child through these stormy emotional moments, but the fact remains that only the peer group can determine appropriate male and female behavior in their own world. The style of expression of masculinity and femininity must be explored by adolescents, as it prepares them for adult decisions in a society that assumes that individuals should have the freedom to select their own partners.

Given the concept of role rehearsal, the exaggerated contrasts in male and female style of expression during adolescence might be interpreted as relatively harmless, except for reports that, in the midst of such role rehearsals, certain serious consequences may simultaneously occur. To begin with, it is widely held that, during adolescence, girls "begin to develop self-doubts about their intellectual competency." This occurs despite the fact that girls tend to perform better in elementary school than boys.[27] It is curious, then, that adolescent boys express greater confidence in their abilities than their female peers despite their generally lower grades and poorer scores on aptitude tests. Boys tend to cite lack of effort and bad luck for their academic failures, but girls tend to cite lack of ability.[28] More seriously, girls also begin to report declining career aspirations during this time, while boys seem to have more optimistic projections for the future.[29]

It is difficult to imagine how such a drastic reversal in achievement and confidence occurs. Some scholars suspect that boys are innately superior at math and science, subjects that are emphasized in middle school, while girls are naturally superior at verbal skills, which are emphasized in elementary school. Therefore, it is somehow natural for girls to face difficulties during middle school and boys to experience success. Others who believe that aggression is innate, cite male persistence and female passivity as side effects of the onset of puberty. But social learning theorists tend to reject explanations favoring innate explanations and instead, offer explanations related to teacher–student interaction, parent–child interaction, and, most pertinent here, peer interaction.

According to one source, there is a clear tendency for all-female peer groups to emphasize social success during adolescence. For certain young women, social success is attainable through adult-sanctioned activities such as school organizations, although positions of power are rare and tend to involve overt adult approval, which may be negatively sanctioned by peers. So, girls may devote more energy to the pursuit of informal positions of influence among their peers.[30] Girls are often accused of forming cliques. Discussion in these cliques often focuses on the physical appearance of the members and, perhaps more so, of the nonmembers. According to one source, "sexual attractiveness is the measure of valued femininity for females in the adolescent culture."[31]

As a logical consequence, talk among adolescent girls inevitably turns to "getting noticed" by boys, in general, and often by one special boy. Girls may even begin to fantasize about "true, lasting" love.[32] It seems very likely that same-sex peer reinforcement plays a vital part in nurturing such fantasies. Girls' activities begin to provide support for male activities; in many adolescent groups, the ultimate role is that of cheerleader, not star female athlete. Logically, time devoted to "male worship" also detracts from schoolwork, and grades decline during this period.[33]

But, if this is the case, why don't girls attribute failure, as boys do, to lack of effort or bad luck? There is something especially disturbing about the way in which adolescent girls simultaneously (1) strive for relationship success and (2) fail to strive for academic success. Carol Gilligan discusses the connection between relationship and competitive achievement in her book *In a Different Voice*. She cites Horner's hypothesis that females believe that "success in competitive achievement activity, especially against men, produces anticipation of certain negative consequences, for example threat of social rejection...."[34] Given the strength of peer sanctioning during this period, it seems possible that female peer groups may, at least indirectly, reinforce in one another the tendency to be passive and noncompetitive, except in the singular pursuit of male attention.

In contrast, male peer groups seem to positively reward tangible indicators of success. Since career is often seen as crucial to male success, and school is seen as an avenue to career success, adolescent males reinforce the importance of academic achievement. At the same time, there is a tendency for all-male groups to shun the "busy work" and "subservience" of school.[35] Thus, the ultimate academic status for boys might be achieved by succeeding with a minimum of effort, as embodied in the expression "Never let them see you sweat."

Athletic activity is equally important, if not more so, in male peer groups, and in that arena, sweating is positively sanctioned. One could argue convincingly that the emphasis on male participation in sports is not a product of peer interaction, but is firmly based in parental socialization, school sanctioning, and media treatment of athletes as heroes.[36] Still, the peer group often provides the most immediate and most influential information about whether or not a young man has what it takes in a given sport. In addition to participating in sports, talking about sports is positively sanctioned in all male groups, so knowledge of sports is a sign of status. As discussed in Chapter Four, it may well be that, to the extent that sports talk takes the place of other types of talk, peer socialization contributes to emotional inexpressiveness and even homophobia among adult men.

Adolescent boys also seem to attribute great status to sexual maturity, so overt signs of development are positively rewarded: muscular development, facial hair, etc. Sexual activity is a topic of conversation in all male groups, but seldom are male adolescents rewarded for fantasizing about "true love" the way girls of the same age are. More often, boys treat sex as just another sport. According to one source, when boys do talk about interaction with girls, they usually focus on the "strategies and techniques of sexual intercourse."[37]

In her book, Gilligan also attempts to portray the messages young men receive from peer socialization: "individual achievement rivets the male imagination, and great ideas of distinctive activity defines the standard of self-assessment and success."[38] Thus, male peer groups reward individual achievement, whether academic, athletic, or sexual. Female peer groups reward achievement as well, but usually achievement in terms of social success, i.e., appearance, popularity, and success with boys. It may be argued that the same criteria for success are part of a well oiled, sociopolitical machinery that keeps women out of positions of power. It may be argued just as violently that these criteria are inevitably linked to natural, biological sex differences. But, it cannot be ignored that peer group interaction during adolescence, in providing the arena for role rehearsal, may contribute irrevocably to stereotypic assumptions about masculinity and femininity.

In addition to providing a compelling statement about the male imagination, the Gilligan quote above introduces an important concept, that of self-assessment. The tendency for individuals to participate in self-sanctioning has been called by various names, but, regardless of the label, it is integral to any social learning approach to the development of gender appropriateness. In the words of George Herbert Mead, each individual creates and carries with him or her the "generalized other," a conceptual entity made possible through "role-taking."[39] In essence, the individual constantly participates in a dialogue with this nonspecific other, as he or she monitors and self-sanctions his or her own behavior.

Many social learning theorists speculate that it is through this *intra*personal interaction, more than through any single *inter*personal interaction, that children learn to internalize sex role stereotypes.[40] Given the capacity to self-sanction gender-appropriate behavior, children can find appropriate models to imitate and shape their own behavior accordingly, without approval from the model. This pursuit is discussed in the next chapter.

C O N D U C T   Y O U R   O W N   R E S E A R C H

1. Keep a diary for one week, recording each day the positive and negative reinforcement you receive from peers pertaining to any stereotypically gender-appropriate or gender-inappropriate behavior. Summarize how often you heard gender messages, who offered them, and how you reacted.

2. Prepare a list of child rearing questions and challenge respondents to answer whether or not they would reinforce a son and daughter differently for these behaviors (e.g., getting in a fistfight, playing with a doll, wearing opposite-sex clothing, having an ear (or both ears) pierced, staying out late at night). Interpret the results.

3. Visit a public area that is frequented by parents with small children (e.g., a playground, a shopping mall, a grocery store). Observe the way parental sanctions vary with gender (both of parent and child), with the child's age, and with the behavior of the child.

DISCUSS THE ISSUES

1. Share childhood messages you remember concerning how you ought to behave. Be sure to identify the source of the message (parents? peers? teachers? older brothers? older sisters?). Also try to remember their exact words, if possible. Why do these messages stand out in your mind? Do they contain sex-specific pronouns? Are they similar to those remembered by opposite-sex members of the group?

2. If everyone suddenly agreed to stop offering sex-specific sanctions to children, would gender differences in behavior completely disappear?

3. Which agents of society do you think have been most powerful in your socialization? Why? Do you imagine that this influence varies across cultures or across historical periods?

CHAPTER 10

EXPLANATIONS BASED ON SOCIAL FACTORS: MODELING THEORY

While most of us are well schooled in the rewards and punishments system, and cannot help but acknowledge its impact on our adult lives, it is clear that this system cannot explain the rate nor the breadth of development of culturally shared sex differences in behavior. According to learning theory, each new citizen, whether male or female, must learn which behaviors are appropriate and which are not through the tedious trial-and-error method. Even if agents of society provide constant reinforcement, with little variation or ambiguity, learning theory cannot explain the early age at which children behave according to societal standards nor the thoroughness with which they learn society's complex lessons. Rather, it stands to reason that each child participates actively in evaluating his or her own behavior as consistent or inconsistent with various acceptable societal models.

Albert Bandura points out that the process he calls *identification,* in which people actively seek models after which to pattern their actions, as well as their thoughts and feelings, is an ongoing process that results in an ever-developing "repertoire of behaviors."[1] Obviously, identification does not replace reinforcement as the mechanism of learning gender appropriateness. The two mechanisms work simultaneously, as the child learns by observing a number of societal models, in addition to receiving rewards and punishments from various societal agents. In essence, the child attempts to impose order on a world of endless action, in search of the desired set of behaviors that constitutes gender appropriateness in the society.

PARENTS AS MODELS

Just as parents are believed to be the most influential sanctioning agents of society, so are they recognized as the most likely models for children to imitate. Their singular status as models is commonly attributed to three factors that researchers have discovered influence model selection: availability, power, and nurturance.[2] In the "typical" American family, it seems reasonable to assume that the parents are the most available adult models for young children. Parents are also likely to be perceived as powerful and nurturant by young children (although probably not at the same moment).

But the combination of availability, power, and nurturance is presumably common to both parents, regardless of sex, so these factors alone cannot explain how parents serve as gender models. Modeling theorists must explain, therefore, why little girls choose mothers as models and little boys choose fathers as models. Certainly, mothers are likely to be available models in our society, and probably nurturant models, so these criteria presumably help to explain how girls learn femininity through modeling their mothers, even though their fathers are likely to appear more powerful. The other task for modeling theorists is somewhat more difficult. They have to explain why little boys choose fathers as models, even though their fathers are likely to be less available and less nurturant.

The relative availability of same-sex parental models has undoubtedly changed and will continue to change as women continue to move into the workforce and as "men's lib" focuses attention on the neglected rights of fathers. According to one source, several recent studies indicate that men are becoming increasingly involved in child care, particularly in educated, middle-class, dual-career families. The same source, though, warns that the situation still falls short of "an equitable division of parenting."[3] Indeed, one scholar proudly reports that "men *are* spending more time in the family" (italics in original), and cites an increase in the proportion of domestic duties performed by husbands from 20% in 1965 to 30% in 1981.[4] This increase seems less than impressive, however, given that the 1980 census demonstrated that "the dual-provider family is rapidly becoming the most prevalent family pattern."[5]

The division of labor in the family is discussed in greater detail in Chapter Fourteen, but here it is important to acknowledge the fact that fathers continue to be, in general, less available as models than mothers. Even if fathers are becoming more available as models and mothers are becoming less available, a gap remains such that little girls are likely to have more same-sex parenting than their brothers. Obviously, since both boys and girls begin to demonstrate knowledge of gender appropriateness quite early in life, the availability criteria is less important than it might seem. Somehow, boys learn to imitate the less available model.

Theorists differ, though, as to whether or not same-sex identification for boys involves a rejection of cross-sex identification.[6] That is, since both boys and girls are likely to spend more time with their mothers initially, it may be that both sexes initially identify with the female model. Lynn reports that many preschool boys seem to be more similar to their mothers than their fathers, although father–son similarity becomes increasingly apparent around age four.[7] It stands to reason that boys around age four, out of diapers and ready for adventure, begin to spend more time with their fathers than they previously had. Possibly, boys simply postpone gender-specific modeling. Thus, same-sex modeling presumably occurs for both boys and girls, but just starts later for boys.

On the other hand, it may be that boys begin same-sex modeling in the absence of a male model, by rejecting identification with the available cross-sex model. This theory is also consistent with the age at which little boys begin to appear increasingly concerned with modeling adult males. Determining the age at which children realize which sex they are and ever shall be is most significant to the cognitive developmental approach, discussed in the next chapter. Here it is important to note that, once they realize that their mothers belong to the opposite sex, boys may use mothers as counter-models.[8]

Either way, it seems that modeling theory provides a depiction of gender learning that is easy and ongoing for females, but complex and problematic for males, based on the relative availability of the same-sex parent. Another theory discussed in the next chapter stresses the implications of these relationship dynamics for eventual adult behavior. Modeling theorists, though, tend to assume the influence of same-sex parental models, regardless of relationship dynamics and availability. Put simply, they conclude that most children seem to figure out which parental model is appropriate and to imitate that parent's behavior whenever possible. To the extent that both parents, as well as other agents, reinforce same-sex modeling, children seem to exhibit sex-appropriate behaviors rapidly and consistently.

Studies have demonstrated, over and over, that children are knowledgeable about gender as early as age two. In fact, they may be knowledgeable about gender restrictions even earlier, but limited in their verbal ability to express that knowledge. Modeling theorists have demonstrated that children offer imitations of sex-stereotyped behavior, however simple and exaggerated, particularly in relation to housework and recreational activities, which are often sex-specific in our society and which are readily available for children to observe. To the dismay of those who believe children of the 1980s and 1990s will be free of stereotypes due to the new model provided by nontraditional mothers who are also successful career women, it seems that little girls still model the behaviors that they see as female: doing housework and caring for children. According to a recent summary, studies comparing the effect of mothers' employment status on daughters' behaviors and attitudes demonstrate that the model provided by the mother "has little impact on the way in which [daughters] perceive adult sex roles."[9] This may be because little girls don't actually see their mothers at work or because they choose to attend to the traditional aspects of femininity.

Studies concerning nontraditional fathers, then, might shed more light on the influence of same-sex parental models. To the extent that fathers participate in household chores and child care, traditionally associated with the female sex role, their sons should model those behaviors. If their sons choose to ignore the performance of traditionally female behaviors by the male model, in favor of more restrictive inter-pretations of appropriateness, modeling theory is dealt a major blow. As you might expect, little evidence has been gathered concerning the influence of the father's participation in housework and diaper changing. Some theorists speculate that men who do perform these duties are forced to hide the fact from the general public or be treated as turncoats. But one recent study was able to gather data from fathers who claimed to share a portion of the daily domestic responsibility and to estimate the impact on children's imitations. The author concluded that "paternal participation in child-caring activities and household tasks contributes independently to reductions in children's stereotyping of the functional and behavioral aspects of the father role."[10] This reduction certainly provides support for modeling theory, although, since all the families studied were dual-career families, it is difficult to be sure of the impact of the mother's behavior on these sons.

Obviously, studies have attempted to depict the influence of parental models on children's portrayal of male and female activities and on children's sex stereotypes. Less information has been gathered concerning the extent to which children actively model specific communication behaviors after same-sex parents. Perhaps children are not skilled enough at subtle verbal and nonverbal communicative acts to accomplish observable imitations. But it stands to reason that children may notice these differences, even if they cannot imitate them. So, to the extent that mothers and fathers do communicate differently, and there is reason to believe that they do, children may learn different lessons about effective communication from parental models.

While the logic of modeling theory seems sound and is largely consistent with our understanding of our own upbringings, critics have pointed out several problems. To begin with, a child's imitation of adult behavior is often laughably unlike the model's and, from a research standpoint, difficult to measure. For example, my little girls thoroughly enjoy the childhood version of washing dishes, complete with suds and splashing. But their pleasure is probably grounded more in the dynamics of the play than in same-sex modeling. From a research standpoint, then, it would be difficult to say that this imitation was anticipatory of adult behavior.

Also, many studies intended to measure the effect of same-sex parental modeling have been survey or interview studies in which parents list or discuss activities and/or opinions and their responses are compared with children's responses. Usually fathers' responses are tabulated and compared with mothers' responses, and sons' responses are tabulated and compared with daughters' responses. Thus, sex-specific results are presented as indicative of modeling: fathers like sports and sons like sports; mothers are afraid of snakes and daughters are afraid of snakes. However, unless specific pairs of fathers and sons and mothers and daughters are examined, studies of this type can hardly attribute similarities to parental modeling. They seem to indicate either cultural trends or innate sex differences. In point of fact, studies of this type may ultimately fail to identify same-sex modeling when it has occurred. What if, for example, Father A likes sports and Son A also likes sports, but Father B and son B both dislike sports? Two cases that provide evidence supporting same-sex parental modeling would cancel one another out in the overall father–son comparison. So, as critics have noted, results of survey studies must be carefully considered.[11]

Those studies that have searched for specific correlations within families have proven disappointing to proponents of modeling theory. Put simply, the results indicate that parents and their children do not seem to be especially similar. Many comparative studies have been conducted among college students, which may be problematic in itself, since college-age students may be well past the time when same-sex parental identification is actively sought or desirable to report. The similarities that have been found are on issues involving values, which are probably shared within the entire family and/or the culture and are not likely to be the result of same-sex modeling.[12]

Other questions abound, such as why brothers differ with regard to visible signs of masculinity or sisters differ with regard to feminine displays. It appears that, within a single family, some children take advantage of their same-sex models and some do not. Apparently, birth order, number of siblings, and sex of siblings must be considered in estimating the influence of parental models. Nevertheless, most of us believe in our potential to influence our children, not only by providing a clear, coherent system of rewards and punishments, but by serving as good models.

OTHER ADULT MODELS

Despite the assumed influence of parental modeling in the American lifestyle, it is important to acknowledge that children are exposed to a great number of adult models, some in face-to-face interaction and some in mediated form. These two groups of adults will be discussed separately, although it is important to stress that today's children often come in contact with nonfamily adult models, both "real" and mediated, at a very young age, so it may be difficult to speculate as to which models are most influential in the communication of gender appropriateness.

A growing number of American children are spending time in the company of parent substitutes while their mothers work. A recent Department of Labor survey indicates that "increases in maternal employment have been greatest among women who previously had very low rates of employment, that is, among mothers with very young children."[13] It follows that some sort of day care must be arranged for the children of these working mothers and that the providers of day care serve as available, powerful, and nurturant models—just the combination that modeling theorists tell us are likely to be selected for imitation.

It would be a mistake to assume that all mothers who surrender day care of their children to a substitute make a deliberate choice to trade their parental role in favor of a career role. In fact, a growing number of mothers are single parents whose financial needs are obvious; others are compelled to work due to economic conditions that threaten the survival of a one-wage family. But a portion of mothers have deliberately and willingly chosen to pursue both family and work without temporary leave from either. This condition is actually chosen less often than you might think, but it has been talked about and written about at length, probably because it is regarded as a future trend—variously treated as a negative and as a positive effect of the feminist movement.[14]

All of this is fascinating in and of itself, but the important point here is that child care is still considered to be the female's responsibility, whether she works or not. So, it is not surprising that most preschool day care is provided by females, either relatives or nonrelatives, either in the child's home or the caregiver's home.[15] Apparently, the philosophy concerning day care in this country is that it ought to be as similar as possible to the care that the child would receive at home from his or her mother. Our child-care policies demonstrate, in part, our confidence in the theory of modeling. We want our children to be cared for in substitute homes, with female providers, while mothers work. Many baby-sitters care for groups of children, so we take added pleasure that our preschoolers have substitute siblings.

In fact, 75% of preschool day care takes place in private homes. The remaining children are cared for in centers specifically intended to promote employment among economically disadvantaged women (often single parents) or in centers specifically intended to make a profit from the economically advantaged.[16] Presumably, the models encountered by children in such centers would vary considerably. Given the recent growth in the day-care industry, it seems likely that even men might seek employment as caretakers. But preschool instruction is a career that continues to be dominated by women, so the rich and the poor alike are still exposed to adult female models during much of the day. Even after work, according to most experts, the majority of child care is conducted by females, be they single mothers or career mothers.[17]

Given this condition, modeling theory need not be reconstructed to consider the influence of substitute models on preschool children. Naturally, girls might encounter some confusion to the extent that the substitute's behavior counters the mother's behavior. But, since most child care is conducted by agents culturally similar to the mother (often from the same family!) this seems unlikely. In the main, learning gender-appropriate behavior from the available adult model is likely to be continuous and unproblematic for girls, but confusing and difficult for boys, regardless of family employment status.

Children of both sexes encounter additional adult models when they reach the age of mandatory formal education. The fact that females continue to dominate the ranks of elementary education was discussed in Chapter Nine. As noted there, children may encounter adult male models in school, but not nearly as often as adult female models. However, often the principal of the school, the ultimate symbol of authority, is male. Modeling theorists speculate that the principal provides much the same kind of model as the traditional father. He is not as available as the female model and probably not as nurturant, although he is very powerful, as his title suggests. Consider the child's perception of the principal of the school. He is seldom seen for more than a moment except on special occasions, including celebrations and disciplinary emergencies, and, when seen, he is visibly the ultimate source of authority over the teachers as well as the students.

Certainly, affirmative action has helped to make it easier for women to become school administrators, although the numbers are still surprisingly low. Most female principals that are hired are at the elementary level, so they provide a model of female authority, but also contribute to the dominance of the female model in the child's life. Conversely, few males have seized the opportunity to break into the female-dominated world of elementary school teaching.[18] So, it is not surprising that "the school environment tends to support stereotyped sex roles,"[19] in part by providing models consistent with the traditional parental models.

MEDIATED MODELS

The influence of the media, particularly television, on children's lives has been well-researched over the last few decades.[20] Social learning theorists are interested in the impact that mediated models have on children's images of masculinity and femininity. Mediated models are certainly available models for children, especially preschool children, given the number of hours they spend being entertained by television, books, and movies. The research suggests that young children encounter sex-typed models in all these genre, a trend that continues as they grow into adolescence and develop an interest in magazines and newspapers.

The prevalence of television models in children's lives is well documented, both in scholarly literature and in casual conversation. Teachers and parents often complain that children are "glued" to the television, and experts generally agree that the average child watches about twenty-five to thirty hours of television per week.[21] The content of these hours varies from child to child, but many studies suggest that most children are exposed to a rather predictable and narrow set of gender models.[22]

It takes only a few hours of Saturday morning viewing to notice that children's programming contains many stereotypic male and female characters. Coincidentally, children's television is becoming more and more closely tied to the commercial toy industry, so children can watch their favorite sex-typed characters, as well as imitate them during playtime. Many shows are referred to by critics as "program-length commercials." The popularity of the "He-Man" television series, according to one source, coincided with a $1 billion sales year for related toy products.[23]

Other popular children's shows and toy lines in the 1985–86 season were "G.I. Joe," "Thundercats," and "Transformers."[24] It would be an understatement to say that both children's cartoons and children's toys continue to have a macho flavor. With the exception of "She-Ra," (a show which resembles "He-Man" in every way except for the obvious curves on the protagonist), children's cartoons continue to feature male characters. These characters continue to conquer evil forces and environmental emergencies, just as Superman did in decades past. The new heroes are rational, competent, and straightforward in their communication style. With a miniature He-Man doll in hand, it is not difficult to imagine how a three-year-old boy will behave. The close link between television and children's toys only magnifies the effect on male children.

Little girls often admire the adventurous and powerful Saturday morning heroes too. The emergence of "She-Ra" undoubtedly sent a message to girls that they could share in the fight against evil, while coincidentally doubling the size of the toy market. But She-Ra's female companions fight evil in remarkably feminine ways. Imagine the tactics used by slim, nonmuscular, nonweaponed characters named Perfuma, Flutterina, and Angelica. It is difficult to render such characters especially powerful. Even the powerful and highly competent She-Ra, before her magical transformation, has a distinctively feminine behavioral style. As She-Ra, though, she assumes a low-pitched voice and traditionally male postures and gestures. Also, her sentences become shorter and her remarks wittier. Thus, while the message is clear that girls can be powerful, it is interesting to note how they display power behaviorally.

For children who tire of heroes and heroines, there are less violent scenarios. One popular show features the Smurfs, an energetic band of little blue creatures, all of whom are male except one. The Smurfs are labeled according to behavioral or dispositional characteristics (much like the Seven Dwarfs): Grouchy, Greedy, Brainy, etc. But the female Smurf is simply identified as Smurfette, which is akin to calling the only girl in a family of boys "Childette." Remarkably, the only parental figure in the tribe is Papa Smurf. For those wondering how little Smurfs are made in the absence of a mother, make a note that a new Baby Smurf (another boy) recently arrived via a stork!

Other shows are apparently intended just for female audiences: "My Little Pony," for example, has a female protagonist, Megan, who both aids and receives aid from mostly female ponies. They are pastel colored and speak in high-pitched, childlike voices. Other characters include Megan's younger sister and brother, and the magical (male) consultant who provides most of the solutions to the problems they encounter. Ladylovely Locks is another female character little girls favor. As the name suggests, she has long, beautiful blond hair and is dressed in full-length, fairy-like clothing. She solves most of her problems (posed by the brunette Duchess Ravenwaves) using goodness and always forgives and forgets.

These isolated examples serve to demonstrate new versions of an established trend in children's cartoons. To begin with, male characters continue to dominate children's programming. Even on public broadcasting shows, specifically designed to be free of stereotypes, male characters appear twice as often as female characters.[25] When females do appear, they are likely to be portrayed as emotionally expressive and not especially powerful. As one source summarizes, "cartoon females are less active than males, complain a lot, and hold fewer positions of responsibility."[26]

Although it is becoming increasingly difficult to separate the commercials from the features in children's television, studies have also focused specifically on sex typing in commercials. The advertisements usually promote toys and food products that appeal to children. You may be surprised to know that the ratio of commercial time to program time tends to be unusually high during children's shows, because children, for some reason, tend to enjoy commercials. Based on the sheer number of commercials and on studies suggesting that young children are very easily persuaded by commercial advertising,[27] a group of Massachusetts mothers formed a group called

ACT (Action for Children's Television). They began a national crusade against all advertising during children's programs, but, over the course of years it has become clear that programming for children just isn't a priority unless product sales are enhanced.[28]

So, commercial advertisements continue to interrupt children's television viewing at an unusually high rate. Both adult and peer models in these brief, highly entertaining messages tend to be sex-typed.[29] Little boys are shown playing with trucks; little girls are shown playing with dolls. Little children who are shown enjoying food products tend to be dressed sex specifically and, as expected, boys are pictured as more independent than girls. When an adult woman appears in children's commercials, she is usually shown in these commercials happily fulfilling the role of wife and mother.[30] In one recent commercial, an apparent attempt to break this trend obviously fails when a working mother tells her friends, "I just told my boss I couldn't miss another one of my daughter's games." But the audience never sees the female child playing the game, nor the mother at work. Instead the mothers proceed to debate the merits of various peanut butter products. In other commercials, little boys push toy lawn mowers as their Dads push real ones. Commercials for boys' toys often feature adult men in sex-typed occupations: athletes, soldiers, heavy machine operators. Toys intended for girls feature little girls helping their smiling, appreciative mothers.

Of course, research has suggested that commercials, in the main, tend to portray men and women in traditional settings, engaged in sex-appropriate activities, dressed in sex-specific attire.[31] So children are exposed to stereotypic models no matter what type of programming they watch. However, commercials during children's programs are likely to be as exaggerated in this regard as the feature programs.

Overall, it seems clear that characters seen in children's programs and in accompanying commercials are likely to look stereotypically male and female. In one of the few studies that has focused on communication behavior, it was also demonstrated that television models are likely to speak in exaggerated versions of the male and female tendencies described in Part Two of this text. After examining transcripts of shows from public television, Saturday morning television, and children's commercials, Mulac et al. reported that "gender-linked differences [in communication] for television characters were on the average 200% greater than corresponding differences for real-world communicators." Specifically, male characters portrayed more "dynamism" via action verbs, present tense verbs, and, yes, grammatical errors. Female characters were rated higher on dimensions of "socio-intellectual status" and "aesthetics," based on predictable linguistic habits: longer sentences, more verbs indicating uncertainty, more polite words, and more evaluative adjectives.[32]

It appears that children can easily find available sex-typed models on television. The programs designed for children are riddled with exaggerated versions of cultural definitions of masculinity or femininity. Other daytime shows that children and/or adolescents may view, most notably soap operas, have also been demonstrated to be remarkably sex-typed, despite the proclaimed changes in women's lives. Women are often labeled doctors, lawyers, and CEOs of large corporations. However, they are usually shown discussing personal matters across their desks and, unlike male characters, are seldom shown competently handling their work.[33] Even more disturbing, women on daytime television are far more likely to be portrayed as victims of illness, crime, mental problems, and loneliness.[34]

Although children are less likely to watch nighttime drama than daytime drama, the prevalence of reruns during the family viewing hour indicates that young children may also be influenced by prime time models. If so, a study by Peevers is highly pertinent here, since it suggests that prime-time male characters are far too "super masculine" to be credible to adult viewers.[35] Perhaps youngsters gathering information about gender appropriateness do not arrive at the same conclusion, but, rather, see the characters as cultural images of masculinity. This could explain why little boys tend to be considerably more macho than most real-life models.

Conversely, what models do girls encounter on prime-time television? A number of analysts have criticized that women are not only underrepresented in prime-time drama, but portrayed as youthful, low status, and dependent on male heroes[36]—an extension of the tradition in which Lois Lane pales in comparison to her Superman. But some critics report that prime-time portrayals of women have improved, such that, at least occasionally, children may view a "mature, financially independent, career woman" on television.[37] In addition, Peevers' data suggests that female television characters are judged to be "within the limits attainable by real people." Adult viewers rate women on television as "diverse, flexible and human."[38] Perhaps the female models children see during prime time, even though they may be subordinate to male characters, are consistent with, or at least not contradictory to, the same-sex parental model. If so, modeling is facilitated for little girls.

Children who turn to books for entertainment are also likely to encounter sex typing, according to most analysts.[39] Although the last decade has seen tremendous pressure for publishers to neutralize children's books, male characters continue to dominate as protagonists, even in award-winning picture books intended for preschoolers.[40] Mothers continue to appear in the home and are usually in dresses; the same is usually true of their daughters. Doctors and policemen continue to be male, whether pictured or referred to by name. As one author points out, children expect to see sex typing in books and notice "mistakes." Also, boys tend to reject stories with female protagonists, but girls are liberal in their acceptance of male protagonists.[41] As with toys, it is difficult to be sure which comes first: the product or the child's desire for the product. But when the product is an instance of children's literature, it is likely to present models that reinforce a young child's already rigid sex-role stereotypes.

As children move from childhood to adolescence, new types of mediated models are introduced via periodical literature, i.e., magazines and newspapers. Extensive research has been conducted concerning the sex typing of models (a term used appropriately here in both a social learning and a Madison Avenue sense). To begin with, magazines intended for sale to adolescents (the popular term is *teen*) tend to be sex specific. Cheris Kramarae reports that leading magazines for teens emphasize "how to" articles, but that the topics vary predictably with the gender of the anticipated reader. Male teens learn "how to" improve their mechanical skills and be successful in sports, while female teens learn "how to" improve their appearance and be successful in relationships. Celebrity models featured in these magazines are also predictably sex specific.[42]

Even more telling than the content of the features in teen magazines, is the content of the advertisements (which tend to take up far more space in most magazines). Jean Umiker-Sebeok has compiled an impressive survey of gender displays in print advertising across what she calls "The Seven Ages of Woman." She points out that "as soon as children are old enough to be considered toddlers...sex distinctions become an important part of the way they are represented" in magazine advertisements. Female children are pictured as small, weak, and passive; male children are shown as adventurous, strong, and competent. Very young children of both sexes are likely to be shown in the safety of the home, but, as they grow older, male models move outside and are often pictured in groups, while female models are still photographed inside with their mothers.[43]

Umiker-Sebeok notes that sex stereotyping of children in American magazines is both cause and effect of the prevailing cultural tendency to see children as boys or girls, not just children. The differences become even more pronounced as they move into adolescence. Advertisements appearing in male magazines feature young men displaying strength and competence in all aspects of life.[44] In a sense, the models mature in line with the assumed maturation of the audience.

However, this trend is not completely true of female models, who are often portrayed as demure and childish, apparently en route to becoming alluring. In some cases, obviously maturing bodies are pictured hugging teddy bears, swinging on swings, or licking ice cream cones in pursuit of cosmetics sales. The trick is to look as soft, pure, and natural as a baby. Also, women's product advertising often articulates a desire to remain private—to keep "beauty secrets"—so young girls continue to be photographed in safe environments.[45]

When young models are photographed outdoors, male models are likely to be doing something—playing ball or fixing something. But young girls just seem to be there, smiling or walking briskly in the midst of the hustle-bustle of life on a busy city street. One analyst, who analyzed 364 contemporary magazine advertisements and compared the results with a similar sample obtained in a 1971 study, reported that "there has been a resurgence of women being portrayed in decorative roles, which is antithetical to the development of an egalitarian society."[46]

Depictions of adults in print advertising also provide sex-stereotypic mediated models. Adult businesswomen may assume male surroundings and display isolated male gestures, but they are usually alone in their offices (which are full of plants and decorative objects) or on street corners or planes gazing into space apparently missing their loved ones. More commonly, women are pictured with children, either in the home or in some consumer marketplace. Men are far more likely to be shown in the midst of work, whether recreational or occupational.[47] In addition, the products these men and women endorse provide subtle messages about the predominant cultural images of adult masculinity and femininity. Women endorse household products, food products, and beauty aids, even as they rush off in their three-piece suits. Male images continue to dominate advertisements for investment firms, insurance companies, car manufacturers, and vendors of other "big ticket" items.[48]

The fact that certain magazines are aimed at particular segments of the population suggests an interaction between sex segregation of activities and interests and advertising practices. In one recent study, sex stereotyping was shown to be more exaggerated in men's magazines (e.g., *Esquire, Sports Illustrated, Field and Stream*) and women's magazines (e.g., *Redbook, House Beautiful, Cosmopolitan*) than in general interest magazines (*Time, Reader's Digest,* and *The New Yorker*).[49] Granted, this is not surprising, since it is only natural for advertisers to adapt messages to predicted audiences. If a magazine is known to have predominantly male readers, why not promote male products in the traditional manly style? It's simply good business.

As one scholar notes, advertising is basically a conservative social force. To succeed, advertisements must be "tied to the prevailing ideology of the culture." But, people also look to advertisements to present new images, not just echo old ones.[50] So, gender must be displayed, within limits, as it is understood to prevail in the culture, i.e., stereotypically. But, it is interesting to wonder how readers, particularly children and adolescents, susceptible to new information about gender, view the models in print advertisements. To the extent that they are recognized as exaggerated and narrow, the only danger may be that of offending the reader. But to the extent that they are thought to be real or even ideal, they may provide dangerously rigid images of gender appropriateness.

Generally, children are exposed to newspaper models well after they have begun to model adult images of masculinity and femininity. But many American children notice a special part of the newspaper even before they can read—the "funny pages"—a brightly colored, picture-filled and highly sex-stereotyped addition to the Sunday paper. Even very recent content analyses demonstrate that characters in comic strips tend to be very rigidly in line with traditional images. To begin with, males dominate in terms of the number of characters portrayed in the comics. When they do appear, female characters are shown inside the home, while male characters are shown outside the home. Indeed, the classic picture of a female in an apron continues to appear, although less so than it did in previous decades. In any case, men do not commonly appear doing housework or caring for children, much less clad in an apron. If they do, this situation is likely to be the butt of the joke.[51]

Even in the news sections—the daily, and supposedly objective, reporting of the factual world—children are exposed to sexist practices. To begin with, news writing has been particularly resistant to gender-neutral pronoun structures, like "he or she." It seems that the extra words offend those who count words. According to a 1985 survey of 120 newspapers and magazines, only about ten of the editors have accepted this style without reservation. Most prefer to use the generic *he*, although they philosophically recognize the limitation, or instruct writers to restructure sentences which present "the problem."[52] As a result, it is possible that news about any unidentified individual is perceived as news about a male individual.

In fact, men are discussed in newspapers far more often than women, except in gossip and advice columns and in the "lifestyle" section.[53] When they do appear, descriptions of women are distinct from descriptions of men; women's descriptions tend to include personal information about their appearance and their marital status.[54] Of course, the conservative voice might argue that women are just not newsworthy. News tends to be about public figures, and women are only recently gaining ground in public affairs. Yet, when a female was included on the 1984 presidential ticket, she was presented quite differently by the press than her male counterparts.

Specifically, the press emphasized the dilemma surrounding the title of respect to be used in referencing Geraldine Ferraro, a married woman who did not take her husband's name. She was referred to as "Miss Ferraro," an obvious error; as "Ms. Ferraro," a feminist statement and a nonstandard style for many newspapers; and as "Mrs. Ferraro" and "Mrs. Zaccaro," both of which stress her marital status, which male titles of respect do not. Stories about Ferraro often included the predictable references to her appearance, including what she wore, not only in terms of style, but size.[55] The same sorts of descriptions tend to accompany stories about first ladies and princesses, but would be laughable in reference to male politicians.

When special female labels were used to refer to Ferraro, the press found it newsworthy. Barbara Bush referred to her as the "$4 million...I can't say it, but it rhymes with rich." This prompted an exaggerated version of the "cat fight" between the two women—clearly not "hard news," but consistent with the prevailing mythology about femininity in America. Other stories about Ferraro stressed that she was "different" from the other candidates. Discussions of her stability in relation to hormonal activity and of her attitude about integrating family and work demonstrated the culture's attitude toward women in politics. One reporter sent her roses to apologize for misquoting her, and included a card that said, "Has anyone ever told you that you are cute when you're mad?"[56]

Again, it may be argued that the news reflects society rather than shapes it, but the influence of mediated models is still powerful. It seems that today's children may find all sorts of mediated models very available, very consistent, and not particularly contradictory to traditional images of men and women.

CONDUCT YOUR OWN RESEARCH

1. Watch five television shows designed especially for children, making notes about each character and paying special attention to the images of masculinity and femininity. Summarize and explain the findings.

2. Repeat the exercise above, making notes about the commercial advertisements accompanying the same five shows.

3. Interview ten children, preferably five of each sex, inquiring about the names and descriptions of their heroes. Describe the trends, noting sex differences in the children's choices and the degree of sex typing apparent in the choices.

D I S C U S S   T H E   I S S U E S

1. What kind of model would you hope to be to a male or female child in your life? Does the model change with the sex of the child? Is it harder for you to imagine yourself as a model for a child of the opposite sex?

2. In small groups, decide on the top ten individuals in each of the following categories: male movie stars, female movie stars, male television stars, female television stars, male athletes, female athletes. What kinds of models have you chosen as male and female "heroes"?

3. Which television commercials do you find most sexist? Is there a relationship between the depiction of masculinity and femininity and the product? the presumed audience? Why does commercial advertising often seem to lag behind social change in terms of gender appropriateness?

CHAPTER 11

EXPLANATIONS BASED ON COGNITIVE FACTORS

Obviously, there is a logical opposition between theories that explain sex differences as biologically innate and theories that explain sex differences as culturally transmitted. In reaction to the ongoing heredity vs. environment debate, Lawrence Kohlberg has proposed that sex-role learning undoubtedly involves an interaction between innate and cultural factors, but that the relative influence of these factors in the development of sex-specific behavior is not conceptually significant. Therefore, cognitive theorists have stressed "the child's cognitive organization of his social world along sex-role dimensions."[1]

COGNITIVE DEVELOPMENT

Lawrence Kohlberg is identified with cognitive developmental theory nearly as closely as Freud is identified with psychosexual theory. Kohlberg argues, as Freud did, that universal cross-cultural patterns surround the development of sex-appropriate behavior. Also like Freud, Kohlberg contends that the child passes through developmental stages en route to developing into a normal sexual adult. But, Kohlberg also recognizes that the child passes through these stages in a complex social world, full of messages about being male or female. The child's cognitive organization of these messages is Kohlberg's primary interest, and the stages he proposes are defined by the child's level of cognitive ability, not by the child's sexual instincts.[2]

Like social-learning theorists, Kohlberg recognizes that children are dependent on observable cultural patterns of adult behavior as they search for information about sex appropriateness. However, in the midst of cultural differences in the content of sex roles, Kohlberg stresses that children everywhere seem to pass through predictable cognitive stages, and that, across cultures, children's attitudes about sex roles change radically with age.[3] These two facts lead Kohlberg to reject a strict social-learning explanation.

Cognitive developmental analysis borrows from the work of Piaget, who is renowned for his developmental theory of children's perceptions of the physical world.[4] Kohlberg adapts Piaget's model to children's perceptions of the social world—a world in which sexual identification seems to be integral to the development of self-perception.[5] The theory of cognitive development emphasizes the child's point of view, as an active participant in his or her own sex-role learning. The focus is on how children seek and organize information about sexual identity within the larger process of seeking a stable and positive self-image.

It may seem unnatural to approach the development of sex differences from the point of view of the student (i.e., the child) since it is inconsistent with the widely held belief that childhood behaviors are shaped by parents and other societal agents. In cognitive developmental analysis, adult models are important, but the child generates his or her own motives, values, and activities with regard to gender learning. Therefore, Kohlberg's analysis proceeds on a chronological basis from the child's point of view.

Gender Identity. Kohlberg believes that children participate in self-socialization, based on their initial cognitive self-categorization according to gender. In early childhood language, this undoubtedly means learning that "I am a boy" or "I am a girl." These words represent nothing more than arbitrary abstract categories, however, at the early age when children first learn them. Kohlberg concludes, based on interview data, that this verbal lesson is learned sometime in the second half of the second year of life. He cites evidence that the majority of two-and-one-half-year-olds do not answer correctly when asked "Are you a little girl or a little boy?"[6] But, the exact age at which children exhibit certain behaviors is less important to cognitive developmentalists than the sequence in which they exhibit the behaviors. So, suffice it to say that children learn to label themselves, in the gender language of their culture, correctly and relatively consistently, during the first three years.

Labeling things correctly is perhaps the most important activity for children aged two to three. One scholar calls this "the name game," and notes that children and adults alike seem to enjoy seeing the child master early semantic relationships.[7] But, as proficient as two-year-olds may be at the name game, they make characteristic mistakes, like calling all dogs by the name of a familiar dog or calling all animals by the name of a familiar animal, such as *dog*. These mistakes help to demonstrate the rudimentary nature of the two-year-old's categorization scheme. Similarly, a child may know that he is a boy or she is a girl but probably does not know the qualities by which the label is discerned, nor the mutual exclusion rule that governs sexual categorization. They are simply not cognitively developed enough to learn these lessons.

According to Kohlberg, children soon learn to apply gender labels to others they encounter on a daily basis—parents, siblings, even pets. It is amusing that the child usually strives for consistency, at first labeling everyone in the immediate environment according to his or her own gender name. In my family, the only man is my husband and, to his dismay, two of our daughters have each taken a turn at announcing "I am a girl. Mommy is a girl. Daddy is a girl." etc., etc. Recently, my two-year-old daughter (now well schooled that Daddy is not a girl) was listing the other children at her baby-sitter's, who are predominantly boys. I was interested to see her mistakenly label two little girls, Julie and Jessica, as boys, but correctly label herself and another little girl who just happens to share her name, "the other" Amanda. Obviously, children actively seek consistency in applying labels, but, as these examples point out, it is a consistency generated, not by adult example or reinforcement, but by the child's own logic.

The child soon develops a set of criteria for classifying people according to gender; Kohlberg estimates this is intact by age four.[8] Children usually determine gender based on simple physical characteristics, such as length and style of hair and type of clothing. They demonstrate remarkable consistency in applying the criteria, as evidenced by my daughter's reaction to a man whose hair length violated her categorization system: "Mommy, why does that lady have a mustache?" Again, the comical mistakes children make provide insight into the logic they use—consistently but incorrectly—to classify various individuals as male and female. Clearly, the rudiments of my daughter's category system had been derived from adult models, i.e., most of those she knows to be men have shorter hair than the individual she saw, and most of those she knows to be women have no facial hair. But it is equally obvious that no adult model or reinforcing agent could have assisted her in reasoning through her response to the long-haired, mustached individual.

Thus, it appears that the average child learns, in a predictable sequence, to apply gender labels to himself or herself, then to significant others, and finally to strangers. But, Kohlberg's cognitive developmental analysis of sex-role learning reaches far beyond the evolution of the child's gender labeling, which, he says, is little more than another instance of Piaget's description of "the child's ability to classify a physical object, the body."[9] Children attach considerable significance to lessons about being male and being female, and these lessons are closely tied to the development of adult "normalcy." Of crucial importance is the understanding that gender is constant and irreversible.

Gender Constancy.   Gender constancy refers to the child's realization that gender classifications are unchanging. Children have to learn that certain classifications disappear with time (i.e., kids grow up to be adults) and certain classifications disappear because of an individual choice (i.e., when I grow up I want to be a particular thing), but that others are unchanging. As adults, we often take the distinctions for granted; it seems silly to believe that we "learned" that gender classifications are irreversible (notwithstanding the wonders of modern science). But, prior to a certain stage of cognitive development, children tend to regard gender as a classification that can be changed. I remember asking my middle child (then aged two-and-one-half) the proverbial question, "What do you want to be when you grow up," to which she thoughtfully answered "a Ryan" (one of her male agemates).

According to Kohlberg's interviews with children, my daughter's response was typical. Prior to age five, most of the children he interviewed responded "yes" when asked if a hypothetical individual could change to the other sex under certain circumstances, specifically, "if he/she wanted to; if he/she played girl/boy games; if he/she wore a girl's/boy's haircut and clothes."[10] Apparently, very young children see sexual assignment as a behavioral achievement—something that can be changed if crucial behaviors are altered.

The realization that sexual assignment as male or female is permanent has been cited by developmental theorists as integral to normal adult sexuality. Kohlberg speculates that "sexual psychopathology" is linked to the failure to understand gender constancy early in life. He finds support for this contention in studies of individuals with ambiguous physical characteristics (i.e., chromosomal and/or hormonal irregularities, some of which were described in Chapter Eight). For example, studies by Money and Hampson indicate that individuals who are sexually reassigned develop normal sexual identities provided the reassignment is complete prior to the age at which children understand gender constancy. After that cognitive stage, Money and Hampson note that sexual psychopathologies are typical.[11]

Thus, Kohlberg reasons that the clinical data concerning sexual psychopathologies, combined with interview data gathered from children at various stages of cognitive development, provide strong support for the contention that the understanding of gender as constant (by a predictable age) is a crucial aspect of the larger process that motivates the child's search for information: the development of the self-concept. Unlike social-learning theorists, who propose that children learn to value gender-appropriate behavior because it yields more rewards and fewer punishments, cognitive developmentalists propose that children value gender-appropriate behavior because (and when) they realize that being male or female is an integral and irreversible aspect of their being.

Gender Valuing. Another important aspect of Kohlberg's cognitive theory lies in his contention that each child "spontaneously" evaluates the world, in conjunction with an ongoing effort to ascribe worth to himself or herself. In this view, children are not the passive recipients of parental values concerning men and women, via reinforcement or modeling. Children are thought to define *worth* in conjunction with a sex-typed social order, but, as Kohlberg points out, children seem to develop standards of self-worth and others' worth according to their own unique view of the world—a highly egocentric world to be sure.[12]

Kohlberg attempts to delineate mechanisms by which the child reasons gender values. In other words, he attempts to recreate the connections made by the child, from the child's viewpoint, as he or she actively seeks information about being male or female, since this information is assumed to be integral to the development of self-worth. These mechanisms are proposed to explain empirical evidence that reflects radical changes in children's perceptions of gender—changes that social learning theorists have been unable to explain, according to Kohlberg. Some of the child's reasoning mechanisms are described below:

1. The child tends to seek consistency, so he or she creates simple categories for information and then evaluates new information according to those categories (two of which are *boy* and *girl*).
2. The child tends to value anything believed to be consistent with himself or herself.
3. The child tends to attribute positive characteristics like prestige, competence, and goodness to sex-role stereotypes.
4. The child tends to value conformity to sex-role stereotypes as "moral."[13]

Taken together, these tendencies suggest that same-sex modeling, both of adults and peers, is a logical outcome of the child's cognitive processes. But, it is important to remember that children actively select and organize information from a number of others; they do not simply imitate the most available, nurturant, and powerful models. This is important because Kohlberg stresses that the child's information gathering is not a neutral activity; it is largely motivated by spontaneous evaluation of self and others in comparison. In a sense, the child is looking for gender-specific information because he or she wants to use it to increase his or her own self-worth. To the extent that parental models provide useful information, the child's search is facilitated, but there is no guarantee that the child will choose to model the same-sex parent.

Through their focus on the child's own motivations and interpretations, cognitive developmentalists have been able to explain some empirical evidence that is inconsistent with social-learning assumptions. As Maccoby and Jacklin report, after reviewing a number of studies intended to demonstrate modeling theory, "masculine and feminine behavior [in childhood] is a qualitatively very different thing from masculinity and femininity in adulthood...the model's behavior has been filtered through childish eyes and the imitative actions are a function of a childish body and a childish level of behavior organization."[14]

According to the mechanisms integral to the theory of cognitive development, not only is the behavior "filtered," but it is selectively chosen in conjunction with what the child knows about himself or herself and schematized to promote consistency with information already held by the child. Therefore, while we might be tempted to see the child's imitation as incomplete or naive, cognitive theory suggests that it is different in predictable ways because of the child's decided purpose. The child may exaggerate or add detail to observed behavior to emphasize sex-role stereotypes because of the logic he or she uses: "I am a man; men are good; I want to act as manly as possible."

Using this logic, cognitive developmentalists have been able to explain why young children tend to demonstrate exaggerated, rigid sex stereotypes in early childhood, which diminish with age. This is apparently true across cultures and environmental situations. Remember that recent studies show that, even in homes with androgynous models and reinforcing agents, young children tend to make arbitrary choices based on an exaggerated view of the genders as traditional opposites.[15] Later, children seem to develop a sense of social awareness that suggests greater freedom and flexibility concerning gender issues.[16]

Given that the child is believed to generate his or her own gender values, it might seem that Kohlberg and his followers ignore societal values concerning sex appropriateness. Whether boy or girl, the child will value his or her own sex-role stereotype, even though society may value one over the other. In fact, Kohlberg recognizes that mechanism #4 on his list eventually carries different implications for boys and girls. He asserts that, for three-to-five-year-olds, "it seems quite reasonable to attribute same-sex preferences...to the child's tendency toward self-projective and identity-maintaining evaluations." However, his interviews with five-to-eight-year-olds indicate an "age-developmental increase in the award of power and competence to the adult male role." It comes as no surprise, therefore, that girls in this age group also "make fewer judgments than boys that their own sex is better..."[17]

As mentioned, the trend toward tomboyism is well established, while the sexual inverse is sure to rock parents and children alike.[18] A boy who would rather play house than baseball? A boy who aspires to be a nurse or a secretary? You may recall reading in Chapter Two that adolescent girls are more likely to project nontraditional career choices than adolescent boys, although younger children of both sexes tend to see themselves "growing up to be" traditional choices. This contrast also supports Kohlberg's contention that, as girls age, they encounter societal messages that contradict early childhood messages that "girls are better." The messages boys receive as they age provide continuous support for their established gender values.

Kohlberg assures us, though, that these societal messages "do not make girls want to give up their own gender identity." He speculates that "adult female stereotypes are positive enough to make femininity attractive to young girls, even though adult females are perceived as less powerful and competent than males." Thus, mechanism #4 involves, for both sexes, associating positive characteristics with their own sex role, but the task is somewhat more challenging for girls. Kohlberg concludes that girls learn to value their "niceness," which is embodied in their lack of aggressive behavior, their "superior attractiveness in the areas of physical beauty, concern with the aesthetic-ornamental in non-body areas, and interpersonal and sexual charm."[19]

Thus, according to cognitive development, the female child's continued effort to promote her self-worth is, at least in part, learning to value those aspects of the adult feminine stereotype that are considered favorable, although she cannot help but acknowledge that adult males are recognized as more powerful and competent. Notably, this creates a difficult, ambivalent situation for girls as their cognitive development allows them to move beyond their egocentric view of the world and see the bigger picture. Boys, in contrast, are unlikely to suffer ambivalence concerning the positive aspects of the adult male role, although the pressure to measure up may emerge as a side-effect of cognitive movement away from the egocentric.

It is interesting to note that, according to the cognitive developmental approach, gender learning is somewhat easier for boys than for girls, due to the coincidence of societal and self-conceptualizations. Kohlberg discounts the influence of female child care in the male experience—a fact that social learning theorists treat as problematic. In fact, using empirical evidence gathered across a variety of familial situations, Kohlberg demonstrates the minimal influence of the same-sex parent's availability on gender learning: "While identification with a like-sex person, and the formation of sex-role values in general, may be facilitated and consolidated by appropriate parental behavior, this process seems to take place without the presence of the same-sex parent, and under a variety of child-rearing conditions."[20]

Obviously, the cognitive developmental approach threatens our assumption that parents are all-powerful figures in children's development. Kohlberg assumes that "basic universal sex-role stereotypes develop" in conjunction with the child's view of his world—a world in which observable body differences are "supported by visible differences in sex assignment of social roles."[21] As children develop a sense of who they are, they seek to value that conceptualization, in large part a gender-specific conceptualization. So, boys and girls alike search for, imitate, and value the positive aspects of masculinity and femininity.

In this way, Kohlberg and his followers imply that the perpetuation of observable sex differences in behavior is motivated from within the child, by his or her own gender valuing. It seems that the theory leaves room for social change, but it is difficult to imagine how societal values are expected to change when new members naturally strive for consistency with accepted standards.

RELATIONSHIP DYNAMICS

Recently, another cognitive theory of sex differences has been given a good deal of attention—a theory that is herein labeled *relationship dynamics* because of its connection to early childhood experiences of relationship. This theory emerges from the work of Carol Gilligan, an education professor at Harvard, who was named *Ms.* magazine's Woman of the Year in 1983 for contributions made in a book called *In a Different Voice*. Although she claims that her "work is not addressed to the issue of sex differences *per se*," (emphasis in original)[22] she helps to articulate sex differences in adult visions of themselves and of the human experience. These visions are unmistakably related to the interpersonal dynamics of early childhood communication and provide a unique view of the impact of those dynamics on adult communication styles.

The dynamics in question concern the widely held understanding that children of both sexes communicate primarily with women, who are largely responsible for child care, during the first three years of life. As Kohlberg suggests, the establishment of self-worth, in conjunction with gender identity, is a major preoccupation during this time. So, it is important to examine the implications of the tradition of assigning women to child-rearing—not only because this assignment is undoubtedly both cause and effect of sex differences in adult communication, but because it may well plant the seed of those differences in children.

Several scholars have attempted to clarify the effects of gender composition in early experiences with dyadic communication, which are essentially same-sex for girls and cross-sex for boys. One of them, David Lynn, is clearly a social-learning advocate. He emphasizes the difficulties faced by little boys in learning masculinity in the traditional family system. Lynn points out that a girl has a highly available model and learns gender appropriateness in a comfortable environment of connection and positive reinforcement. Since, in Lynn's view, children usually have a "moderately distant" father and a "close" mother, the situation is problematic for boys. A boy initially identifies with the mother and suffers negative sanctioning from both parents unless he breaks away. The father may be particularly anxious about this break, according to Lynn, since culturally remaining a "mama's boy" is a tremendous threat to masculinity.[23]

From a social-learning standpoint, the gender dynamics of early childhood certainly facilitate the female child's effort to learn the culture's behavioral definition of femininity, while complicating the male child's effort to learn its gender complement. However, according to Lynn, boys solve the puzzle as they search for any and all information about the cultural definition of masculinity. Such information is available from observing the father, when available, and paying special attention to the father's evaluations of the child's behavior. It is also available through the media, through peers, and through anti-modeling and negative sanctions provided by the more available mother.[24]

Although he takes a social learning, not a cognitive, view, Lynn points out that the "mental exercise" necessary to solve the puzzle concerning gender definition may result in superior rationality among males. On the downside, he adds that the emphasis on separation from the mother during this critical period of self-identity formation may hinder the adult male's need for affiliation.[25] With these assumptions, Lynn apparently focuses on aspects of the child's cognition of the situation, rather than on sanctions or on imitation.

Another scholar, Nancy Chodorow, has contributed more directly to the theory that relationship dynamics in early childhood communication result in sex differences in adult behavior. Like Kohlberg, she reports that there appear to be certain "universal differences" in masculine and feminine roles and "personalities." But, in contrast to Kohlberg, Chodorow attributes these differences to the gender dynamics of early child care, not to the child's perception of the body in conjunction with the larger social order.

She concludes that female children concurrently learn important lessons about themselves, about femininity in general, and about significant others in their lives. At the same time they are developing a sense of self, they are enjoying a sense of continuity and strong feelings of relationship to those around them. Boys, on the other hand, learn about themselves and about masculinity in the midst of others with whom they must feel unconnected. For them, the feelings of relationship and empathy are threats to definitions of masculinity. Hence, in Chodorow's view, the development of gender appropriateness necessarily entails a sense of discontinuity, or individuation, for boys.[26]

The theoretical stances taken by Lynn and Chodorow are grounded in the empirical observation that certain aspects of masculinity and femininity are more universal than social-learning theory can explain. Couple these regularities with the fact that, across cultures (and in our culture, across career arrangements), women are the primary child-care providers. The connection suggests that females may experience a different world from the very beginning than their brothers. Of course, a reversal in child-care policy would undo these theories. Theoretically, boys with "close" fathers and "moderately distant" mothers would develop a strong sense of empathy and connection, while girls in the same situation would develop superior problem-solving ability along with a strong sense of individuation. However, the situation remains a rarity in a culture that emphasizes work in the male experience. Even if full-time, stay-at-home fathers really did exist (and were willing to be studied), their children would encounter females as soon as paid child care entered their lives, which is often at or before age four.

Gilligan recognizes the logical implications of the gender dynamics of early child care. But she takes a somewhat different approach to elucidating sex differences in "personality." Troubled by the tendency for scholars like Freud, Erikson, and Kohlberg to ignore women's development or treat it as a problem, Gilligan attempts to clarify sex differences in the "interaction of experience and thought." In this way, she treats "women's development" as qualitatively different from (but not inferior to) "men's development." She notes that the latter term may sound silly since, in most psychological discussions, male development is simply called *development*.[27]

Gilligan examines, through interview data, women's "voices," based on the belief that what people say about their lives is significant, that talk contains valuable information about the world as people experience it. As you might expect, she finds considerable evidence that women experience a world of connection with others and define themselves in terms of responsibilities. In contrast, male "voices" in Kohlberg's research (and in one of Gilligan's studies) echo an understanding of the world in terms of individuation and rights.[28]

It is certainly easy to see how the tension between connection and individuation is tied to early childhood experience. The implications for sex differences in communication are also obvious: men are logically more self-centered; women are logically more other-centered. In Gilligan's view, the definition of *self* for a female is practically inseparable from the relationships in her life. In contrast, men tend to separate themselves from others, which allows them to emphasize individual rights and deemphasize contingencies based on relationships to others. In a sense, this is the same psychological sex difference that Lionel Tiger attributes to genetic evolution, i.e., the tendency for women to bond on a private level and for men to bond on a public level.

Tiger concludes that women are poorly suited for positions of power because of their tendency to stress personal relationships. Historians have noted that politically empowered women have been few in our society and that, even when women have entered public life, their most important political contributions have surrounded moral issues: temperance, human rights, suffrage. Gilligan acknowledges that the world as we know it (a man's world) is a "competitive and hierarchical system," difficult to break into if you care too much about other people. She adds that, since women "don't have much power, it's difficult to change anything." But she, and others, have suggested that the female voice, which emphasizes responsibility and caring, may be the loudest voice in the coming decades.[29] After all, the struggle for "justice" and "position" has resulted in a world which can destroy itself hundreds of times over; new issues surround how to cooperatively "undo" that accomplishment.

CONDUCT YOUR OWN RESEARCH

1. Interview two children, one male and one female, asking questions about the relative permanency of gender assignment. For instance, ask them "Will you always be a boy or girl?" or "Could you be a boy or girl if you wanted to be?" or "Do you think your sister will ever become your brother?"

2. Write a hypothetical scene that involves a character faced with a moral dilemma. Make sure that the character has to make a choice concerning the lesser of two evils or the greater of two goods. Present the scene to 10 men and 10 women, requesting that they explain how and why they would choose to act in the situation. Characterize the apparent sex differences in their sense of morality (if any).

3. Watch four different television games shows. Have a tape recorder handy and record each contestant's self-introduction, i.e., responses to questions like "tell us a little about yourself." Contrast the introductions by male and female contestants, using Gilligan's hypothesis that women tend to define themselves as members of relationships and that men tend to define themselves as individuals.

DISCUSS THE ISSUES

1. Do relationships matter more to women than to men? Discuss all types of relationships as you defend your answer.

2. What are the implications of the cognitive developmental perspective for achieving social change? As compared to the social-learning or modeling perspectives? As compared to the biological perspectives?

3. According to Chodorow's theory, what would happen if we suddenly redefined the child care practices of our culture, such that men assumed the role of primary caregiver and women assumed the role of breadwinner?

SUMMARY OF PART III

The various competing explanations are not necessarily mutually exclusive; in some respects, the theories overlap. For instance, the theory of psychosexual development, the theory of cognitive development, and the social theories all acknowledge that adult models influence children's behaviors. The theorists explain the role of models differently, but share a belief that gathering information about adult behavior is part of learning gender-appropriate standards. In some respects, though, the theories may clash rather directly. Certainly, theories that emphasize innate sex differences are countered by theories that stress learned sex differences.

Each reader is encouraged to reexamine the prevailing cultural stereotypes and the empirical evidence of sex differences in communication in light of the various explanations, not so much to select the best, but to become more aware of the important link between communication and gender in the human experience. As stated at the onset, communication and gender are believed to be mutually influential. Regardless of which theory you favor, you will notice that they all stress the importance of communication. In reality, whether they originate from biological roots or not, sex differences are realized, lived, and experienced in interaction with others. Communication provides the vehicle for making sex differences personal and meaningful in our lives. At the same time, there is little doubt that communication is influenced by gender. Otherwise, why is it utterly impossible to communicate with another comfortably unless we feel secure about their sexual assignment?

Meanwhile, as the debate concerning explanations continues, we still find ourselves in the midst of messages about gender appropriateness. Even if we dedicate ourselves to eliminating gender prescriptions in our own behavior and our own expectations of others' behavior, we can hardly hope to experience overnight freedom. So, it seems worthwhile to consider the implications of sex differences in communication for the various male–female relationships we encounter.

The next three chapters focus on the specifics of male–female interaction in various types of relationships. Of course, relationships are very complex and defy ready typification, yet we do tend to refer to others using certain possessive pronouns that focus on their meaning in our lives—*my* colleague, *my* husband, *my* friend, etc. Sometimes, using such relationship language is problematic. Colleagues can also be friends, or even spouses. Surely it is best if a spouse is also a friend. The labels simply don't reflect the fact that people can have multiple meanings in our lives. Also, the labels tend to be treated as static, so it is sometimes problematic to attend to the inevitable change in relationships. Friends grow close and grow apart. As coworkers move up and down the proverbial ladder, their relationships change. Parent–child relationships seem to be in a constant state of change.

Having acknowledged the difficulties, it seems worthwhile to discuss male and female communication in the context of three common relationship types: relationships at work, relationships between friends, and relationships in the family. These are not only categories that have helped to structure the literature on male–female interaction, they are also labels that most people use in daily conversation as they talk about communication with others.

CHAPTER 12

RELATIONSHIPS AT WORK

The term *work* can be defined in a number of ways. In contemporary America it usually refers to employment for pay. But, as the reader is undoubtedly well aware, work can also mean involvement in education, where the worker pays for the opportunity to be employed. Also, individuals who receive neither dollars nor credits often complain about being overworked: parents, for instance, come to mind. Just as the meaning of work in our lives varies from individual to individual, it also varies from group to group. So, it will come as no surprise that work has held different meanings for men and women throughout history.

GENDER INTEGRATION IN THE WORKPLACE

Most of my students are firmly sold on the philosophy of progress in this regard. They argue that women have moved into the paid work force, through employment and educational opportunity, and that freedom from restrictions according to sex is an ever-growing achievement in a democratic society. Our forefathers (and foremothers?) were understandably narrow in defining the work-related roles as solely male, and our grandfathers and grandmothers were somewhat "old-fashioned." Even our own parents are not totally "liberated," but the new generation is moving steadily toward that end.

Yet, even a quick glimpse at history reveals that the theory of steady progress is flawed. Most of those who envision the progressive integration of women into the workforce seem to begin American history in the 1960s, citing the poor status of women in work and education, comparing their position after two decades of increasing awareness, and assuming that the same logic characterized the years prior to 1960. In fact, attention to women's rights was feverish in the early part of the 1900s when the now-famous suffragettes campaigned for the right to vote, which was awarded in this country in August 1920. Ironically, obtaining the right to vote seemed to calm the women's movement, rather than excite it. As one source explains, "Most women innocently believed the right to vote gave them the equality they had long sought. Consequently,...over the next forty years, the women's movement remained dormant and public interest in sexual equality waned."[1]

In truth, the number of employed women did increase between 1920 and 1960, but probably not because of political awareness. Economists cite the depression and World War II as major motivations for women to join the world of work. By 1960, 33.4% of all American workers were women, but the prevailing image of the successful American woman was not nearly as work related as the statistic suggests. The housewife was revered by both men and women as the ultimate nurturing, yet pampered, female. She was financially supported by her successful husband, allowed to devote herself entirely to her home, her children, and, oh yes, to shopping. When the Kennedy administration established a commission to investigate the status of women in 1961, the report "reinforced traditionally held assumptions about women and their roles as mothers and homemakers."[2] Clearly, working women were not admired during this period of "Leave it to Beaver" and "Father Knows Best."

Even more troublesome is the observation by one analyst that "As the 1960s opened, the position of women in higher education was weaker than it had been three decades before. In 1960, women received 35 percent of all bachelor's degrees awarded; in 1930 they had received 40 percent."[3] A popular expression was coined during this time, to the effect that "Women only attend college for their MRS. degrees anyway." College may have been a place to meet a suitable husband, but was not necessarily perceived as professional training for women. To compound the problem, the professions that were usually pursued by women were often extensions of the nurturant female image, e.g., teachers, nurses, and secretaries.

So, there is reason to believe that the women of the 1950s and 1960s may not have been as work-oriented as the women of the 1920s. But, the myth of the "happy homemaker" was challenged by the rebirth of the women's movement in the mid-sixties. Many cite the formation of the National Organization of Women in 1966 as a crucial turning point. The decade of unrest was ideal for attacking an image that kept women in one of several powerless positions: in the home; in employed positions deemed undesirable for men; in employed positions shared by men, but earning less for the same work.

It should be stressed that the feminist movement brought into public debate not only the status of women and work, but related personal and family issues, such as birth control and abortion. In the midst of increasing freedom of choice concerning childbearing, women of the 1970s and 1980s moved into the worlds of work and education with increasing frequency. But, the integration of American women into the arenas traditionally dominated by men is still not as complete as one might expect. To begin with, although the exact numbers vary, most analysts report that women continue to earn fewer dollars per hour than men. The following report is typical:

> A puzzling contradiction characterizes the situation of working women in the United States in the 1980s. Despite impressive gains in the numbers of women entering the professions and the once exclusively masculine ranks of commerce, women's income vis-à-vis men's is *declining*. The wage gap is sizable, and it is growing: In 1955 women full-time workers earned 64 cents for every dollar men earned, and by 1980 that gap had widened to 59 cents for every dollar (emphasis in original).[4]

Explanations for this gap vary. Some believe that women are more likely than men to accept low-paying jobs because, in some families, the woman's income is used as extra spending money. These same analysts emphasize the inequity in pay between traditionally female jobs (teacher, secretary, etc.) and traditionally male jobs, even those requiring less education (sanitary engineer, construction worker, etc.) Traditionalists, in contrast, often speculate that women by choice do not pursue advancement opportunities in order to avoid excessive work-related pressure. Still others cite the failure of affirmative action legislation to correct a situation of obvious and illegal discrimination. Regardless of the explanation, employment records of the 1980s unmistakably point to the continued existence of "pink ghettos" in the world of work, i.e., low-paying, female-dominated jobs. In fact, Department of Labor statistics indicate that, while women are steadily moving into male-dominated fields, the number of women moving into traditionally female-dominated fields reflects a parallel growth.[5] So, women are continuing to replace women in the female ghettos.

It seems logical that equal employment, seemingly mandated according to the Civil Rights Act of 1964 (specifically, Title VII), could never be realized in the absence of legislation mandating equal educational opportunity. But this legislation was not passed until the Education Amendments of 1972 (specifically, Title IX). Thus, it may be that gender integration in employment has been necessarily delayed while women achieve integration into educational domains that prepare them for high-paying, prestigious careers. Women do seem to be creeping slowly but steadily into such domains. According to the Department of Education, women constituted about one-third of all law school graduates and one-fourth of all medical school graduates in 1982, but only about one-tenth of those receiving engineering degrees.[6] Less encouraging though, is the continued dominance of women in college programs such as education (especially elementary education), nursing, and library science. In the early 1980s women still comprised between 75% and 90% of those who received degrees qualifying them for traditionally female jobs.[7]

Nevertheless, it may well be that slow change will prove effective, and the next decade will mark the end of sex-segregated work, just as the sixties marked the end of legally mandated sex-segregation in employment and the seventies marked the end of legally mandated sex segregation in education. It should be stressed, though, that laws are not self-executing. Indeed, despite strict laws, we have failed miserably at putting an end to less controversial social problems: drugs and crime, for example.

Enforcement of legislation depends on judicial interpretations, administrative competence, and budget support. Also, no equality can be achieved, in a legal sense, unless individual citizens force the issue, and many have been reluctant to do so.

Despite the barriers, optimism about gender integration in the American workplace continues to abound, especially among young Americans, as they imagine themselves free to pursue any career avenue they choose. The rest of this chapter is dedicated to the young men and women who will find themselves employed in mixed-sex settings. Presumably, an examination of sex differences in communication may be very helpful in developing male–female relationships in the workplace.

WOMEN AS SUBORDINATES

The term *subordinate* generally means "underneath" or "in support of," and is seemingly analogous to the stereotypic female position in American society. In fact, based on empirical evidence, many critics agree that women's work has traditionally been the work of providing various kinds of support for the men in their lives. Labels like *the better half* and *the woman behind the man,* regardless of their good intentions, clearly express the subordinate role of women in male–female relationships. In their vocational pursuits, women have typically extended the support role. As mentioned, women have dominated as career nurturers in elementary classrooms and hospitals. Ultimately, many women have found work as "career housekeepers." In one moving account, an educated, talented woman reports that domestic servant may be the only vocation in which high-quality performance is truly appreciated by male employers: "in other jobs, workers and bosses resented excellence. With household work the better a woman is at it, the less trouble she has."[8]

Even the political pursuits of women can be interpreted as extensions of their subordination. History leaves little doubt that women have entered the world of politics sparingly, but when they have campaigned, it has seldom been for self-interest. Women have campaigned for the prohibition of social ills, the abolition of discrimination, and the vote for themselves and minorities, but they have not campaigned for position or pay in significant numbers.

Fishman's metaphoric title, "Interaction: The Work Women Do," suggests that certain sex differences in communication behavior may be either cause or effect of women's supporting role in relation to men. Clearly, subordination may be a communicative achievement that women have unknowingly pursued in the process of acting gender appropriately. This possibility suggests a self-fulfilling prophecy, i.e., women have occupied positions subordinate to men because they are good at providing support; and they are good at providing support because, historically, that has been the cultural definition of *women's work.*

Currently, despite legal prohibitions against discrimination, women continue to find themselves subordinate to men in our society. Granted, the number of women in positions of prestige and control is growing, but most female readers (and many male readers due to lack of experience) will find themselves entering the world of paid employment as subordinates to men. So, it seems worthwhile to examine studies focusing on the interaction between men as superiors and women as subordinates.

Sexual Harassment. When women's rights activists first began campaigning for equal employment, many women opposed legal change because they feared the consequences of removing restrictions thought of as protective. Women were treated, under the law, as potential victims, much like children. Similarly, a good deal of female opposition to the Equal Rights Amendment is grounded in the fear of equality. It seems that the integration of women and men in the same setting has hidden dangers for women, one of which is sexual harassment. Granted, men may be victims of sexual harassment, but there is little doubt that cultural images depict men as aggressors and women as sex objects and that these images hold serious consequences for women whenever they interact with men. Sexual harassment at work is especially troublesome for women, because, to the extent that it deters them from achieving success, it contributes to its own perpetuation. In other words, women are harassed because they are seen as the controlled, not the controllers.

Sexual harassment at work may be communicated in a number of ways. In fact, although many individuals can describe the details of behavior they believe to be harassment, the courts differ somewhat on the exact definition of the term and the Supreme Court has not yet addressed the issue.[9] In 1981, the Equal Employment Opportunity Commission provided guidelines that define sexual harassment as: (1) unwelcome sexual advances; (2) requests for sexual favors; and (3) other verbal or physical contact of a sexual nature, provided the behavior interferes with the harassed person's continued employment, ability to conduct his/her work, or right to work in a nonhostile environment.[10] (Please note the use of the gender-neutral form, even though the victim is far more likely to be a female than a male; certainly, the generic *he* would be ill-advised in this discussion.)

From a communication standpoint, these guidelines cite both verbal and non-verbal behaviors that are either implicitly or explicitly sexual in nature and that are not welcome by one party—usually the subordinate party who has something to lose unless he or she tolerates the behaviors. Of course, outright sexual propositions, particularly with an "either-or" clause, constitute harassment. But, according to the EEOC guidelines, sexual joking, certain compliments of a very personal nature, and gratuitous touching, all of which women are likely to encounter in the workplace, also constitute harassment.

Woodrum stresses that harassment involves the deliberate repetition of unwanted verbal comments, gestures, or physical contact in the face of expressed unwelcomeness.[11] This definition emphasizes the responsibility of the harassed person to draw attention to the harassment. But, as one analyst points out, "negative reactions to such sexual advances may violate expectations for 'feminine' behavior as well as expectations for appropriate 'subordinate' behavior."[12] So, the subordinate female is especially limited in her communicative choices, and it is not surprising that many women report on confidential surveys that, although their superiors violated the EEOC guidelines, the incidents were tolerated.[13]

Granted, unwanted sexual advances are inherent in a society that sanctions flirtatious behavior, idealizes romantic seduction, and covets sexual prowess as a sign of power. In such a society, male subordinates are also likely victims of harassment from superiors. But, keep in mind that empirical evidence discussed in this text suggests that women are approached more closely by others, touched more by others (particularly male others), and disclosed to more by others. Compared to men, women are called by their first names more often (as are subordinates), are called by pet names more often (as are children), are metaphorized more often as cuddly animals and edible objects, and are more often the object of sexual jokes. Arguably, none of these communicative trends alone causes sexual harassment of women in any setting, but the combination of these communicative habits certainly establishes women as probable victims of unwelcome sexual innuendo.

Perhaps many male superiors unknowingly treat female subordinates in line with their own experience of women, but if women and men are to work in a nonhostile environment, it seems that men must learn to make their communication specific to the audience as co-workers, instead of as women. As Farley depicts the situation, sexual harassment is evidence that, at work, a woman's sex role is more communicative than her function as a worker.[14] A simple awareness of the communicative behaviors that constitute treating an individual more like a female than like a co-worker may assist male readers in successfully avoiding unintentional harassment.

Female readers may be left wondering how to simultaneously cope with illegal practices and succeed, interpersonally and professionally, in a male-dominated workplace. Short of filing a formal lawsuit, how can a woman communicate that certain verbal and nonverbal behaviors are unwelcome? The most obvious and direct course of action seems to be a nonblaming statement to the offender specifically about those behaviors that make you feel uncomfortable. It may be helpful to consult sources in assertive communication to develop skills in phrasing an appropriate message. Generally, you should state your feelings and the behavior you prefer: "I feel uncomfortable with pet names. Would you mind calling me by my real name?" Of course, certain unwanted behaviors are more difficult to confront. Perhaps you just can't picture yourself saying, "It really bothers me when you put your hands on me." In such situations, it might be possible to indirectly communicate displeasure, either through another individual or by complaining to the offender about another individual—perhaps even a fictional character—who does the same thing. Neither of these methods is direct or honest, but for topics like touching and sexual joking that you may prefer not to raise directly, complaining to or about someone else may effectively end unintentional hostility.

On the other hand, if both direct and indirect messages fail and harassment continues, there are other communication options available short of filing a suit. According to Jones, "if [direct confrontation] fails, the victim can write a letter concerning the problem and the fact that initial confrontation with the harasser was ineffective in gaining his or her cooperation. The letter should...list names and dates of harassment incidents...[and] should be sent to the personnel department, to the harasser's direct superior, and to the harasser."[15] Such a letter makes use of the proper channels to attack behaviors that violate policy and threaten the organization. After all, studies reveal that sexual harassment is extremely costly for organizations in terms of absenteeism from work, diminished performance, and turnover—all of which women tend to treat more as individual problems than as organizational problems, both in terms of causes and effects.

Granted, some women may find no organizational support against harassment, because the organization is too small or the harasser is too important. In such cases, bringing formal charges may be the only recourse. Too few women have chosen this avenue and judicial interpretations continue to leave room for doubt about what constitutes harassment. But, in some cases, the employing agency has been held legally and financially responsible for the behavior of their employees, so the threat of liability has begun to function as an internal deterrent to sexual harassment.

Obscene Language and Humor.   Although the uttering of obscene language and humor in the workplace has been interpreted as a form of sexual harassment directed at women, it is more often taken as a communicative reality in male-dominated settings. Indeed, some scholars have explained that men display their masculinity to one another linguistically, through such practices. Others have gone so far as to argue that the shared freedom to use expressions generally deemed unacceptable in the culture serves to promote a healthy sense of identity in the workplace.[16] In a sense, the freedom to break the rules is an indication of trust.

Still, for a woman entering a male-dominated workplace, she may feel victimized, offended, or just plain embarrassed by the expressions and jokes she hears. Her sense that she is a victim seems logical in light of the analysis of many scholars that sexual joking tends to be designed by men for male consumption and, as most humor, promotes group unity by making outsiders the "objects" of their laughter.[17] The fact that women are offended by obscene language and joking is also logical, according to Fine, who generalizes that across cultures "participation in obscene banter is limited to certain individuals and certain situations...[and] in Anglo-American culture, sexual humor has been primarily a male prerogative, usually found at such times when females are not present."[18]

Thus, the expression "not for mixed company," frequently used to acknowledge the impact of sexual expressions and jokes on women, also signifies the in-group identity that results when men tell jokes about "outsiders." Granted, some women report that they are feeling increasingly free to utter profanities and tell sexual jokes, particularly to other women.[19] If so, it might be assumed that such practices increase their sense of in-group identity. But, since women are still likely to be the object of sex jokes, it stands to reason that sexual humor does not function to this end in all-female groups as effectively as it does in all-male groups. Also, there is little doubt that discussing sexual conquests remains largely a male practice; even in same-sex groups, women tend to discuss romance rather than sex.

When the mixed group is a work group, where females are likely to be both outsiders and subordinates, dealing with obscene interaction may be especially important. According to studies conducted in male-dominated settings ranging from restaurant kitchens to police precincts to large corporate offices, women are confronted with obscene discourse. Since women have typically been absent from male-dominated work settings, abusing females via jokes seems to have become a well-developed form of entertainment. But, when women enter the setting, their presence draws attention to behavior that had formerly been treated as harmless. As one analyst writes, "it is reasonable to assume that most men felt no unfriendly intent in their joking. They were, after all, only having a good time, and building a work community in the process."[20]

Researchers find that women who express disapproval of this behavior report feeling like outsiders. In contrast, the men in their midst report that disapproving women "have no sense of humor," or just "don't fit in" and that they "cannot be themselves" around such women.[21] The question remains as to whether or not cultural traditions are hopelessly contradictory in this case. Nevertheless, women continue to find the pressure on them when it comes to obscene joking. As with many other forms of traditionally male behavior, women find themselves in a double bind, or a lose–lose situation. If they join in, they risk being perceived as unfeminine and, more seriously, may endorse the escalation of behaviors they find offensive. If they express their disapproval, they risk being perceived as humorless, or, more seriously, one who just doesn't fit in.

Again, the dilemma of individual vs. group choice is not unique to women and not unique to this situation, but, in this case, it seems to be inherently part of being female in a society that legally mandates equal opportunity in employment although well-entrenched sex-segregated values and communication practices still exist.

Cooperation and Competition.   Organizations tend to be highly structured settings in which most individuals know exactly where they stand in relation to others. In fact, researchers may refer to the "organizational chart," but most subordinates simply refer to the "ladder." Communication with superiors may be especially "upward" for women if sex is perceived as a status factor in and of itself. Conversely, communication with female subordinates may be perceived as particularly "downward" by male superiors. This inequity is enforced by opposing communication styles: the highly cooperative, other-centered female style vs. the more competitive, self-centered male style.

Although cooperation and competition seem to be logical opposites, analysts concur that both are healthy for group "productivity."[22] A similar logic suggests that individual advancement within the organization may depend on the proper mix of cooperative and competitive behavior. But studies show that the mix may be predictably "improper" for women. To begin with, most paid employment is contingent on successful performance during an interview. Yet, interviewers report that women are noticeably more nervous and less confident during these interactions.[23] Some women are inexperienced at interviewing, which may account for some of their nervousness. Also, it stands to reason that, to the extent that the interviewee is other-centered, communication focusing on one's own abilities and behaviors may be particularly stressful and full of doubt.

One analyst suggests that women are understandably nervous during employment interviews because they are often asked stressful (and illegal) questions that put them on the defensive—questions concerning marital status or even "dating" status, plans to have a family, etc.[24] Even legal questions, concerning willingness to travel, relocate, or work extra hours may involve stress for women. If a female appears too eager and available, too dedicated to career, she may appear unfeminine. In fact, some of the most important questions in the interview, ones that call for a strong statement of ambition and drive from the interviewee, require adopting a traditionally masculine pose.

It seems that women are particularly ill-equipped for the employment interview to the extent that they are other-centered in their communication style. Excessive question asking, expressions of uncertainty, incessant smiling, and closed postures are just a few of the behaviors that are not particularly desirable in this competitive setting but have been well cultivated in most female communication.

Despite the obstacles, women are currently negotiating employment in nearly every male-dominated field. But, I would be remiss not to note that the law requires that employers integrate women into the workforce, unless sex is a "bona fide occupational qualification," and I challenge the reader to name five such jobs. (Stripper? prostitute? escort? surrogate mother?) Indeed, males have roared "Reverse discrimination!" in the face of specific goals and timetables for integrating women into traditionally male occupations.[25]

Whether or not affirmative action legislation actually results in hiring less-qualified candidates just because they're female is debatable. The labeling of women as *tokens* and *affirmative action candidates* has consequences nevertheless. According to Putnam, "in many instances this token status works for the advancement of women, but it can also hinder a woman's efforts."[26] In other words, although affirmative action may create opportunities for women, it also carries implications about their work, such that it is "good (especially for a woman)" or "not good enough (just because it's a woman's)."

In light of their status as tokens, and their noncompetitive behavior during interviews, it is not surprising that women report that they have to work harder than the men around them to achieve the same rewards. As mentioned, sources agree that women earn less on the average than men, whether for part-time or full-time employment. Also, women often fail to be competitive in the pursuit of raises, promotions, and other forms of recognition in the workplace.[27] Admittedly, they ask for such recognition less often than men. This may be because they are not privy to information about the potential for advancement, or because they fear rejection more than men. Both theories have been advanced, along with the theory that women may honestly devalue their own worth.[28] In one study, female candidates, in a simulated employment situation, asked for a lower starting salary than male candidates with the same qualifications.[29] But, even when they do request equal recognition, in the form of salary, travel expenses, or adoption of their ideas, female subordinates are granted their requests far less often than males of comparable status.[30]

For many women, the natural opposition between simultaneously wanting to succeed in a competitive environment and operating from a cooperative stance is sadly resolved by devaluing their own work and/or finding a comfortable supporting role and working like crazy. Indeed, studies show that working women tend to attribute success to effort, while working men (the adjective is noticeably awkward here) tend to attribute success to talent. Moreover, women tend to attribute the lack of recognition to their own failures, while men tend to blame organizational barriers.[31]

In sum, women will probably continue to find themselves as subordinates to men in the world of work, in part because women are still relative newcomers and in part because their communication behaviors may be ill-suited to advancement in the competitive, male-dominated structure of the public sector. Vertical communication is inevitable in organizations, but women can present themselves favorably in these situations if they develop a sense of self-awareness and actively pursue a communication approach that is appropriately subordinate without being self-defeating.

Putnam suggests that women need to learn to see events at work as "integrated," not simple "cause-effect" and "either-or" depictions of isolated communication behaviors. Also, women need to project self confidence, even in situations in which they are apprehensive. She suggests that women communicate any self doubts only to a select support group, not with superiors or even with peers. Finally, she advises women to actively improve their bargaining skills, learning "rules of thumb" that men have traditionally used, such as asking for more than they would actually accept.[32] Granted, these rules may not be appropriate in all situations involving subordinate women, but they target the typical behaviors which have served to inhibit women from succeeding in the competitive workplace.

The advice for men who find themselves with female subordinates is less available, except in legally binding documents. It may well be that dealing with women as subordinates comes naturally, or at least is well modeled and well practiced in a patriarchal society. But, it seems advisable to reconsider habits that, as cited earlier, Farley defines as "asserting a woman's sex role over her function as a worker."[33] For instance, men who ask female subordinates to select gifts or advise them on office furnishings are undoubtedly treating that female like a female, unless such duties are in her job description. The secretary may not be willing to assert "I don't make coffee," but the boss should honestly confront the fairness of expecting such domestic help. After all, would a male secretary be expected to do the same?

Another common practice is calling female subordinates by first names (or even pet names), but calling male subordinates by last names. Name-calling is, in part, a linguistic practice bound by tradition. Even formal terms of address draw attention to a woman's marital status. But male superiors who wish to establish equity in their communication practices can benefit from examining the implications of name-calling. Nonverbal behaviors can also inhibit effective communication between a male superior and female subordinate. Inappropriate touching and failure to award appropriate space are habits that superiors ought to be aware of with all subordinates, but especially with those subordinates with whom these behaviors are most likely to occur, namely females.

WOMEN AS SUPERIORS

A growing number of women have "made it" in the competitive world of work, although the number of upper-level executive positions held by women continues to be remarkably low—about 1%.[34] My students, both male and female, are particularly curious about the behavior of these few successful, powerful women. The mythology would have us believe that they are cold-hearted, emasculating females, even though various optimists predict that the female communication style will achieve recognition in the coming decades of uncertainty and rapid change during which cooperative, not competitive, interaction will be more effective.

A good deal has been written by and about the few highly visible women who have competed and won in a man's world. Suzanne Gordon characterizes two emerging views concerning what she labels *The New Corporate Feminism*. According to one view, "the managerial woman [is] less competitive and callous, more humane and supportive, than the managerial man." To demonstrate this view, Gordon cites interviews with powerful women who describe other centered strategies for leading, such as "trying to reach consensus [in order to] build a team," creating "the opportunity for all members to participate and contribute their skills and knowledge to the processes affecting them," and "paying close attention to others in order to understand their motivations and predict what is apt to happen."[35]

The other view cited by Gordon is critical of the style that successful women have typically adopted. Some voices accuse them of compromising the principles of the feminist movement. As Gordon puts it, "feminism's promise was a life that balanced love, friendship and work."[36] She provides quotes from powerful women that suggest they have adopted traditionally male behaviors and attitudes, such as "the separation of personal, private self from public self," the eagerness for "long hours, travel outside work hours and public review of one's action," the development of "relationships which emphasize...position not emotion" and "a degree of social distancing from subordinates."[37]

As the number of empowered females grows, gender may cease to be so noticeable. But, at present, these women are drawing a good deal of attention. Traditionalists label them *feminists,* and feminist critics call them *careerists.* Regardless of the label or evaluation of these females, it is important to note that female CEOs continue to be exceptional. Women are integrating the ranks of lower-level management, but American organizations continue to be male dominated. According to one pessimistic source, public awareness has forced the token acceptance of women's potential, but "male power is constantly perpetuated [in informal communication]...strengthened in the 'old boy' networks of schools, pubs and clubs." Consequently, females must be very resilient to rise above lower-management level—positions at which they are still likely to be subordinate to men.[38]

In effect, then, research concerning male–female interaction in which the former is subordinate to the latter is available, but it is important to remember that this pair is likely to be fairly low on the proverbial totem pole. Numerous researchers have concentrated on the perceptions that others hold of women with power, indicating that they continue to be a curiosity. Don't forget that these women are, at once, exceptional within their gender category and interesting representatives of that category.[39]

They are also perceptual contradictions in another sense. For most people, leadership and masculinity, as concepts, tend to be logical correlates: "Leadership is associated with high status, expertise, dominance, independence and assertiveness. These are traits of the traditional male stereotype."[40] So, the successful female represents an inherent paradox due to the "basic contradiction between abstract social definitions of 'woman' and normative behavioral expectations of 'professional.' "[41]

Of course, this analysis proceeds purely on a logical basis, examining stereotypic judgments of perceptual categories. There does exist a growing body of research that reports actual expressed perceptions of female superiors, usually those of their subordinates. Several studies indicate that women are seen as less competent managers, particularly in the judgment of male subordinates.[42] This perceptual bias is especially prevalent in traditionally male-dominated organizations, according to Brown's review of the research. He explains that females are more likely to be pronounced effective leaders in typically female occupations: "Data obtained from mental hospitals, civil service organizations and schools show no sex bias in [perceptions of] leadership effectiveness."[43]

Of course, given enough time women can prove themselves to be expert, dominant, etc. Indeed, one recent study revealed that experience working under a female manager was positively correlated with positive attitudes about female managers. Those who had never worked under a female, or who had had a female superior for a short period of time, were less likely to see females as competent than those who had worked with female managers for a longer period.[44] In fact, college students tend to be more stereotypical in their judgments of female managers than subjects in the workplace[45]—a finding my students typically find quite disturbing, since they take pride in their cohort group being liberal-minded.

Across contexts, stereotypes have been found to be more influential in the absence of information, so those who have little or no experience with a particular category of people (in this case, female bosses) are likely to hold perceptions based on cultural stereotypes. Many organizational scholars stress that subordinates' perceptions of female ineffectiveness will gradually diminish as women gain managerial status. But, this prediction is contingent on the fact that male and female leadership styles will be experienced as similar. So, research that examines the female management style, as opposed to expressed perceptions of that style, must be considered.

Some scholars have characterized women as distinctly interpersonal in their style of management, i.e., more open and responsive.[46] Others have reported that women are less assertive in dealing with subordinates.[47] These observations may be related to research suggesting that female bosses are more "approachable" in the judgment of both male and female subordinates.[48] Once again, stereotypes appear to interact with lived experience in creating a self-fulfilling prophecy.

Ultimately, women may be able to overcome the preconceived notion that they are not born leaders. But, Wood and Conrad suggest that a woman who is currently serving in management continues to encounter the inherent paradox—the double bind—that demands she pay a price for her behavioral choices: if she acts too capable, she risks being perceived as unfeminine; if she acts too feminine, she risks being perceived as incompetent.[49]

Some studies, such as the one conducted by Hagen and Kahn, report that competent women may be perceived as unpleasant and may be excluded from social groups within the organization.[50] Spence, Helmreich and Stapp characterized the typical male reaction to female competence as "indifference."[51] In sharp contrast, Deutsch and Leong found that, in laboratory dyads, competent women were particularly well liked, even more so than competent men. But, as the researchers acknowledged, female competence was probably not threatening to the men in their study, because it contributed to their successful completion of an assigned shared task. Thus, the competent women in their study were probably seen as teammates, which is consistent with both the stereotype that females are cooperative and the empirical evidence as to the work women do when they talk with men. In contrast, the male–male dyads were characterized by competition between the pair. Competence in this situation was probably viewed as an effort to "outshine" the other. In any case, Deutsch and Leong admit that their laboratory study may not be applicable to situations in which females are not expected to be competent—i.e., "fields that are traditionally male dominated."[52] It certainly stands to reason that women may pay a higher price for being judged competent in a male-dominated area than in laboratory exercises.

According to Wood and Conrad, the double bind is not easily resolved for most female superiors, and, in fact, many women may "complete the double bind" with their own behaviors. They inadvertently opt to behave like either a "nonfemale professional" or a "nonprofessional female." In doing so, they reinforce the belief that the two are contradictory and perpetuate the paradox. While men undoubtedly feel a conflict, at times, between being too familiar with subordinates and being unresponsive, they seldom encounter this dilemma as part of self-definition. Wood and Conrad point out that many women withdraw from the situation, psychologically or physically, which again completes the double bind with information that "women just aren't cut out to withstand the pressure."[53]

Many social analysts point out that we are in a state of flux, that when the dust settles contradictions between success in the world of work and success as a woman will be reconciled. Expectations will merge, and both perceptions will be better for the merging. In the meantime, communication scholars have offered advice to women who must resolve the contemporary state of affairs and break the ground for others. Wood and Conrad suggest that women who are very skilled at "analyzing the situation" can adopt a flexible position that lets them choose which role (woman or boss) to assert in any given situation. The analysts admit, though, that this calls for a good deal of awareness and certainly doesn't resolve the problem. They also point out that a woman can "clearly, repeatedly and forcefully communicate both that she is a professional and that she is a woman...at times a woman professional may need to instigate an open confrontation regarding the discrepancy...." But, again, calling attention to the dilemma may present an image that she is hypersensitive about the double bind—a disposition that reinforces her ill-placement in management in the first place.[54]

Another communication expert, Mary Anne Fitzpatrick, recommends that women (and men for that matter) might benefit from paying close attention to their immediate goals in work-related interaction. She sees these goals as being of three types: task goals, relational goals, and impression-management goals. Women, stereotypically, tend to overemphasize relational goals, so Fitzpatrick suggests that most women need to concentrate on task and impression-management goals to achieve balance in their communication. On the other hand, it stands to reason that women who find themselves perceived as "bitches" can benefit from de-emphasizing task goals and concentrating on relational and impression-management goals.[55]

Once identified, Fitzpatrick acknowledges that women cannot realistically expect to adopt traditionally male behaviors to achieve their goals. She suggests that managerial women "think like men," but "act like ladies." Specifically, this amounts to developing strategies that utilize traditionally other-centered behaviors to one's own advantage. For instance, questions can be used strategically, perhaps to reintroduce topics that had been ignored or interrupted by male subordinates.[56] Fitzpatrick makes a convincing case in arguing for a goal-oriented yet nonthreatening style as the answer to the double-bind of the female manager. Positions of power allow flexibility in communication and women, to the extent that they are process analysts, can benefit from constant self-evaluation in their communication with subordinates.

WOMEN AS PEERS

Analysts have emphasized the importance and prevalence of vertical communication in organizations, as the ladder metaphor stresses. But a good deal of interaction at work, both formal and informal, can be classified as horizontal. The interactants may be equal in status, or they may cooperate in ignoring their status temporarily, i.e., talk "man to man." Of course, this expression becomes problematic when one participant is a female. How would you react to the proposal that you have a "man to woman" talk with a coworker?

Predicting the strategies and outcomes likely in a man-to-woman talk in work-related settings has been the goal of a number of communication research studies. Researchers have typically identified stereotypic aspects of masculinity and femininity and attempted to establish or disestablish their application in the lived experience of working men and women. For example, the cultural myth that men are more aggressive than women has provided the motivation for investigations of "trait argumentativeness."[57] Argumentativeness is an observable communication behavior often associated with the invisible psychological construct aggression. Nonverbal behaviors such as punching or pushing are also taken as evidence of aggression, but arguing is more likely to be allowed, even expected, in task-related pursuits. Thus, researchers have focused on the extent to which men and women display argumentativeness and on how they react to argumentativeness from others.

According to several studies, females argue less than males, perhaps because they believe that "arguing is a hostile, combative communication encounter...employed as a means of controlling and/or dominating another."[58] This theory has special implications for women in the competitive working world, since researchers also propose that argumentative individuals tend to be selected as leaders more often than less argumentative members and to have greater influence on group decision making.[59] Some scholars even argue that argumentativeness has intrinsic value for the individual, facilitating self-concept development and promoting creativity and clear thinking.[60]

It seems inevitable that working peers will be confronted with both conflicts of ideas and conflicts of interests. If females are less likely to participate in, or even tolerate, arguing, it stands to reason that the task-group will suffer a loss of valuable input. By the same token, if females are less likely to argue for advancement, it stands to reason that they will suffer a loss of recognition in the form of raises, promotions, etc. Both conditions have prompted experts to design programs intended to encourage women to view arguing as a desirable activity.[61]

A related research interest is negotiation, a skill area in which experts also believe women workers may be noticeably weak. Women's failure to negotiate their own advancement troubles Nadler and Nadler, who write: "We contend that obtaining raises, promotions and other forms of organizational support are at least partially related to the individual's negotiation ability and that women are at a negotiation disadvantage relative to men."[62] As proof of the proposed disadvantage, Nadler and Nadler cite a recent study in which subjects were asked to name the hypothetical raise they would request, based on a performance rated "good" in a company whose average raise was 6%. Each subject was also asked to name a figure he or she thought represented a realistic negotiation outcome and a minimum figure he or she would expect. It may not be surprising that male subjects indicated that they would request a figure higher than that indicated by female subjects. Stereotypically men are portrayed as greater risk-takers and empirically, they consistently demonstrate their assertiveness in stating their own worth.[63] Similarly, history has shown that women will, and do, settle for less than men in terms of financial recognition. This trend has already been discussed. But it is certainly telling that women underrated the realistic figure, in comparison to men—a finding that Nadler and Nadler take as evidence that they are inexperienced negotiators.[64]

In subsequent research, Nadler and Nadler determined that successful negotiators not only demonstrate effective interpersonal strategies, but they effectively anticipate the strategies of the opponent and often are able to predict the overall outcome of the encounter.[65] The fact that negotiation requires superior strategizing helps to explain an apparent contradiction in the literature concerning sex differences in negotiation. It seems that, in some studies, males tend to be more cooperative negotiators than females, while, in other studies, they tend to be less cooperative than females. Rubin and Brown propose that men orient themselves to "the impersonal task of maximizing their own earnings," and adopt the negotiation style that will benefit them most. Women demonstrate a more consistent tendency to adopt an attitude "sensitive to the other" as a person, but not sufficiently analytic or strategic to result in a high payoff.[66]

Obviously, in negotiations, both the ability to persuade the other and the openness to being persuaded (sometimes labeled *persuasability*) impact on the outcome. Stereotypically, women are believed to be easy marks for a persuasive male. Indeed, some communication research indicates that women are more easily persuaded than men, particularly by men.[67] But, women have also been portrayed as skilled manipulators in male–female interaction, "batting their eyelashes" or "acting like a helpless child" in order to get their way. Perhaps because women are believed to have "special tools" available for persuasion, it is not surprising that many men have welcomed them as coworkers into a business realm that requires constant negotiation—that of sales. Of course, women have long dominated retail sales, in low paying jobs where "the customer is always right." But, recently, there has been a rapid influx of women into the world of manufacturer's representatives and industrial sales.

Many forward thinkers have recognized that women can make superior sales representatives, regardless of the product, provided that they are well schooled in compliance-gaining techniques. A good deal of literature has been amassed which summarizes strategies for gaining the customer's compliance—for a demonstration, visit any big-ticket item sales showroom or pay close attention the next time you receive one of those annoying telephone sales calls. These strategies range from the very affective (e.g., the "liking" strategy in which the sales representative acts as friendly and helpful as possible in hopes that the customer will purchase the product because he or she likes the representative) to the purely cognitive (e.g., the "reason" strategy in which the salesperson presents rational arguments for buying the product). They range from nonassertive (e.g., "hinting" and "evasion") to aggressive (e.g., "threat" and "manipulation")."[68]

As women move into the sales force, it is fascinating to wonder whether certain strategies are more suited to the feminine style of communication, while others are more suited to the masculine style. A recent investigation of self-reports by salespeople indicates that there are clear sex differences in the use of compliance-gaining strategies, but not in terms of "thematic" analysis. That is, female sales reps are not necessarily more affective, more nonassertive, or more manipulative than their male counterparts. Rather, the main distinction is in terms of the range of strategies used. While women tend to be more limited, preferring one or another strategy to the others, men use many strategies, sometimes during a single sales interaction![69] Again, this supports the notion that men analyze the situation in terms of the payoff, while women may be hyper-sensitive to relationship issues in the customer–salesperson dyad.

Whether women are superiors, subordinates, or peers with respect to the men with whom they interact, both sexes will need to challenge traditional gender stereotypes if they hope to experience a tolerable mix of cooperative and competitive interaction in a gender-integrated workplace. Lest the reader become too optimistic about the ease of gender integration, however, keep in mind that, according to Risman and Schwartz, as of 1989, "men and women [still] do not have access to identical settings or opportunities" and "even when men and women are in identical settings, they often face differential expectations."[70]

Granted, this chapter has emphasized the settings to which women may have limited or difficult access. Granted, even further, that force-fitting women into traditionally male domains may be inevitably difficult at first. Still, unless we each confront our differential expectations and recognize behavioral evidence that the collective has differential expectations, it seems unlikely that we will be able to make the most of any work experience that involves male–female interaction.

Male voices have argued, in noticeably small numbers, that there also continue to be settings to which they have limited or difficult access. Limited expectations may indeed minimize a man's ability to become active in the private, female-dominated, realms of family and social interaction. In the next chapters, sex differences in communication are discussed in terms of their implications for male–female interaction in the nonworking world.

CONDUCT YOUR OWN RESEARCH

1. Interview three women you consider to be successful in the working world. To what do they attribute their success? To what do you, as a communication analyst, attribute their success?

2. Observe male–female interaction in three business settings you consider to be distinct from one another (e.g., a classroom, a store, an office). Write down and hand in (before the observation) your expectations for contrast. Compare your findings to your expectations.

3. Ask a group of friends to role play scenes that you create, staged in the workplace and varied as to gender composition and status composition of the characters. Record the role playing (either on videotape or audiotape) and discuss the apparent connections between gender, power, and communication.

DISCUSS THE ISSUES

1. Why haven't women achieved true equality with men in the workplace, be it political, professional, or educational? Is it just a matter of time? If women do achieve equality, how will it affect their lives? men's lives?

2. Share your attitudes about reverse discrimination. Do you believe that women (and/or minorities) should receive preferential treatment in applying for jobs? Should organizations be forced to meet specified quotas?

3. When does playful communication become sexual harassment? What would you do if you were the victim of sexual harassment, or a witness to it?

CHAPTER 13

RELATIONSHIPS BETWEEN FRIENDS

Lillian B. Rubin labels friendship "the neglected relationship" because "there are no social rituals, no public ceremonies to honor or celebrate friendships of any kind...not even a linguistic form that distinguishes the formal, impersonal relationship from the informal and personal one."[1] The shortage of descriptive labels for this neglected relationship is particularly apparent in a project like this, since clarity in distinguishing categories of relationships is desirable. The linguistic forms chosen within this chapter (indeed, those that distinguish this chapter from the two adjacent chapters) represent the inadequacy of the names by which we call those around us who are neither kin nor strangers. Certainly, some of the male–female relationships we develop during working hours move in substance toward friendships. Similarly, it stands to reason that marriages may begin as friendships in a society that allows an individual to select his or her spouse.

Rawlins points out that friendship and love are similar in that both are "personal relationships privately negotiated between particular individuals."[2] Unlike professional relationships, there are no interviews or advertisements for friendships, and there are no preexisting rules or roles that limit and define communication between friends. Also, friendships are assumed, at least ideally, to be cooperative units, characterized by loyalty and equality, not competition and hierarchy. Clearly, we take pleasure in believing that friends are distinct from coworkers in these respects.

As mentioned, it is somewhat more difficult to distinguish friends from lovers, although we have a very popular religious and legal ceremony to formalize the latter. Even after marriage, partners often refer to themselves as "best friends."[3] (Please note that the discussion of lovers, by whatever inadequate label, is apologetically limited to heterosexual lovers, not because homosexual relationships are considered unimportant, but because it stands to reason that the social and political dynamics of these relationships are significantly unique to warrant a separate discussion).[4] In fact, the connection between kinship and friendship is especially complex in the sense that, although the nuclear family is considered to be the primary unit of emotional support and may be threatened by emotional bonds with outsiders, it is largely through friendship that nuclear families perpetuate themselves. After all, marriage within a family unit is not permitted; in the absence of prearranged marriage, individuals are largely on their own to find potential mates and often use friendship as a vehicle to romance.

Despite the acknowledged overlap between friendship and other types of relationships, this chapter is devoted to the depiction of nonkin relationships between men and women—relationships that are primarily personal, as opposed to professional.

PLATONIC RELATIONSHIPS

Many people are unaware of the origin of the term we often use to describe nonsexual friendships between men and women. A brief lesson in the classics provides not only an aid to spelling the word, but also information about its meaning and even its significance in our lives. Long ago, the Greek philosopher Plato described a type of deep, spiritual love that transcends earthly desire (i.e., sex). At the time, he referenced *love between men,* although it remains in doubt whether this construction constitutes an instance of the generic *he* or acknowledges the prevalence of homosexuality in Plato's community. In any case, the term is now used to distinguish a type of male–female relationship. We would not describe male–male or female–female friendships as platonic, which demonstrates our predisposition toward heterosexuality. In fact, we usually don't use the term *platonic* to describe a relationship unless we suspect that someone else might suspect that it is not platonic; hence, the addition of an adverb when we feel the need to assert information about the relationship's type.

The current usage patterns surrounding this term are subtle, but clear indicators that we tend to treat adult male–female interaction, except interaction between family members, as potentially sexual. Rawlins provides a useful typology that positions the platonic relationship (he calls it "platonic love," consistent with Plato's original treatise on the subject) between friendship, which presumably knows no gender-bounds in a heterosexual society, and relationships which traditionally necessitate one partner of each sex:

1. *Friendship* is a voluntary, mutual, personal, and affectionate relationship devoid of expressed sexuality....
2. The *Platonic Love* relationship includes high emotional commitment without sexual activity. A deeper intimacy and a movement toward greater exclusivity characterizes platonic love.

3. *Friendship-Love* is a potentially unstable interplay between emotional and sexual expression of affection...the appellations 'boyfriend' or 'girlfriend' express well the fluid and transitional state of such a relationship....

4. *Physical Love* is the sexual counterpart of platonic love. Here, there is a high sexual involvement with little emotional commitment.

5. Finally, *Romantic Love* implies an exclusive sexual and emotional relationship. (emphasis in original)[5]

Obviously, in a chapter titled "Friendship" it serves no purpose to begin with a section labeled "Friendship." Therefore, it seems worthwhile to include a category "platonic relationships," which merges Rawlins' notions of "friendship" and "platonic love." Relationships discussed in this section, then, may vary as to exclusivity and degree of emotional commitment. But, they are distinguishable (at least theoretically) from various stages of romantic relating in a heterosexual society that emphasizes the importance of love and marriage in the pursuit of happiness.

As stated in Chapter Two and again in Chapter Nine, female–female friendships have been proposed to differ from male–male friendships in several ways. Research indicates that female friendships are both more exclusive[6] and more emotionally committed[7] than male friendships. Researchers also distinguish same-sex friendships according to communication variables (proposed variously as both the cause and effect of exclusivity and commitment) including self-disclosure,[8] emphasis on talk as an activity,[9] and supportive communication.[10]

In some studies, cross-sex friendships have been compared with same-sex friendships, with the former usually rated between female–female and male–male friendships on the variable of interest. For example, Fisher and Narus described male–female friends as "closer" than male–male friends, but "more distant" than female–female friends.[11] This conclusion indicates that platonic relationships are characteristically a compromise between the male's vision of friendship and the female's vision of friendship.

But a number of studies, that focus directly on cross-sex friendship, provide a different perspective on this relatively rare and unique type of relationship. To begin with, the median ratings obtained from male–female friends as to their degree of "closeness" may not represent a "median" common to both partners. That is, one partner may perceive the relationship as "very close," while the other may perceive it as "not very close," the end result being an interpretation of "medium closeness." This possibility takes on significance in light of the proposal of some critics that men may perceive cross-sex friendships as "closer" than women do.[12] This theory is supported by recent research in which male partners found their friendships with women more "therapeutic" than their same-sex relationships, but the women found friendships with men less so than their same-sex relationships.[13]

Safilios-Rothschild explains that, in cross-sex friendships, women tend to provide support, to serve as an emotional outlet where men can freely express feelings that they tend to keep hidden from same-sex friends. But, the favor is seldom returned, i.e., the same male partners are not as willing to indulge emotional outpourings from their female friends.[14] Consistent with this interpretation, Rawlins suggests that men clearly distinguish between the type of communication that characterizes their same-sex and cross-sex friendships, while women tend to distinguish between friendships without making generalizations based on gender composition.[15] Rawlins concludes that "males and females seem to bring different agendas to their cross-sex friend-ships...It appears that males typically rely on heterosexual relationships for emotional gratification whereas women can be intimate with members of both sexes."[16]

Buhrke and Fuqua note a similar trend in their recent study: "both women and men were more likely to seek out women than men when under stress." The researchers speculate that women are seen as the "nurturers and care givers and thus it may be more socially acceptable for women to be approached for support than men...Also, given that women are more frequently sought out for support, it may be that women have learned to be better supporters."[17] In short, a self-fulfilling prophecy may influence the level of emotional sharing in cross-sex friendships, such that women provide support for male partners, because they are experienced at providing support for others.

If men do, indeed, obtain nurturance and care-giving in platonic relationships with women, at least more so than vice versa, it stands to reason that men should actively seek these relationships, at least more so than vice versa. Especially in light of the reports that men express greater dissatisfaction with same-sex friendships than women, platonic friendships might fill an important void in the male experience. Ironically, scholars have discovered that men tend to be more ready than women to push for platonic relationships to become physical or romantic (using Rawlins' typology).[18]

Herein, it seems, lies the biggest threat to enduring platonic friendships. Al-though women find communication with cross-sex friends less satisfying and less reciprocal than communication with their same-sex friends, they seem to be willing to work at friendships with men, at least according to survey data. Women reportedly indicate that they "want more male friendships" and "want closer male friendships."[19] But, the potential for romance may create a tension in these relationships, which makes being "just friends" especially difficult for men.

The fact is that the literature on platonic friendship, which is admittedly rare, states quite clearly that friendships between men and women, devoid of any hint of sexual attraction, are relatively rare and short-lived. According to one authority, who recently interviewed 300 men and women (ages twenty-five to fifty-five), sexual innuendo continues to provide a major deterrent to the formation of long-term platonic bonds:

> The history of conquest and seduction that has for so long dominated relations between women and men is not easily left behind. Therefore, when I asked about friendships with the opposite sex, most people's thoughts turned quickly to the ways in which sex, whether acted on or not, both gives the relationship a special charge and also creates difficulties that are not easily overcome.[20]

It is only fair to note that many young people object vehemently to this generalization, assuring me that they have many long-standing, cross-sex relationships in which sex is not an issue. However, when pressed as to the history of the friendship, an interesting trend emerges: platonic friends are often former boyfriends or girlfriends. Thus, the sexual status of the pair may have already been established. Other platonic pairs began in early childhood; some are distant cousins or neighbors. In some cases, according to my students' reports, cross-sex friendships are linked to same-sex friendships, i.e., a bond may evolve with a friend's romantic partner. To the extent that the same-sex friendship is valued and secure, affection for the boyfriend or girlfriend is desirable.

Of course, the "green monster" may rear its ugly head, since jealousy tends to accompany the intense emotions associated with romantic love. Theorists speculate that the jealousy of a significant other may constitute a second major deterrent to enduring platonic friendship. In a society that holds monogamy sacred, even young people seem to be sold on the value of investing most of their time and affection in a single heterosexual relationship.[21] In fact, giving up other friends is often a prerequisite to developing a romance. According to Hansen, "the expectation that one's partner will give up close opposite-sex friendships develops in the early stages of any intimate relationship."[22] This exclusivity logically intensifies as partners grow older and confirm their commitment to one another in some sort of culturally significant ritual.[23]

Therefore, it is not surprising that never-married individuals tend to report more cross-sex platonic friendships than married individuals, as do divorced and widowed individuals.[24] It stands to reason that devotion to a single, consuming relationship drains time and energy from all other relationships, but cross-sex friendships are especially vulnerable after marriage. This is most true for the female partner, who tends to give up her male friends along with her surname, after she says her vows.[25] When a married woman does speak of friendships with other men, they tend to be with individuals she has met through her husband. Married men, in contrast, report that most platonic friendships with women are born of interaction at work.[26]

Sociologists firmly acknowledge that participation in the public sphere facilitates all networking, including the formation of cross-sex friendships. Therefore, to the extent that the traditional definition of being married and mothering young children logistically inhibits women from forming platonic bonds with men, this sex difference may be reversed by the movement of women into the workforce. The desegregation of work, should it be successfully legislated, may provide some fascinating new data concerning cross-sex friendships. As yet, there has been a good deal more interest in sexual harassment, which again speaks to our cultural preoccupation with the physical aspects of male–female interaction.

Nevertheless, it will be interesting to observe the male–female friendships which develop in the "post-Feminist" era. Dated research only reveals that such friendships tend to be class-specific (i.e., both white collar or both blue collar), and they tend to be more numerous in white-collar professions.[27] It is possible that white-collar interaction may be governed by norms of politeness and gentility, at least more so than blue-collar interaction, and thereby may be more suitable to the integration of females. Also, since white-collar jobs usually require extended education, which is increasingly open to both sexes, platonic bonding may have been practiced first in the classroom.

The data that have been discussed seem to suggest that cross-sex friendships are most likely to form (and most desirable, at least to men) to the extent that they approximate female–female friendships. Yet, as women move into male-dominated arenas, there is no reason why they should not develop an aptitude and an appreciation for cross-sex relationships that more nearly approximate male–male friendships. Conceivably, the same sort of numerous "weak ties" that typify male friendship groups could provide women with professional and social links to others.

In one recent study, women reported that their cross-sex friendships provided more "companionship" than their same-sex friendships, although the women also reported men as less accepting and less intimate friends. Apparently, men are enjoyable companions, even though they are not particularly nurturant or supportive. The researcher speculates further that women may receive, not only companionship, but also status benefits from cross-sex associations.[28] The capacity for forming male–female bonds, may be particularly rewarding for women in the workplace, because, some scholars point out, there exist "unofficial, unstated, but crucial values" in the workplace that are only shared informally.[29] Thus, cultivating friends with men may function to enlarge a female worker's network, improve her status, and create a more comfortable professional atmosphere.

It seems that women may have a good deal to gain from cross-sex friendships. Logically, as women integrate male-dominated realms, they may develop an increasing appreciation for cross-sex friendships that resemble male–male friendships, i.e., are less intimate and less demanding than the friendships they have known with other women. Such friendships may require "speaking the other's language," whether that means talking about sports, sharing an off-color joke, or even adopting a posture of relaxed aggressiveness. Personal experience suggests that this type of interaction facilitates a distinct and valued brand of closeness between cross-sex individuals. After all, such exchanges are usually enjoyable, short-lived, and nonthreatening. They do not call for high levels of self-disclosure, nor its reciprocal—trust. They communicate a degree of association that is appropriate and comfortable in many integrated workplaces and many mixed social settings. Eventually, relationships grounded in this sort of interaction may grow into something closer, but they need not be devalued because they do not.

In sum, male–female platonic friendship may provide an important context in which all individuals can develop a sense of flexibility in relating to members of the opposite sex. At present, these relationships are threatened by romance and sexual innuendo. Conversely, they may be perceived as threatening, most often by romantic partners, but also by same-sex friends and family members. However, as men and women begin to work and recreate together in increasing numbers, platonic relationships may be the source of many gratifying, though distinctly nonsexual, experiences.

ROMANTIC RELATIONSHIPS

There is little doubt that our cultural mythology reserves a special status for romantic relationships. We are weaned on the magical fantasies of Cinderella, Sleeping Beauty, and Snow White, each of whom gets her man (a prince at that!) and lives happily ever after. The element of free choice may be woven into such tales, but the emphasis is on some mystical, unpredictable, highly emotional event—a kiss, a shoe that fits "just right," etc. In fact, the metaphoric language of romantic relationships indicates the assumption of nonrational behavior: "crazy-in-love," "falling in love," "head-over-heels-in-love."

Perhaps it is because we hold the mythology of love so dear that the realities of romantic interaction are often so difficult to accept. Relating in romantic dyads is sometimes conflict-ridden to the point that bonds intended to last forever cannot always endure the strain. Even those that do endure are likely to be quite volatile. Researchers agree that, as the degree of intimacy in a male–female relationship increases, so does the threat of violence. In one recent survey, nearly one-half of the respondents reported that they had experienced violence in a dating relationship. Both men and women revealed having made or received threats of physical abuse, witnessed violent destruction of inanimate objects, and/or experienced "real violence."[30]

The apparent contradiction between the culture's love fantasy and the personal reality of romantic interaction is not difficult to understand in light of two considerations: (1) these relationships are assumed to be exclusive and (2) the communication in these relationships is likely to be extremely emotional. The former assumption often leads to a sense of possessiveness by one or both partners and/or a tremendous fear of losing the other. Perhaps the tendency for romantic pairs to experience extremely positive and extremely negative emotions logically leads, from time to time, to "temporary insanity."

Keep in mind that individuals in our culture are pressured to find and win a desirable mate. Courtship in other cultures may amount to the negotiation of goods or the introduction of preassigned partners, but here it involves identifiable communication events—attempts to appear attractive to members of the opposite sex, strategies to win the affections of desired individuals, and ultimately the negotiation of social and personal connection with a significant other—all events that are both a product of and an influence on each individual's self-image. In a very real sense, succeeding at love is integrally tied to succeeding at life.

Naturally, success at love may be defined differently for different individuals, or even for the same individual at different points in time. In fact, Lee describes six distinct types of love, metaphorically referred to as the *colors of love:* (1) *erotic love,* which is driven by intense desire for the chosen partner; (2) *storge,* a love that develops slowly and is often preceded by friendship; (3) *pragmatic love,* in which practical issues are tantamount; (4) *ludus,* in which love is played like a game (derived from the Greek word for *sport*); (5) *mania,* a sort of crazed love accompanied by possessiveness and jealousy; and (6) *agapic love,* which is more spiritual than sexual and is characterized by self-sacrifice.[31]

By adulthood, most of us have at least witnessed, if not experienced, each color of love described above. Yet, despite the knowledge that people sometimes play games, that love sometimes hurts, and even that people feign love in order to obtain practical ends, love remains an undeniable cultural fantasy—one that most men and women hope to make real. It seems worth noting that sexual activity and marriage (not necessarily in that order) are key components in the fantasy. Certainly, these components are not necessarily present in all romances, but they are issues that become increasingly urgent to individuals as they approach adulthood in a society that places great emphasis on the nuclear family. Therefore, keep in mind that romantic relationships are discussed in the chapter titled "Friendship" because they are bonds created, negotiated, and maintained or dissolved by choice, as are all friendships. It is assumed that both partners volunteer their participation, as they do in platonic friendships, and that sexual activity is a type of participation often associated with courtship or dating or whatever name is in vogue.

Due to their voluntary nature, both romantic involvements and platonic friendships are distinct from kinship ties, which are legal institutions either contracted through the courts or established in bloodlines. Although this logic suggests that heterosexual romance is appropriately labeled a type of *friendship,* and thereby separated from the next chapter titled "Family," it is important to remember that part of the traditional love myth is that its ultimate trajectory is marriage. Thus, the full ending to most fairy tales reads, "They were married and lived happily ever after." Once their relationship is acknowledged in a formal ceremony, that man and woman who stood at the alter take their place in the social world (and with the IRS) as a basic family unit. Because marriage marks the onset of a new family, it marks the onset of the next chapter. However, it is important to remember that, according to our culture's fantasy, love and marriage are hopelessly connected, as are love and sex, sex and children, etc.

As mentioned, even youngsters seem to be cognizant of the significance of experiencing a special male–female relationship, perhaps because they've been read too many fairy tales. Most children begin to rehearse exclusive romantic bonding just after the years of voluntary sex segregation. In other words, almost immediately after they decide they don't hate the opposite sex, they select a singular representative to love.[32] Of course, these pairings seldom feature the sort of "extended, social interaction which might let [them] explore mutual interests and lay the foundation for a friendship."[33] In fact, Zick Rubin speculates that romantic interest during this period does more to facilitate same-sex relating than cross-sex relating.[34]

The discussion of peer socialization in Chapter Nine suggests that same-sex peer interaction, not cross-sex peer interaction, provides the major source of learning during this all-important period in adolescent development. The familiar tease, "So-and-so has a boy/girlfriend," demonstrates both the novelty of such relationships in this age group (just adding the prefix *boy-* or *girl-* effectively creates the tease) and the recognition that this is a one-of-a-kind relationship (it changes the meaning entirely to say "so-and-so has some boy/girlfriends"). Even when the dreaded accusation is admitted, both boys and girls tend to converse more with same-sex peers about the boyfriend or girlfriend than with the admired other. More often than not, they will send messages and notes through same-sex confederates and arrange meetings in groups. Thus, the mystical nature of romance is created and preserved, to a great extent, in the midst of the adolescent's developing sense of himself or herself as male or female.

Perhaps because they are often more "talk than action," adolescent flirtations are seldom taken seriously by research scholars. Most of what we claim to know about how people view courtship behavior has been learned from individuals between the ages of sixteen and twenty-six.[35] The lower limit of this range undoubtedly stands as a comment about the age of presumed sexual activity, although it by no means matches the onset of puberty nor the average age of first marriage. The norms that govern participation in sex are too complex and transitory to present here, but researchers seem to imagine that dating takes on a serious flavor around the age of sweet sixteen. The upper limit of the research group may be a matter of convenience (after all, college students are highly accessible) or may communicate an inherent bias that courtship is still a pastime primarily for the young. Certainly, we can assume that older people continue to enjoy one another's company, but surprisingly little attention has been paid to exactly how they negotiate or terminate dating relationships. If the age of first marriage continues to climb, and the ranks of single adults continue to grow due to divorce or death of partners, researchers will undoubtedly develop an interest in courtship after age twenty-six.

At present, we continue to view the dating relationship as either a rehearsal for marriage, where we get to practice the various activities associated with that institution, or a tryout for marriage, where we assess various individuals as potential partners. In either case, romantic pairings tend to be marked by rituals and ceremonies, even in this modern day and age. Young lovers trade symbolic gifts, share secrets, and even call each other by special names.[36] The perception that romances have clear beginnings (and perhaps endings) distinguishes them from plain-old friendships, as do various verbal declarations that seem to be associated with developmental stages. Perhaps we view romances as relationships that must grow, while we allow friendships to remain stable. Similarly, trouble in a romance is almost always an immediate concern. If a problem cannot be resolved, the relationship is threatened. But, disagreements with friends may simply cause the participants to distance themselves; they seldom declare an end to the relationship. Romantic partners, in contrast, apparently imagine that they must be free before they can pursue another, which also supports the theory that romantic relationships simulate marriages.

Since, romantic interaction is intertwined, sometimes explicitly and sometimes only implicitly, with the institution of marriage, it is hardly surprising that male–female communication in courtship relationships tends to be highly susceptible to traditional images of masculinity and femininity. Recall the research presented in Chapter Two indicating that today's college students, who fancy themselves to be extremely liberal in their ideas about men and women, tend to become fairly conservative on issues involving interaction between dating couples. Even college women— consistently the most liberal group when it comes to occupational, educational, and leadership issues—take a conservative position concerning romantic interaction, including paying for date expenses, proposing marriage, and engaging in sexual intimacy before marriage.[37]

In the same vein, although a recent study reports that women typically feel free to "initiate" various events in platonic friendships,[38] research suggests that it is still the man's place to take the initiative in dating relationships.[39] In romantic relationships, initiating includes behaviors such as asking for the first date and moving in for the first kiss. Ultimately, initiating may boil down to proposing a more extended physical encounter, which, according to a 1988 study, men continue to be far more likely to do than women.[40]

It seems that the gender stereotypes aggressive and passive may take on special significance in romantic relationships given the potential for sexual intimacy. A recent article by Grauerholz and Serpe reports that men continue to be sexually "proactive," while women continue to be "reactive." This boils down to greater freedom for men to initiate sex and greater freedom for women to refuse sex—both perrogatives that ideally should be available to either a male or a female in a free society. The researchers conclude that the proposed "single sexual standard does not yet exist."[41] Indeed, there is evidence that the traditional double standard continues to operate in creating and perpetuating images of men as aggressive and women as passive.

Predictably, research suggests that the more sex-typed the participants, the more likely they will approve of male aggression and female passivity.[42] Therefore, it might be argued that change is imminent—i.e., individuals born into a gender-neutral world will be less sex-typed and a single standard will govern initiation in romantic relationships. If so, we would expect to see a single standard emerging among the nation's youth. But attitudes favoring male initiation appear to be especially rigid among adolescents girls and boys.[43] Perhaps newcomers need to play by established rules before they gain the confidence to improvise, or perhaps romantic interaction is highly resistant to change.

The obvious question is, then, why do women cling to tradition, or at least not campaign for equal power, when it comes to romantic relationships? Why accept a passive position in initiating these all-important relationships and controlling events in ongoing relationships? According to feminist critiques, "efforts to equalize women's status through legal reforms guaranteeing equal rights and formal equality may be insufficient for creating true sex equality since in the private and intimate spheres of life...women still find themselves subordinate to their boyfriends, lovers and husbands."[44] Of course, the issue of subordination is not settled by simply citing that men tend to be proactive and women tend to be reactive. The young men in my classes are quick to inform me that it is the woman who truly holds the power in dating relationships, since she can either accept or reject the advances of the man. Also, men must be subordinate, because they have to pick up the check!

In fact, the very issues raised by these students were investigated in a recent study. Traditionally, researchers have defined power in male–female interaction as a function of controlled resources. Thus, since the male dating partner controls the "asking" as well as the money, and usually drives the car, he may be assumed to be more powerful than the female.[45] But, as the young men in my classes suggest, actually providing resources may be seen as negatively correlated with having power, in the sense that the giver is less powerful than the taker. In fact, Sprecher found this to be the case in dating relationships for both males and females. However, her interviews also suggested a predictable twist to this scenario. To the extent that the male dating partner perceived that he had other options, the responsibility to initiate encounters and control the resources was seen as empowering. Apparently, a key factor in determining power in dating relationships is the perceived dependency of the partners on one another, not in terms of money, but in terms of social companionship. Since women have to "wait passively for someone else to show an interest," they perceive themselves as more dependent.[46]

Notably, the above discussion of power in dating relationships defines resources in seemingly traditionally male terms. But, the ultimate power cited by male students—the female's right to turn them down—has been identified by Safilios-Rothschild as one of several "feminine resources." She argues that, by the same tradition that renders men in control of certain resources, women are granted control of resources associated with love. In addition, women may control certain services that men want but cannot (or would rather not) buy.[47] It is interesting to note that nearly any service traditionally provided by women, even giving birth to children, can now be purchased for the right price.

Obviously, the resources labeled *feminine* are valuable commodities in romantic relationships, i.e., commodities that might be used for bargaining. But it is not difficult to imagine how, once "contributed," these resources reduce the power of the giver. According to Sprecher's respondents, male and female alike, women who give a great deal in relationships tend to surrender power. They tend to become highly dependent on their male partner for the very same resources they formerly controlled.[48]

Although the feminist movement promised sexual freedom for women, it seems important to note that the surrender of sexual favors continues to be understood as a gift given by a woman to a man—and a gift which, if given to too many men, serves to harm the reputation of the generous provider. As discussed in Chapter Three, linguistic labels for women who "give" a great deal are plentiful, but seldom have gender complements. The negative image of women who engage in sex with many partners, and the absence of a male counter-image, are probably related to another well-established cultural myth about romantic entanglements. Women, at least stereotypically, are supposed to attach sex to love, while men are expected to equate sex with pleasure, separable from love.

In line with these conceptualizations, college women, across studies conducted as recently as 1988, typically cited "emotional reasons" for engaging in sex, while college men cited "pleasure" far more often.[49] In fact, in one study this trend was one of the few correlated with biological sex, not psychological gender. This means that even men and women who presented themselves as androgynous conformed to gender-specific standards in explaining the reasons for sexual activity.[50]

Thus, romantic relationships continue to involve different motivations and different consequences for men and women, even as the relative educational, political, and economic status of women continue to improve. In 1978, a study conducted by Peplau reported that, to the extent that the female dating partner was career oriented and well educated, she was perceived as more powerful by both participants in the relationship.[51] But more recent studies suggest distinct limitations on the expression of power by women in dating relationships. The failure of women to initiate action in intimate relationships, the negative attitudes voiced by women concerning contributing certain resources, and the unchanging conceptualizations of male and female desires in dating relationships all seem to have countered the impact predicted by Peplau a decade ago.

So, in love relationships, which are held in very high esteem in our culture's fantasies, little has changed over the years. Tradition continues to dominate not only the fantasies, but the lived behaviors of men and women. Remarkably, young women often comment that they don't want to pursue power in these special relationships—that power ought not be an issue when it comes to love. They report that they enjoy being taken care of by men and see issues of equality as threatening or trivial. The reactions of men to this stance vary. Some counter that today's women are hypocrites; they want to assert their independence when it's convenient and be taken care of, too! Other young men admit that they are looking for an "old-fashioned girl." Still others acknowledge the value of an egalitarian relationship, where men and women share power and responsibility equally.

Various models of male–female couples are discussed in the next chapter, with specific reference to marriage. But, the same tension that characterizes the struggle between tradition and change in marriage tends to affect communication in dating relationships. Remember that love relationships are negotiated informally; acceptable standards of equality cannot be mandated by law. Each pair must struggle to create rules by which they can be together comfortably. At present, it seems fair to say that traditional images continue to influence the interaction of men and women in the private sphere of love and marriage.

Yet economic and social factors are simultaneously pushing women into the public sphere and demanding that men make room for them. So, women and men will have to learn to balance tradition and change as they pursue an exclusive attachment with a member of the opposite sex. Most of the young women in my classes voice their desire to "have it all." However, to the extent that "having it all" for a woman involves a dating or marital relationship with a man, she may encounter contradictory self-images as she seeks to be both a successful career woman and a successful significant other. Also, according to Duck, it is noteworthy that loving couples must display their relationship, at least in part, before interested friends and family. Aspects of the relationship are visible to others, and despite vehement protests to the contrary, the judgments of others are difficult to ignore.[52] So, it may be very unrealistic to believe that we can maintain traditional sex role divisions in the realm of love, as we pursue equality in the world of work.

Although feminist authors have stressed that most male–female relationships—including romantic relationships—are inherently unsatisfying to women,[53] heterosexual love continues to dominate the culture. Granted, women, as well as men, are pursuing career goals in increasing numbers, while postponing marriage and planning childbearing. Moreover, alternative lifestyles are becoming more prevalent. People variously choose to or at least come to terms with remaining single, remaining childless, becoming single parents, maintaining long-distance romances, etc. Still, the love fantasy persists and continues to be tied to the nuclear family. Therefore, establishing an exclusive male–female relationship continues to be a major pastime among Americans. It will be fascinating to observe how young lovers of the future reconcile issues of gender equality with traditional images of romance.

CONDUCT YOUR OWN RESEARCH

1. Construct a survey in which you ask respondents to identify and answer questions about their closest same-sex friend and their closest opposite-sex friend. Ask them to cite the length and nature of the relationship. Then ask them to respond to questions you deem pertinent to the investigation of sex differences in friendship.

2. For a period of one week, keep a diary in which you record "relationship stories" that people share with you. At the end of the week, compare the number and quality of the stories about same-sex vs. cross-sex friendships and about platonic vs. romantic friendships. Also, make a note of the gender compositions of the situations in which you heard the stories.

3. Write a brief fictional scenario in which two lovers part. Try to incorporate some of the evidence about romantic relationships discussed in this chapter. Then, prepare a version of the scenario, in which the characters behave according to opposite-sex tendencies. Ask readers to rate the two versions as realistic or unrealistic and explain the ratings.

DISCUSS THE ISSUES

1. Share your views on chivalry. Is it dead or alive? In what forms is it desirable? objectionable?

2. Are women today more liberated in terms of sexuality than their mothers and grandmothers were? If not, why not? If so, what factors have contributed to their liberation?

3. Discuss your experiences with platonic friendships. Be specific about how they began, how long they lasted, and, if appropriate, how they ended.

CHAPTER 14

RELATIONSHIPS IN THE FAMILY

The family continues to occupy a special status in our culture, despite rumblings of its demise. To begin with, the legal and economic structure dictates that family members be connected, even though they may wish to disavow their ties. (This is often most apparent during income tax preparation.) But it is more than a legal connection that links members of families. By tradition, they are symbolically identified by the same name and, according to social norms, they are perceived as a unit. One family member's actions impact on the others, whether they bring pride or shame, wealth or poverty. So, it would be an oversimplification just to say that family relationships involve blood ties or legal substitutes.

Relationships in families are governed by tradition, often by religion, and certainly by law in many respects, but each family experience is presumably created by the participants. Many college students discover, often in late-night talks, that the family relationships experienced by one individual, although called by the same label as those experienced by another individual, are distinctly different in form and meaning. Perhaps because we experience family interaction from the very beginning (most of us are born into a family or placed in one soon after birth), we take for granted that our experiences with parents, siblings, aunts and uncles, and so on, are typical, having known no others. We seldom question the nature of family interaction until we are already deeply committed to membership in a particular family.

The truth is that American families come in many forms. The nuclear family, portrayed in Dick and Jane storybooks, is only one of America's families, one that is becoming less dominant. Galvin and Brommel point out that alternate family formations are appearing in increasing numbers: the single-parent family (one parent with one or more children), the blended family (two parents with children, at least one of one of whom is not the product of their union), the extended family (a family unit that includes relatives beyond the nuclear unit), and the couple without children.[1]

Thus, families differ widely in form and function. It is somewhat ironic that, despite their growing prominence, alternate family formations are typically talked about in relation to the nuclear family. Hence, we may hear a single-parent identified as "both mother and father" to a child, or we may point out that a child was "raised by an aunt" or we may happily report that a stepfather is "just like a real father." In the same vein, couples without children, although increasingly common, are often a curiosity. Only recently have researchers taken an interest in the small, but reportedly growing, number of couples who are voluntarily childless, i.e., biologically capable of reproduction, but not willing to conceive. Often researchers present explanations for the decision, in terms of negative family experiences, unusual devotion to career (but only for the potential mother), expiration of the biological clock (but only for the potential mother), etc.[2]

In keeping with the feminist emphasis on choice for women, a few analysts have pointed out that childless couples are not necessarily failures of society, but rather, tend to include highly educated, otherwise successful individuals (particularly the women). The marriages are neither unstable nor unhappy, but these couples often find themselves rejected by family and friends who simply don't understand this violation of societal norms.[3] It is most telling that, when they encounter a childless couple, well-intentioned outsiders invariably suspect infertility, and may suggest adoption, proof that having children continues to be viewed as an integral part of married life in our culture.[4]

Another choice violating the norms of the traditional family is the choice to live as a family, without the sanction of formal marriage vows. Commonly referred to as *cohabitation,* the practice in which unrelated adults share a household is becoming more prevalent. Cohabitants range in age, marital status, and degree of commitment to one another. According to a recent analysis by Yelsma, cohabiting individuals fall into two categories: (1) "those who want to fulfill their own needs and tend to reject marital commitment" and (2) "those who want to grow and develop a relationship with their partner and view cohabitation as a prelude to marital commitment."[5] It seems logical that the former group should have been discussed (and was to some degree) in the last chapter. Like dating couples, these pairs tend to be quite young and are often transient. Individuals in this category generally acknowledge openly that they will remain together as long as the rewards (e.g., satisfaction and enjoyment) outweigh the costs (e.g., social sacrifices, exclusion of other relationships). In this sense, cohabitating may be seen as an extension of dating.[6]

More appropriate in this chapter is the discussion of cohabitating couples who view living together as a prelude to marriage. Presumably, they may adopt all of the characteristics of a family, although they may not be held legally responsible for their connection unless the union is determined to be marriage by "common law." In some cases, cohabitating couples have children in residence, either mutually conceived or the result of "blending." For these couples the choice to cohabitate may be driven by legal matters concerning former marriages. Older couples are also choosing cohabitation more often than they had in previous decades. For many elderly couples, a legal and financial union is not feasible, but the social and emotional bonding is desirable.[7]

In terms of communication behaviors, cohabitation, at least for young couples, functions as a rehearsal for marriage; it serves as a transitional period in which individuals do not feel pressured to resolve issues and coordinate their behavior. Research suggests that cohabitants are less patterned in their communication, and less influenced by sex-specific standards than married individuals. Both of these conclusions were supported in a recent study comparing self-reported couple communication between married couples and unmarried couples. Across items, although unmarried women and men portrayed their behavior as traditionally feminine and masculine, respectively, they proved to be considerably less traditional than married women and men. Also, there was a greater tendency for inconsistency between the accounts provided by the cohabiting partners as compared to those provided by the husbands and wives. These two trends emerged regardless of the length of the relationship. Therefore, it seemed to be the marital status, not the time together, that was associated with resolving gender-related issues in the relationship.[8]

Notably, although voluntary childlessness and cohabitation are becoming increasingly common, they remain, at present, violations of the family myth in our culture. When couples choose these alternatives, regardless of the validity of their reasons, they are likely to suffer disapproval and isolation. Other alternate family forms, such as single-parenthood and blending, are somewhat more acceptable, particularly when the individuals in question are viewed as victims of bad marriages (in the case of divorce) or ill fortune (in the case of death of the spouse). It seems worth stating again, however, that the prevailing myth identifies the traditional family—an exclusive, loving, legal male–female partnership complete with offspring—as the model to which all alternatives are compared. Even though the alternatives may threaten the traditional family in terms of statistics, they do not appear to have threatened the fairy tale image. Let us consider, therefore, the implications of the "ideal" boy-meets-girl scenario, noting exceptions and probable obstacles as we examine issues that impact on male–female communication in the family context.

THE TRADITIONAL MARRIAGE MYTH

The cultural myth that a new family is grounded in the love and mutual commitment of a man and woman has already been discussed at length. Whether sanctioned by religion or not, this commitment is assumed to be exclusive and lifelong, "forsaking all others until death do you part." In some ceremonies, future children of the union are blessed in advance. Although the bride's and groom's parents may participate in the ceremony (and usually pick up the bill), part of the love myth is that the newlyweds leave their parents to begin their new life together. For the bride, this exit is symbolized by trading her father's name for her husband's name.

The marriage ceremony symbolizes the special status of the spousal relationship in our culture, and the accompanying assumptions concerning love, sex, and children.

This male–female relationship, conceived in love and dedicated to the pursuit of shared well-being, is recognized as the most significant, albeit the most difficult, pairing in society. This joining is expected to be intense, to include the integration of goals and dreams, the cooperative management of shared responsibility, the mutual fulfillment of individual needs, the merging of two formerly single entities into a couple.

It stands to reason that traditions, learned from parents who learned them from parents, might be very valuable in assisting newly married couples to achieve these difficult ends. But part of the love myth is that each new pair must make it work on their own. "Going home to mother" is considered a last resort, not a fact-finding mission. Worse yet is asking for help or support from in-laws, even though they may be quite familiar with the problems of living with the new husband or wife. Also, if today's newlyweds do go back to yesterday's experts for advise, it seems that tradition may conflict with modern egalitarian ideas about marriage. After all, newlyweds are not immune to the redefinition of men and women that is presumably part and parcel of legislative reform. Although the extent of the liberalizing effect of the feminist movement remains debatable, it logically suggests certain difficulties for husbands and wives of the future—and the present.

In the absence of acceptable traditions about roles and rules in marriage, individuals may have to negotiate the relationship, complete with expectations about each individual's behavior. Survey evidence suggests that this is the case in contemporary America. Whereas married respondents of past decades endorsed societal standards, today's couples "largely reject normative standards and societal values about marriage...and are more prone to use interpersonal communication to negotiate role definitions than rely on the traditionally defined marital and family roles."[9] In this chapter, some of the issues that may be targeted for negotiation are examined.

THE DIVISION OF LABOR

One issue that invariably warrants considerable attention in today's marriages is the division of labor. Indeed, this is an issue that recurs in this text and seems to impact on all sorts of other issues. At a societal level, the sex segregation of labor is often cited as the primary factor keeping women from equal status. Regardless of the importance attached to integrating various workplaces, few contemporary voices would argue (at least not publicly) that discrimination ought to be allowed without good reason. Discussed at length in Chapter Twelve, arguments against integrating work typically hinge on assumptions that women (or, less often, men) are not biologically suited to certain types of work. Within the family, there is one job for which women are particularly well suited and men are distinctly ill equipped. It is often through an indirect connection to childbearing that sex role traditions in the family are justified.

Child Care. Over the years, the biological reality that women carry children and possess the physical capability to sustain them after birth (i.e., breast-feed them), has been the basis for assuming that women are better suited than men to nurture young children. As Stephen and Harrison point out, social-biologic theory does suggest that females "biologically invest more in reproduction than males"—presumably more time and more physical risk.[10] But, feminists argue that, in a patriarchical society, this investment is extended beyond reason. Granted, caring for children need not be seen as a "sentence" that men have imposed on women. For many of us, it constitutes the single greatest joy in our lives. However, to the extent that providing that care full-time confines females to the privacy of their homes, excluding them from participating in the wage-earning world, it certainly serves to foster female dependency and keep women from positions of power.

In the extreme, according to Perkins, this division of labor effectively creates the prevailing sex stereotypes. Men function in a world that calls for them to be strong, competitive, and unemotional; women's settings call for them to be nurturing, emotional, and even "flighty," since they may have to relate on the level of a preschooler and simultaneously act as the model of adult decorum. Thus, stereotypes are not completely fictional, according to Perkins, but they do invert cause and effect. Sex-stereotypic qualities do not cause an individual to seek a particular environment. Rather, women and men find themselves confined to different worlds and develop qualities and self-images appropriate to the requirements of those worlds.[11]

To consider the dilemma from a more neutral stance, creating and caring for children is part of the myths of the traditional marriage and family. But, children require near constant care at first, and the parents are expected, morally and legally, to provide that care. At the same time, parents are required to provide support in the form of hard, cold cash to purchase shelter, food, etc. The traditional model, the one that the feminists condemn, is a complementary partnership, prescribing that the male parent assume the role of breadwinner and the female parent assume the role of caregiver to the children. This model continues to characterize American family life, despite the cries of women's rights activists that it subordinates women. Incidentally, even feminists are divided on this issue. Many women argue that it is women themselves, not men, who have given the housewife a bad name; that women ought to campaign for more recognition of the valuable services they have traditionally performed, instead of implying that only work outside the home is worthwhile.[12]

An alternate solution to the problem is to adopt a symmetrical model, in which partners share both the wage-earner role and the caregiver role. As this model becomes more prevalent, so do the labels by which it is identified: dual-worker, dual-earner, dual-career, dual-provider. But, it is interesting to note that all these labels focus on the external employment status of the couple, not on their relative positions inside the home. More importantly, the same analysts who identify families in which both partners are employed as "dual-whatever," often adopt the term *traditional* for families in which the husband works for pay and the wife does not.[13] Some forward-thinkers are opting for a parallel term, *one-provider,* but recognize that the overwhelming number of these couples are traditional in that the man is the breadwinner.[14]

The ramifications of the traditional model are also apparent in the choices made by women who have opted to pursue work outside the home. It seems that many young women who plan to become career women also intend to have children. A 1988 survey of 250 college women indicates that respondents have various plans for achieving both goals—not one of which involves finding a full-time househusband. Many plan to postpone childbirth and/or take temporary breaks from established careers; others plan to work part time while their children are young; still others hope to find partners willing to share the child-rearing responsibilities.[15] Keep in mind that a survey of male college students as to the same dilemma would seem ill conceived.

Scientific technology has made it easy for women to plan childbirth, but, once the child is born, it continues to be primarily the mother's life that is affected by the addition of a child to the marriage. Indeed, although feminists have argued that the traditional division of labor in the family subordinates women, many important legal battles have centered on the recognition that child care is a woman's issue. After years of rigorous campaigning, women are now guaranteed, by law, maternity leave. The minimum time allowed is typically six weeks, but, in many cases, women leave work with or without compensation for several years. At present, the gender complement, paternity leave, is neither legally mandated nor socially acceptable. Imagine the reaction to a man who wanted to take six weeks off from work to feed and change a new baby, much less to abandon his breadwinner status altogether until the child was an adult. (We might allow this choice, if the wife had a better job than the husband, but statistics show that this is highly unlikely.)[16]

Obviously, even in families that opt for a symmetrical model, a working father is probably never asked to explain or defend his choice. The term itself sounds silly. Fathers work; that's part of the traditional makeup of the family. On the other hand, the rare young man who opts to assume the primary caregiver role full time and abandon work outside the home will undoubtedly be questioned by his peers, even today. More commonly, though, it is the young woman who believes she can "have it all" who will feel the tension between career and child care, experiencing the guilt that accompanies leaving her baby or suffering the occupational setbacks that accompany the interruption of her career. Perhaps the opportunity to make the choice is evidence of progress. According to one recent report, "the majority now tolerates or approves of mothers working and no longer believes that children are necessarily harmed if their mothers are employed."[17] Still, the very suggestion that young children could be harmed by maternal employment but not, presumably, by paternal employment, is evidence that women are expected to take the primary responsibility for child care in our culture.

It seems clear that the cultural image of Mother Nature as nurturer is alive and well, both in theory and practice. There is overwhelming evidence that early child care remains women's work. Based on recent interview data obtained from new mothers and fathers, LaRossa and LaRossa report that "both parents assume that Mom is the one to orchestrate and implement the childcare." This is true regardless of her employment status. Although housewives assume a greater portion of the child-care work (7:1 compared to their husbands), young working mothers also assume a disproportionate share (2:1).[18] When fathers do spend time with children, it is often labeled *helping*. Remarkably, this arrangement seems to be very acceptable to women. In fact, mothers indicate less dissatisfaction with this imbalance than fathers. The reason for this discrepancy is unclear, but it must be noted that the failure of men to assume an equal partnership in care-giving may not be entirely due to their negative valuation of the nurturer role. For whatever reason, women reserve their special status in this realm of family interaction, regardless of their employment status.[19]

It is certainly intriguing that women outnumber men when it comes to favoring the status quo in terms of the traditional division of labor, but this should not cloud that fact that the vast majority of both men and women still believe that caring for young children remains women's work. Nevertheless, a recent report suggests that a portion of today's fathers are becoming more involved with child care. Sadly, the surveys also indicate that fathers experience a great deal of stress as a result of their attempts to schedule working hours around their wife's work and/or around the demands of being a parent.[20] Couples with small children logically experience tremendous pressure as they negotiate work schedules, private time, family time, and couple time. Experts agree that the loss of available time is the single greatest challenge faced by married couples as they make the transition to parenthood.[21] From personal experience and numerous interviews with married couples, the author can state, without pause, that it is couple time that is most often sacrificed in families with small children. According to one source, these "couples report unusually high levels of marital distress, with levels for both the husbands and the wives approaching the cutoff typically predictive of future divorce."[22]

It stands to reason that having to negotiate child care, an issue that traditionalists don't have to negotiate, would seem troublesome, especially to the male partner. But there is reason to believe that the successful sharing of this endeavor, as difficult as it may be, improves marital relationships. According to Hertz, couples who adopt the symmetrical model, thereby negotiating the details of marriage in accord with the demands of dual employment outside the home, "understand each other's lives and experience a high degree of empathy."[23] Also, young fathers stand to gain, personally as well as relationally, from this arrangement. To begin with, analysts point out that "the father in a dual-career family has a wife who is a co-provider, emancipating him from the strains of total economic responsibility for the family."[24] Of course, this emancipation may be difficult to enjoy for many men, given the stereotypic image of masculinity in America. Sometimes equally difficult to enjoy for the particularly macho man, and sadder by far, are the benefits of sharing time with children, especially babies. Arguably, the male experience could be "enhanced [by] opportunities to enjoy the development of the child, to experience genuine human interaction, often lacking in the alienating workplace, and to develop the nurturant side of his personality."[25]

Research conducted among single fathers, which admittedly does not focus on the dynamics between a husband and wife, clearly indicates that, in the absence of a female partner, men are very capable caregivers. Contrary to the rumor, they seldom recruit girlfriends or female relatives to nurture the children in their place. According to all indications, single fathers are as competent as single mothers in performing the role of primary caregiver. They are open and caring with children, spend time with them in family activities, and enjoy the father role.[26] In intact traditional families, with father and mother both available, it remains debatable whether women hinder men from usurping the pleasure of child care or whether men opt out when the traditional caregiver is available. But, there is little doubt that fathering need not be restricted to earning a good living.

At present, young couples are certainly not free of prescriptions about success as either breadwinner or nurturer, but the door has been opened for them to question the traditional division of labor and adopt a model that each finds personally satisfying and that, together, they deem beneficial to their children. This may be the single greatest challenge facing marriages in the coming decades.

Household Responsibilities.   Child care seems to constitute the most-talked about, and arguably the most pressing, labor issue that young married couples must negotiate. But, the sharing of a single household also necessitates that domestic work be distributed between the partners, and this topic often rivals the discussion of children when young women discuss their lives with one another. Traditionally, our culture distinguishes "men's work" from "women's work." Coincidentally, the lines of division are not unrelated to the assumption that women care for children, even in homes in which no children exist. For example, even in these liberal times, men continue to do the outdoor work around the home—yard work, automobile mainte- nance, snow removal, etc. Women continue to do the indoor work.[27] According to one analyst, women continue to be assigned to "the constantly repetitive and much more time-consuming tasks":[28] meal preparation, cleaning, laundry, grocery shopping, etc.

Keep in mind, as well, that the responsibilities traditionally assigned to the female partner seem to be more confining than those assigned to the male partner; notice the obvious similarity between the terms *housework* and *housewife*. When it comes to the daily maintenance of the home, researchers agree that today's liberated woman continues to struggle for assistance from her husband, even when both work.[29] It seems that women, in increasing numbers, have been either emancipated from the home or pushed out the door by financial necessity to enter the ranks of the employed. Those who argue that the traditional division of labor indirectly influences images of men and women ought to praise the flood of women into the public realm. However, the expected reallocation of work on the home front has not kept pace. As House phrases it, "the preponderance of evidence suggests that women generally assume the additional responsibility of provider without a commensurate reduction in their responsibility for the traditionally feminine domestic...functions."[30] In other words, even working women continue to be tied to their homes.

Thus, the cooperative distribution of the domestic work necessary to manage a home, with or without children, remains a challenge for most married couples. In a fascinating article titled "What Do Women Want from Men?," Kathleen Gerson points out that, as contemporary women experience "changing social position," they will also experience "changes in their expectations of and relationships with men." In the future, more women will not need to marry a man for financial support. Consequently, women will experience greater freedom to choose a life-style compatible with their own self-perception. Women who want to divide the work according to tradition, may opt for the standard complementary marriage; women who want symmetrical relationships can seek men who are willing to assume equal responsibility for domestic chores, in exchange for financial benefits and, very likely, a partner who shares similar experiences.[31] It remains curious, though, why so many women currently settle for less: partnerships in which they work outside the home (usually full time) and continue to perform a disproportionate amount of the domestic work.

Notwithstanding the argument that the traditional division of work contributes to narrow stereotypes, either union, complementary or symmetrical, seems a workable solution. Logically, the freedom to choose is progress in and of itself, but, as many grandparents and greatgrandparents have voiced, there was a certain comfort to the traditional arrangement. Given the growing range of choices, married couples will have to rely on interpersonal communication, as Petronio suggests, to negotiate a mutually acceptable division of the work involved in establishing and maintaining a family unit.[32] In the absence of traditional gender specifications, it remains to be seen exactly how couples will (and do) divide the work inherent in a marriage. Nyquist et al. cite personal expertise as a logical determinant of which partner will perform a particular task in an egalitarian relationship. However, they add that, at present, there is little evidence that "permissive attitudes" expressed about egalitarianism per se actually make their way into "actual changes in practice" concerning household management.[33]

Understandably, to the extent that traditional parents have taught children to help around the house in gender-specific ways, the expertise criteria will probably result in the perpetuation of the traditional, sex-stereotyped division of household work.[34] Furthermore, as Denmark et al. speculate, a period of "uncertainty" is required in order for liberal sex-role attitudes to effect real changes in behavior, and, in the case of tasks deemed "trivial," it may be easier to follow tradition than to deal with the uncertainty.[35] If so, couples may not be willing to invest the time and energy needed to negotiate a reasonable distribution of household chores.

DECISION MAKING AND POWER

Because marriage, by definition, involves a legal and financial connection, even the most independent individuals must make certain decisions in tandem with a partner. The degree of interdependence in a marriage often grows beyond the obligatory legal commitment, and couples find themselves making daily decisions about the allocation of their time, the coordination of their social activities, the distribution of their money, the use of the bathroom, etc. Some analysts believe that the degree of *marital interaction* (defined as "the amount of joint participation in day-to-day activities") is an important factor in determining the quality of a marriage.[36] If so, the communication that facilitates joint decision making is also very important.

Although few couples, even dual-career couples, can be classified as egalitarian when it comes to dividing the housework, some studies report that decision making is more likely to be shared, particularly when the wife works. According to Nyquist et al., in the typical contemporary marriage, the "wife and husband have relatively equal input on most decisions.[37] However, it would be hasty to interpret reports of equal input as indicative of equal influence. Rather, the discussion of relative power in a relationship must accompany the discussion of decision making, because when joint input leads to disagreement, partners often attempt to influence one another in the desired direction.

Of course, it would be naive to wager that the partners in a given marriage necessarily wield equal power at the onset. As an extension of romantic love, marriage is seldom characterized by the equal distribution of power, in sharp contrast to platonic friendship.[38] As explained in the last chapter, many analysts believe that power in relationships is related to the control of resources. Therefore, if husbands have "easier access to sources of influence, such as money and position, [they also have] more opportunity to exercise power over others" with less access to the same resources— namely, their wives.[39]

Although this was found to be the case in foundational research conducted by Blood and Wolfe in a widely cited 1960 study, it stands to reason that the distribution of resources should have changed by now.[40] However, in a 1980 review, McDonald reported that studies over the decades continued to indicate that men have the upper hand in controlling resources and, presumably, decisions within the family.[41] Remember that, although a growing number of women are attaining money and position through employment outside the home, even the most recent reports indicate that the average man still earns more than his wife and is likely to advance farther in his career than she does. As recently as 1986, the majority of employed married women characterized themselves as grossly underpaid and rated their chances for promotion as either nonexistent (31%) or not very good (26%)."[42] Thus, the operative concept at present may be the male's easier access, as opposed to absolute access, to resources, and, therefore, power, in the family.

Although it may be somewhat distasteful, it is widely accepted by scholars that, if power is defined as the access to tangible resources obtained outside the relationship, women continue to occupy subordinate positions. However, to the extent that the egalitarian image is judged positively by the participants, young men and women may choose to ignore the import of money and position when it comes to making decisions within the relationship. Young couples could view traditional, complementary relationships as equal, with otherwise unemployed homemakers wielding the same degree of influence as their breadwinning husbands. But it is interesting to note that there is a strong connection between a couple's claim to egalitarianism and the female partner's educational level, her income, and the number of children in the home. Apparently, women with money, position, and relative freedom either seek out egalitarian partners or earn equal position in the family based on the same access to resources as men.[43]

As the debate pertaining to the balance of power in marriage rages on, other analysts have investigated influence as a communicative achievement. It has been suggested that men and women use different strategies to "get their way." The resultant research is not totally unrelated to the power-distribution issue, since we know that superiors and subordinates tend to use different persuasive strategies, regardless of gender.[44] But, it may well be that, even in situations involving equal partners, there are distinct male and female styles of influence. People seem to believe, at least, that "men-in-general" use different power strategies than "women-in-general." According to Gruber and White, a survey of nearly 300 respondents verified the belief that, even in relationships they label "intimate," men use direct, rational, assertive, and sometimes even aggressive strategies to "get their way," while women use indirect, subtle, emotional appeals.[45]

Coincidentally, the very same respondents described themselves as exceptions to these rules. Both females and males reported that they used socially desirable strategies most often: "reason and logic" was the most frequently reported strategy for both sexes, with "compromise" a close second. Females admitted resorting to a stereotypically feminine ploy, "plead, beg or pray," more often than males, but did not indicate that they frequently used flattery or deceit, like "women-in-general." According to their expressed self-perceptions, the males in the study were most reasonable; they seldom used "threats" or "physical force" to get their way, in sharp contrast to their judgments about "men-in-general."[46]

As is often the case, self-reports differ sharply from stereotypic images when it comes to sex differences in style of exerting power in intimate relationships. It may well be the case that closed-ended surveys are inappropriate for gathering detailed information about how individuals act in intimate contexts. Many researchers are opting to collect and analyze detailed open-ended descriptions either in place of or in conjunction with closed-ended surveys. For example, Falbo and Peplau asked individuals to write lengthy essays entitled "How I Get My Way." After careful consideration of the content of these essays, the analysts concluded that there is empirical support for the stereotype that men use direct approaches in decision making. A male is more likely than a female to ask the partner for concessions, to try to persuade the partner to see the opposing view, etc. Women use indirect approaches more often. A female is more likely to hint at what she wants, attempt to divert the partner, or create a positive mood. In this respect, the essays seem to merge self-reports and stereotypes with specific examples.[47]

However, Falbo and Peplau report another dimension of sex differences in power strategies. It seems that men tend to use bilateral strategies in attempting to influence a female partner. Bilateral strategies are interactive; they require that the partner participate, e.g., "persuading" or "bargaining." Women tend to use unilateral strategies, which require no cooperation, e.g., "withdrawing" or "telling."[48] This contrast is fascinating, and somewhat surprising, in terms of the stereotype that women are more relationship-oriented and men are more self-oriented. At first glance, the essays written by men seem to contain proof that they are more concerned than women about adopting a relationship-centered approach to decision making. However, the analysts point out that "the results can be best explained in terms of power differences." Apparently, "because men expect compliance to their influence attempts," they use the most direct and expedient approach: confront the partner and state your case. "Conversely, because women anticipate noncompliance, they are more likely than men to report in their essays the use of unilateral strategies": since he probably won't budge no matter what you do, there's no point in making moves that depend on the partner's cooperation. This may seem a rather arbitrary conclusion, but consider the related finding that "Individuals [male or female] who reported having greater power than their partner in their relationship were likely to report using bilateral power strategies."[49]

As mentioned in the discussion of dating relationships, it would be a mistake to assume that all resources in a marriage are characteristically masculine, nor that direct strategies are necessarily more effective than indirect strategies. Although the metaphors are clear about which partner "wears the pants," and "is the boss" and ultimately "knows best," researchers have discovered that women have not allowed themselves to be totally dominated by intimate partners without developing characteristically feminine countermoves based on traditionally feminine resources. However, critics have pointed out that women's influence strategies are related to communicative behaviors that are not only indirect, but also manipulative. One indirect influence strategy, reportedly used by women is labelled *expressed helplessness*. In a sense, women use the stereotypic image of dependence on men in order to obtain a desired outcome. According to Weimann, when women ask men for assistance, they often mention that they "have a problem" or "need help" whereas, when men ask women for assistance, they directly ask for or demand help or state that they would be grateful for help.[50]

Johnson concurs that women use the resources they possess in the culture to communicate persuasively toward desired ends.[51] If helplessness can be seen as a "resource," it may be a strategy that women can use within the limits of perceived sex appropriateness. Certainly, showing concern for the other as an individual and expressing a positive affect toward the other are potentially influential strategies that women often use.[52] One research team hypothesized that women also use self-disclosure, an affiliative behavior at which women are most likely more skilled than men, to achieve persuasive ends in cross-sex interaction.[53]

Perhaps, as most subordinate populations, women have cultivated strategies that are nonthreatening to their "superiors," but also effective in obtaining desired outcomes. Certainly, children across the ages have learned how to get what they want from parents, and few critics would question the distribution of resources and power in the typical parent–child dyad. According to one recent study, children, as women, are slightly more likely to be influential in family decisions to the extent that they contribute to the pool of family resources.[54] So, the husband–wife relationship may resemble the parent–child relationship more closely than most married women would like to acknowledge. In any case, women may have less to lose by avoiding strategies traditionally masculine; in experimental settings, both men and women have been critical of females who use direct power strategies, evaluating them less favorably and judging them less competent.[54]

Marriage may constitute the most demanding, most constant, and most important context for decision making between adult men and women. Mutual decisions are continually required, except in very independent unions, which are difficult to maintain in our couple-oriented society. The partners may have separate jobs, separate friends, and even separate bedrooms, but they will find themselves invited in tandem to most social events. Similarly, they may be able to negotiate separate bank accounts, but they will find it difficult to be treated as independent financial entities when they file for credit ratings. Perhaps most seriously, if they share children, they share a responsibility and, one would hope, a dedication to the same goals for them.

Despite the prevalence of decision-making communication in married life, marriage may constitute the most difficult of decision-making contexts. To begin with, it involves two individuals who probably use different styles of influence and who may have difficulty empathizing with one another because they live traditionally dissimilar lives. Even if they are more alike than different, married partners may find that the decisions they make together are stressful precisely because each must bargain with the other for free time, individual space, etc. In short, mutual decisions often involve individual sacrifices, and achieving an acceptable balance is crucial.

MARITAL SATISFACTION

Because the marital dyad constitutes the cornerstone of the family and because we are weaned on stories of "true love," the absence of marital bliss may be doubly difficult to accept. Ironically, sustaining a marriage simultaneously represents success as an individual and a threat to individuality. So, marital discord is very common and is usually charged with emotion. Giving in to the discord, denying the union, places a stigma on both individuals and entails long-term repercussions for the entire family. Yet, it is a well-known fact that a large percentage of marriages do not last forever. Indeed, roughly half end in divorce before ten years have passed. The prevalence of divorce in our culture has been the subject of a good deal of informal debate and the motivation for a huge body of formal research. Frankly, there is little consensus in either arena as to what factor(s) cause divorce or about how to avoid divorce. Yet married couples and scholars alike continue to search for the perfect "formula" to produce strong, durable marriages, apparently convinced that longevity is the mark of a successful marriage. In many minds, longevity is taken to be indicative of stability and fulfillment. It follows that the marriages that last longest are best.[56]

Of course, we all know couples who remain together but aren't satisfied with their relationships. Booth and White point out that divorce is not the only sign of instability. They argue that "thinking about divorce" is also evidence that the marriage is unstable.[57] Consider the individual who spends a great deal of time regretting the marriage, wishing divorce was possible, reviewing the reasons why divorce is impossible, etc. Surely this individual is not part of a highly stable marriage, even though the marriage may endure. Still, a golden anniversary represents an "accomplishment" in our culture—something to be proud of regardless of other measures of relationship quality.

Duck raises an interesting question about longevity in relationships when he asks whether relationships stay together due to the absence of negative factors or come apart due to the absence of positive factors?[58] The distinction may be especially pertinent to marital relationships since the myth is that love sustains the relationship. To the extent that couples believe this myth, they may assume that little effort should be required, even in the face of negative events. Yet, considerable attention has been devoted to determining both the negative factors that can deter a couple from its golden anniversary, and the positive factors that can make a lifetime together fulfilling to the participants. Many of these factors are intertwined with the traditions of masculinity and femininity and affected by sex differences in communication.

Commitment.   It may sound foolish to name commitment as a factor that may or may not influence the only relationship to which individuals voluntarily vow, before witnesses, to be committed exclusively and permanently. But, though all married couples promise to be exclusively and deeply devoted to one another, the depth and steadfastness of that devotion varies considerably from couple to couple. Obviously, the exchange of loyalty between the partners is tremendously valuable to a marriage. According to Rusbult, partners who hold fast to their vows of loyalty can compensate for other factors that cause dissatisfaction in a marriage. Having promised to stay married for the duration of their lives, "for better or for worse," these individuals weather the storm and/or overlook long-term shortcomings of the union. As Rusbult points out, this is a relatively passive approach to marital dissatisfaction, but, nevertheless, it results in longevity.[59]

Finlay, Starnes and Alvarez explain that women are more likely than men to remain loyal in hard times, due to inequities in the division of labor and the distribution of resources in the traditional family. Until recently, they argue, a woman had little choice but to remain married, due to economic dependence and to the stigma attached to divorce, which has traditionally been more salient for women.[60] Even now, many women find that divorce is not feasible or is not worth the price. The majority of today's women, working women notwithstanding, remain financially dependent on their spouses. If a woman does opt to disavow her loyalty to a bad marriage and is able to support herself (and her children), statistics indicate that she is likely to remain lonely and isolated. It is not difficult to understand why most divorced individuals, male or female, hope to remarry. After all, our society is centered around family life. But it is ironic that a divorced woman is less likely to remarry than her ex-husband, particularly if she earns a good living and is well educated.[61]

It seems that a decided sex difference characterizes the rates of remarriage in our supposedly liberated society. Men are more likely than women to find a second partner, and they are far more successful at this endeavor if they are well educated. This is true regardless of the divorced man's age or his status as a parent. However, for women, remarriage is greater among younger women, particularly those of lower economic status who have no children.[62] One explanation for the statistical contrast is that men find the divorcee in question unattractive or unsuitable as a wife. Perhaps she is too independent, too aggressive, too unfeminine. More likely, though, these statistics provide support for Jesse Bernard's theory, first voiced during the 1970s. Bernard suggested that marriage is qualitatively different for men and women. She argued that, despite the commonly held belief that women are constantly trying to "trap" men into marriage and men are constantly trying to avoid the trap, on the whole marriage is good for men and bad for women.[63] Indeed, if marriage is so repulsive to men and so attractive to women, why do so many divorced men, "free at last" and capable of supporting themselves, opt to rejoin the ranks of the marrieds? And why do divorced women in the same condition remain single?

One decided benefit of the women's movement, for both "traditionalists" and "feminists," is the attention being paid to the female experience in our culture. Regardless of the lifestyle a young woman chooses for herself, public awareness that marriage is not without costs for women can only result in more informed decision making. We are just recently learning about the number of women who remain in highly abusive marriages, demonstrating the power of "commitment." In this extreme, commitment may be viewed as positive for the marriage, but extremely dangerous and destructive, especially for the fragile, dependent partner. Battered wives and wife batterers seem to symbolize, in the clearest terms, the danger of overly rigid sex stereotypes.

Although cases of blind loyalty and commitment are intriguing (and disturbing), cases of infidelity are far more numerous. Typically, marital infidelity is operationalized, both in the everyday world and the scholarly literature, as participation in extramarital sex. But, just as "thinking of divorce" is evidence of instability, Glass and Wright argue that many individuals abandon their marital commitment emotionally. These analysts point out that emotional infidelity has been neglected by researchers, although, in their study, it was more likely than sexual infidelity to accompany marital dissatisfaction. Ultimately, it is the combination of sexual and emotional noncommitment that is most threatening to a marriage.[64]

Coincidentally, a fascinating sex difference characterizes reports of infidelity. Men report a greater incidence of extramarital intercourse than women; not only do more men than women say they have engaged in extramarital sex, but many say they did so early in the relationship and continued the practice, with numerous partners.[65] This evidence is not surprising, since self-reports about sexual activity usually reinforce the myth that sex is a male perogative. Whether offered on an anonymous questionnaire or over a pitcher of beer, males may believe that accounts of sexual activity (factual or fictional) increase their status, while women withhold the same reports in an effort to portray themselves in a socially desirable light.

In any case, the more telling information about sexual infidelity is contained in the motivation to be unfaithful. Men often seek sex outside of the marriage, thereby denying their commitment, although they are generally satisfied with the marriage in other respects. They reportedly seek sexual excitement and diversity not available within the relationship, but consider themselves still committed to the marriage.

Remarkably, unfaithful men are less likely than their female counterparts to feel guilty about this choice. In contrast, women who engage in sexual activity outside of marriage, tend to perceive the involvement as an "affair," a relationship that competes with the marriage and is initiated in conjunction with marital dissatisfaction. Women are far more likely to become emotionally involved with the extramarital partner, to attribute "love" to the involvement, and to feel guilty.[66]

Lest we immediately condemn husbands as unfaithful, unfeeling so-and-so's, keep in mind that, although men are a better bet to report extramarital sex, women are more likely than men to report emotional noncommitment while denying sexual noncommitment. In essence, both men and women probably experience feelings that threaten the exclusive commitment promised in marriage. Both men and women variously act on or deny attraction to others. However, women are more likely to seek love, while men are more likely to seek pleasure. Most threatening to the marriage, according to Glass and Wright, is the "combined-type involvement"—love and sex.[67] After all, this dual involvement with another individual closely resembles the myth on which the marriage was supposedly founded.

Flexibility.   One of the most widely cited "positive" traits an individual can bring to a marriage is flexibility. Logically, since marriage constitutes a life-long commitment, the partners need to be able to adapt to changes, not only as individuals, but as a couple. As mentioned, couples who adopt a symmetrical model, whether they be dual-career couples or not, are likely to rely on ongoing negotiation of time, resources, responsibilities, freedoms, etc. Couples who adopt a complementary model usually follow traditional sex-role prescriptions (or reverse them) and probably don't stress negotiation to the same extent. So, it is not surprising that flexibility seems to be especially valuable in symmetrical pairs.

Arguably, the woman in the traditional marriage is expected to be flexible; in a sense, that is part of her role. The male role is to be strong, competent, and resistant, presumably to outside threats against the family, but perhaps within the family as well. Coincidentally, a number of items believed in our culture to be stereotypically feminine (see Chapter Two) are associated with behavioral adaptability, while a number of items believed to be masculine are associated with behavioral strength. Similarly, the female communication style (see Chapters Four through Eight) is clearly other-centered while the male communication style is decidedly self-centered.

Given the logical association of femininity with flexibility, it is not especially shocking that individuals who report high levels of marital satisfaction, tend to score high on femininity measures.[68] (They may be classified either *feminine* or *androgynous* depending on their score on masculinity measures.) In addition, individuals with a good dose of feminine characteristics are perceived positively by their spouses.[69] Hence, marriage seems to have become a female institution. Stereotypically female characteristics are valuable in marriage: tenderness, affection, and, foremost, flexibility.

In a fascinating book that students usually find far too radical, Ann Douglas provides an historical account of *The Feminization of American Culture*. She explains that when women were segregated to the private sphere, they created a culture in which powerlessness was valuable. As caregivers and homemakers, women prided themselves on serving the needs of others. To the extent that they were thoughtful and generous and cooperative, they were not only feminine, but successful at their "work." The same, of course, does not hold true in the public sphere, which has become masculinized—a survival of the fittest culture.[70] Inherent in this dichotomy are deficiencies for both sexes. Feminine women are, logically, not well suited to the dog-eat-dog routine, while masculine men are, logically deficient as nurturers and flexible partners. Certainly, the suitability of femininity in the public sphere has been the source of debate (see Chapter Twelve), but few scholars have defended the suitability of masculinity in the private sphere.

One recent study, conducted among newly wed couples, indicated that independent wives were positively perceived by their new spouses. Young husbands were more satisfied with wives who had their own interests and activities and solved their own problems—all masculine characteristics. The researcher, Patricia Parmelee, points out that this may be evidence that masculinity has its place in the modern marriage of sex-role equals. She adds, though, that the same masculine qualities valued by newly married couples may be discounted when children arrive, since research indicates a greater need for coordination of activity during that transition.[71]

In conclusion, although family communication is apparently private, and thereby immune to legal interference, it stands to reason that marriages have been and will continue to be affected by legal changes pertaining to sexual equality. Most likely, in our lifetimes, traditions will be challenged and defended. Change will result, but slowly and deliberately and not without a struggle. Each of us, female or male, will make choices, some of them intellectual, some of them emotional. Each of our choices, because we are ultimately family-bound, will affect others and we, in turn, will find ourselves troubled or enriched by the choices made by those to which we are connected.

The logic and integrity of the traditional marriage is worthy of study, and may be appealing to individuals who admire the balance provided by allocating family roles and responsibilities according to gender. I have learned from interacting with students of all ages that those who emerged (or wish they had) from traditional families take comfort in the stability of the institution as it stands. Others may value continuity across generations even though they see the wisdom of change; still others may opt to preserve relationships with parents and grandparents by accepting traditional customs and passing them along through the next generation. For each of us, the issues surrounding male–female interaction in the family are complex. There are no immediate nor easy solutions, but there is clearly a sense of urgency about gender issues in marriage. They demand our thoughtful and personal attention, since no government body nor social reform movement can fulfill our vision of the family, nor fill the void if we sacrifice that vision.

C O N D U C T   Y O U R   O W N   R E S E A R C H

1. Collect as many wedding ceremonies as you can find. Survey different religious groups, if possible. Do a content analysis of the references to gender.
2. Conduct a survey of married couples, asking both the husband and wife to designate a list of chores as his, hers, or theirs. Then ask for a short statement about their degree of satisfaction with the apparent division of labor. Discuss the role of gender in dividing the work and the extent to which the two partners agree.
3. Ask five females and five males to answer the question: "How do you get your way when you want something?" If necessary, ask them to enlarge on their answers or give examples. Record and compare the responses.

D I S C U S S   T H E   I S S U E S

1. How do you feel about alternative life-styles to the traditional nuclear family? Single parents, childless couples, cohabitating couples, polygamy? etc. What plans do you have for living arrangements in the future? How does your future differ from your present and your past in this regard?
2. Some critics argue that the women's movement has resulted in the decline of the family in our culture. Do you agree or disagree? Cite specific evidence.
3. How would you define *marital satisfaction?* What constitutes a good marital relationship? Is it different from a good friendship or a good dating relationship?

SUMMARY OF PART IV

As we go about living our everyday lives, we seldom stop to think about the interface between society and the individual, but scholars have long debated whether society creates the individual or a group of individuals create society. Sometimes a media event, such as the Watergate scandal or the execution of mass-murderer Ted Bundy, prompts us to stop and ponder the reasons for individual behavior. Is society, the invisible collective, really to blame for all the negative aspects of our lives? In truth, though I've never met society personally, I often think he or she gets too much of the blame. In any case, those of us who make a living by communicating about communicating like to believe that it is the way people interact together, on a day-to-day basis, that provides the vehicle for creation, regardless of the direction you favor. In other words, the various personal relationships in which we create and share, challenge or perpetuate meaning, allow individuals to form a society, or society to shape individuals, or, most likely, both.

It is an oversimplification and an understatement to remark that gender is significant in our individual lives and in our society. Gender matters. We need to learn (and teach) the meaning of maleness and femaleness in a world in which people care about gender appropriateness—whether that means believing in tradition or challenging tradition. At the same time, one human being cannot stand face-to-face with another without being aware of his or her sexual assignment. Gender communicates.

Similarly, relationships matter and relationships communicate. Adult male–female relationships, whether professional or personal, are likely to be especially important in our lives, but also especially difficult, given that men and women are stereotypically portrayed as opposites, spoken of as opposites, and are arguably somewhat opposite in terms of their communication styles. To complicate matters, each of us is inconsistent in terms of our own emphasis on the importance of gender from relationship to relationship, from issue to issue and from moment to moment. So, as much as we may want to resolve questions about gender restrictions in our own personal relationships, we may find it frustrating and difficult to be all things to all people and still be true to ourselves.

Questions surrounding gender pervade our relationships and, yet, relationships provide the communication in which we come to understand gender, to develop a sense of self, and to feel connected and fulfilled in a social world. The discussion of male–female relationships in the last three chapters of this book constitutes just the tip of the iceberg—and the iceberg is moving, albeit slowly, through the icy waters of change. In the coming decades, more than ever, individuals will need to talk about gender issues, and perhaps more importantly, to listen to one another.

NOTES

Chapter 1

[1]Madeline Shakin, Debra Shakin, and Sarah Hall Sternglanz, "Infant Clothing: Sex Labeling for Strangers," *Sex Roles* 12 (1985): 955–64.

[2]Shakin, Shakin, and Sternglanz, 962.

[3]Jacqueline McGuire, "Gender Stereotypes of Parents with Two-Year-Olds and Beliefs about Gender Differences in Behavior," *Sex Roles* 19 (1988): 233–40.

[4]Karen A. Foss and Sonja K. Foss, "The Status of Research on Women and Communication," *Communication Quarterly* 31 (1983): 195–206.

[5]W. Barnett Pearce and Sharon M. Rossi, "The Problematic Practices of Feminism: An Interpretive and Critical Analysis," *Communication Quarterly* 32 (1984): 277–86.

[6]Pearce and Rossi, 278–79.

[7]Barrie Thorne, Cheris Kramarae, and Nancy Henley, "A Second Decade of Research," in *Language, Gender and Society,* ed. Barrie Thorne, Cheris Kramarae, and Nancy Henley (Rowley, Mass.: Newbury House, 1983), 7–24.

[8]Ibid., 16–17.

[9]Ray L. Birdwhistell, *Kinesics and Context* (Philadelphia: University of Pennsylvania Press, 1970), 42.

[10]Ann Oakley, *Sex, Gender and Society* (New York: Harper & Row, 1972).

Chapter 2

[1]Ellen Seiter, "Stereotypes and the Media: A Re-evaluation," *Journal of Communication* 36 (1986): 14–26.

[2]Ibid., 15–17.

[3]Patricia Smith and Elizabeth Midlarsky, "Empirically Derived Conceptions of Femaleness and Maleness: A Current View," *Sex Roles* 12 (1985): 313–27.

[4]David M. Siegler and Robert S. Siegler, "Stereotypes of Males' and Females' Speech," *Psychological Reports* 39 (1976): 167–70.

[5]Claire M. Renzetti, "New Wave or Second Stage? Attitudes of College Women Toward Feminism," *Sex Roles* 16 (1987): 265–77; M. Dwayne Smith and George D. Self, "Feminists and Traditionalists: An Attitudinal Comparison," *Sex Roles* 7 (1981): 183–88.

[6]e.g., Sandra L. Bem, "The Measurement of Psychological Androgyny," *Journal of Consulting and Clinical Psychology* 42 (1974): 155–62; Inge K. Broverman, Susan Raymond Vogel, Donald M. Broverman, Frank E. Clarkson, and Paul S. Rosenkrantz, "Sex-Role Stereotypes: A Current Appraisal," *Journal of Social Issues* 28 (1972): 59–78; Jeffrey A. Kelly and Judith Worrell, "New Formulations of Sex Roles and Androgyny: A Critical Review," *Journal of Consulting and Clinical Psychology* 45 (1977): 1101–15; Janet T. Spence and Robert L. Helmreich, "On Assessing Androgyny," *Sex Roles* 5 (1979): 721–38.

[7]Broverman et al., 64.

[8]Broverman et al; Paul S. Rosenkrantz, Susan R. Vogel, H. Bee, Inge K. Broverman, and Donald M. Broverman, "Sex-Role Stereotypes and Self-Concepts in College Students," *Journal of Consulting and Clinical Psychology* 32 (1968): 287–95.

[9]L. Gilbert, C. Deutsch, and R. Strahan, "Feminine and Masculine Dimensions of the Typical, Desirable and Ideal Woman and Man," *Sex Roles* 4 (1978): 767–78.

[10]A. L. Comrey, *Manual for Comrey Personality Scales* (San Diego: Educational and Industrial Testing Service, 1979); *Gough Manual for the California Psychological Inventory* (Palo Alto, Calif.: Consulting Psychological Press, 1969).

[11]Bem, 155–56.

[12]Broverman et al., 75.

[13]Bem, 156.

[14]Sandra Lipsitz Bem, "Gender Schema Theory and the Romantic Tradition," in *Sex and Gender,* ed. Philip Shaver and Clyde Hendrick (Newbury Park, Calif.: Sage, 1987), 251–71.

[15]Linda Putman, "In Search of Gender: A Critique of Communication and Sex-Roles Research," *Women's Studies in Communication* 5 (1982): 1–9; Lana F. Rakow, "Rethinking Gender Research in Communication," *Journal of Communication* 36 (1986): 11–26; Barrie Thorne, Cheris Kramarae, and Nancy Henley, "A Second Decade of Research," in *Language, Gender and Society,* ed. Barrie Thorne, Cheris Kramarae, and Nancy Henley (Rowley, Mass.: Newbury House, 1983), 7–24.

[16]Bem, 1974, 156.

[17]Patricia Gaudrea, "Factor Analysis of the Bem Sex Role Inventory," *Journal of Consulting and Clinical Psychology* 45 (1977): 299–302; Elazar Pedhazur and Toby Tetenbaum, "Bem Sex Role Inventory: A Theoretical and Methodological Critique," *Journal*

of Personality and Social Psychology 37 (1979): 996–1016; Virginia Wheeless and Kathi Dierks-Stewart, "The Psychometic Properties of the BSRI: Questions Concerning Reliability and Validity," *Communication Quarterly* 29 (1981): 173–85.

[18]Kathleen McKinney, "Age and Gender Differences in College Students' Attitudes Toward Women: A Replication and Extension," *Sex Roles* 17 (1987): 353–58.

[19]Donald G. Ellis and Linda McCallister, "Relational Control Sequences in Sex-Typed and Androgynous Groups," *Western Journal of Speech Communication* 44 (1980): 35–49; Lynda Greenblatt, James Hasenauer, and Vicki Freimuth, "Psychological Sex Type and Androgyny in the Study of Communication Variables: Self Disclosure and Communication Apprehension," *Human Communication Research* 6 (1980): 117–29; Carol L. Montgomery and Michael Burgoon, "The Effects of Androgeny and Message Expectations on Resistance to Persuasive Communication," *Communication Monographs* 47 (1980): 56–67; Linda Putnam and Linda McCallister, "Situational Effects of Task and Gender on Nonverbal Display," in *Communication Yearbook 4*, ed. Dan Nimmo (New Brunswick, N.J.: Transaction Books, 1980).

[20]Lisa A. Serbin and Rhoda K. Unger, "Social Change: Introduction," *Sex Roles* 14 (1986): 561–66.

[21]Paul D. Werner and Georgina Williams LaRussa, "Persistence and Change in Sex-Role Stereotypes," *Sex Roles* 12 (1985): 1089–99.

[22]Ibid., 1089.

[23]Ibid., 1093–94.

[24]Ibid., 1097.

[25]Smith and Midlarsky, 325–27.

[26]McKinney, 356–57.

[27]Robert L. Helmreich, Janet T. Spence, and R. H. Gibson, "Sex Role Attitudes: 1972–1980," *Personality and Social Psychology Bulletin* 8 (1982): 656–63.

[28]McKinney, 356.

[29]Renzetti, 265.

[30]Alice G. Sargent, Diane Kravetz, and Dorothy Diemer, "A Short History of the Women's Movement," in *Beyond Sex Roles,* ed. Alice Sargent (St. Paul: West, 1984), 190–98.

[31]Alexa A. Albert and Judith R. Porter, "Age Patterns in the Development of Children's Gender Role Stereotypes," *Sex Roles* 9 (1983): 59–67.

[32]Bem, 1987, 265–66.

[33]Deanna Kuhn, Sharon C. Nash, and Laura Brucken, "Sex-role Concepts of Two- and Three-Year Olds," *Child Development* 49 (1978): 445–51.

[34]Harry T. Reis and Stephanie Wright, "Knowledge of Sex-Role Stereotypes in Children Aged 3 to 5," *Sex Roles* 8 (1982): 1049–56.

[35]Cynthia J. Archer, "Children's Attitudes Toward Sex-Role Division in Adult Occupational Roles," *Sex Roles* 10 (1984): 1–10; Winifred O. Shephard and David T. Hess, "Attitudes in Four Age Groups Toward Sex Role Division in Adult Occupations and Activities," *Journal of Vocational Behavior* 6 (1975): 27–39; Leslie S. Tremaine, Candace Garrett Schau and Judith Wilde Busch, "Children's Occupational Sex-Typing," *Sex Roles* 8 (1982): 691–710.

[36]Ronald S. Drabman, Stephen J. Robertson, Jana N. Patterson, Gregory J. Jarvie, David Hammer, and Glenn Cordua, "Children's Perceptions of Media-Portrayed Sex Roles, *Sex Roles* 7 (1981): 379–89.

[37]Diana M. Zuckerman and Donald H. Sayre, "Cultural Sex-Role Expectations and Children's Sex-Role Concepts," *Sex Roles* 8 (1982): 853–62.

[38]Ibid., 859.

[39]Ibid., 857.

[40]Shephard and Hess, 38.

[41]Mary Lynn Crow and Kay Taebel, "Sex-Role Stereotyping is Alive and Well in Sixth Graders," *Elementary School Journal* 76 (1976): 359–64; Shephard and Hess, 38–39.

[42]Miriam Lewin and Lilli M. Tragos, "Has the Feminist Movement Influenced Adolescent Sex Role Attitudes? A Reassessment After a Quarter Century," *Sex Roles* 16 (1987): 125–35; Eileen O'Keefe and Janet Shibley Hyde, "The Development of Occupational Sex-Role Stereotypes: The Effects of Gender Stability and Age," *Sex Roles* 9 (1983): 481–92.

[43]Lewin and Tragos, 132.

[44]Ibid., 135.

Chapter 3

[1]For an excellent summary of the discussion of Linguistic Relativity, and examples from anthropological linguistics, see Roger Brown, *Words and Things* (Glencoe, Ill.: The Free Press, 1958), 229–63.

[2]Pamela Schroeder Kingsolver and Harold V. Cordry, "Gender and the Press: An Update," in *Advances in Gender and Communication Research,* ed. Lawrence B. Nadler, Marjorie Keeshan Nadler, and William R. Todd-Manchillas (Langham, Md.: University Press of America, 1987), 307–16.

[3]Virginia P. Richmond and Joan Gorham, "Language Patterns and Gender Role Orientation Among Students in Grades 3–12," *Communication Education* 37 (1988): 143.

[4]Wendy Martyna, "Beyond the He/Man Approach: The Case for Nonsexist Language," in *Language, Gender and Society,* ed. Barrie Thorne, Cheris Kramarae, and Nancy Henley (Rowley, Mass.: Newbury House, 1983), 25–37.

[5]Donald G. MacKay, "Psychology, Prescriptive Grammar and the Pronoun Problem," *American Psychologist* 35 (1980): 444–49.

[6]Wendy Martyna, "What Does 'He' Mean?" *Journal of Communication* 28 (1978): 131–38; Alleen P. Nilsen, "Sexism in Children's Books and Elementary Teaching Materials," in *Sexism and Language,* ed. Alleen P. Nilsen, Haig Bosmajian, H. Lee Gershuny, and Julia P. Stanley (Urbana, Ill.: National Council of Teachers of English, 1977), 161–79.

[7]Jeanette Silveria, "Generic Masculine Words and Thinking," *Women's Studies in International Quarterly* 3 (1980): 165–78; William R. Todd-Mancillas, "Masculine Generics = Sexist Language: A Review of Literature and Implications for Speech Communication Professionals," *Communication Quarterly* 29 (1981): 107–15.

[8]Richmond and Gorham, 145.

[9]Ibid.

[10]Harry T. Reis and Stephanie Wright, "Knowledge of Sex-Role Stereotypes in Children Aged 3 to 5," *Sex Roles* 8 (1982): 1049–56.

[11]Jesse Bernard, *The Sex Game* (New York: Atheneum, 1973).

[12]*The American Heritage Dictionary* (New York: Dell 1983), 448.

[13]*The American Heritage Dictionary*, 439.

[14]Barbara Bate, "Nonsexist Language in Transition," *Journal of Communication* 28 (1978): 139–49.

[15]Amy Vanderbilt, *Amy Vanderbilt's Everyday Etiquette* (New York: Bantam Books, 1974).

[16]*The American Heritage Dictionary*, 208.

[17]*The American Heritage Dictionary*, 337.

[18]*The American Heritage Dictionary*, 337.

[19]George Lakoff and Mark Johnson, *Metaphors We Live By* (Chicago: University of Chicago Press, 1981).

Chapter 4

[1]Cheris Kramarae, "Wishy-Washy Mommy Talk," *Psychology Today* 8 (1974): 82–85.

[2]Janet Saltzman Chaefetz, *Masculine, Feminine or Human?* (Itasca, Ill.: F. E. Peacock Publishers, 1974), 79.

[3]Janet Lever, "Sex Differences in the Games Children Play," *Social Problems* 23 (1976): 478–87; Marsha B. Liss, "Learning Gender-Related Skills Through Play," in *Social and Cognitive Skills: Sex Roles and Children's Play*, ed. Marsha B. Liss (New York: Academic Press, 1983); Cynthia Miller, "Qualitative Differences Among Gender-Stereotyped Toys: Implications for Cognitive and Social Development in Girls and Boys," *Sex Roles* 16 (1987): 473–87.

[4]Michael Messner, "The Life of a Man's Seasons: Male Identity and the Life Course of a Jock," in *Changing Men: New Directions in Research on Men and Masculinity*, ed. Michael S. Kimmel (Newbury Park, Calif.: Sage, 1987, 53–67.

[5]Donna Eder and Maureen T. Hallinan, "Sex Differences in Children's Friendships," *American Sociological Review* 43 (1978): 237–50.

[6]Zick Rubin, *Children's Friendships* (Cambridge, Mass.: Harvard University Press, 1980), 104–5.

[7]Mayta A. Caldwell and Letita Anne Peplau, "Sex Differences in Same-Sex Friendship," *Sex Roles* 8 (1982): 721–32.

[8]Ladd Wheeler and John Nezlek, "Sex Differences in Social Participation," *Journal of Personality and Social Psychology* 35 (1977): 742–54.

[9]Adelaide Haas and Mark A. Sherman, "Reported Topics of Conversation Among Same-Sex Adults," *Communication Quarterly* 30 (1982): 341.

[10]Barbara Eakins and Gene Eakins, "Verbal Turn-Taking and Exchanges in Faculty Dialogue," in *The Sociology of the Languages of American Women*, ed. Betty Lou Dubois and Isabel Crouch (San Antonio, Tex.: Trinity University Press, 1976), 53–62.

[11]Raphaela Best, *We've All Got Scars: What Boys and Girls Learn in Elementary Schools* (Bloomington, Ind.: Indiana University Press, 1983).

[12]Thomas L. Good, J. Neville Sikes, and Jere E. Brophy, "Effects of Teacher Sex and Student Sex on Classroom Interaction," *Journal of Educational Psychology* 65 (1973): 74–87.

[13]Virginia R. Brooks, "Sex Differences in Student Dominance Behavior in Female and Male Professor's Classrooms," *Sex Roles* 8 (1982): 683–90.

[14]Marlaine E. Lockheed, *A Study of Sex Equity in Classroom Interaction, Final Report to the National Institute of Education* (Princeton: Educational Testing Service, 1984).

[15]Constantina Safilios-Rothschild, *Sex Role Socialization and Sex Discrimination: A Synthesis and Critique of the Literature* (Washington, D.C.: National Institute of Education, 1979).

[16]Dee Boersma, Debora Gay, Ruth A. Jones, Lynn Morrison, and Helen Remick, "Sex Differences in College Student-Teacher Interactions: Fact or Fantasy?" *Sex Roles* 7 (1981): 775–84.

[17]David A. Karp and William C. Yoels, "The College Classroom: Some Observations on the Meanings of Student Participation," *Sociology and Social Research* 60 (1976): 421–39.

[18]Elizabeth Aries, "Interaction Patterns and Themes of Male, Female and Mixed Groups," *Small Group Behavior* 7 (1976): 7–18.

[19]Charlan Nemeth, Jeffrey Endicott, and Joel Wachtler, "From the 50's to the 70's: Women in Jury Deliberations," *Sociometry* 39 (1976): 293–304.

[20]Carole Edelsky, "Who's Got the Floor?" *Language in Society* 10 (1981): 383–421.

[21]William F. Soskin and Vera P. John, "The Study of Spontaneous Talk," in *The Stream of Behavior*, ed. Roger Barker (New York: Appleton-Century-Crofts, 1963), 228–81.

[22]Helena M. Leeft-Pellegrini, "Conversational Dominance as a Function of Gender and Expertise," in *Language: Social Psychological Perspectives,* ed. Howard Giles, W. Peter Robinson, and Philip M. Smith (New York: Pergamon Press, 1980), 97–104.

[23]Joseph Berger, Susan J. Rosenholtz, and Morris Zeleditch, Jr., "Status Organizing Processes," in *Annual Review of Sociology,* ed. Alex Inkeles (Palo Alto, Calif.: Annual Reviews, 1980), 479–508.

[24]e.g., P. E. Jose, F. Crosby, and W. J. Wong-McCarthy, "Androgyny, Dyadic Compatibility and Conversational Behavior," in *Language: Social Psychological Perspectives,* ed. Howard Giles, W. Peter Robinson, and Philip M. Smith (New York: Pergamon Press, 1980), 74–96.

[25]H. T. Moore, "Further Data Concerning Sex Differences," *Journal of Abnormal and Social Psychology* 4 (1922): 81–89.

[26]H. M. Landis and H. E. Burtt, "A Study of Conversations," *Journal of Comparative Psychology* 4 (1924): 81–89.

[27]Haas and Sherman, 332–42.

[28]Adelaide Haas, "Partner Influences on Sex-Associated Spoken Language of Children," *Sex Roles* 7 (1981): 925–35; Fern L. Johnson and Elizabeth J. Aries, "Close Friendship in Adulthood: Conversational Content between Same-Sex Friends, *Sex Roles* 9 (1983): 1183–96; Mirra Komarovsky, *Blue Collar Marriage* (New York: Vintage Books, 1967).

[29]Haas and Sherman, 341.

[30]Michael Messner, "The Life of a Man's Seasons: Male Identity in the Life Course of a Jock," in *Changing Men: New Directions in Research on Men and Masculinity,* ed. Michael S. Kimmel (Newbury Park, Calif.: Sage, 1987), 37–52.

[31]Haas and Sherman, 341.

[32]Jack Levin and Arnold Arluke, "An Exploratory Analysis of Sex Differences in Gossip," *Sex Roles* 12 (1985): 281–87.

[33]Haas and Sherman, 340.

[34]Ibid., 340.

[35]Ibid., 342.

[36]Robin Lakoff, "Language and Woman's Place," *Language in Society* 2 (1973): 45–80.

[37]Ibid., 49.

[38]Roger Brown, *Words and Things* (Glencoe, Ill.: The Free Press, 1958), 229–63.

[39]Lakoff, 49.

[40]Ibid., 50–51.

[41]Gary W. Selnow, "Sex Differences in Uses and Perceptions of Profanity," *Sex Roles* 12 (1985): 303–12.

[42]Lakoff, 51–52.

[43]Ibid., 54–56.

[44]Faye Crosby and Linda Nyquist, "The Female Register: An Empirical Test of Lakoff's Hypothesis," *Language in Society* 6 (1977): 313–22.

[45]Crosby and Nyquist, 316–18.

[46]William M. O'Barr and Bowman K. Atkins, "Women's Language or Powerless Language?" in *Women and Language in Literature and Society,* ed. Sally McConnell-Ginet et al. (New York: Praeger, 1980), 93–110.

[47]Barbara W. Eakins and R. Gene Eakins, *Sex Differences in Human Communication* (Boston: Houghton Mifflin, 1978), 45.

[48]Lakoff, 54.

[49]Ibid., 55

[50]Julie R. McMillan, A. Kay Clifton, Diane McGrath, and Wanda S. Gale, "Women's Language: Uncertainty or Interpersonal Sensitivity and Emotionality?" *Sex Roles* 3 (1977): 545–59; Don H. Zimmerman and Candace West, "Sex Roles, Interruptions and Silences in Conversations," in *Language and Sex: Difference and Dominance,* ed. Barrie Thorne and Nancy Henley (Rowley, Mass.: Newbury House, 1975), 105–29.

[51]Betty Lou Dubois and Isabel Crouch, "The Question of Tag Questions in Women's Speech: They Don't Really Use More of Them, Do They?" *Language in Society* 4 (1975): 289–94.

[52]Lakoff, 57.

[53]McMillan et al., 551.

[54]Crosby and Nyquist, 319.

[55]Mary Ritche Key, *Male/Female Language* (Metuchen, N.J.: Scarecrow Press, 1975).

[56]McMillan et. al., 547–48.

[57]Lakoff, 47.

[58]Jesse Bernard, *The Sex Game* (New York: Atheneum, 1972); Carol Gilligan, *In a Different Voice: Psychological Theory and Women's Development* (Cambridge, Mass.: Harvard University Press, 1982).

Chapter 5

[1]Harvey Sacks, Emmanual Schegloff, and Gail Jefferson, "A Simplest Systematics for the Organization of Turn-Taking for Conversation," *Language* 50 (1974): 696–735.

[2]Candace West and Don H. Zimmerman, "Small Insults: A Study of Interruptions in Cross-Sex Conversations Between Unacquainted Persons," in *Language, Gender and Society,* ed. Barrie Thorne, Cheris Kramarae, and Nancy Henley (Rowley, Mass.: Newbury House 1983), 102–17.

[3]Don H. Zimmerman and Candace West, "Sex Roles, Interruptions and Silences in Conversations," in *Language and Sex: Differences and Dominance,* ed. Barrie Thorne and Nancy Henley (Rowley, Mass.: Newbury House 1975), 105–29.

[4]Kathryn Dindia, "The Effects of Sex of Subject and Sex of Partner on Interruptions," *Human Communication Research* 3 (1987): 345–71; C. W. Kennedy and C. T. Camden, "A New Look at Interruptions," *Western Journal of Speech Communication* 47 (1983): 45–48.

[5]Zimmerman and West, 107.

[6]Michael Natale, Elliot Entin, and Joseph Jaffe, "Vocal Interruptions in Dyadic Communication as a Function of Speech and Social Anxiety," *Journal of Personality and Social Psychology* 37 (1979): 865–78.

[7]John E. Baird, "Sex Differences in Group Communication: A Review of Relevant Research," *Quarterly Journal of Speech* 62 (1976): 179–92; Barbara Eakins and Gene Eakins, "Verbal Turn-taking and Exchanges in Faculty Dialogue," in *The Sociology of the Languages of American Women,* ed. Betty Lou Dubois and Isabel Crouch (San Antonio, Tex.: Trinity University Press, 1976), 53–62; Dale Spender, *Man Made Language* (London: Routledge and Kegan Paul, 1980).

[8]Anita Esposito, "Sex Differences in Children's Conversation," *Language and Speech* 22 (1979): 213–20.

[9]Zimmerman and West; West and Zimmerman; Eakins and Eakins.

[10]West and Zimmerman, 103.

[11]Dindia, 366; Kennedy and Camden, 47.

[12]Dindia, 367.

[13]Marianne LaFrance, "Gender Gestures: Sex, Sex-role, and Nonverbal Communication," in *Gender and Nonverbal Behavior,* ed. Clara Mayo and Nancy M. Henley (New York: Springer-Verlag, 1981), 129–50.

[14]Esther Blank Greif, "Sex Differences in Parent-Child Conversations," *Women's Studies International Quarterly* 3 (1980): 253–58.

[15]Pamela Fishman, "Interaction: The Work Women Do," in *Language, Gender and Society,* ed. Barrie Thorne, Cheris Kramarae, and Nancy Henley (Rowley, Mass.: Newbury House, 1983), 89–102.

[16]Robin Lakoff, *Language and Women's Place* (New York: Harper & Row, 1975).

[17]Fishman, 94.

[18]Ibid., 95.

[19]Ibid., 89.

[20]Ibid., 96.

[21]Zimmerman and West, 114.

[22]Fishman, 96.

[23]Zimmerman and West, 114.

[24]Fishman, 96.

[25]Esposito, 219.

[26]Eakins and Eakins, 1977; Zimmerman and West, 1975; West and Zimmerman, 1983.

[27]Kennedy and Camden, 53.

[28]Fishman, 97.

[29]Ibid.

[30]Rose Laub Coser, "Laughter Among Colleagues," *Psychiatry* 23 (1960): 81–95.

[31]Carol Edelsky, "Who's Got the Floor?" *Language in Society* 10 (1981): 383–421.

[32]Starkey Duncan and Donald W. Fiske, *Face-to-face Interaction* (Hillsdale, N.J.: Erlbaum, 1977).

[33]Paul E. McGhee, "Sex Differences in Children's Humor," *Journal of Communication* 26 (1976): 176–89.

[34]McGhee, 179.

[35]Antony J. Chapman, "Humorous Laughter in Children," *Journal of Personality and Social Psychology* 31 (1975): 42–49; Adelaide Haas, "Production of Sex-Associated Features of Spoken Language by Four-, Eight- and Twelve-Year Old Boys and Girls," *Dissertation Abstracts International* (1978) 39: 23A.

[36]James Hassett and John Houlihan, "Different Jokes for Different Folks," *Psychology Today* 12 (1979): 64–71.

[37]Larry Wilde, *The Great Comedians Talk About Comedy*, (New York: Citadel Press, 1968), quoted in Joan B. Levine, "The Feminine Routine," *Journal of Communication* 26 (1976): 173–75.

[38]Levine, 174.

[39]Joanne R. Cantor, "What is Funny to Whom? The Role of Gender," *Journal of Communication* 26 (1976): 164–72.

[40]Hassett and Houlihan, 70.

[41]Dolf Zillman and S. Holly Stocking, "Putdown Humor," *Journal of Communication* 26 (1976): 154–58.

[42]Mei-Jung Chang and Charles R. Gruner, "Audience Reaction to Self-Disparaging Humor," *The Southern States Speech Communication Journal* 46 (1981): 419–26.

[43]Sidney M. Jourard, *The Transparent Self* (Princeton: Van Nostrand, 1971).

[44]Robert A. Lewis, "Emotional Intimacy Among Men," *Journal of Social Issues* 34 (1978): 108–20.

[45]Lynda Greenblatt, James E. Hasenauer, and Vicki S. Freimuth, "Psychological Sex Type and Androgyny in the Study of Communication Variables: Self-Disclosure and Communication Apprehension," *Human Communication Research* 6 (1980): 117–28.

[46]Paul Cozby, "Self-Disclosure: A Literature Review," *Psychological Bulletin* 79 (1973): 73–91; Lynne R. Davidson and Lucile Duberman, "Friendship: Communication and Interactional Patterns in Same-Sex Dyads," *Sex Roles* 8 (1982): 809–23; Brian S. Morgan, "Intimacy of Disclosure Topics and Sex Differences in Self-Disclosure," *Sex Roles* 2 (1976): 161–66.

[47]Valerian J. Derlega and Alan L. Chaiklin, "Privacy and Self-Disclosure in Social Relationships," *Journal of Social Issues* 33 (1977): 102–15; A. George Gitter and Harvey Black, "Is Self-Disclosure Self-Revealing?" *Journal of Counseling Psychology* 23 (1976): 327–32; Edward A. Powers and Gordon L. Bultena, "Sex Differences in Intimate Friendships of Old Age," *Journal of Marriage and the Family* 38 (1976): 739–44.

[48]Helen Mayer Hacker, "Blabbermouths and Clams: Sex Differences in Self-Disclosure in Same-Sex and Cross-Sex Friendship Dyads," *Psychology of Women Quarterly* 5 (1981): 385–401.

[49]Morgan, 162.

[50]Cozby, 74.

[51]Sidney M. Jourard and R. Friedman, "Experimenter-Subject Distance and Self-Disclosure," *Journal of Personality and Social Psychology* 8 (1971): 278–82; Joan Held Kopfstein and Donald Kopfstein, "Correlates of Self-Disclosure among College Students," *Journal of Consulting and Clinical Psychology* 41 (1973): 163; W. H. Rivenback III, "Self-Disclosure among Adolescents," *Psychological Reports* 28 (1971): 35–42.

[52]Judith L. Fischer and Leonard R. Narus, Jr., "Sex Roles and Intimacy in Same-Sex and Other-Sex Relationships," *Psychology of Women Quarterly* 5 (1981): 444–55; Greenblatt, Hauser, and Freimuth, 126.

[51]Hacker, 385.

[52]Nancy Henley, *Body Politics: Power, Sex and Nonverbal Communication* (New York: Touchstone Press, 1986), 72–73.

[53]Hacker, 392.

[54]Ibid., 393.

Chapter 6

[1]Ray L. Birdwhistell, *Introduction to Kinesics* (Louisville: University of Louisville Press, 1952).

[2]Ray L. Birdwhistell, *Kinesics and Context* (Philadelphia: University of Pennsylvania Press, 1970).

[3]Birdwhistell, 1970, 42.

[4]Dale G. Leathers and T. H. Emigh, "Decoding Facial Expressions: A New Test with Decoding Norms," *Quarterly Journal of Speech* 66 (1980): 418–36.

[5]Marianne LaFrance and Clara Mayo, *Moving Bodies: Nonverbal Communication in Social Relationships* (Monterey, Calif.: Brooks/Cole, 1978).

[6]Nancy Henley, *Body Politics: Power, Sex and Nonverbal Communication* (New York: Touchstone Press, 1986), 169.

[7]Kathi Dierks-Stewart, "Sex Differences in Nonverbal Communication: An Alternative Perspective," in *Communication, Language and Sex: Proceedings of the First Conference,* ed. Cynthia Berryman and Virginia A. Eman (Rowley, Mass.: Newbury House, 1979), 112–21; Susan J. Frances, "Sex Differences in Nonverbal Behavior," *Sex Roles* 5 (1979): 519–35; Judith Hall and Amy Halberstadt, "Sex Roles and Nonverbal Communication Skills," *Sex Roles* 7 (1981): 273–87; Henley, 1986, 174; Anneke Vrugt and Ada Kerlstra, "Sex Differences in Nonverbal Communication," *Semiotica* 50 (1984): 1–41; Miron Zuckerman, Richard S. Frank, Nancy H. Spiegel, and Deborah T. Larrance, "Masculinity-Femininity and Encoding of Nonverbal Cues," *Journal of Personality and Social Psychology* 42 (1982): 548–56.

[8]Paul Ekman and Wallace V. Friesen, *Unmasking the Face* (Englewood Cliffs, N.J.: Prentice Hall, 1975).

[9]"Women's Faces Show Emotions; Men Hide Theirs," *Phoenix Gazette,* December 13, 1974, quoted in Barbara Westbrook Eakins and R. Gene Eakins, *Sex Differences in Human Communication* (Boston: Houghton Mifflin, 1978), 155.

[10]Ross Buck, Robert E. Miller and William F. Caul, "Sex, Personality and Physiological Variables in the Communication of Affect via Facial Expression," *Journal of Personality and Social Psychology* 30 (1974): 587–96.

[11]David C. Bellinger and Jean Berko Gleason, "Sex Differences in Parental Directives to Young Children," *Sex Roles* 8 (1982): 1123–39; Margaret Snow, Carol Jacklin, and Eleanor Maccoby, "Sex of Child Difference in Father-Child Interaction at One Year of Age," *Child Development* 54 (1983): 227–32.

[12]Birdwhistell, 1970, 43–44.

[13]Paul Ekman, Wallace V. Friesen, and S. Ancoli, "Facial Signs of Emotional Experience," *Journal of Personality and Social Psychology* 39 (1980): 1125–34.

[14]Kathleen P. Hoover-Dempsey, Jeanne M. Plas, and Barbara Wallston, "Tears and Weeping Among Professional Women: In Search of New Understanding," *Psychology of Women Quarterly* 10 (1986): 19–34.

[15]Gary A. Crester, William K. Lombardo, Barbara Lombardo, and Sharon C. Mathis, "Fer Cryin' Out Loud—There is a Sex Difference," *Sex Roles* 9 (1983): 987–95; Gary A. Crester, William K. Lombardo, Barbara Lombardo, and Sharon C. Mathis, "Reactions to Men and Women Who Cry: A Study of Sex Differences and Perceived Societal Attitudes versus Personal Attitudes," *Perceptual and Motor Skills* 55 (1982): 479–86; Ekman, Friesen, and Ancoli, 1980; Catherine Ross and John Mirowsky, "Men Who Cry," *Social Psychology Quarterly* 47 (1984): 138–46.

[16]Dierks-Stewart, 1976; Judith A. Hall, *Nonverbal Sex Differences: Communication Accuracy and Expressive Style* (Baltimore: Johns Hopkins University Press, 1984); Frances, 1979; LaFrance and Mayo, 1979.

[17]Amy Halberstadt, Cynthia W. Hayes, and Kathleen M. Pike, "Gender and Gender Role Differences in Smiling and Communication Consistency," *Sex Roles* 19 (1988): 589–603; Hall, 1984.

[18]LaFrance and Mayo, 1979, 101.

[19]Daphne E. Bugenthal, Jacques W. Kaswan, and Leonore R. Love, "Perception of Contradictory Meanings Conveyed by Verbal and Nonverbal Channels," *Journal of Personality and Social Psychology* 16 (1970): 647–55; Daphne Bugenthal, Jacques W. Kaswan, Leonore R. Love, and Michael N. Fox, "Child Versus Adult Perception of Evaluative Messages in Verbal, Vocal and Visual Channels," *Developmental Psychology* 2 (1970): 367–75; Daphne E. Bugenthal, Leonore R. Love, and Robert M. Gianetto, "Perfidious Female Faces," *Journal of Personality and Social Psychology* 17 (1971): 314–18.

[20]Jeanette Silveria, "Thoughts on the Politics of Touch," *Women's Press* 1 (1972): 13.

[21]Mary B. Parlee, "Women Smile Less for Success," *Psychology Today* 12 (1979): 16.

[22]Judith A. Hall, "On Explaining Gender Differences: The Case of Nonverbal Behavior," in *Sex and Gender*, ed. Philip Shaver and Clyde Hendrick (Newbury Park, Calif.: Sage 1987), 177–200.

[23]Adam Kendon, "Some Functions of Mutual Gaze in Social Interaction," *Acta Psychologica* 26 (1967): 22–63.

[24]Phoebe C. Ellsworth and L. M. Ludwig, "Visual Behavior in Social Interaction," *Journal of Communication* 22 (1971): 375–403.

[25]Phoebe C. Ellsworth, "Eye Contact and Gaze Aversion in an Aggressive Encounter," *Journal of Personality and Social Psychology* 28 (1973): 280–92.

[26]Ralph V. Exline, Steve L. Ellyson, and Barbara Long, "Visual Behavior as an Aspect of Power Role Relationships," in *Advances in the Study of Communication and Affect*, ed. P. Pilner, L. Krames, and T. Alloway (New York: Plenum Press, 1975).

[27]Michael Argyle and J. Dean, "Eye-contact, Distance and Affiliation," *Sociometry* 28 (1965): 289–304; Ralph V. Exline, "Explorations in the Process of Person Perception: Visual Interaction in Relation to Competition, Sex and Need for Affiliation," *Journal of Personality* 31 (1963): 1–20.

[28]Ralph V. Exline, D. Gray, and D. Schuette, "Visual Behavior in a Dyad as Affected by Interview Content and Sex of Respondent," *Journal of Personality and Social Psychology* 1 (1965): 201–9.

[29]Albert Mehrabian, "Nonverbal Betrayal of Feeling," *Journal of Experimental Research in Personality* 5 (1971): 64–73.

[30]Michael Argyle and Roger Ingham, "Gaze, Mutual Gaze and Proximity," *Semiotica* 6 (1972): 32–49; L. M. Coutts and F. W. Schneider, "Visual Behavior in an Unfocused Interaction as a Function of Sex and Distance," *Journal of Experimental Social Psychology* 11 (1975): 64–77; Marion Heineman Levine and Brian Sutton-Smith, "Effects of Age, Sex and Task on Visual Behavior during Dyadic Interaction," *Developmental Psychology* 9 (1973): 400–5; Zick Rubin, "Measurement of Romantic Love," *Journal of Personality and Social Psychology* 16 (1970): 265–73.

[31]Hall, 1987, 182.

[32]Albert Mehrabian, *Silent Messages* (Belmont, Calif.: Wadsworth, 1971), 67.

[33]Rubin, 265–73.

[34]Ralph V. Exline and Lewis C. Winters, "Affective Relations and Mutual Glances in Dyads," in *Affect, Cognition and Personality*, ed. Silvan S. Tomkins and Carroll E. Izard (New York: Springer, 1965), 319–30.

[35]Exline, Gray, and Schuette, 202–5.

[36]Exline, 1963, 1–20.

[37]Ibid., 15.

[38]Mehrabian, 1971, 71.

[39]Michael Argyle and Mark Cook, *Gaze and Mutual Gaze* (Cambridge, England: Cambridge University Press, 1976), 149.

[40]Henley, 1986, 163.

[41]Rubin, 270.

[42]Henley, 1986, 165.

[43]Patricia G. Webbink, "Eye Contact and Intimacy," quoted in Nancy Henley, *Body Politics: Power, Sex and Nonverbal Communication* (New York: Touchstone Press, 1986), 162.

[44]Michael Argyle and M. Williams, "Observer or Observed? A Reversible Perspective in Person Perception," *Sociometry* 32 (1969): 396–412.

[45]Steve L. Ellyson, John F. Dovidio, and B. J. Fehr. "Visual Behavior and Dominance in Women and Men," in *Gender and Nonverbal Behavior,* ed. Clara Mayo and Nancy M. Henley (New York: Springer-Verlag, 1981), 63–74.

[46]Ellyson, Dovidio, and Fehr, 73–74.

[47]Henley, 1986, 163.

[48]Julius Fast, *Body Language* (New York: Evans, 1970).

[49]Dane Archer, *How to Expand Your Social Intelligence Quotient* (New York: Evans, 1980); Julius Fast, *Body Language of Sex, Power and Aggression* (New York: M. Evans, 1977); Michael Korda, *Power! How to Get It and How to Use It* (New York: Random House, 1975); L. Lee and J. Charlton, *The Handbook: Interpreting Handshakes, Gestures, Power Signals and Sexual Signs* (Englewood Cliffs, N.J.; Prentice Hall, 1980); B. R. Schenkler, *Impression Management* (Monterey, Calif.: Brooks/Cole, 1980).

[50]Leathers, 64–66.

[51]Gerald I. Nierenberg and Henry H. Calero, *How to Read a Person Like a Book* (New York: Pocket Books, 1973).

[52]John Spiegel and Paul Machotka, *Messages of the Body* (New York: Free Press, 1974).

[53]Mehrabian, chapter 1.

[54]Leathers, 63.

[55]Adam Kendon, "Movement Coordination in Social Interaction: Some Examples Described," *Acta Psychologica* 32 (1970): 101–25.

[56]Leathers, 63.

[57]Birdwhistell, 1970, 39–47.

[58]Susan J. Frances, "Sex Differences in Nonverbal Behavior," *Sex Roles* 5 (1979): 519–35.

[59]C. E. Fortier, "Male-Female Differences in Movement," quoted in Martha Davis and Shirley Weitz, "Sex Differences in Body Movements and Positions," in *Gender and Nonverbal Behavior,* ed. Clara Mayo and Nancy M. Henley (New York: Springer-Verlag, 1981), 81–82.

[60]Davis and Weitz, 90.

[61]Henley, 1986, 141.

[62]Peter Collett and Peter Marsh, "Patterns of Public Behavior: Collision Avoidance on a Pedestrian Crossing," *Semiotica* 12 (1974): 281–99.

[63]Nierenberg and Calero, 59–61.

[64]Henley, 1986, 136–38; Adam Kendon and Andrew Ferber, "A Description of Some Human Greetings," in *Comparative Ecology and Behavior in Primates,* ed. R. P. Michael and J. H. Cook (London: Academic Press, 1973), 591–668; Mary Ritchie Key, *Male/Female Language* (Metuchen, N.J.: Scarecrow Press, 1975).

[65]Kendon and Ferber, 600.

[66]Henley, 1986, 138.

[67]Ibid., 139.

[68]Davis and Weitz, 86–87.

[69]Ibid., 86.

[70]Ibid., 87.

[71]Ignatius M. Mattingly, "Speaker Variation and Vocal Tract Size," *Journal of the Acoustic Society of America* 39 (1966): 1219; Sally McConnell-Ginet, "Intonation in a Man's World," in *Language, Gender and Society,* ed. Barried Thorne, Cheris Kramarae, and Nancy Henley (Rowley, Mass.: Newbury House, 1983), 69–88.

[72]Harry Hollien and R. Shipp, "Speaking Fundamental Frequency and Chronological Age in Males," *Journal of Speech and Hearing Research* 15 (1972): 155–59.

[73]Jacqueline Sachs, "Cues to the Identification of Sex in Children's Speech," in *Language and Sex: Difference and Dominance,* ed. Barrie Thorne and Nancy Henley (Rowley, Mass.: Newbury House, 1975), 152–71.

[74]Charles D. Aronovitch, "The Voice of Personality: Stereotyped Judgments of their Relation to Voice Quality and Sex of Speaker," *Journal of Social Psychology* 99 (1976): 207–220.

[75]Henley, 1986, 74.

[76]Ibid., 75.

[77]Ralph O. Coleman, "A Comparison of the Contributions of Two Voice Quality Characteristics to the Perception of Maleness and Femaleness in the Voice," *Journal of Speech and Hearing Research* 19 (1976): 168–80; Sachs, 1975; Larry Terango, "Pitch and Duration Characteristics of the Oral Reading of Males on a Masculinity-Femininity Dimension," *Journal of Speech and Hearing Research* 9 (1966): 590–95.

[78]McConnell-Ginet, 75.

[79]Ruth Brend, "Male-Female Intonational Patterns in American English," in *Language and Sex: Difference and Dominance,* ed. Barrie Thorne and Nancy Henley (Rowley, Mass.: Newbury House, 1975), 84–87.

[80]Carole Edelsky, "Question Intonation and Sex Roles," *Language in Society* 8 (1979): 15–32.

[81]Aronovitch, 218–19.

[82]David W. Addington, "The Relationship of Selected Vocal Characteristics to Personally Perception," *Speech Monographs* 35 (1968): 492–503.

[83]Brend, 86; Lakoff, 1973; McConnell-Ginet, 1983.

[84]Edelsky, 30; McConnell-Ginet, 75.

[85]McConnell-Ginet, 74.

[86]Ross Buck, *The Communication of Emotion* (New York: The Guilford Press, 1984); Joel Davitz, *The Communication of Emotional Meaning* (New York: McGraw-Hill, 1964); Miron Zuckerman, Marsha S. Lipets, Judith Hall Koivoumaki, and Robert Rosenthal, "Encoding and Decoding Nonverbal Cues of Emotion," *Journal of Personality and Social Psychology* 32 (1975): 1068–76.

[87]Buck, 1984; Judith A. Hall, "Gender Effects in Decoding Nonverbal Cues," *Psychological Bulletin* 85 (1978): 845–57; Patricia Noller, "Sex Differences in Nonverbal Communication: Advantage Lost or Supremacy Regained?" *Australian Journal of Psychology* 38 (1986): 13–22; Zuckerman et al., 1975.

[88]Addington, 1968, 1976; Aronovitch, 1976; Susan Batstone and Seppo K. Tuomi, "Perceptual Characteristics of Female Voices," *Language and Speech* 24 (1981): 111–23.

[89]Aronovitch, 217.

[90]Addington, 1968, 497.

[91]Ibid.

[92]Eakins and Eakins; Henley, 1986, 77; William Labov, *Sociolinguistic Patterns* (Philadelphia: University of Pennsylvania Press, 1972); Peter Trudgill, "Sex, Covert Prestige and Linguistic Change in the Urban British English of Norwich," in *Language and Sex: Difference and Dominance,* ed. Barrie Thorne and Nancy Henley (Rowley, Mass.: Newbury House, 1975), 88–104.

[93]Labov, 242–43.

[94]Trudgill, 100.

[95]Kenneth Kidd, Judith Kidd, and Mary Ann Records, "Possible Causes of the Sex Ratio in Stuttering and It's Implications," *Journal of Fluency Disorders* 3 (1978): 13–23.

[96]Ibid., 22–23.

Chapter 7

[1]Mark Knapp, *Nonverbal Communication in Human Interaction* (New York: Holt, Rinehart and Winston, 1978), 258.

[2]James J. Gibson, "Observations on Active Touch," *Psychological Review* 69 (1962): 477–91.

[3]Kay Deaux, *The Behavior of Men and Women* (Monterey, Calif.: Brooks/Cole, 1976), 64.

[4]Dale G. Leathers, *Successful Nonverbal Communication: Principles and Applications* (New York: Macmillan, 1986), 137.

[5]Sidney M. Jourard, "An Exploratory Study of Body-Accessibility," *British Journal of Social and Clinical Psychology* 5 (1966): 221–31; Lawrence B. Rosenfeld, Sallie Kartus, and Chett Ray, "Body Accessibility Revisited," *Journal of Communication* 26 (1976): 27–30.

[6]Nancy M. Henley, "Status and Sex: Some Touching Observations," *Bulletin of the Psychonomic Society* 2 (1973): 91–93.

[7]Brenda Major, "Gender Patterns in Touching Behavior," in *Gender and Nonverbal Behavior*, ed. Clara Mayo and Nancy M. Henley (New York: Springer-Verlag, 1980), 3–37.

[8]Nancy Henley, *Body Politics: Power, Sex and Nonverbal Communication* (New York: Touchstone Press, 1986)

[9]Major, 18–20.

[10]Frank N. Willis and G. E. Hofmann, "Development of Tactile Patterns in Relationship to Age, Sex and Race," *Developmental Psychology* 11 (1975): 866.

[11]Frank N. Willis, D. L. Reeves and D. R. Buchanan, "Interpersonal Touch in High School Relative to Sex and Race," *Perceptual and Motor Skills* 43 (1976): 843–47.

[12]Albert Mehrabian, *Nonverbal Communication* (Chicago: Aldine-Atherton, 1972); Ashley Montagu, *The Human Significance of the Skin* (New York: Columbia University Press, 1971).

[13]Henley, 1986, 110.

[14]Mary Ritchie Key, *Paralanguage and Kinesics* (Metuchen, N.J.: Scarecrow Press, 1975), 103.

[15]Desmond Morris, *Intimate Behavior* (New York: Random House, 1971), 104–5.

[16]Morris, 74.

[17]Jesse Bernard, *The Sex Game* (New York: Atheneum, 1973), 60.

[18]Robert Baker, " 'Pricks' and 'Chicks': A Plea for 'Persons,' " in *Sexist Language: A Modern Philosophical Analysis*, ed. Mary Betterling-Braggin (Totowa, N.J.: Littlefield-Adams, 1981), 161–82.

[19]Julia Stanley, "Gender Marking in American English: Usage and Reference," in *Sexism and Language*, ed. Alleen P. Nilsen et al. (Urbana, Ill.: National Council of Teachers of English, 1977), 43–74.

[20]Shere Hite, *The Hite Report* (New York: Macmillan, 1976).

[21]Henley, 1986, 203–4.

[22]Major, 21.

[23]M. N. Blondis and B. E. Jackson, *Nonverbal Communication with Patients: Back to the Human Touch* (New York: Wiley, 1977); L. M. Verbrugge and R. P. Steiner, "Physician Treatment of Men and Women: Sex Bias or Appropriate Care?" *Medical Care* 19 (1981): 609–32.

[24]Deaux, 82; T. Tieger, "On the Biological Basis of Sex Differences in Aggression," *Child Development* 51 (1980): 943–63.

[25]Eleanor E. Maccoby and Carol N. Jacklin, "Sex Differences in Aggression: A Rejoinder and Reprise," *Child Development* 51 (1980): 964–80.

[26]Deaux, chapter 8.

[27]Henley, 1986, 183.

[28]Major, 1981, 23.

[29]Henley, 1986, 104.

[30]Major, 1981, 24.

[31]Edward T. Hall, "Proxemics," *Current Anthropology* 9 (1968): 83.

[32]Henley, 1986, 29.

[33]Edward T. Hall, *The Hidden Dimension* (Garden City, N.J.: Doubleday, 1966).

[34]Judee K. Burgoon and S. B. Jones, "Toward a Theory of Personal Space Expectations and Their Violations," *Human Communication Research* 4 (1976): 131–46.

[35]Robert Sommer, "Leadership and Group Geography," *Sociometry* 24 (1961): 99–110; Robert Sommer, "The Distance for Comfortable Conversation: A Further Study," *Sociometry* 25 (1962): 111–16.

[36]Hall, 1966.

[37]Frank N. Willis, "Initial Speaking Distance as a Function of the Speaker's Relationship," *Psychonomic Science* 5 (1966): 221–22.

[38]Billy S. Barrios, L. Claire Corbett, J. Philip Estes, and Jeff S. Topping, "Effect of Social Stigma on Interpersonal Distance," *The Psychological Record* 26 (1976): 343–48; Stanley Heshka and Yona Nelson, "Interpersonal Speaking Distance as a Function of Age, Sex and Relationship," *Sociometry* 35 (1974): 92–104; Gloria Leventhal and Michelle Matturro, "Differential Effects of Spatial Crowding and Sex on Behavior," *Perceptual Motor Skills* 51 (1980): 111–19; Darhl Pederson and Anne Heaston, "The Effects of Sex of Subject, Sex of Approaching Person, and Angle of Approach upon Personal Space," *Journal of Psychology* 82 (1972): 277–86.

[39]Gary W. Evans and Roger B. Howard, "Personal Space," *Psychological Bulletin* 80 (1973): 334–44; Martin Giesen and Harry A. McClaren, "Discussion, Distance and Sex: Changes in Impressions during Small Group Interaction," *Sociometry* 39 (1976): 60–70; Henley, 1986, 36–38.

[40]Janet Saltzman Chaefetz, *Masculine, Feminine or Human?* (Itasca, Ill.: F. E. Peacock, 1974), 35.

[41]Henley, 1986, 38–39.

[42]Teresa J. McCroskey and James C. McCroskey, "The Effect of Race and Sex on Proxemics Behavior in an Interview Setting," *Southern Speech Communication Journal* 40 (1975): 408–20.

[43]Irwin Altman, *The Environment and Social Behavior* (Monterey, Calif.: Brooks/Cole, 1975).

[44]Leathers, 82.

[45]Jeffrey D. Fisher and Donn Byrne, "Too Close for Comfort: Sex Differences in Response to Invasions of Personal Space," *Journal of Personal and Social Psychology* 32 (1975): 15–21; Frank Prerost, "The Effects of High Spatial Density on Humor Appreciation: Age and Sex Differences," *Social Behavior and Personality* 8 (1980): 239–44.

[46]Jeanette Silviera, "Thoughts on the Politics of Touch," *Women's Press* 13 (1972): 13.

[47]Paul R. Bleda and Sharon Estee Bleda, "Effects of Sex and Smoking on Reactions to Spatial Invasions at a Shopping Mall," *The Journal of Social Psychology* 104 (1978): 311–12.

Chapter 8

[1]J. D. Wilson, F. W. George, and J. E. Griffin, "The Hormonal Control of Sexual Development," *Science* 211 (1981): 1278–84.

[2]John Nicholson, *Men and Women: How Different Are They?* (Oxford: Oxford University Press, 1984), 10.

[3]Betty Yorburg, *Sexual Identity* (New York: Wiley, 1974).

[4]Ashley Montagu, *The Natural Superiority of Women* (New York: Macmillan, 1968).

[5]B. Childs, "Genetic Origins of Some Sex Differences Among Human Beings," *Pediatrics* 35 (1965): 798–812.

[6]Yorburg, 16.

[7]United States Department of Health and Human Services, "Advance Report on Final Mortality Statistics." Monthly Vital Statistics Report, 1980, 1–3.

[8]Norma L. McCoy, "Innate Factors in Sex Differences," in *Beyond Sex Roles*, ed. Alice Sargent (St. Paul: West, 1985), 121–68.

[9]Montagu, 1968.

[10]Nicholson, 42.

[11]McCoy, 126–27.

[12]"Growth Charts with Reference Percentiles for Girls Birth to 36 Months of Age," National Center for Health Statistics (Evansville, Ind.: Mead Johnson, 1988); "Growth Charts with Reference Percentile for Boys Birth to 36 Months of Age," National Center for Health Statistics (Evansville, Ind.: Mead Johnson, 1985).

[13]"Growth Charts with Reference Percentiles for Girls 2 to 18 Years of Age," National Center for Health Statistics (Evansville, Ind.: Mead Johnson, 1988); "Growth Charts with Reference Percentiles for Boys 2 to 18 Years of Age," National Center for Health Statistics (Evansville, Ind.: Mead Johnson, 1985).

[14]Nicholson, 29–31.

[15]Ibid., 34.

[16]K. Dyer, "Female Athletes are Catching Up," *New Scientist* 22 (1977): 722–23.

[17]Nicholson, 38.

[18]E. O. Reiter and M. M. Grumbach, "Neuroendocrine Control of Mechanisms and the Onset of Puberty," *Annual Review of Physiology* 44 (1982): 595–613.

[19]J. M. Tanner, "Sequence, Tempo and Individual Variation in the Growth and Development of Boys and Girls Aged Twelve to Sixteen," in *Twelve to Sixteen: Early Adolescence*, ed. Jerome Kagan et al. (New York: Norton, 1972), 907–30.

[20]McCoy, 127.

[21]Lionel Tiger, *Men in Groups* (New York: Vintage Books, 1970), chapter 3.

[22]Anke A. Ehrhardt, "Gender Differences: A Biosocial Perspective," in *Psychology and Gender*, ed. Theo B. Sonderegger (Lincoln, Nebr.: University of Nebraska Press, 1984), 37–57.

[23]Ibid., 39.

[24]F. A. Beach, "Historical Origins of Modern Research on Hormones and Behavior," *Hormones and Behavior* 15 (1981): 325–76.

[25]Ehrhardt, 47.

[26]John Money and Anke A. Ehrhardt, *Man and Woman, Boy and Girl: The Differentiation and Dimorphism of Gender Identity from Conception to Maturity* (Baltimore: Johns Hopkins University Press, 1972).

[27]Ehrhardt, 48.

[28]Anke A. Ehrhardt and H. F. L. Meyer-Bahlburg, "The Effects of Prenatal Hormones on Gender Identity, Sex-Dimorphic Behavior, Sexual Orientation and Cognition," *Science* 211 (1981): 1312–18; Money and Ehrhardt, 52–6.

[29]McCoy, 129.

[30]Ibid., 130.

[31]Ehrhardt, 40.

[32]Nicholson, 62.

[33]R. N. Walsh, I. Budtz-Olsen, C. Leader, and R. A. Cummins, "The Menstrual Cycle, Personality and Academic Performance," *Archives of General Psychiatry* 38 (1981): 219–21.

[34]Alice S. Rossi and Peter E. Rossi, "Body Time and Social Time: Mood Patterns by Menstrual Cycle Phase and Day of Week," *Social Science Research* 6 (1977): 273–308.

[35]John Nicholson and L. O. Ward, "Do Women Go Mad Every Month?," *New Society* February 11, 1982: 226–28.

[36]C. J. Doering, H. K. Brodie, H. C. Kramer, R. H. Moos, H. B. Becker, and D. A. Hamburg, "Negative Affect and Plasma Testosterone: A Longitudinal Human Study," *Psychosomatic Medicine* 37 (1975): 484–91.

[37]Estelle Ramey, "Men's Cycles (They Have Them Too You Know)," in *Beyond Sex-Role Stereotypes,* ed. Alexandra Kaplan and Joan Bean (Boston: Little Brown, 1976).

[38]Daniel R. Miller, "Psychoanalytic Theory of Development: A Re-Evaluation" in *Handbook of Socialization Theory and Research,* ed. David Goslin (Chicago: Rand McNally, 1971), 481–502.

[39]Carol Gilligan, *In a Different Voice* (Cambridge, Mass.: Harvard University Press, 1982), 7.

[40]Janet Saltzman-Chaefetz, *Masculine, Feminine or Human?* (Itasca, Ill.: F. E. Peacock Press, 1974), 14.

[41]Leonard D. Goodstein and Alice G. Sargent, "Psychological Theories of Sex Differences," in *Beyond Sex Roles,* ed. Alice Sargent (St. Paul: West, 1985), 140.

[42]Nicholson, 23.

[43]Ibid.

[44]Gilligan, 7.

[45]Goodstein and Sargent, 141.

[46]Ibid.

[47]Sigmund Freud, "Some Psychical Consequences of the Anatomical Distinction Between the Sexes," *The Standard Edition of the Complete Psychological Works of Sigmund Freud,* ed. and trans. James Strachey (London: Hogarth Press, 1961), quoted in Gilligan, 7.

[48]Goodstein and Sargent, 141.

[49]Miller, 500.

Chapter 9

[1]Leonard D. Goodstein and Alice G. Sargent, "Psychological Theories of Sex Differences," in *Beyond Sex Roles,* ed. Alice Sargent (St. Paul: West, 1985), 142.

[2]Eleanor Emmons Maccoby and Carol Nagy Jacklin, *The Psychology of Sex Differences* (Stanford: Stanford University Press, 1974), 304–5.

[3]Ibid., 308–9.

[4]Judy Cornelia Pearson, *Gender and Communication* (Dubuque, Iowa: W. C. Brown, 1985), 38; J. Z. Rubin, F. J. Provenzano and Z. Luria, "The Eye of the Beholder: Parents' Views on Sex of Newborns," *American Journal of Orthopsychiatry* 44 (1974): 512–19.

[5]John Condry and S. Condry, "Sex Differences: A Study of the Eye of the Beholder," *Child Development* 47 (1976): 812–19.

[6]Nancy J. Bell and William Carver, "A Reevaluation of Gender Label Effects: Expectant Mothers' Responses to Infants," *Child Development* 51 (1980): 925–27.

[7]Norma McCoy, "Innate Sex Differences," in *Beyond Sex Roles,* ed. Alice Sargent (St. Paul: West, 1985), 124.

[8]Maccoby and Jacklin, 305.

[9]Cynthia Miller, "Qualitative Differences Among Gender-Stereotyped Toys: Implications for Cognitive and Social Development of Girls and Boys," *Sex Roles* 16 (1987): 473–87; Peter O. Peretti and Tiffany M. Sydney, "Parental Toy Choice Stereotyping and its Effect on Child Toy Preference and Sex-Role Stereotyping," *Social Behavior and Personality* 12 (1985): 213–16.

[10]Marion R. Bradbard, "Sex Differences in Adults' Gifts and Children's Toy Requests at Christmas," *Psychological Reports* 56 (1985): 969–70; Ramona S. Frasier, Joanne R. Nurss, and Donna R. Brogan, "Children's Toy Preferences Revisited: Implication for Early Childhood Education," *Child Care Quarterly* 9 (1980): 26–31; Miller, 475–6; Clyde C. Robinson and James T. Morris, "The Gender-Stereotyped Nature of Christmas Toys Received by 36-, 48-, and 60-Month-Old Children: A Comparison Between Nonrequested vs. Requested Toys," *Sex Roles* 15 (1986): 21–32.

[11]Janet Saltzman Chaefetz, *Masculine, Feminine or Human?* (Itasca, Ill.: F. E. Peacock, 1974), 81.

[12]Lori A. Schwartz and William T. Markham, "Sex Stereotyping in Children's Toy Advertisements," *Sex Roles* 12 (1985): 157–70.

[13]Maccoby and Jacklin, 338.

[14]Ibid., 335–38.

[15]See reviews in Maccoby and Jacklin, and in Constantina Safilios-Rothschild, *Sex Role Socialization and Sex Discrimination: A Synthesis and Critique of the Literature* (Washington, D.C.: National Institute of Education, 1979).

[16]Lisa Serbin, Daniel O'Leary, Ronald Kent, and Illene Tonick, "A Comparison of Teacher Response to the Preacademic and Problem Behavior of Boys and Girls," *Child Development* 44 (1973): 796–804.

[17]Maccoby and Jacklin, 335.

[18]Terry N. Saario, Carol N. Jacklin, and Carol Kehr Tittle, "Sex Role Stereotyping in the Public Schools," *Harvard Educational Review* 43 (1973): 386–416.

[19]Serbin et al., 800.

[20]Roy Martin, "Student Sex and Behavior as Determinants of the Type and Frequency of Teacher-Students Contacts," *Journal of School Psychology* 10 (1972): 339–47.

[21]Louis V. Paradise and Shavaun M. Wall, "Children's Perceptions of Male and Female Principals and Teachers," *Sex Roles* 14 (1986): 1–7.

[22]Boyd R. McCandless, "Childhood Socialization," in *Handbook of Socialization Theory and Research,* ed. David A. Goslin (Chicago: Rand McNally, 1971), 808–9.

[23]Ibid., 809.

[24]For a comprehensive discussion see *Gender and Nonverbal Behavior,* ed. Clara Mayo and Nancy M. Henley (New York: Springer-Verlag, 1981).

[25]McCandless, 808.

[26]Nancy Felipe Russo, "Sex-Role Stereotyping, Socialization and Sexism," in *Beyond Sex Roles,* ed. Alice Sargent (St. Paul: West, 1985), 155.

[27]Carol S. Dweck and Diane Gilliard, "Expectancy Statements as Determinants of Reactions to Failure: Sex Differences in Persistence and Expectancy Change," *Journal of Personality and Social Psychology* 32 (1975): 1077–85.

[28]Julia Sherman, "Girls Talk about Mathematics and Their Future: A Partial Replication," *Psychology of Women Quarterly* 7 (1983): 338–42.

[29]Earnest Q. Campbell, "Adolescent Socialization," in *Handbook of Socialization Theory and Research,* ed. David A. Goslin (Chicago: Rand McNally, 1971), 821–83.

[30]Ibid., 839.

[31]McCandless, 810.

[32]Sherman, 340.

[33]Matina Horner, "Toward an Understanding of Achievement-Related Conflicts in Women," *Journal of Social Issues* 28 (1972): 157–72, quoted in Gilligan, 15.

[34]Campbell, 840.

[35]Michael Mesner, "The Life of a Man For All Seasons: Male Identity in the Life Course of the Jock," in *Changing Men: New Directions in Research on Men and Masculinity,* ed. Michael S. Kimmel (Newbury Park, Calif.: Sage, 1987), 53–67.

[36]McCandless, 810.

[37]Gilligan, 163.

[38]George Herbert Mead, *Mind, Self and Society* (Chicago: University of Chicago Press, 1934).

[39]Chaefetz, 71.

Chapter 10

[1]Albert Bandura, "Social-Learning Theory of Identificatory Processes," in *Handbook of Socialization Theory and Research,* ed. David A. Goslin (Chicago: Rand McNally, 1971), 213–262.

[2]Walter Mishel, "A Social Learning View of Sex Differences in Behavior," in *The Development of Sex Differences,* ed. Eleanor E. Maccoby (Stanford: Stanford University Press, 1966), 56–81.

[3]Teresa L. Jump and Linda Haas, "Fathers in Transition: Dual Career Fathers Participating in Child Care," in *Changing Men,* ed. Michael S. Kimmel (Newbury Park, Calif.: Sage, 1987), 98–114.

[4]Joseph Pleck, "American Fathering in Historical Perspective," in *Changing Men,* ed. Michael S. Kimmel (Newbury Park, Calif.: Sage, 1987), 83–99.

[5]Jeylan T. Mortimer and Hayne London, "The Varying Linkages of Work and Family," in *Work and Family: Changing Roles of Men and Women,* ed. Patricia Voyanoff (Palo Alto, Calif.: Mayfield Publishing Company, 1984), 20–35.

[6]Joseph Pleck, "The Theory of Male Sex-Role Identity: Its Rise and Fall, 1936–Present," in *In the Shadow of the Past: Psychology Views the Sexes,* ed. Miriam Lewin (New York: Columbia University Press, 1983), 205–25.

[7]David B. Lynn, *Parental and Sex Role Identification: A Theoretical Formulation* (Berkeley: McCitchan Publishing Company, 1969).

[8]Lynn, 21–23.

[9]Bonnie E. Carlson, "Preschoolers' Sex Role Identity," in *Two Paychecks: Life in Dual-Earner Families,* ed. Joan Aldous (Beverly Hills: Sage, 1982), 207–25.

[10]Ibid., 221.

[11]Maccoby and Jacklin, 292.

[12]Ibid., 293.

[13]Mortimer and London, 27.

[14]Rosanna Hertz, "Dual-Career Couples: Shaping Marriages Through Work," in *Gender in Intimate Relationships: A Microstructural Approach,* ed. Barbara J. Risman and Pepper Schwartz (Belmont, Calif.: Wadsworth, 1989), 193–204.

[15]Karen Wolk Feinstein, "Directions for Day Care," in *Work and Family: Changing Roles of Men and Women,* ed. Patricia Voyanoff (Palo Alto, Calif.: Mayfield Publishing Company, 1984), 304.

[16]Ibid., 305–6.

[17]Clyde Franklin II, *The Changing Definition of Masculinity* (New York: Plenum Press, 1987), 112.

[18]Louise Cherry Wilkinson and C. Marrett, eds., *Gender Influences in Classroom Interaction* (New York: Academic Press, 1985).

[19]Franklin, 43.

[20]Ronald E. Frank and Marshall G. Greenberg, *The Public's Use of Television: Who Watches and Why* (Beverly Hills: Sage, 1980).

[21]Mark A. Runco and Kathy Pezdel, "The Effect of Television and Radio on Children's Creativity," *Human Communication Research* 11 (1984): 109–20.

[22]Susan A. Basow, *Sex-Role Stereotypes: Traditions and Alternatives* (Monterey, Calif.: Brooks/Cole, 1980); Faye H. Dambrot, Diana C. Reep, and Daniel Bell, "Television Sex Roles in the 1980's: Do Viewers' Sex and Sex Role Orientation Change the Picture?" *Sex Roles* 19

(1988): 387–401; K. Durin, "Television and Sex-Role Acquisition," *British Journal of Social Psychology* 24 (1985): 101–13.

[23]Dale Kunkel, "From a Raised Eyebrow to a Turned Back: The FCC and Children's Product-Related Programming," *Journal of Communication* 38 (1988): 90–108.

[24]Kunkel, 101.

[25]C. Cathey-Calvert, "Sexism on Sesame Street: Outdated Concepts in a 'Progressive' Program," (ERIC, No. ed. 168–683, 1979).

[26]Anthony Mulac, James J. Bradac, and Susan Karol Mann, "Male/Female Language Differences and Attributional Consequences in Children's Television," *Human Communication Research* 11 (1985): 481–506.

[27]Roger Jon Desmond and Suzanne Jeffries-Fox, "Elevating Children's Awareness of Television Advertising: The Effects of a Critical Viewing Program," *Communication Education* 32 (1983): 107–16.

[28]Kunkel, 95–97.

[29]Leslie Zebrowitz McArthur and Susan V. Eisen, "Television and Sex-Role Stereotyping," *Journal of Applied Social Psychology* 6 (1976): 329–51.

[30]William J. O'Donnell and Karen J. O'Donnell. "Update: Sex-Role Messages in TV Commercials," *Journal of Communication* 28 (1978): 156–58.

[31]Daniel J. Bretl and Joanne Cantor, "The Portrayal of Men and Women in U.S. Television Commercials: A Recent Content Analysis and Trends over 15 Years," *Sex Roles* 18 (1988): 595–609.

[32]Mulac et al., 500–2.

[33]Laurie P. Arliss, Mary Cassata, and Thomas Skill, "Dyadic Interaction on the Daytime Serials: How Men and Women Vie for Power," in *Life on Daytime Television: Tuning-in American Serial Drama*, ed. Mary Cassata and Thomas Skill (Norwood, N.J.: Ablex, 1983), 147–56.

[34]Mary Cassata, Thomas Skill, and Samuel Osei Boadu, "Life and Death in the Daytime Television Serial: A Content Analysis," in *Life on Daytime Television: Tuning-in American Serial Drama*, ed. Mary Cassata and Thomas Skill (Norwood, N.J.: Ablex, 1983), 47–70.

[35]Barbara Hollands Peevers, "Androgyny on the TV Screen? An Analysis of Sex-Role Portrayal," *Sex Roles* 5 (1979): 797–809.

[36]For a review see Durkin, 1985.

[37]Diana C. Reep and Faye J. Dambrot, "Television's Professional Women: Working with Men in the 1980's," *Journalism Quarterly* 64 (1987): 376–81.

[38]Peevers, 807.

[39]Sheila Egoff, *Thursday's Child: Trends and Patterns in Contemporary Children's Literature* (Chicago: American Library Association, 1981).

[40]Leonore J. Weitzman, Deborah Eifles, Elizabeth Hokada, and Catherine Ross, "Sex-Role Socialization in Picture Books for Preschool Children," *American Journal of Sociology* 77 (1972): 1125–50.

[41]Barbara Grizzuti Harrison, "Early Stereotypes," in *Women and Men: Traditions and Trends*, ed. Suzanne Fremon (New York: H. W. Wilson Company, 1977).

[42]Cheris Kramarae, *Men and Women Speaking* (Rowley, Mass.: Newbury House, 1981), 82–89.

[43]Jean Umiker-Sebeok, "The Seven Ages of Women: A View from American Magazine Advertisements," in *Gender and Nonverbal Behavior*, ed. Clara Mayo and Nancy Henley (New York: Springer-Verlag, 1981), 209–52.

[44]Ibid., 213.

[45]Ibid., 212–17.

[46]Gary L. Sullivan and P. J. O'Connor, "Women's Role Portrayals in Magazine Advertising: 1958–1983," *Sex Roles* 18 (1988): 181–88.

[47]Umiker-Sebeok, 218.

[48]Sullivan and O'Connor, 187.

[49]Gerald U. Skelly and William J. Lundstrom, "Male Sex Roles in Magazine Advertising, 1959–1979," *Journal of Communication* 31 (1981): 52–57.

[50]Umiker-Sebeok, 210.

[51]Sarah Brabant and Linda Mooney, "Sex Role Stereotyping in the Sunday Comics: Ten Years Later," *Sex Roles* 14 (1986): 141–48.

[52]Pamela Schroeder Kingsolver and Harold V. Cordry, "Gender and the Press: An Update," in *Advances in Gender and Communication Research*, ed. Lawrence B. Nadler, Marjorie Keeshan Nadler, and William R. Todd-Mancillas (Lanham, Md.: University Press of America, 1987), 307–16.

[53]Junetta Davis, "Sexist Bias in Eight Newspapers," *Journalism Quarterly* 59 (1982): 456–60.

[54]Karen G. Foreit, Terna Agor, Johnny Byers, John Larue, Helen Lokey, Michael Palazzini, Michael Patterson, and Lillian Smith, "Sex Bias in Newspaper Treatment of Male-Centered and Female-Centered News Stories," *Sex Roles* 6 (1980): 475–80.

[55]T. M. Mathews, "A Team Player," *Newsweek* (July 23, 1984), quoted in William G. Davey and Michael E. Mayer, "Campaign 1984: The Ferraro Factor—The Politics of Pragmatism and Prejudice," in *Advances in Gender and Communication Research*, ed. Lawrence B. Nadler, Marjorie Keeshan Nadler, and William R. Todd-Mancillas (Lanham, Md.: University Press of America, 1987), 278.

[56]William G. Davey and Michael E. Mayer, "Campaign 1984: The Ferraro Factor—The Politics of Pragmatism and Prejudice," in *Advances in Gender and Communication Research*, ed. Lawrence B. Nadler, Marjorie Keeshan Nadler, and William R. Todd-Mancillas (Lanham, Md.: University Press of America, 1987), 273–90.

Chapter 11

[1]Lawrence Kohlberg, "A Cognitive-Developmental Analysis of Children's Sex-Role Concepts and Attitudes," in *The Development of Sex Differences*, ed. Eleanor E. Maccoby (Stanford: Stanford University Press, 1966), 82–173.

[2]Ibid., 83.

[3]Jean Piaget, *The Construction of Reality in the Child* (New York: Basic Books, 1954).

[4]Kohlberg, 83.

[5]Lawrence Kohlberg, "The Cognitive-Developmental Approach to Socialization," in *Handbook of Socialization Theory*, ed. David A. Goslin (Chicago: Rand McNally, 1971), 349.

[6]Kohlberg, 1966, 93.

[7]John Condon, *Semantics and Communication* (New York: Macmillan, 1985).

[8]Lawrence Kohlberg and E. Ziegler, "The Impact of Cognitive Maturity on Sex-Role Attitudes in the Years Four to Eight," *Genetic Psychology Monographs* 75 (1967): 89–165.

[9]Kohlberg, 1966, 94.

[10]Ibid., 95.

[11]John Money, Joan Hampson, and J. L. Hampson, "Imprinting and the Establishment of Gender Role," *Archives of Neurological Psychiatry* 77 (1957): 333–36, quoted in Kohlberg, 1966, 87.

[12]Kohlberg, 1966, 108.

[13]Ibid., 111.

[14]Eleanor Emmons Maccoby and Carol Nagy Jacklin, *The Psychology of Sex Differences* (Stanford: Stanford University Press, 1974), 299.

[15]Alexa A. Albert and Judith R. Porter, "Age Patterns in the Development of Children's Gender Role Stereotypes," *Sex Roles* 9, (1983): 59–67; Cynthia J. Archer, "Children's Attitudes toward Sex-Role Division in Adult Occupational Roles," *Sex Roles* 10, (1984): 1–10; Glenn D. Cordua, Kenneth O. McGraw, and Ronald S. Drabman, "Doctor or Nurse: Children's Perceptions of Sex Typed Occupations," *Child Development* 50 (1979): 590–93.

[16]Ruth J. Coles, "Occupations in Regard to Ethnic Groups," *Journal of Vocational Behavior* 14 (1978): 43–45; M. E. Umstot, "Occupational Sex Role Liberality of Third, Fifth and Seventh-Grade Females," *Sex Roles* 8, (1982): 691–710.

[17]Kohlberg, 1966, 120.

[18]John K. Antill, "Parents' Beliefs and Values about Sex Roles, Sex Differences and Sexuality: Their Sources and Implications," in *Sex and Gender,* ed. Phillip Shaver and Clyde Hendrick (Newbury Park, Calif.: Sage, 1987), 294–328.

[19]Kohlberg, 1966, 121.

[20]Ibid., 165.

[21]Ibid.

[22]Martha Saxton with Carol Gilligan, "Are Women More Moral than Men?: An Interview," *Ms. Magazine*, (December, 1981) 63–64.

[23]David B. Lynn, *Parental and Sex Role Identification: A Theoretical Formulation* (Berkeley: McCuthan Press, 1969).

[24]Ibid., 24–25.

[25]Ibid., 50.

[26]Nancy Chodorow, *The Reproduction of Mothering* (Berkeley: University of California Press, 1978).

[27]Carol Gilligan, *In a Different Voice* (Cambridge, Mass.: Harvard University Press, 1982).

[28]Ibid., 173.

[29]Saxon with Gilligan, 62.

Chapter 12

[1]Alice G. Sargent, Diane Kravetz, and Dorothy Diemer, "A Short History of the Women's Movement," in *Beyond Sex Roles*," ed. Alice Sargent (St. Paul: West, 1984), 190–98.

[2]Sargent, Kravetz, and Diemer, 191–92.

[3]Maurine H. Beasley, "The Gender Shift in Journalism Education," in *Advances in Gender and Communication Research*, ed. Lawrence B. Nadler, Marjorie Keeshan Nadler, and William R. Todd-Mancillas (Lanham, Md.: University Press of America, 1987), 57–73.

[4]Ann Crittenden, "The Unfinished Revolution," in *Beyond Sex Roles*, ed. Alice Sargent (St. Paul: West, 1985), 497–502.

[5]U. S. Department of Labor, "Perspectives on Women: A Databook," Bulletin 2080 (Washington D.C.: Bureau of Labor Statistics, 1980).

[6]Beasley, 63.

[7]Anne E. Thorkelson, "Women Under the Law: Has Equity Been Achieved?" in *Beyond Sex Roles*, ed. Alice Sargent (St. Paul: West, 1984), 477–96.

[8]Jill Nelson, "I'm Not Your Girl," in *Images of Women in American Popular Culture*, ed. Angela G. Dorenkamp, John F. McClymer, Mary M. Moynihan, and Arlene C. Vadum (San Diego: Harcourt Brace Jovanovich, 1985), 294–300.

[9]Michele Hoyman and Ronda Robinson, "Interpreting the New Sexual Harassment Guidelines," *Personnel Journal* 59 (1980): 990–98.

[10]United States Equal Employment Opportunity Commission, "Rules of the Equal Employment Opportunity Commission." (Washington, D.C.: Bureau of National Affairs, 1981), 13–15.

[11]Robert L. Woodrum, "Sexual Harassment: New Concern About an Old Problem," *S.A.M. Advanced Management Journal* 46 (1981): 23–32.

[12]Tricia S. Jones, "Sexual Harassment in the Organization," in *Women in Organizations*, ed. Joseph J. Pilotta (Prospect Heights, Ill.: Waveland Press, 1983), 23–38.

[13]Ibid., 28–31.

[14]Lin Farley, *Sexual Shakedown: The Sexual Harassment of Women on the Job* (New York: McGraw-Hill, 1979), 14.

[15]Jones, 35–36.

[16]Elizabeth Mechling and J. Mechling, "Shock Talk: From Consensual to Contractual Joking Relationships in the Bureaucratic Workplace," *Human Organization* 34, (1986).

[17]Antony J. Chapman and Nicholas J. Gadfield, "Is Sexual Humor Sexist?" *Journal of Communication* 26 (1976): 141–53.

[18]Gary Alan Fine, "Obscene Joking Across Cultures," *Journal of Communication* 26 (1976): 134–40.

[19]Fine, 134.

[20]Gary Alan Fine, "One of the Boys: Women in Male-Dominated Settings," in *Changing Men: New Directions on Men and Masculinity*, ed. Michael S. Kimmel (Newbury Park, Calif.: Sage, 1987), 131–47.

[21]Ibid., 134.

[22]B. Aubrey Fisher, *Small Group Decision Making* (New York: McGraw-Hill, 1976), chapter 2.

[23]Judy Cornelia Pearson, *Gender and Communication* (Dubuque, Iowa: W. C. Brown, 1983), 335.

[24]Laura Garrison, "Recognizing and Combatting Sexist Job Interviews," *Journal of Employment Counseling* 17 (1980): 270–76.

[25]Thorkelson, 482.

[26]Linda L. Putnam, "Lady, You're Trapped: Breaking Out of Conflict Cycles," in *Women in Organizations*, ed. Joseph J. Pilotta (Prospect Heights, Ill.: Waveland Press, 1983), 39–53.

[27]Natalie Porter and Florence Geis, "Women and Nonverbal Leadership Cues: When Seeing is Not Believing," in *Gender and Nonverbal Behavior*, ed. Clara Mayo and Nancy M. Henley (New York: Springer-Verlag, 1981), 39–57.

[28]Kay Deaux, "Self-Evaluations of Male and Female Managers," *Sex Roles* 5 (1979): 571–80.

[29]Kay Deaux, "Internal Barriers," *Women in Organizations*, ed. Joseph J. Pilotta (Prospect Heights, Ill.: Waveland Press, 1983), 11–22.

[30]Porter and Geis, 44.

[31]Deaux, 1983, 14.

[32]Putnam, 38–40.

[33]Farley, 14.

[34]Julia T. Wood and Charles Conrad, "Paradox in the Experiences of Professional Women," *Western Journal of Speech Communication* 47 (1983): 305–22.

[35]Suzanne Gordon, "The New Corporate Feminism," in *Images of Women in American Popular Culture*, ed. Angela G. Dorenkamp, John F. McClymer, Mary M. Moynihan, and Arlene C. Vadum (San Diego: Harcourt Brace Jovanovich, 1985), 321–26.

[36]Ibid., 323.

[37]Ibid., 323–24.

[38]Jeff Hearn and P. Wendy Parkin, "Gender and Organizations: A Selective Review and Critique of a Neglected Area," *Organization Studies* 4 (1983): 219–42.

[39]Wood and Conrad, 313.

[40]Porter and Geis, 42.

[41]Wood and Conrad, 307.

[42]Cynthia Berryman-Fink, Mary A. Heintz, Marc Steven Lowy, Monica Louise Seebohm, and Virginia Eman Wheeless, "Perceptions of Women as Managers: Individual and Organizational Implications," in *Advances in Gender and Communication Research*, ed.

Lawrence B. Nadler, Marjorie Keeshan Nadler, and William R. Todd-Mancillas (Lanham, Md.: University Press of America, 1987), 3–11; Otto C. Brenner and John A. Bromer, "Sex Stereotypes and Leaders' Behavior as Measured by the Agreement Scale for Leadership Behavior," *Psychological Reports* 48 (1981): 960–62; Gary N. Powell and D. Anthony Butterfield, "The 'Good Manager': Masculine or Androgynous?" *Academy of Management Journal* 22 (1979): 395–403; Virginia Eman Wheeless and Cynthia Berryman-Fink, "Perceptions of Women Managers and their Communicator Competencies," *Communication Quarterly* 33 (1985): 137–48.

[43]Stephen M. Brown, "Male Versus Female Leaders: A Comparison of Empirical Studies," *Sex Roles* 5 (1979): 608.

[44]Berryman-Fink et al., 7.

[45]Brown, 595.

[46]John Baird and Patricia Hayes Bradley, "Styles of Management and Communication: A Comparative Study of Men and Women," *Communication Monographs* 46 (1979): 101–11; William R. Todd-Manchillas and A. M. Rossi. "Gender Differences in the Management of Personnel Disputes," *Women's Studies in Communication* 8 (1985): 25–33.

[47]A. S. Baron and R. L. White, "The New Work Dynamic: Men and Women in the Workforce," *Business Horizons* (August 1980): 56–60.

[48]Putnam, 48.

[49]Wood and Conrad, 320.

[50]Randi L. Hagen and Arnold Kahn, "Discrimination Against Competent Women," *Journal of Applied Social Psychology* 5 (1975): 362–376.

[51]Janet T. Spence, Robert Helmreich, and J. Stapp, "Likability, Sex-Role Congruence of Interest and Competence: It all Depends on How You Ask," *Journal of Applied Social Psychology* 5 (1979): 93–109.

[52]Francine M. Deutsch and Frederick T. Leong, "Male Responses to Female Competence," *Sex Roles* 9 (1983): 89.

[53]Wood and Conrad, 320.

[54]Ibid., 314–15.

[55]Mary Anne Fitzpatrick, "Effective Interpersonal Communication for Women in the Corporation: Think Like a Man, Talk Like a Lady…" in *Women in Organizations*, ed. Joseph J. Pilotta (Prospect Heights, Ill.: Waveland Press, 1983), 73–84.

[56]Ibid., 82–83.

[57]D. A. Infante and Andrew S. Rancer, "A Conceptualization and Measure of Argumentativeness," *Review of Educational Research* 46 (1982): 72–80.

[58]Andrew S. Rancer, Robert A. Baukas, and D. A. Infante, "Relations between Argumentativeness and Belief Structures about Arguing," *Communication Education* 34 (1985): 37–47.

[59]Beatrice Schultz, "Argumentativeness: Its Effect on Group Decision Making and Its Role in Leadership Perception," *Communication Quarterly* 30 (1982): 368–75.

[60]David W. Johnson and Roger T. Johnson, "Conflict in the Classroom: Controversy and Conflict," *Review of Educational Research* 49 (1979): 51–70.

[61]Andrew S. Rancer and Kathi J. Dierks-Stewart, "The Influence of Sex and Sex-Role Orientation on Trait Argumentativeness," *Journal of Personality Assessment* 49 (1985): 69–70.

[62]Marjorie Keeshan Nadler and Lawrence B. Nadler, "The Influence of Gender on Negotiating Success in Assymetric Power Situations," in *Advances in Gender and Communication Research*, ed. Lawrence B. Nadler, Marjorie Keeshan Nadler, and William R. Todd-Mancillas (Lanham, Md.: University Press of America, 1987), 189–218.

[63]Lynn McFarlane Shore and George C. Thornton III, "Effects of Gender on Self- and Supervisory Ratings," *Academy of Management Journal* 29 (1986): 115–29.

[64]Nadler and Nadler, 192.

[65]Ibid., 203.

[66]J. Rubin and B. Brown, *The Social Psychology of Bargaining and Negotiation* (New York: Academic Press, 1975), 172–74.

[67]Carol L. Montgomery and Michael Burgoon, "The Effects of Androgeny and Message Expectations on Resistance to Persuasive Communication," *Communication Monographs* 47 (1980): 56–67.

[68]John P. Sprowl, "Women, Men and Personal Sales: An Analysis of Sex Differences in Compliance Gaining Strategy Use," in *Advances in Gender and Communication Research*, ed. Lawrence B. Nadler, Marjorie Keeshan Nadler, and William R. Todd-Mancillas (Lanham, Md.: University Press of America, 1987), 243–57.

[69]Ibid., 251–53.

[70]Barbara J. Risman and Pepper Schwartz, *Gender in Intimate Relationships* (Belmont, Calif.: Wadsworth, 1989): 1.

Chapter 13

[1]Lillian B. Rubin, *Just Friends* (New York: Harper & Row, 1985), 4.

[2]William K. Rawlins, "Cross-Sex Friendship and the Communicative Management of Sex-Role Expectations," *Communication Quarterly* 30 (1982): 343–52.

[3]Rubin, 133.

[4]For a discussion of homosexual friendships see Alan P. Bell and Martin S. Weinberg, *Homosexualities: A Study of Diversity Among Men and Women* (New York: Simon & Schuster, 1978); John Malone, *Straight Women/Gay Men* (New York: Dial Press, 1981).

[5]Rawlins, 344.

[6]Robert J. Barth and Bill N. Kinder, "A Theoretical Analysis of Sex Differences in Same-Sex Friendships," *Sex Roles* 19 (1988): 349–63; Mayta A. Caldwell and Letita A. Peplau, "Sex Differences in Same-Sex Friendship," *Sex Roles* 8 (1982): 721–32; Dorie Giles Williams, "Gender, Masculinity-Femininity, and Emotional Intimacy in Same-Sex Friendships," *Sex Roles* 12 (1985): 587–600; Paul H. Wright, "Men's Friendships, Women's Friendships and the Alleged Inferiority of the Latter," *Sex Roles* 8 (1982): 1–20.

[7]Robert R. Bell, "Friendships of Women and Men," *Psychology of Women Quarterly* 5 (1981): 402–17; Robin A. Buhrke and Dale R. Fuqua, "Sex Differences in Same- and Cross-Sex Supportive Relationships," *Sex Roles* 17 (1987): 339–51; Judith L. Fisher and Leonard R. Narus,

Jr., "Sex Roles and Intimacy in Same-Sex and Other-Sex Relationships," *Psychology of Women Quarterly* 5 (1981): 444–55; Williams, 588–89.

[8]Lynda Greenblatt, James E. Hasenauer and Vicki S. Freimuth, "Psychological Sex Type and Androgyny in the Study of Communication Variables: Self-Disclosure and Communication Apprehension," *Human Communication Research* 6 (1980): 117–28; Helen Mayer Hacker, "Blabbermouths and Clams: Sex Differences in Self-Disclosure in Same-Sex and Cross-Sex Friendship Dyads," *Psychology of Women Quarterly* 5 (1981): 385–401.

[9]Elizabeth J. Aries and Fern L. Johnson, "Close Friendships in Adulthood: Conversational Content between Same-Sex Friends," *Sex Roles* 9 (1983): 1183–96; Richard Aukett, Jane Ritchie, and Kathryn Mill, "Gender Differences in Friendship Patterns," *Sex Roles* 19 (1988): 57–66; Caldwell and Peplau, 730; Davidson and Duberman, 809; Mark L. Knapp, Donald G. Ellis, and B. A. Williams, "Perceptions of Communication Behavior Associated with Relationship Terms," *Communication Monographs* 47 (1980): 262–78.

[10]Buhrke and Fuqua, 339; Wright, 19; J. P. Stokes and D. G. Wilson, "The Inventory of Socially Supportive Behaviors: Dimensionality, Predictions and Gender Differences," *American Journal of Community Psychology* 12 (1984): 53–69.

[11]Fisher and Narus, 451.

[12]Buhrke and Fuqua, 339.

[13]Aukett, Ritchie, and Mill, 64.

[14]Constantina Safilios-Rothschild, "Toward a Psychology of Relationships," *Psychology of Women Quarterly* 5 (1981): 377–84.

[15]Rawlins, 347.

[16]Ibid.

[17]Buhrke and Fuqua, 348–49.

[18]Zick Rubin, Letita Peplau, and Charles T. Hill, "Loving and Leaving: Sex Differences in Romantic Attachments," *Sex Roles* 6 (1980): 821–35.

[19]Buhrke and Fuqua, 350.

[20]Lillian Rubin, 149.

[21]Zick Rubin, *Children's Friendships* (Cambridge, Mass.: Harvard University Press, 1980), 105.

[22]Gary L. Hansen, "Dating Jealousy Among College Students," *Sex Roles* 12 (1985): 713–21.

[23]Robert R. Bell, *Worlds of Friendship* (Beverly Hills: Sage, 1981), 97–99.

[24]Beth B. Hess, "Sex Roles, Friendship and the Life Course," *Research on Aging* 1 (1979): 494–515.

[25]Alan Booth and Elizabeth Hess, "Cross Sex Friendship," *Journal of Marriage and the Family* 36 (1974): 38–47.

[26]Lillian Rubin, chapter 8.

[27]Booth and Hess, 38–39.

[28]Suzanna M. Rose, "Same and Cross-Sex Friendships and the Psychology of Homosociality," *Sex Roles* 12 (1985): 63–74.

[29]Gary Alan Fine, "One of the Boys: Women in Male-Dominated Settings," in *Changing Men: New Direction in Research on Men and Masculinity,* ed. Michael S. Kimmel (Newbury Park, Calif.: Sage, 1987), 131–47.

[30]J. E. Deal and K. S. Wampler, "Dating Violence: The Primacy of Previous Experience," *Journal of Social and Personal Relationships* 3 (1986): 457–71.

[31]J. A. Lee, *The Colors of Love: An Exploration of the Ways of Loving* (Toronto: New Press, 1973).

[32]Zick Rubin, 105.

[33]Janet Ward Schofield and H. Andrew Sagar, "Peer Interaction Patterns in an Integrated Middle School," *Sociometry* 40 (1977): 130–38, quoted in Zick Rubin, 105.

[34]Zick Rubin, 106.

[35]Steve Duck, *Relating to Others* (Chicago: The Dorsey Press, 1988), chapter 4.

[36]Robert Hopper, Mark L. Knapp, and Lorel Scott, "Couples' Personal Idioms: Exploring Intimate Talk," *Journal of Communication* 13 (1981): 23–33.

[37]Kathleen McKinney, "Age and Gender Differences in College Students' Attitudes Toward Women: A Replication and Extention," *Sex Roles* 17 (1987): 353–58.

[38]Buhrke and Fuqua, 350.

[39]Susan K. Green and Philip Sandos, "Perceptions of Male and Female Initiators of Relationships," *Sex Roles* 9 (1983): 849–52.

[40]Bernard E. Whitley, Jr., "The Relation of Gender-Role Orientation to Sexual Experience Among College Students," *Sex Roles* 19 (1988): 619–38.

[41]Elizabeth Grauerholz and Richard T. Serpe, "Initiation and Response: The Dynamics of Sexual Interaction," *Sex Roles* 12 (1985): 1041–59.

[42]Elizabeth Rice Allgeier, "The Influence of Androgynous Identification on Heterosexual Relations," *Sex Roles* 7 (1981): 321–30; Letita A. Peplau, Zick Rubin, and Charles T. Hill, "Sexual Intimacy in Dating Relationships," *Journal of Social Issues* 33 (1977): 211–22; L. J. Snow and J. L. Parsons, "Sex Role Orientation and Female Sexual Functioning," *Psychology of Women Quarterly* 8 (1983): 133–43.

[43]Whitley, 620.

[44]Judith A. DiIorio, "Being and Becoming Coupled: The Emergence of Female Subordination in Heterosexual Relationships," in *Gender in Intimate Relationships,* ed. Barbara J. Risman and Pepper Schwartz (Belmont, Calif.: Wadsworth, 1989), 94–107.

[45]Gerald W. McDonald, "Family Power: The Assessment of a Decade of Theory and Research, 1970–1979," *Journal of Marriage and the Family* 42 (1980): 841–54.

[46]Susan Sprecher, "Sex Differences in Bases of Power in Dating Relationships," *Sex Roles* 12, (1985): 449–61.

[47]Constantina Safilios-Rothschild, *Love, Sex and Sex Roles* (Englewood Cliffs, N.J.: Prentice Hall, 1977).

[48]Sprecher, 458–59.

[49]J. C. Carroll, K. A. Volk and J. S. Hyde, "Differences Between Males and Females in Motives for Engaging in Sex," *Archives of Sexual Behavior* 14 (1985): 131–39; Janice L.

DeLucia, "Gender Role Identity and Dating Behavior: What is the Relationship?" *Sex Roles* 17 (1987): 153–61; Lillian Rubin, 154–57; Whitley, 633–34.

[50]Whitley, 634.

[51]Letita A. Peplau, "Power in Dating Relationships," in *Women: A Feminist Perspective*, ed. Jo Freeman (Palo Alto, Calif.: Mayfield, 1978), 106–21.

[52]Duck, 75–76.

[53]Adrienne Rich, "Compulsory Heterosexuality and Lesbian Existence," *Signs* 5 (1980): 62–91.

Chapter 14

[1]Kathleen M. Galvin and Bernard J. Brommel, *Family Communication: Cohesion and Change* (Glenview, Ill.; Scott, Foresman, 1982), chapter 1.

[2]e.g., Susan Bram, "Voluntarily Childless Women: Traditional or Nontraditional?" *Sex Roles* 10 (1984): 195–206; Eleanor D. Macklin, "Nontraditional Family Forms: A Decade of Research," *Journal of Marriage and the Family* 42 (1980): 905–22; Lisa Kay Rogers and Jeffry H. Larson, "Voluntary Childlessness: A Review of the Literature and a Model of the Childlessness Decision," *Family Perspective* 22 (1988): 43–58.

[3]Diana Burgwyn, *Marriage Without Children* (New York: Harper & Row, 1981); Marian Faux, *Childless By Choice* (New York: Anchor/Doubleday, 1984).

[4]Sharon K. Houseknecht, "Voluntary Childlessness in the 1980's: A Significant Increase?" *Marriage and Family Review* 5 (1982): 51–69; Rogers and Larson, 56; J. Veevers, "Voluntary Childlessness: A Review of Issues and Evidence," *Marriage and Family Review* 2 (1979): 3–26.

[5]Paul Yelsma, "Marriage Vs. Cohabitation: Couples' Communication Practices and Satisfaction," *Journal of Communication* 36 (1986): 94–107.

[6]Barbara J. Risman, Charles T. Hill, Zick Rubin, and Letita Peplau, "Living Together in College: Implications for Courtship," *Journal of Marriage and the Family* 43 (1981): 77–83.

[7]Yelsma, 94–95.

[8]Florence L. Denmark, Jeffrey S. Shaw, and Samuel Ciali, "The Relationships Among Sex Roles, Living Arrangements and the Division of Household Responsibilities," *Sex Roles* 12 (1985): 617–25.

[9]Sandra A. Petronio, "The Effect of Interpersonal Communication on Women's Family Role Satisfaction," *Western Journal of Speech Communication* 46 (1982): 208–22.

[10]Timothy Stephen and Teresa M. Harrison, "A Longitudinal Comparison of Couples with Sex-Typical and Non–Sex-Typical Orientations to Intimacy," *Sex Roles* 12 (1985): 195–206.

[11]T. E. Perkins, "Rethinking Stereotypes," in *Ideology and Cultural Production*, ed. Michele Barrett et al. (New York: St. Martin's Press, 1979), 135–59 quoted in Ellen Seiter, "Stereotypes and the Media: A Re-evaluation," *Journal of Communication* 38 (1986): 14–26.

[12]Kristine M. Baber and Patricia Monaghan, "College Women's Career and Motherhood Expectations: New Options, Old Dilemmas," *Sex Roles* 19 (1988): 189–203.

[13]Joan Aldous, "From Dual-Earner to Dual-Career Families and Back Again," in *Two Paychecks: Life in Dual-Earner Families*, ed. Joan Aldous (Beverly Hills: Sage, 1982), 11–26.

[14]Elizabeth A. House, "Sex Role Orientation and Marital Satisfaction in Dual- and One-Provider Couples," *Sex Roles* 14 (1986): 245–59.

[15]Baber and Monaghan, 189.

[16]Howard Hayghe, "Dual-Earner Families," in *Two Paychecks: Life in Dual-Earner Families*, ed. Joan Aldous (Beverly Hills: Sage, 1982), 27–40.

[17]Linda Nyquist, Karla Slivken, Janet T. Spence, and Robert L. Helmreich, "Household Responsibilities in Middle-Class Couples: The Contribution of Demographic and Personality Variables," *Sex Roles* 12 (1985): 15–34.

[18]Ralph LaRossa and Maureen Mulligan LaRossa, "Baby Care: Fathers vs. Mothers," in *Gender in Intimate Relationships: A Microstructural Approach*, ed. Barbara J. Risman and Pepper Schwartz (Belmont, Calif.: Wadsworth, 1989), 138–54.

[19]Ibid., 144–45.

[20]Kristina Cooper, Laurie Chassin, and Antonette Zeiss, "The Relation of Sex-Role Self-Concept and Sex-Role Attitudes to the Marital Satisfaction and Personal Adjustment of Dual-Worker Couples With Preschool Children," *Sex Roles* 12 (1985): 227–41.

[21]Lynda Cooper Harriman, "Personal and Marital Changes Accompanying Parenthood," *Family Relations* 32 (1983): 387–94; Ralph LaRossa, "The Transition to Parenthood and the Social Reality of Time," *Journal of Marriage and the Family* 45 (1983): 579–89.

[22]Cooper, Chassin, and Zeiss, 237.

[23]Rosanna Hertz, "Dual-Career Corporate Couples: Shaping Marriages Through Work," in *Gender in Intimate Relationships: A Microstructural Approach*, ed. Barbara J. Risman and Pepper Schwartz (Belmont, Calif.: Wadsworth, 1989), 193–204.

[24]Teresa L. Jump and Linda Haas, "Fathers in Transition: Dual Career Fathers Participating in Child Care," in *Changing Men*, ed. Michael S. Kimmel (Newbury Park, Calif.: Sage, 1987), 98–114.

[25]Ibid., 110–11.

[26]Geoffrey Greif, *Single Fathers* (Lexington, Mass.: Lexington Books, 1985).

[27]Denmark et al., 620.

[28]Nyquist et al., 31.

[29]G. W. Bird, G. A. Bird and M. Shruggs, "Determinants of Family Task Sharing: A Study of Husbands and Wives," *Journal of Marriage and the Family* 46 (1984): 345–56; E. Maret and Barbara Finlay, "The Distribution of Household Labor Among Women in Dual-Career Families," *Journal of Marriage and the Family* 46 (1984): 357–64; Suzanne Model, "Housework by Husbands: Determinants and Implications," in *Two Paychecks: Life in Dual-Earner Families*, ed. Joan Aldous (Beverly Hills: Sage, 1982), 193–206; Nyquist et al., 31; Sara Yogev, "Do Professional Women have Equalitarian Marital Relationships?" *Journal of Marriage and the Family* 43 (1981): 865–72.

[30]House, 246.

[31]Kathleen Gerson, "What Do Women Want from Men? Men's Influence on Women's Work and Family Choices," in *Changing Men: New Directions in Research on Men and Masculinity*, ed. Michael S. Kimmel (Beverly Hills: Sage, 1987), 115–30.

[32]Petronio, 221.

[33]Nyquist et al., 31.

[34]Marianne N. Bloch, "The Development of Sex Difference in Young Children's Activities at Home: The Effect of Social Context," *Sex Roles* 16 (1987): 279–302.

[35]Denmark et al., 624.

[36]David R. Johnson, Lynn K. White, John N. Edwards, and Alan Booth, "Dimensions of Marital Quality: Toward Methodological and Conceptual Refinement," *Journal of Family Issues* 7 (1986): 31–49.

[37]Nyquist et al., 31.

[38]Toni Falbo and Letita Anne Peplau, "Power Strategies in Intimate Relationships," *Journal of Personality and Social Psychology* 38 (1980): 618–28; William K. Rawlins, "Cross-Sex Friendship and the Communicative Management of Sex-Role Expectations," *Communication Quarterly* 30 (1982): 343–52.

[39]Kenneth J. Gruber and Jacquelyn W. White "Gender Differences in the Perceptions of Self's and Others' Use of Power Strategies," *Sex Roles* 15 (1986): 109–18.

[40]Robert O. Blood and Donald M. Wolfe, *Husbands and Wives* (Glencoe, Ill.: The Free Press, 1960).

[41]G. W. McDonald, "Family Power: The Assessment of a Decade of Theory and Research, 1970–1979," *Journal of Marriage and the Family* 42 (1980): 841–54.

[42]Joseph P. Stokes and Judith S. Peyton, "Attitudinal Differences Between Full-Time Homemakers and Women Who Work Outside the Home," *Sex Roles* 15 (1986): 299–310.

[43]Stokes and Peyton, 306. Yogev, 866.

[44]Falbo and Peplau, 619.

[45]Gruber and White, 112–113.

[46]Ibid.

[47]Falbo and Peplau, 625.

[48]Ibid., 625.

[49]Ibid., 627.

[50]Gabriel Weimann, "Sex Differences in Dealing with Bureaucracy," *Sex Roles* 12 (1985): 777–90.

[51]Paula Johnson, "Women and Power: Toward a Theory of Effectiveness," *Journal of Social Issues* 32 (1976): 99–106.

[52]Leonard H. Chusmir and Barbara Parker, "Dimensions of Need for Power: Personalized versus Socialized Power in Female and Male Managers," *Sex Roles* 11 (1984): 759–69.

[53]Melissa Dingler-Duhon and Barbara B. Brown, "Self-Disclosure as an Influence Strategy: Effects of Machiavellianism, Androgyny and Sex," *Sex Roles* 16 (1987): 109–23.

[54]Gary L. Hansen and Janet L. Bokemeier, "Children's Influence in Family Decision Making," *Family Perspective* 22 (1988): 131–43.

[55]Toni Falbo, D. Hazen, and D. Linimon, "The Costs of Selecting Power Bases or Messages Associated with the Opposite Sex," *Sex Roles* 8 (1982): 147–57.

[56]Steve Duck, *Relating to Others* (Chicago: The Dorsey Press, 1988), chapter 5.

[57]Alan Booth and Lynn White, "Thinking About Divorce," *Journal of Marriage and the Family* 42 (1980): 605–16.

[58]Duck, 88.

[59]C. E. Rusbult, "Response to Dissatisfaction in Close Relationships: The Exit-Voice-Loyalty-Neglect Model," in *Intimate Relationships: Development, Dynamics, and Deterioration,* ed. Dan Perlman and Steve Duck (Beverly Hills: Sage, 1987).

[60]Barbara Finlay, Charles E. Starnes, and Fausto B. Alvarez, "Recent Changes in Sex-Role Ideology Among Divorced Men and Women: Some Possible Causes and Implications," *Sex Roles* 12 (1985): 637–53.

[61]Ibid., 641.

[62]Lynn White, "Sex Differences in the Effect of Remarriage on Global Happiness," *Journal of Marriage and the Family* 41 (1979): 869–76.

[63]Jesse Bernard, *The Future of Marriage* (New York: World, 1972).

[64]Shirley P. Glass and Thomas L. Wright, "Sex Differences in Type of Extramarital Involvement and Marital Dissatisfaction," *Sex Roles* 12 (1985): 1101–20.

[65]Ibid., 1103.

[66]Graham B. Spanier and Randie L. Margolis, "Marital Separation and Extramarital Sexual Behavior," *Journal of Sex Research* 19 (1983): 23–48.

[67]Glass and Wright, 1116–17.

[68]B. I. Murstein and P. E. Williams, "Sex Roles and Marital Adjustment," *Small Group Behavior* 14, (1983): 77–94.

[69]J. K. Antill, "Sex Role Complementarity vs. Similarity in Married Couples," *Journal of Personality and Social Psychology* 45 (1983): 145–55.

[70]Ann Douglas, *The Feminization of American Culture* (New York: Knopf, 1977).

[71]Patricia A. Parmelee, "Sex Role Identity, Role Performance and Marital Satisfaction of Newly-Wed Couples," *Journal of Social and Personal Relationships* 4 (1987): 429–44.

AUTHOR INDEX

SUBJECT INDEX